W9-ADP-796

Media Messages

Media Messages

What Film, Television, and
Popular Music Teach Us About
Race, Class, Gender and
Sexual Orientation

Linda Holtzman

M.E. Sharpe
Armonk, New York
London, England

Library of Congress Cataloging-in-Publication Data

Holtzman, Linda, 1949–
Media messages : what film, television, and popular music teach us about race, class,
gender, and sexual orientation / Linda Holtzman.
p. cm.
Includes bibliographical references and index.
ISBN 0-7656-0336-5 (hardcover : alk. paper)
ISBN 0-7656-0337-3 (paperback : alk. paper)
    1. Mass media and race relations—United States. 2. Mass media and sex—United
States. 3. Mass media—Social aspects—United States. 4. Popular culture—United States.
5. Social classes—United States. 6. United States—Social conditions—1980– I. Title.

P94.5.M552 U646 2000
302.23—dc21   00-037155

To my teachers Ernest Calloway, George Gerbner, and Grandma Dora

Table of Contents

List of Tables, Figures, Personal Inventories, and Media Activities

Media Activities

Photographs follow Page 50

Preface

This is a book about ideas, histories, theories, ideologies, beliefs, personal experiences, and values. It is academic and it is deeply personal. I have offered information and perspectives that are often untold in our schools, neighborhoods, families, and places of worship and are invisible and inaudible on our televisions, in our movie theaters, and on our radios. I have explored the various ways we arrive at what we know to be "fact," as well as how we come to the deep convictions in our hearts about difference, diversity, and oppression. I have tried to be accurate and fair with this information, but I do not claim to be objective, nor do I think objectivity is possible or desirable. This is value-heavy terrain. Claims of objectivity and declarations of truth about diversity often lead to oversimplifications and distortions. On the other hand, the explicit and thorough scrutiny of the sources and derivation of our beliefs and values can lead us to more complexity and higher and deeper levels of understanding about gender and class and race and sexual orientation and ourselves.

The fabrication of "the other" has caused enormous pain and tragedy throughout history. The death of millions of Africans at sea as they were taken from their homes and brought to the United States to be sold as merchandise, as slaves; the murder of millions of Jews in the Holocaust; the so-called ethnic cleansing in Bosnia; the murder of gay Wyoming student Matthew Shepard. How is it that otherwise decent people can be convinced that a group that is different from them is less than human and deserves lower status, hate, or violence? How is it that some people, in the midst of the most violent and venomous of times, are determined and able to do whatever is in their power to interrupt the smallest individual acts of hate and the largest systemic kinds of violence and injustice?

I have asked my students these questions, and as often happens they have been my best teachers. One student said, "If we can just get people to look into the eyes of the people they hate, they would see their humanity and the difference would just be difference, not something worthy of violence." Another student wrote, "Humanity is our basic understanding; compartmentalizing people is something that's taught." He went on to say that he did not fully understand how and why hate and violence could be directed at whole groups because of their race or religion or sexual orientation and concluded that he was glad he did not understand because "it would be as if I had a hole in my soul."

The possibility of seeing this humanity in ourselves and in each other is what interests me and is what this book is about. This book is about reflecting on and repairing the "holes in our souls" that have been drilled there by misinformation and repeated negative messages. It is about examining, revisiting, and at times reconstructing the explicit and subtle partial truths and lies that we have been told in school, by our families, by our peers, and in movies and situation comedies and popular songs. It is about developing the tools to scrutinize the information and the sources and to determine their impact on our own convictions and values. It is not about political correctness. It is not about replacing one set of simple myths for another. It is about seeing the serious consequences of hate and oppression for those who have been segregated, lynched, ostracized, marginalized, laughed at, and murdered, and it is about the serious consequences—the "hole in the soul" that becomes a part of those of us who hate and obliterate the humanity of others. It is about weighing what we have learned in the past in light of what we are learning in the present and making our own independent choices about what to think and believe and how to act.

I have used language that is both academic and personal. I have told parts of my personal story and have encouraged readers to think about their own stories. So many textbooks and academic articles and theological analyses and films and television programs and songs and authorities in our lives have given us partial information, theories, beliefs, and feelings as if they were facts, the truth. But as you will see, much of the information and meaning about diversity and oppression is socially and politically constructed, contested, fluid and dynamic through history and across cultures. I think it is important for you to know my academic and media sources and citations as is conventionally provided and also to know my personal sources, experiences, and perspectives so that you can more readily evaluate what I say in the same way I have encouraged you to evaluate your other sources of information. Because of this, I have intentionally used the first person so that you will know that this is *my* interpretation and *my* understanding. I am present in this book. I hope you will be, too.

Acknowledgments

As this book is organized in three directions—personal experience, reconstructing knowledge, and entertainment media—so are the people I want to thank for their help and support

I wish to thank the late Ernest Calloway for teaching me to reconstruct knowledge by looking below the surface and to understand that information, knowledge, and truth are not always the same. I wish to thank George Gerbner (Temple University) for responding to my out-of-the-blue letter expressing the desire to study with him and for accommodating my life and schedule. George taught me how to study and analyze the "stories" in media, how to discover rather than "cover," and he demonstrated how one could be a scholar and a passionate agent for change.

Many thanks to my editor at M.E. Sharpe, Peter Coveney, for his support and graciousness in providing all of the extensions when I wanted to research "just a few more things."

Thanks to my good friend and colleague, Art Silverblatt (Webster University) for his thorough reading of many drafts, helpful comments, and off-the-wall humor. Many thanks to Sylvia Shepard and Tracy Ronvik, my sisters-in-law, who clarified my thinking and organization with their thoughtful, detailed comments. A very special thank you to my research associate, Janis Valdes, who conducted painstaking research, provided excellent feedback, and has been one of the best cheerleaders for my work. Many thanks to the "daughter of my heart," Sheila Magrath, for her clear illustrations. Thanks to Bill Barrett for guiding me through the digital maze of photography. Thanks to Rachel Sierra and Laurie Smith for the depth and wisdom of their comments and for challenging my thinking as only true, smart friends can do.

For sharing their personal experiences and wisdom about what it means to be the "other" and about the possibilities of transformation, I wish to thank my mentors and "femtors" Deborah Allen, Jeri Au, Otis Bolden, Ernest Calloway, Shawn D'Abreu, Donna Lacy, Deke Law, Winnie Lipman, Velma Miles, Aliah Mubarak Tharpe, Erma "Tiny" Motton, James Motton, Rudy Nickens, Mike Savage, Rachel Sierra, Charlie Silverman, Margie Silverblatt, Laurie Smith, Rabbi Susan Talve, Karen Techner, Reverend Chuck Watt. I wish to thank my grandfather, Irving Goldman, for having breakfast with me every Sunday during the last year of his life and telling me what it was like for him to leave Russia and come to St. Louis in the early 1900s. I wish to thank my grandmother, Dora Holtzman, for showing me through her life what it meant to truly love people. I wish to thank my mother, Evelyn Holtzman, for continuing the traditions of matzo ball soup, gefilte fish, chopped liver, brisket, and kumish bread. I wish to thank my father, Donald Holtzman, for the many stories he told about being a soldier during World War II—fighting the German army and its virulent anti-Semitism, being one of the first soldiers to liberate the concentration camp at Buchenwald, and fighting anti-Semitism within the U.S. army.

I wish to thank my good friends Rudy Nickens and Judy El Amin for listening to me on a weekly and daily basis as I struggled with some of the concepts in the development of the book.

My children and my students have always been my best teachers. They have taught me that age is no barometer of wisdom and challenged me and made me listen even when I have traveled to my separate adult world.

I want to thank my husband, Mike Magrath, for bringing cappuccino and setting it next to the computer as I waved him away with the gesture that said, "Don't break my concentration." Thanks to my children Dora and Alex Magrath for telling me how "cool" it is to write a book and believing that I will be a famous author. Thanks to my husband and children Mike, Pat, Sheila, Bernadette, Ken, Dora, and Alex for living their lives in such a way that embraces diversity and offers different ways of challenging, interrupting, and transforming oppression.

Media Messages

Introduction

When most Americans turn on the television in the evening, they want to be entertained, lulled, or simply anesthetized. Following a day of work or studies or simply walking through the complexities of life's daily challenges, many of us need and desire a break. Prime time television seems to offer the perfect solution: perhaps mindless fun, perhaps a few laughs, and even the occasional meaty thought to ponder. But as we sit curled up on the couch relaxing after a long day, what are the messages that we are receiving and what impact do they have on us?

Cultural studies scholar Douglas Kellner says, "Radio, television, film and other products of the culture industries provide the models of what it means to be male or female, successful or a failure, powerful or powerless . . . media culture helps shape the prevalent view of the world and its deepest values: it defines what is considered good or bad, positive or negative, moral or evil" (Kellner 1995, 1).

According to media scholar George Gerbner, television has become the primary storyteller for children in the late twentieth century, a common source of information and socialization in an otherwise diverse population (Gerbner et al. 1986, 17). Other researchers observe that while television may be only one of many things that serve to explain the world, it is "special because its socially constructed version of reality bombards all classes, groups, and ages with the same perspectives at the same time. . . . What makes television unique, however, is its ability to standardize, streamline, amplify, and share common cultural norms with virtually all members of society" (Morgan and Signiorelli 1990, 13).

The average American household has the television on for seven hours each day. Most people choose to watch television according to when they have leisure time available, not by specifically selecting programs of their choice. There are a series of homogeneous, consistent messages conveyed during prime time television regardless of the network or program selected. Even the smartest and most aware television viewers can experience television in two seemingly contradictory ways. On the one hand, most of us know and can articulate that the programs we are watching are fictional; yet we often believe and internalize the invisible messages we are receiving. This same process occurs as we listen to popular music or watch a feature film.

We will examine the stories and messages conveyed on prime time television, in popular film, and in music and their potential impact on the audience—the

3

American public. This information and analysis is for the media producer, student, and media consumer alike, providing methods to critically examine entertainment media and decipher what is being portrayed. We will explore accessible methods to analyze the content and impact of images of gender, socioeconomic class, race, and sexual orientation in entertainment media.

Readers are invited to actively engage in the text in three ways, exploring how we see ourselves and others through (1) *personal experience,* (2) *reconstructing knowledge,* and (3) *entertainment media assessment tools.* These three components are inextricably linked and add up to primary forces that shape who we are and how we think, act, and see the world around us.

In each chapter we will observe and analyze our *personal experiences* with individuals and groups that are different from us. Examining personal experience allows us to determine what we have learned informally about various groups according to race, gender, economic status, and sexual orientation. A variety of exercises and quizzes will provide a foundation for understanding how where we lived and what we were told by our parents, peers, teachers, and religious leaders has shaped how we see the world. For example, what beliefs do you have about the nature and capabilities of men and women? What did your parents teach you about appropriate roles for boys and girls, both through what they told you and how they behaved themselves? What did your peers tell you was out of line for boys' and girls' behavior? We will look at experiences such as these and determine how they contributed to what you believe to be true and right and possible for men and women.

Through the exploration of personal experience we will examine informal education, information, and misinformation that each of us has received about gender, race, class, and sexual orientation. Readers will be invited to examine their own experiences, what they learned about various groups from family, friends, and faith-based organizations. A variety of experiential exercises are designed to offer thoughtful processes for reflection regarding this informal education. Later in each chapter, we will begin to consider the meaning and impact of various forms of popular media, and you will be asked to refer back to your own personal experience as the foundation and context for understanding your relationship to the messages conveyed in film, music, and television.

This process will begin to identify what we have learned through our own direct contact and personal experience. As we do these exercises, we will begin to identify where there are gaps and voids in our experiential learning. For example, if you are white, African American, or Asian American, did you grow up without any contact with American Indians? If so, where did you get information or misinformation about American Indians? Most likely, it was through what people told you, what you learned in school, and what you saw and heard in the media.

After exploring and assessing personal experience, a second kind of analysis will be offered that examines more formal sources of information (and, again, misinformation) concerning gender, race, class, and sexual orientation. This method of investigation involves *reconstructing knowledge* through analyzing explicit information we have been taught in school and other formal learning organizations.

For example, most U.S. students were taught in school about the Civil War and slavery, but the majority of us were not taught about the Middle Passage (Zinn 1995, 29). During the Middle Passage, the journey in which captured Africans were brought to North America by white Americans and Europeans to become slaves, an estimated 50 million Africans died at sea. As part of reconstructing knowledge, you will be asked to consider critical questions about such an historic tragedy. Why is this information rarely included in high school history books? How has this and other missing information contributed to our beliefs about slavery, the treatment of African Americans, and contemporary racism?

As you review what you have been formally taught, you will be asked to consider the source of your information and beliefs and place it into the context of reconstructing knowledge. No one is ever pressured or required to change their values or convictions. Rather, you are invited to assimilate new information and analyze and square it with what you have already been taught and come to believe. Through this process of evaluating information, we have the opportunity to reconsider our beliefs and to independently reconstruct our own knowledge.

After examining personal experience and formal education, we will focus on assessing entertainment media: prime time television, popular film, and music. These forms of popular culture are common sources of education and socialization that stretch across the United States, forming the media culture in which we are all immersed, with or without our consent. While the intent of entertainment media may not be explicitly to educate us, it often fills the voids and gaps in our formal and informal learning. For example, if we did not have any direct contact with Asian Americans as we were growing up, where will we learn about this group? We will learn from what people tell us, from school, and from media. What we learn in this way may or may not correspond to the actual history and contemporary circumstances of Asian Americans.

Entertainment media (prime time television, popular film, and music) are a primary fact of life in most U.S. homes. Much of our sense of personal and group identity, our beliefs about what is "normal," and our understanding of groups that are different from us is created and/or reinforced by the pervasive entertainment media culture. The ability and the skills to critically observe and analyze these messages and their impact are integral to becoming informed citizens striving for independence in thought, values, and behavior. We will explore the many theories available for examining popular media culture and its vast impact. In addition, tools and exercises to assess entertainment media are offered to provide accessible methods for decoding the messages that surround us in entertainment media. For example, most of the families portrayed on prime time television are nuclear families with mother, father, children, and an income that is at least middle or above. What do we learn about what it means to be a "normal" family from these repeated images? What are the messages inherent in the invisibility of single parent families, extended families, working class and low income families, and gay and lesbian families?

This book is divided into six chapters. Chapter One establishes the framework and foundation for the strong and essential links between personal experience, reconstructing knowledge, and entertainment media. Key terms that will be used throughout the book are introduced in this chapter. Chapters Two, Three, and Six are organized around gender, socioeconomic class, and sexual orientation, respectively. Each of these chapters explores the particular issue in our personal experience, formal education, and its reflection in entertainment media. Chapters Four and Five are both about race. In an effort to explore personal experience, formal education, and entertainment media as they relate to African Americans, Asian Americans, American Indians, Latinos, multiracial Americans, and European Americans, I have divided this mountain of information into two chapters for easier readability.

Many researchers have maintained that the common messages in entertainment media have a homogenizing or "mainstreaming" affect on the American public. This means that popular television, film, and music help shape what we think of as "true" and "normal." Mainstreaming creates and reinforces an invisible set of values that are so firmly entrenched in our culture and belief systems that they seem indisputable to us. This homogeneity and these invisible values influence the way we think and act on personal, public, and political levels. We make personal choices, we vote and take political action, and we form public policy based on our values and beliefs. To the extent that these messages, values, and norms are invisible, our choices and actions are automatic, dependent, and less than conscious.

We will learn about diversity in the United States through this blend of experience and information. As we look at gender, class, race, and sexual orientation, we will investigate our interactions and experiences with groups who are different from us, examine and critique what we have been taught about various cultures in school and through religious organizations, and finally decode the messages about diversity in entertainment media. We will investigate the meaning, influence, and impact of the information and misinformation received and learn new tools to determine our own values and beliefs and make our own life choices. It is that independence and those choices that are central to this book.

Chapter 1

The Connections: Life, Knowledge, and Media

Once you have learned how to ask questions—relevant and appropriate and substantial questions—you have learned how to learn, and no one can keep you from learning whatever you want or need to know.

—Postman and Weingartner

When individuals engage diversity, tension can result from new information about others that is contrary to the learner's previous understanding of their identity, the world and the relationship between the two . . . if we find that the others are not who we thought them to be, perhaps we are not who we define ourselves to be.

—(N)ISM Toolkit

Each chapter begins with the inquiry about your personal experience so that you can explore what you were explicitly and implicitly taught, how you were socialized, what you absorbed, what you resisted, and ultimately what you learned to be true about gender or class or race or sexual orientation.

Personal Experience

Take a journey to your childhood and think about what, if any, holiday your family celebrated during December. Think of the kind of celebration that it was. Remember the foods, the smells, the people, the decorations. What was everyone doing? Was there a religious element to the holiday? Was there gift giving? Did the family gather together? Were there songs or prayers? Were there any special family traditions involved? Do you have other significant memories associated with this holiday? Write or tape record your answers to these questions.

Groups that are predominantly white, middle class, and Christian often assume that Christmas is the December holiday. Often people in such homogeneous groups will answer the above questions prefaced with statements such as, "It was your *average* Christmas," or "We ate the *usual* foods," or "The only thing different about my family was we ate duck instead of turkey," or "We were pretty *typical, nothing exciting.*"

Yet there are many other possibilities for holidays and celebrations around December. These include Chanukah, celebrated by Jews; Kwanzaa, celebrated by many African Americans; and the Winter Solstice, celebrated by many individuals who are part of organized religions and many who are not. During Chanukah, candelabra known as menorahs are lit for eight consecutive days, potato pancakes or latkes are eaten, and a game is played with a toplike "dreidl." During Kwanzaa, a kenora is lit and families celebrate seven principles including unity, self-determination, and cooperative economics (Salzman, Smith, and West 1996, 2475). For some faiths, agnostics, or atheists, there may be no traditional December holiday.

If you grew up celebrating Christmas in a predominantly Christian community, most likely you understood your experience to be the norm. Perhaps you never heard of Chanukah or Kwanzaa until you were much older. Perhaps you still are not completely sure what those holidays are about and why Christmas is not celebrated by everyone. Perhaps you felt sorry for people who did not have Christmas trees. Or perhaps you thought that people who celebrated other non-Christian holidays were interesting, exotic, odd, or even un-American. As part of the dominant Christian culture in the United States, your early holiday experiences were part of the construct of what you believed to be average and normal and how you understood the "other," or people and groups that were different from you.

If you grew up non-Christian in the United States you knew, at least for a month or so, what it was like to be different. You heard Christmas music and saw lights and Santa Claus everywhere you went. In stores, schools, and offices, people with the warmest of intentions said "Merry Christmas." Maybe you smiled and nodded politely or maybe you said, "I don't celebrate Christmas." Maybe you went to a school in which Christmas carols were sung and you had to decide whether to participate in the more religious of the songs. These examples illustrate the media and cultural saturation of Christmas images and messages and their acceptance as "normal." If you were part of a minority group in a predominantly Christian culture, you learned early on what it was like to be different, to stand outside of the norm, to be the "other."

In fact, there is great variation among how Christians observe Christmas. Some celebrate Christmas as a deeply meaningful religious holiday while others celebrate it is a secular midwinter holiday of gift giving, food, and festivities.

Your position in this December scenario is a critical element in the establishment of your personal identity and your sense of where you belong in your neighborhood, school, and in the larger community and culture. Depending on how the adults in your life helped to explain your experience, it may have been positive, negative, or a mix. But whatever it was, it contributed to shaping how you see both yourself and people who are different from you.

Exploring how we see ourselves and others is an important first step in understanding diversity. Later in the chapter we will examine related issues in reconstructing knowledge and entertainment media and make the important connections between your personal experiences and your formal and mediated learning.

Your place as inside or outside the "norm" of the Christmas holiday will contribute to how you regard what you learn in school and the workplace. For example, most public and private schools in the United States are organized around the Christian calendar. School breaks and holidays usually correspond with Christmas, Good Friday, and Easter rather than Yom Kippur, Kwanzaa, or Ramadan. This conveys to us that the Christian holidays are "normal," while the other holidays are at best for minorities and at worst seen as unusual or strange. On a more practical level, Christians generally have time off school and work to celebrate important holidays while people who observe other faiths have to figure out how to accommodate their religious observances. A question often asked by non-Christians is, "Should I miss an important test, blow my perfect attendance record, or take a personal leave day to observe my holiday?" Your standpoint in the holiday scenario above also has an enormous impact on how you see the "holiday specials" on television, hear the Christmas music on the radio and in department stores, and feel about the release of December seasonal films. For Christians, this may seem like either an overcommercialization of a deeply religious holiday or wonderful examples of holiday spirit. For non-Christians, the media saturation may be disturbing and disorienting. Some non-Christians may feel almost invisible during December. To continue this process of understanding diversity in an experiential context, I invite you to take the multicultural quiz in Personal Inventory 1.1.

After completing the quiz, total your score. The highest possible score is 100. If you scored 90–100 you have lived in a highly multicultural world. If you scored 80–89, your life has been filled with diversity. If you scored 70–79 you have been exposed to people who are different from you. If you scored 60–69 you have been exposed to some diversity, but have primarily lived among people much like you. If you scored under 60, you have lived primarily among people who are very much like you in race, religion, sexual orientation, and social and economic class or you have been in the minority among others who were quite similar.

And, if you scored under 60, you are similar to over 90 percent of the people who have taken this quiz—you have lived in a unicultural world.

What does this all mean? People of all different ages, races, ethnicities, genders, economic and social classes, religions, and sexual orientations have taken this quiz, and, repeatedly, most people find that they have grown up among others who are in fundamental ways very much like them. This simple and unscientific quiz underscores that U.S. society is still largely structured in a way that separates and segregates people who are different from each other. Often people actively and explicitly choose to live among others who are similar to them. Sometimes

Personal Inventory 1.1
The Multicultural Quiz

Instructions

Answer each question below to the best of your ability. If you lived in many different places during the time period described, give yourself a score that averages your experiences. Leave blank any experiences (e.g., preschool, religious institution, etc.) that don't pertain to you.

For each answer score yourself as follows:

1 point: Experience was largely unicultural; most people were of my race, religion, sexual orientation, economic, and social class.

2 points: Experience was largely unicultural, but most people were of a different race, religion, sexual orientation, economic, or social class than I was.

2 points: Experience was largely unicultural; but there were a few people who were different from me in race, religion, sexual orientation, or economic and social class.

3 points: In at least 2 categories (race, religion, sexual orientation, economic, and social class) there were people present different from me.

4 points: In at least 3 categories there were people present who were different from me.

Ages 1–5   **Score**

1. The neighborhood where you lived   _____
2. The children with whom you played   _____
3. Your parents' friends   _____
4. The preschool or day care you attended   _____
5. The religious institution you attended   _____

(cont'd)

people make residential choices based on the limits of their income or as a result of discrimination in real estate or lending. Yet, just as often, the choices for diversity continue to be exceedingly limited in this society. People who have lived in communities with great diversity have generally made very deliberate choices to do so, in order to expose themselves and their families to a multicultural world.

If most American's experiences are, in fact, unicultural; how do people learn about the nature of *difference?* Young people learn about people and groups that are different from them in several ways:

Ages 6–10

6. The neighborhood where you lived _____
7. The children with whom you played _____
8. The school you attended _____
9. Clubs or organizations to which you belonged _____
10. Religious institution _____

Ages 11–14

11. The neighborhood where you lived _____
12. Your friends _____
13. The school you attended _____
14. Clubs or organizations to which you belonged _____
15. Religious institution _____

Ages 15–18

16. The neighborhood where you lived _____
17. Your friends _____
18. The school you attended _____
19. Clubs or organizations to which you belonged _____
20. Religious institution _____

Ages 19–25

21. The neighborhood where you lived. _____
22. Your friends _____
23. The school you attended _____
24. Clubs or organizations to which you belonged _____
25. Religious institutions _____
26. Your parents' friends _____

TOTAL SCORE _____

Source: Presentation by Barbara Love, 1989.

- from their families;
- from their peers;
- from their religious institutions;
- from school;
- from the media.

Through the process of socialization, we grow up learning the values of our culture. The vast majority of us grew up with little diversity, and the values and beliefs we were taught seemed real, central, and "normal." Often we experienced no sense of a pluralist community that included different foods, religious practices, beliefs, or customs. Rather, these invisible norms instilled a sense that our way was the right or only way and that other ways were unusual, weird, abnormal, or wrong.

This exercise is not intended to provoke guilt or to evoke the specter of political correctness. In fact, since most of the United States is quite segregated residentially particularly by race, ethnicity, and religion, the exercise points out that cultural isolation is a common experience shared both by groups in the majority and by groups in the minority. This isolation denies most of us the personal opportunity to be neighbors, friends, peers, or classmates with people who are different from us. This cultural isolation is critical to remember as later in this section we begin to examine what we were taught formally in school and what we have learned about one another from the media. For many of us, the voids and gaps in our personal experience are filled exclusively by formal education and media. These sources of information shape what we "know" and believe regardless of whether they are solid, accurate, and factual or sketchy, inaccurate, and fictional.

The final experiential exercise in this section, Personal Inventory 1.2, begins the process of developing your autobiography, which can be written in a notebook or tape recorded. The development of autobiographies and their exchange with others from similar and different backgrounds is encouraged over the course of the six chapters of this book. Our sense of individual and cultural identity is integral to how we understand the world we live in and its portrayal in entertainment media.

A closer examination of a few of these questions uncovers some common issues regarding difference, isolation, and our consequences. Number four invites us to report on the treatment of elders in our family and community. Some families and groups are informal in addressing older people and commonly refer to parents' friends, neighbors, friends' parents, and even aunts and uncles by their first names. Other families consider it an essential sign of respect for children to address all elders as Mr. or Mrs., Ms., sir, or ma'am. Violation of this sign of respect is regarded as an affront and extraordinarily rude.

Over the centuries, many African American families have seen their elders treated with disrespect by being called by their first names by very young white children or by being called "boy" or "girl." Historically, titles of respect accorded to European Americans were rarely used for African Americans. As a result of this history, some contemporary African American families are emphatic that courtesy titles (Miss, Ms., Mrs., Mr.) be used at all times as a sign of respect and as an important compensatory gesture of courtesy.

Consider a scenario between individuals who have been taught to address elders in very different ways. While in first grade an African American child, John Harris, and a European American child, Alex Rosen-Fox, become friends in school and begin to visit each other's homes to play. John has been explicitly told that all male adults should be addressed as Mr. and all married women should be addressed as Mrs. Alex's family has roots in the political and social change move-

---

Personal Inventory 1.2
Developing an Autobiography: Part One

Instructions

Answer the questions below in as much detail as you can remember. Write or record your responses. There are no right or wrong answers.

---

1. Describe the neighborhood(s) in which you were raised. Were there houses, apartments, farms? How many generations lived in a single dwelling? Who was at home in your neighborhood on weekdays? On weekends? Describe the roads and the shops. How did neighbors interact? How did children play? What smells, foods, activities, events do you remember from your childhood?

2. What religious institutions were in your neighborhood? Were there churches, temples, synagogues, mosques? What religions did your neighbors and friends observe?

3. How were children treated in your community? How were they disciplined?

4. How were older adults or elders addressed (e.g., first name, sir, ma'am, titles, etc.) and how were they treated?

5. What were the spoken and unspoken rules about dating, courtship, and marriage?

6. What were the expectations for your generation regarding education? How many generations of your family have attended college?

7. What holidays did your family celebrate? Describe the rituals, gathering, and food of these celebrations.

8. What music did you grow up listening to among your family and friends? What did you and your family do with your leisure time?

---

ments of the 1960s and he has been taught to call adults, including his parents, by their first names. His parents believe this informality in language across ages is a symbol of equality and not one of disrespect. His mother has kept her original or "maiden" last name and technically is a "Ms." rather than a "Mrs."

So when John comes to visit Alex and refers to the adults as Mr. and Mrs. Fox, the adults immediately say, "Call us Larry and Susan," unwittingly putting John in conflict between what his parents have taught him about respect and what other adults are asking him to do. John decides to obey his parents and continues to call Alex's parents Mr. and Mrs. Fox. Susan corrects John and tells him her last name is Rosen. John is very confused.

When Alex plays at John's house, he hears the adults call each other by their first names, Renee and Herb, and immediately begins to address them as such. Renee and Herb Harris are disturbed that Alex, who otherwise seems to be a nice little boy, is so disrespectful. They are perplexed by this apparent disrespect and begin to wonder if Alex is calling them by their first names because they are African American.

Something that on the surface may seem simple can cause two families from different cultures to draw very different conclusions about behavior. If the Harrises understand Alex's background, they will know that he means no disrespect but rather that his family has a different set of traditions, beliefs, and practices around the treatment of elders. If the Harrises are unaware of this, they may conclude that while Alex is a nice boy, his parents, at best, have not taught him respect and, at worst, are racist. If the Rosen-Foxes understand some of the historical realities for African American families they will know the significance of courtesy titles and may explain this to their son, Alex, teaching him to respect different histories and cultural traditions. However, if the Rosen-Foxes are unaware of these cultural differences, they may decide that while John is a nice boy, his parents must be old-fashioned and overly formal. They may continue to insist that John call them by their first names or that he call Susan "Ms. Fox."

Difference in cultural practices, personal histories, or racial history can be spun into many scenarios that can result either in greater understanding of diversity or in harsh judgment and offensive behavior. We bring these experiences and understandings with us as a filter every time we got to school, to church, temple, or mosque; every time we go to a movie, watch television, or listen to music; and every time we meet someone who is different from us.

Reconstructing Knowledge

Ronald Takaki describes a personal encounter with a narrowly constructed view of what it means to be American. Takaki, a second generation Japanese American, relates an experience in a taxi in Norfolk, Virginia, in which the taxi driver asks Takaki what country he is from and compliments him on his English. Because Takaki's face is Asian, the driver assumes that he is not American (Takaki 1993, 1). The driver, like many others in U.S. society, has "learned" that appearances of certain groups are un-American or foreign. The driver meant no harm. In fact, he thought he was flattering Takaki by complimenting his English.

The driver's comments disclosed what his formal and informal education taught him about what it means to be American. Takaki says, "What happens . . . when someone with the authority of a teacher describes our society, and you are not in it? Such an experience can be disorienting, a moment of psychic disequilibrium, as if you looked in a mirror and saw nothing" (Takaki 1993, 53). Many groups who have made vital contributions to American society and culture have been excluded from the American curriculum and common knowledge pool. "The result is that what we know—about the experience of both these silenced groups and the dominant culture—is distorted and incomplete" (Andersen and Collins 1995, 1).

Reconstructing knowledge involves another kind of journey through the past in which we examine the explicit information we learned in school and from other formal learning experiences and review it in light of new information. As we assess what we were formally taught and what was omitted in the past we gain a clearer picture about what we bring to our understanding of people and groups who are different from us. We can begin to ask the questions:

- Does our formal learning reinforce or contradict what our personal experience has taught us?
- How do the messages in entertainment media square with this formal and informal learning?

This process requires an openness to questioning what has been learned before, a willingness to assess and incorporate new information, a tolerance for interim confusion, and ultimately the ability to make shifts in how we view the world. Using your developing autobiography as background, reconstructing knowledge invites you to evaluate both your formal and informal education. Each subsequent chapter of this book will include information that is not typically provided in elementary and high school textbooks on the topics of gender, class, race, and sexual orientation. You are never required to change what you think or believe, only to consider new information, to weigh it, and to determine how it fits with what you already "know."

We can begin reconstructing knowledge by looking at a socioeconomic example: the American Dream. What were you taught that this "dream" includes? Were you taught that it could, in fact, be yours someday?

What most Americans are taught in school about the American Dream is that every American, regardless of economic status, race, or family background, can rise to great heights. It is the story of the poor boy who grows up to be President (of the United States or of Ford Motor Company). The American Dream, a central tenet of American culture, suggests that we all begin from a level playing field. According to the Dream, it is hard work and virtue that determines who succeeds rather than gender, race, ethnicity or economic background. The American Dream focuses on the power of the individual and assumes that American society is classless and that upward mobility is fluid. Regardless of our own personal experience—our race, our economic status or family background—we are all taught these same lessons.

The first step in reconstructing knowledge is to identify these explicit and implicit lessons in our formal learning, to tease out what up till now may have been invisible assumptions. Have you always just "known" that hard work and virtue would result in upward mobility and success? Has it seemed to you that only "lazy" people fail in this society? Do you believe that most people get what they deserve in their lives?

The next step in reconstructing knowledge is to place these lessons about the American Dream in the context of some newer, perhaps less well-known information that examines economic issues in the United States. For example, the wealthiest public schools in the United States spend $15,500 per pupil and the poorest public schools spend an average of $7,000 per pupil (Adams, Bell, and Griffin 1997, 253). Some of the poorest city and rural school districts have lost or are in danger of losing their state accreditation. With poor resources and poor education for some, is it possible for all Americans to begin on a level playing field? Does a child who goes to a school with tattered books, few pencils, and no library have the same life chances as a child who goes to school with the newest textbooks and curriculum, a wealth of supplies, a large library, and computers and VCRs in every classroom? (Additional information regarding economic stratification in the United States is provided in Chapter Three.)

The process of reconstructing knowledge helps us to understand our relationship to the American Dream. What were you taught about opportunity in the United States? How did your family's economic position affect what you believed to be possible? What, if anything, were you taught in school and at home about race and class disparities in income, education, health care, and housing? What did you believe about who is responsible for poverty or wealth? Were poor people to blame for their lack of resources? Did people of wealth have any responsibility to address inequities in income?

If the American Dream teaches us that virtue, merit, and hard work are the key ingredients in achieving economic and material success, then what does that dream say about people who do not achieve such success? The flip side of the Dream is that poor people lack virtue, merit, and the industriousness to succeed. Do you believe that to be true?

Reconstructing the American Dream does not mean giving up hope or indulging in cynicism. Challenging the myths attached to the Dream means carefully examining and reconsidering what we have been taught about economics and class in the United States and rethinking how opportunity is structured. In much the same way that we have examined the American Dream, you will be invited to reexamine and rethink many issues related to your own experiences, American culture, entertainment media, and the powerful connections between these three topics. Reconstructing knowledge offers you a chance to view familiar terrain, to try it on, and to see if it still fits. Once again, if our personal lives have not allowed us the opportunity to get to know people and groups that are different from us, something must fill the void. Most often the void is filled with formal education and entertainment media. It is part of our task to determine accuracy, gaps in information, distortion, and misinformation in the lessons we have learned.

In order to examine and evaluate information and knowledge, it will be useful to provide a foundation of terms, language, and theories that can serve as a basis for reconstructing knowledge. This will be the focus of the next section of this chapter. This terrain of diversity or multiculturalism is a contested terrain; one in which even the overarching categorical terms of diversity, multiculturalism, or anti-oppression are in dispute by experts and practitioners alike. While it is not always possible to include every perspective, conflicting theories will be acknowledged as such in order to give the reader every opportunity to evaluate the information provided and to engage in critical and autonomous thinking. Our goal in reconstructing knowledge is not to exchange one set of myths for another, but to encourage analytical skills and independence of thought.

The Process of Socialization

As individuals we develop our sense of personal *identity* from our social interactions with others and the information we receive about ourselves. Our sense of our own biological sex, gender, race, ethnicity, class, and sexual orientation unfolds as our parents, siblings, peers, teachers, and others begin to paint a picture of who we are. For example, when a child is born, often parents and grandparents buy pink for girls and blue for boys; dolls for girls and footballs for boys. A children's book, *Baby X,* tells the story of an adorable newborn whose parents would not disclose whether "X" was a girl or a boy. Visitors did not know what to say. Should they say, "Oh, she's so beautiful!" or "Look at his grip!" (Gonzales et al. 1993, video)? This same basic confusion, curiosity and discomfort is evoked in the *Saturday Night Live* portrayal of the character "Pat." Like Baby X, Pat's sex is withheld from the audience and while this gender confusion creates many humorous situations it also creates social discomfort (Cader 1994, 244). We are accustomed to responding, at least in part, to babies, children, and adults based on conclusions we draw from their sex. From the time of birth, a child is told what it means to be male or female in his or her family and community.

This process is called *socialization.* Socialization is the total set of experiences in which children become clear about norms and expectations and learn how to function as respected and accepted members of a culture. Through socialization, children learn to choose a more limited set of behaviors based on these expectations. Children are socialized at both conscious and unconscious levels to internalize the dominant values and norms of their culture and, in so doing, develop a sense of self (Croteau and Hoynes 1997, 18).

There are many theories of how socialization works and how we learn to adapt to our culture. We will explore some of the classic sociological theories as well as newer theories that offer explanations of this phenomenon. Most of these theories include descriptions of the common agents of socialization that strongly influence our cultural adaptation. These agents are the family, the school, the peer group, and the mass media. The peer group and the family correspond with our personal experience and informal learning, and the school is clearly an important source of formal education.

Social Learning Theory

One sociological theory that provides a general explanation of human behavior is *social learning theory* developed by Albert Bandura (Grusec 1992, 776–86). According to this theory, the individual notices something external and after repetition begins to internalize it and mimic it. If the individual receives external rewards for this behavior, the learning will be internalized. This constitutes "social learning." For example, if a little boy is told repeatedly that big boys do not cry and notices that men in his world never cry when they are sad or hurt, he will begin to consider that behavior as a model for his own. When very young, when his body or feelings are hurt, he will cry. But if he is told that is wrong and "big boys don't cry," or if he simply observes that his tears somehow embarrass or anger his parents, the next time he is hurt he will try very hard not to cry. If he is successful in holding back the tears, the adults around him might say, "Good boy. You are such a big boy, just like a little man." He will enjoy this reward and begin to internalize it as part of the definition of who he is, who boys are, and how men behave. Social learning will have occurred.

In this scenario it is easy to see many other ways in which external events could create different kinds of social learning. For example, adults could have told the little boy that it is good to cry when he is hurt and that it helps release the pain. Or in an example that may seem far-fetched given American socialization, it is possible for adults to tell the little boy that it is manly to cry.

Social learning theory is a fairly straightforward way of understanding the socialization process. It explains how we take in what we are told and what we observe and that with enough repetition, this perspective becomes how we understand "truth" and "reality." As we will see in later chapters, much of this kind of learning is cultural and varies from culture to culture; yet it is our socialization process that often causes us to hold steadfast to our beliefs that this information is "fact."

The Social Self

Another classic socialization theory is George Herbert Mead's analysis of the social self. According to Mead, it is our sense of self that differentiates humans from animals. This theory asserts that our identity consists of our self-awareness and self-image, our interaction with others, and our ability to conceive of, understand, and respond to others.

As in social learning theory, children begin to mimic behavior of the adults around them as part of their early development of self. But the self continues to develop as our consciousness of our own self and others evolves. Essential to the development of self is our ability to imagine other people's response to us. For example, if we say "Good morning" to someone, we can imagine that person will say "Good morning" in response. If we throw a ball to someone, we can imagine them catching it and throwing it back. In this way we learn certain rituals of human behavior as well as the norms of interaction.

Another feature of the development of the social self is that the way others think of and respond to us strongly influences our identity and self-image. If, as we grow up, we are told that we are a good friend, then that will contribute to our identity, which will include being a good friend. A negative self-identity can also develop if we are consistently told that we are not smart or that we are unattractive.

One key element of the theory of the social self is the belief that the self continues to evolve throughout our lives as a result of changing circumstances and changing social experiences. A final and hopeful step in this theory is the conviction that as social experiences and society influence us, we too interact with society and other people and can influence and change people, culture, and institutions. This theory views socialization as interactive and regards each individual as potentially powerful (Mead 1995, 63).

Liberation Theory

Liberation theory is a newer theory of socialization that builds on social learning and social self theory and adds a political element to it. Liberation theory presumes that individuals from any and every group are born with innate qualities of brilliance and the infinite capacity to be happy and successful. The theory, developed as a construct of Reevaluation Counseling (also known as RC), maintains that brilliance and the capacity to succeed are *innate,* while misinformation that is oppressive is *learned.* The conclusion of liberation theory is that because this information and behavior are learned, they can also be unlearned (Marcuse).

Liberation theory maintains, as does social self theory, that infants, children, and adults receive messages that shape their sense of identity. When a baby boy is born, he may be dressed in blue and told all of the things that boys can and cannot do. From the time of birth, some parents express disappointment when their new baby, especially a firstborn, is a girl. Many adult women casually report, "I was supposed to be a boy." This early socialization process around sex establishes a set of messages about how boys are supposed to behave and how girls are supposed to behave, and in some instances assumes male superiority. Such information is learned and according to liberation theory can be unlearned.

Liberation is the process by which we can individually and institutionally observe, recognize, rethink, and interrupt the misinformation and negative messages around us, changing how we see ourselves and others. Engaging in liberation requires:

- an awareness and understanding of the socialization process;
- the belief that some of the ways we are socialized are limiting, deadening; and
- the desire, commitment, and the deliberate choice to exchange misinformation for accurate information in ways that dismantle oppression and liberate ourselves and other people.

For some people, liberation may be something as simple as interrupting a joke that makes race or gender or ethnicity the offensive brunt of the humor. Others may embark on a self-education process, seeking alternative sources of information to better understand sexual orientation, race, or religion. Some may choose to lead or participate in organizations or movements for liberation and change. Others may introduce policies at work that acknowledge same sex partnerships and offer health insurance to an employee's life partner.

Liberation theory examines the roles of privileged and targeted groups. Members of *privileged groups* have greater access to the resources and power to get what they want in the world because of their membership in a particular group. Persons in *targeted groups* have less access to privileges, resources, and power to get what they want because of their membership in a particular group. For example, in the United States, men have traditionally had greater access to positions of power (e.g., senators, CEOs of corporations, presidents of universities) and are therefore considered members of a privileged group. Conversely, women have had less access to positions of power and constitute a targeted group.

Individuals may belong to some privileged groups and some targeted groups. A white, low-income man belongs to two privileged groups by virtue of his race and gender and one targeted group by virtue of his economic class. A wealthy lesbian belongs to two targeted groups by virtue of her gender and sexual orientation and one privileged group by virtue of her economic class.

According to liberation theory, we learn messages about our identity and place in the world through a thorough and comprehensive socialization process based on our membership in privileged and targeted groups. But because this socialization is *learned,* it can also be *unlearned.* Liberation theory is an action theory and offers hope for change that is based on individual and/or collective action.

Cultural Competence Theory

Cultural competence theory is another relatively new socialization theory. Like liberation theory, cultural competence theory is based on the premise that society will be better when we understand, respect, and become knowledgeable in each other's cultures. What differentiates this theory is that rather than describing the socialization process itself, it describes a continuum of behavior that characterizes how individuals and institutions may behave and interact with others different from them.

Important to this theory is the understanding that *culture* is the integrated pattern of human behavior that includes thought, communication, actions, customs, beliefs, values, and institutions of a racial, ethnic, religious, or social group (Adams, Bell, and Griffin 1997, 254). "Culture provides the overall framework in which we imagine what we do not encounter directly, and interpret what we do encounter directly. It is the context in which experience becomes consciousness. Culture, then, is a system of stories and other artifacts—increasingly mass-produced—that mediates between existence and consciousness of existence, and thereby contributes to both" (Gerbner 1995, 4).

Culture can be bisected into *surface* culture and *deep* culture. Think of culture as a tree in which surface culture is the above-ground part of the tree and deep culture is the roots below the surface (see Figure 1.1). Surface culture is easily visible in the form of clothing, food, language, music, and dance. When you visit an ethnic festival, you are observing and participating in surface culture. Deep culture reflects less observable values, beliefs, and customs and includes child rearing practices, rules about courtship and marriage, treatment of elders, and proxemics (the physical distance from which conversation and other interaction feels most comfortable). This image can help us understand that in order to become culturally competent, we need to learn about both the surface and deep culture of groups that are different from us. This learning takes more effort than attending an ethnic festival or reading one book.

The cultural competence continuum (Figure 1.2) helps us identify where we are in this cultural learning process both as individuals and as institutions. Individuals and institutions can be identified according to various points on the continuum.

The cultural competence continuum is a scale of attitudes and behaviors that describe an individual or a system. As you view the continuum and the points along it, think first of yourself and ask where you belong. Then think of institutions or organizations in which you are involved. This can be a place of employment, a school, a welfare department, or a bank. Ask yourself where the policies of this system fit on the continuum.

On one end of the continuum is *cultural destructiveness* which is based on the belief that one group is better than another. An individual who is at this point on the continuum may belong to a white supremacist group or assume that working class people are ignorant and lazy. A system that is culturally destructive is one in which there are many cultures present, but only one is recognized as legitimate. All other cultures are rejected and regarded as inferior.

For example, in 1620 the Wampanoag Indians were a farming people with a representative political system and a division of labor with workers specializing in arrowmaking, woodwork, and leathercrafts. "However, many colonists in New England disregarded this reality and invented their own representations of Indians. What emerged to justify dispossessing them was the racialization of Indian 'savagery,' Indian heathenism and alleged laziness which came to be viewed as inborn group traits that rendered them naturally incapable of civilization" (Takaki 1993, 37).

The midpoint of the continuum is *cultural neutrality.* Those organizations and individuals who are culturally neutral take the stance that there are no differences between groups and all approaches are equally effective for all people. This is perhaps the trickiest point on the continuum, and even the word *neutrality* is itself misleading. Many of us were taught that for people who believe in equality, cultural neutrality is and should be the desired endpoint; a place where everyone is

Figure 1.1   **Deep and Surface Culture**

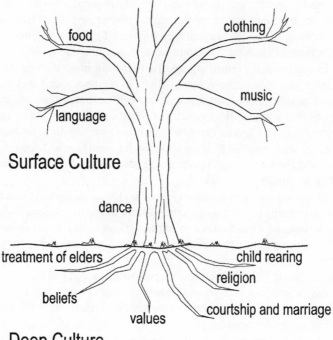

the same and difference does not matter. You may have heard people say, "I do not notice color when I meet a person; I just see a person." Yet for many people of color, racial identity is a source of pride that represents a history of struggle and survival against great odds. While on the surface it may seem noble or benign to ignore or "not see" racial difference, this act of so-called cultural neutrality may render invisible important aspects of a person's racial identity and heritage.

Many groups wish to maintain the food, music, and language of their culture and proudly wish them to be visible for others to see. Cultural neutrality can also obliterate these manifestations of heritage and pride. On a deeper level, there are many historically significant events that shape the experiences of a group in ways that contribute to both individual and cultural identity. These may be events that evoke pride as in the development of the women's movement. These may also be events that evoke pain and perhaps even shame, as in World War II when the U.S. government interred more than 110,000 Japanese Americans (Hamamoto 1994, 75). Cultural neutrality on an individual level, while often motivated by kindness, requires that people flatten these differences and agree to be the same. However, sameness and equality are very different phenomena.

When cultural neutrality is embedded in a system, it can be quite dangerous. A

Figure 1.2 **Cultural Competence Continuum**

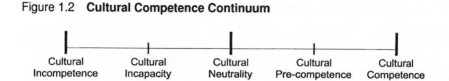

Cultural	Cultural	Cultural	Cultural	Cultural
Incompetence	Incapacity	Neutrality	Pre-competence	Competence

college or university may decide to treat each entering first-year student exactly the same and that policy will reflect a commitment to equality and equity. If, in fact, the structural differences in prior public education reflect that schools in poor communities and communities of color tend to have fewer educational resources and lower academic achievement, this color-blind policy may be the *same* for everyone, but not *equitable* for everyone. Recognition of these differences and their translation into just policies is challenging and complex.

The issue of cultural neutrality is important to our further discussions of assimilation and diversity. Some immigrant groups, Western Europeans for example, may choose to assimilate for a variety of reasons. After a generation or two, these groups may be fully assimilated if they choose to give up the language, clothing, and food (surface culture) of their country of origin. Other groups, Asians and Africans for example, may also choose to assimilate and give up elements of their surface culture, but their skin color makes it impossible for them to fully assimilate into American culture, that defines white skin as the norm. Cultural neutrality ignores the complexity of assimilation and diversity.

Cultural competence is the practice of actively understanding the integrated set of human values and behaviors belonging to a particular group *and* the capacity to function effectively and respectfully in other cultures. The ultimate goal on this continuum is *cultural competence* in both individuals and institutions. This takes us full cycle to the acceptance of and respect for difference. Cultural competence necessitates ongoing self-assessment and learning. Individuals and organizations that are culturally competent pay attention to the dynamics of difference and are committed to the expansion of cultural knowledge. Organizations that are culturally competent review and, when necessary, adapt policies and procedures with regard to employment, promotion, programming, products, and services.

A culturally competent individual is actively committed to understanding other cultures by reading, studying, asking questions, attending cultural events, and interacting. This individual understands the difference between surface and deep culture and does not assume that one interaction makes him or her an expert. A culturally competent individual is not required to know everything about other cultures, but rather to have an openness and a commitment to learn.

A culturally competent system or organization includes a plan to expand and act on cultural knowledge by adapting individual and institutional policies, structure, and services to meet culturally diverse needs and audiences. A culturally competent organization would closely resemble the proportion of the surrounding population at every level of employment. For example, a public school system in the southwest United States may develop a culturally competent plan that is bilingual (English and Spanish), studies and displays Mexican and Indian art, and includes Mexican and Indian history and literature as an integral part of the mainstream curriculum. For this school system to fully succeed at cultural competence there would need to be bicultural and bilingual employees at every level of the organization.

It is possible, and not uncommon, for an individual or organization to be culturally competent in one area and culturally neutral or even destructive in another area. For example, a heterosexual white male may feel knowledgeable and competent regarding women, African Americans, and Asian Americans but have little knowledge and much discomfort regarding Latinos, gays, and lesbians. The concept of cultural competence is not static; it is dynamic. Maintaining cultural competence requires continued openness and commitment to learning and rethinking what has been learned.

Cultural competence differs from the theories studied so far because it applies to both individuals and organizations. As you read through the various definitions, at what point on the continuum did you find yourself? How does that impact how you see people who are different from you in the world and in the media?

The Fabric of Oppression

The *fabric of oppression* is another theory of socialization that describes the structural arrangement of privileges, resources, and power. This theory is based on a liberal or left political understanding of how institutions, systems, and policies can create inequities according to group membership (National Conference on Community and Justice 1994). While liberation theory is based primarily on the individual, the fabric of oppression revolves around organizations and institutions. However, like liberation theory, this theory identifies the potential for each individual to either collude with oppression or participate in activism for change.

In order to fully understand the fabric of oppression, some basic definitions are essential. These terms will be used in subsequent chapters to examine and rethink issues of gender, race, class, and sexual orientation both in our culture and in the media. Often people use these terms interchangeably, causing some confusion. Table 1.1 provides definitions that distinguish the meanings of these terms.

The fabric of oppression is a systematic phenomenon that creates some groups that are dominant or privileged by it and other groups that are targeted or oppressed by it. It is possible to be part of a dominant group and benefit from that system of privileges without ever behaving in a way that is mean, prejudiced, or hateful. Conversely, one can also be part of a targeted group without ever experiencing a hateful act.

For example, because I am a heterosexual, married woman I can count on these attributes working in my favor and for the benefit of my children as we work our way through life. If I refer to "my husband" when speaking to my children's teach-

Table 1.1

The Fabric of Oppression and Definitions

Bigotry is the intolerance and prejudice that glorifies one's own group and disparages members of other groups.

Discrimination is the negative and harmful treatment of other groups that serves to provide an advantage to one's own group.

Prejudice is an attitude, opinion, or feeling based exclusively on an individual's membership in a particular group; it precludes prior knowledge, thought, or reason.

Social groups are groups of people who share a common social identity. Any group of people set apart by socially defined boundaries such as race, gender, sexual orientation, religion, age, ethnicity, ability, or socioeconomic class constitutes a social group. The number of dominant groups that an individual identifies with establishes that individual's amount of social power in American society.

Social power is the access to resources that increase one's chances of getting what one wants and influencing others. Social power is based on social group standing.

Resources and privileges are unearned benefits that accrue to people who belong to dominant groups. For example, white people can count on their skin color working for them when they apply for a bank loan or register a complaint at a restaurant or department store.

Oppression is a structural arrangement characterized by unequal access to resources, privilege, and social power. Like social power, oppression is also based on social group standing.

Source: Information is based on definitions provided in unpublished manuscripts and workshops provided by the National Conference on Community and Justice in St. Louis, 1994.

ers, they assume that we are a two parent, nuclear family—part of a dominant group that automatically triggers comfort and respectability. My lesbian friends with children experience something very different. When one parent is in a conference with a teacher and refers to her partner as "she," she cannot count on the teacher's acceptance or goodwill regarding her family in the same way I can.

It is important to note that membership in a dominant group does not guarantee wealth, power, and success but rather increases the opportunities for such gains. Similarly, membership in a targeted group does not guarantee failure but implies fewer chances and necessitates harder work. There is an anecdote attributed to Texas gubernatorial candidate Ann Richards that illustrates how this operates. Richards was running against George W. Bush, who was from a family of great wealth. Using a baseball analogy to describe Bush's advantage, Richards said that to this day George W. Bush believes he hit a triple when, in fact, he was born on third base.

Institutionalized oppression refers to the web of organizations and systems that perpetuate unequal access. There are three different kinds of institutionalized oppression. It can be *legal,* overt, and intentionally built into various institutions. An example of this is early laws that prohibited women from voting. Institutionalized oppression can be *illegal,* covert, and intentional, such as the refusal of certain organizations to hire gays and lesbians or African Americans even though they may be fully qualified for a job. The third kind of institutionalized oppression is *self-perpetuating* and systemic. This kind of oppression is built deeply into existing structures and is more difficult to identify and change. For example, some institutions that regard themselves as committed to racial equity still find that their highest ranking officials and employees are European American. These organizations have not been willing or able to figure out how to put verbal commitment to diversity into action.

Along with the external lack of access to power, resources, and privilege, members of targeted groups may experience *internalized oppression.* This phenomenon occurs when an individual takes the external misinformation, stereotypes, and negative images about their group and turns them inward. Internalized oppression is never voluntary, but rather a result of the same misinformation that is conveyed to members of the dominant group.

For example, until the 1960s middle class men and women were told that women's work was to stay at home, raise the children, and to cook and clean. As many women in the 1960s began to break out of this singular role and seek meaningful work outside of the home, others condemned them for failing their families and failing to be sufficiently feminine. While this issue was and continues to be politically charged, it is clear that many women believed that to be "real women" they must do women's work as assigned by society. According to the fabric of oppression, a particular woman's difficulty in recognizing alternative gender roles is a function of the misinformation she has received over time and a reflection of internalized oppression.

The process by which those in power secure the consent or social submission of those who are not in power is called *hegemony.* Hegemony is not secured through force but rather through the way that values get taught in religious, educational, and media institutions—through socialization. The structure and values of hegemony are often invisible. For example, until the 1960s, force was rarely needed to convince women to defer to men in financial or business matters. Women and men were socialized to understand their roles and to act them out accordingly.

As you look at the diagram below, think of the upper spaces as representing those groups that are privileged and have greater access to social power and resources, and the lower spaces as representing those groups that are targeted by oppression and that have less access to privileges, social power, and resources (see Figure 1.3). As you determine which groups are privileged and which are targeted, it is useful to think of major corporations, Congress, state legislatures, and other institutions and to think about who typically holds the highest positions in these

Figure 1.3   **The Fabric of Oppression and Social Group Membership**

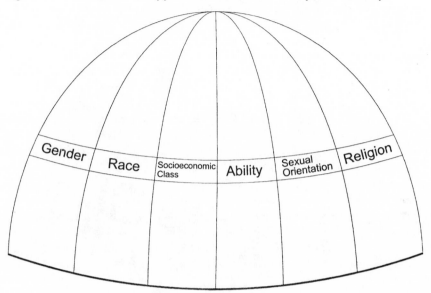

Source: Adapted from unpublished workshop material created by Joan Olsen.

organizations. Complete the upper spaces in the diagram according to which groups are privileged and the lower spaces according to which groups are targeted by oppression. Now look at the completed diagram in Figure 1.4.

According to theory of the fabric of oppression, the vast majority of those in power and with access to social power in the United States are male, white, physically and mentally able, and perceived to be heterosexual and part of the owning class. A few of these dominant group descriptions require explanation. *Owning class* refers to those individuals whose wealth is such that there is no financial need to work. Working class consists of that group of people who need to work to survive and are typically two to three paychecks away from poverty. The dominant group with regard to sexual orientation refers to individuals who are *perceived* to be heterosexual. This perception or appearance affords individuals access to social power. This does not mean that membership in any one of these groups absolutely guarantees or predicts that an individual will become the president of the United States or the CEO of General Motors. Rather, it describes the group memberships of those who are in positions of power and those who have greater access to it.

The same holds true for individuals who are members of the targeted groups described in the lower spaces of the diagram. The fact that there is less access to resources, power, and privilege does not imply that there is no access, nor does it forecast inevitable failure. Rather, the listing of targeted groups describes social power and its access in contemporary U.S. society.

Figure 1.4   **The Fabric of Oppression and Impacted Groups**

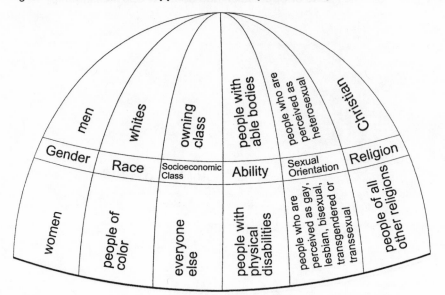

Source: Adapted from unpublished workshop material created by Joan Olsen.

The fabric of oppression further describes the vast majority of those who are targeted by oppression and have less access to social power, resources, and privileges as female; people of color; individuals with physical and/or mental disabilities; individuals who are perceived to be gay, lesbian, or bisexual; non-Christians; and individuals who are middle class, working class, or poor.

As you review the completed chart, notice where your group membership fits in the various categories. Most people find that they have membership in a variety of groups, some privileged and some targeted. Upon further review, observe that the diagram is in the shape of a bird cage. Carrying this image one step further, regardless of where any of us sits in this picture, we are all inside the cage (Olsen). This image is compatible with liberation theory in that it compels all people, privileged or targeted, to find ways to work toward liberation—in order to exist outside the cage.

This conceptualization of oppression is integral to all of the theories that analyze oppression and advocate social justice. Because oppression limits the human possibilities of all people—those with greater and lesser advantage—it is to everyone's advantage to pursue information and activities that will dismantle this system of oppression. These theories hold that this pursuit restores wholeness to humanity.

The Cycle of Oppression

The *cycle of oppression* is another theory of socialization. This theory describes the stages of socialization and their relationship to oppression. According to this cycle, during our early years we receive misinformation, and biased history, as well as stereotypes. Through the socialization process this information or misinformation is reinforced by people, systems, and institutions that we know, love, and trust. These distortions are provided to us, often unwittingly, by our families and neighbors through education, media, government, and our places of worship. In the next phase of the cycle, we internalize what we have learned and through this internalization we collude with the socialization process. We view misinformation as the truth and often see difference as wrong or abnormal. When we reach this stage in the cycle, we pass on the misinformation as truth and the cycle begins again (National Conference on Community and Justice 1994).

For example, an American Indian child may be taught early on not to speak her native language or wear any native clothing. Her family, with her best interest at heart, may tell her that she will fit in better, be accepted more, and have a better chance of success if she appears and acts "white." She may live in a mostly white neighborhood, attend a church that is predominantly white, and go to school with white classmates. Some of her friends may play "cowboys and Indians" in which the Indians wear feathers and have war cries and get shot by the "good guy" cowboys. In school, she may learn that most of the important people in American history and science have been white. In television and movies, most of the heroes she sees are white. When she does see American Indians in the media, they are typically dressed in buckskin and speak broken English. Most of the messages from the people and institutions she trusts reinforce what her parents told her; that it is better for her if people think she's white. If nothing happens in her life to interrupt this distortion of information, she will pass along these same messages to her own children.

What has she lost in this process, this cycle of oppression? First, regardless of her attempts to pass as "white," she is still American Indian. Her sense of self, authenticity, and self-esteem may be seriously shaken. She may, in fact, internalize oppression and think that deep down she must be "bad" if it is so terrible to be who she really is. This internalized oppression may reflect itself in many different ways. She could become personally withdrawn or depressed. It could result in deep prejudice and bigotry toward American Indians as a group. She may demonstrate disdain toward American Indians who maintain their original culture. If she is ever in a policymaking position, she may decide that American Indians are not worthy of any special consideration. This same cycle can occur with regard to gender, other races and ethnicities, class, and sexual orientation.

Theories regarding oppression state emphatically that no one is naturally oppressive or oppressed but rather subject to systematic and pervasive mistreatment based on membership in various groups. The perpetuation of oppression is made possible by the conditioning of new generations into dominant or targeted roles, which is then perpetuated through hegemony and the recycling of systematic misinformation about the nature, history, and abilities of dominant and targeted groups.

The classic theories of socialization described above include:

- social learning theory; and
- the social self.

The newer theories of socialization include:

- liberation theory;
- cultural competence;
- the fabric of oppression; and
- the cycle of oppression.

Socialization teaches us the culture and norms of our society. It may teach us that honesty and hard work are valued in U.S. society. But it can also lead to the misinformation that contributes to racism, sexism, homophobia, and class oppression.

Each of these theories explains ways that we learn who we are as individuals and the meaning of our membership in various groups. They also explain how we come to understand the "other," those whose social group membership is different from ours. Some of the theories, such as liberation theory and cultural competence, have strong value-based foundations that mandate individual and institutional action to increase equity and freedom. The theories of oppression often have a political foundation that is liberal or left.

Most of these theories mention media as an institution of socialization. The final and critical piece of the socialization puzzle is understanding the role and pervasiveness of entertainment media and how they reinforce or challenge our socialization in U.S. society.

Reconstructing knowledge is an invitation to critical thinking and emotional autonomy. It invites us to review what we have learned about history and politics and current events and to understand that there is almost always some combination of accurate information, misinformation, and distortion. Reconstructing knowledge asks us to not simply believe everything we are told, even by teachers and parents, or the author of this book; but rather implores us to carefully sift out truth from myth. Our personal experiences in life provide the informal lessons, and school provides the more formal lessons, that we inevitably bring with us every time we turn on a radio, buy a ticket to a movie, or sit at home watching television.

Entertainment Media

As we have seen, our personal experiences and formal education often create voids and distortions in information about people and groups that are different from us. Studying entertainment media is a third way to examine how these voids and distortions are challenged or reinforced. For example, if we have little contact with gays and lesbians in our personal lives and there is no information about sexual orientation provided in school, images of gays and lesbians in the media will become more powerful.

Our quest to analyze images of race, gender, class, and sexual orientation in the media constitutes more than a simple appreciation of diversity. It requires inquiry into our own life experiences, exploration and reevaluation of what we have been formally and informally taught about various groups, and an examination of how these messages appear in entertainment media. This section provides a variety of theories and perspectives that assess entertainment media, experience, and knowledge. These theories and tools will be utilized to examine the connection between the standing of a particular group and its portrayal in "media reality."

I have focused on entertainment media because of the pervasiveness of this aspect of popular culture in American lives through the entire span of our lives. News media has an increasing impact on our view of groups that are different from us as we grow older. However, as we learned through theories of socialization, the messages we receive in early developmental stages have extraordinary influence on how we see the world. From the cradle to the grave, entertainment media in the form of prime time television and popular music and film offers images that are often repeated over and over. These images can either fill in the gaps of our learning, reinforce what we have already learned, or challenge previous learning.

In the 1950s and early 1960s, the American family was conveyed in television programs such as *Father Knows Best, Leave it to Beaver, The Donna Reed Show,* and *Ozzie and Harriet.* In these programs, the family was portrayed as white, middle class, with two parents and two to three children. The father worked outside the home and the mother worked in the home; most often the mother wore a dress and sometimes she wore pearls as accessories. In these families, people rarely quarreled or shouted, and wise parents resolved problems in a quick thirty minutes. Sibling conflict ended with a brotherly punch on the arm and a sheepish, "Gee, Beav." Imagine that in the 1950s and 1960s, many people watched these programs and more every week for weeks and weeks and weeks.

Now recall what was discussed earlier in the chapter about social learning theory. According to this theory, repetition followed by reward becomes internalized learning. Also, recall that in liberation theory, misinformation gets taken in and internalized both by privileged and targeted groups. The 1950s television family became a perceived norm, what was regarded in American society as "normal" or "average." If your family was working class or poor, African American or Latino, if there was a single parent or extended family in your home or a language spoken other than English—you were different, abnormal, the "other."

The 1998 film *Pleasantville* offers a critical look at the perfect, simple world portrayed in these early television programs. When two teens get transported into the black-and-white life represented in the TV program *Pleasantville,* they compare the simplicity and predictability of television life to the complexity and unpredictability of their lives in the 1990s. Through a series of conflicts and revelations, the film conveys a strong message about what it means to be human. To be human is to be full of contradictions, to experience a range of feelings and sometimes messy emotions, and to face unpredictability. The film clearly prefers this complexity with all its chaos and pain to the black-and-white barrenness of the fantasy world of 1950s television.

Television viewers frequently hold contradictory beliefs about the materials they view. On the one hand, we know and can articulate that the program we are watching is fiction; yet on the other hand we often believe the messages that we are receiving (Jhally and Lewis 1992,15). This is key to understanding the impact of entertainment media on consumers. We may say of television, music, or film, "I know it's not real," and yet with heavy consumption of the media the repetition of the images will influence us in spite of that understanding.

This section of the chapter reviews various forms of entertainment assessment theory and offers some accessible, consumer-friendly tools for analyzing media content. These theories and tools provide qualitative, quantitative, and anecdotal methods of assessing the meaning and impact of media culture. Current and potential media producers can use these tools to analyze programs they are developing and considering. Media consumers can use these tools to dissect the messages and information they receive from media on a daily basis.

Entertainment assessment, then, is the third component of the three-part analysis system of this book. It is the combination of classic and new theories, approaches, and practical tools to determine messages in and impact by the media. By itself it provides us with some interesting analytical possibilities. Combined with our understanding of our personal experiences, informal learning, and reconstructing knowledge, it offers us a comprehensive method of investigation that opens enormous possibilities for critical and independent thinking in all aspects of life. And it is people with these skills who create, invent, discover, and solve problems at every level.

Entertainment Assessment Theories

Research in entertainment media has grown tremendously in the last half of the twentieth century. Given the growth in prime time television, cable television, popular music, film, and computer games, researchers focus on: (1) the industries that produce these materials; (2) the messages they contain; and (3) their impact. Some theories offer anecdotal and qualitative means of media analysis, while others construct methods to quantify media messages. Some of the theories claim political neutrality or objectivity, while others begin from a clear and unabashedly political standpoint. The theories and approaches we will consider are: media literacy, cultural studies, media production and economy theories, and the cultural indicators approach. We will use these entertainment assessment theories to gain a better understanding of how we interact with entertainment media.

Media Literacy

One relatively new approach to analyzing the messages in entertainment media is *media literacy.* Media literacy is an international field of study that involves observing media content, production, and impact as well as the industry itself. According to media literacy scholar Art Silverblatt, media literacy includes five elements:

1. *Awareness of the impact of media* on the individual and society involves educating media students, consumers, and producers to understand the enormous influence of media and to learn independence from its impact on us.
2. *Understanding the process of mass communication* involves learning the ways that messages are sent and received in both interpersonal and mass communication.
3. *Developing strategies to understand and interpret media messages* utilizes detailed analytical questions or keys that revolve around process, context, framework, and production values.
4. *Using media to understand contemporary culture and ourselves* reviews media texts and images to unravel cultural values, beliefs, and attitudes.
5. *Enhanced appreciation and enjoyment of the media* is one of the aims of media literacy that is advanced by the insights that are integral to the process (Silverblatt 1995, 2–3).

The application of media literacy is highly adaptable from elementary through graduate school. Given the pervasiveness of media and its influence on young people, some states are beginning to include media literacy as an element of their required public school curriculum. The purpose of teaching the tools of media literacy to students early in their lives is to help them make sense of the maze of media messages they receive and to sift out fiction from fact. This is a relatively new curriculum in the United States, and while it is too early to determine results, there is anecdotal information to suggest that even young children are enthusiastic about playing media detective to uncover hidden messages. For example, children who are glued to video games are intent on winning and are often only semiconscious in the process. Children who learn about the roles of women and messages of violence in these games may be more aware of the messages in the game, may discuss what they think about these messages, and may at times make different choices.

Media literacy does not take an explicitly political or activist stand. Rather, media literacy provides a wide array of methods and tools to analyze media texts and serves as a foundation for education from elementary school through college. But although the methodology is apolitical, what this analysis uncovers can have strong political ramifications.

Cultural Studies

Another approach to understanding the messages conveyed through media is *cultural studies*. Understanding the *ideology* that is present in various forms of entertainment media is an important aspect of cultural studies. Ideology is "a system of meaning that helps define and explain the world and that makes value judgments about the world" (Croteau and Hoynes 1997, 163). We can examine programs, songs, or films to see how they demonstrate certain kinds of thinking about cultural issues and about the social order of things and people. The ability and tools to discern this ideology are central to the understanding of cultural studies that allows media scholars and consumers to see beyond the surface entertainment value.

The analysis of political economy and production, analysis of media texts (e.g., film, music, television), and understanding of audience reception are the main components of cultural studies. Cultural studies examine the content of media within a framework of media ownership by analyzing how ownership and economic self-interest in the industry itself influence decisions about media format, content, and distribution.

Unlike media literacy, cultural studies theorists do not claim political neutrality but rather build their analyses from an explicit political position. One cultural studies scholar, Douglas Kellner, defines it as a critical endeavor with particular views and values which include: criticism of media as it recreates images of dominance, repression, and oppression; a critical perspective of media that advances democracy; and an understanding of the potential that media culture has to advance the interests of oppressed groups (Kellner 1995, 2).

One unique aspect of cultural studies is this forthright claim that it is not neutral. In fact, most theories about media and about diversity, multiculturalism, and oppression are not neutral. Just as you and I bring our personal experiences and values to our understanding of media, so do the researchers who study media and develop theories. In cultural studies, the politics and values are explicit.

Another important contributor to the development of cultural studies, Stuart Hall, defines ideology as "those images, concepts, and premises which provide the frameworks through which we represent, interpret, understand and 'make sense' of some aspect of social existence" (Hall 1993, 18). According to Hall, while ideological statements in the media may be made by individuals, they are the product of the conditions of socialization and the way the society and culture have formally and informally taught individuals to make sense of the world. Ideology works best when it operates at a less than conscious level—that is, when our socialization has been so thorough that we do not identify our positions as ideology but rather, see them as the articulation of "truth." Hall uses the example, "Little boys like playing rough games; little girls, however, are full of sugar and spice." While to some this may seem like a reflection of "truth," according to cultural studies it is largely based on a series of ideological beliefs about the nature of boys and girls (Hall 1993, 19).

Media is an important source of information for introducing and replicating a society's dominant ideologies, and as cultural studies theorists point out, these ideologies are often invisible to the media consumer. They often simply confirm what the consumer already "knows" to be true.

Television is the most pervasive form of contemporary media. A popular TV show can reach 15–20 million households. "One reason why television is considered to be so ideologically charged is that it relies, almost exclusively, on conventional 'realist' forms of image construction that mask the workings of the camera" (Croteau and Hoynes 1997, 180). For example, most of us know from our own experience that problems rarely resolve themselves neatly in a thirty-minute format. But to the extent that the characters and plot closely resemble "real people," the leaps from realism often seem more credible to the audience.

Prime time television tells stories that create a sense of what is normal and acceptable. For example, until recently, gay and lesbian couples did not exist in prime time television. By the 1990s, some programs such as *Northern Exposure, thirtysomething,* and *Roseanne* featured minor, recurring characters who were gay or lesbian, and by 1996 the program *Ellen* depicted the coming out of its main character. Yet, throughout most of prime time, gays and lesbians have remained relatively invisible. By 1998 *Ellen* was off the air. The program's ratings were down and network executives claimed the character was "too gay" each week. This under-representation of gay and lesbian characters underscores a central ideology that characterizes the heterosexual couple and family as normal and marginalizes other kinds of couples and families. The way that television orders its realities and tells its stories thus creates a central and dominant ideology with few opportunities for alternate stories to be told.

However, there are some forms of entertainment that offer alternative voices and ideologies. One such example is rap music. Some forms of rap and hip-hop music criticize the dominant culture and ideology. "In essence, rap presents an ideological critique from below; it is a musical form that criticizes social institutions from the perspective of those who have comparatively little power in contemporary society" (Croteau and Hoynes 1997, 184–85).

Cultural studies theorists say that media hold multiple meanings, which in turn offer the raw material for multiple interpretations. This empowers the audience to create meaning by bringing their formal learning, socialized experience, and critical and independent thinking to their media experience. With this in mind, audiences can interpret or "read" media in three different ways (Croteau and Hoynes 1997, 233).

The first kind of media reading is the *dominant reading* in which the media consumer is relatively passive and takes in the content without consciously thinking or processing the messages. In this case, the consumer almost always takes in the dominant message that was intended by the media producer. A *negotiated reading* of media assumes a more active consumer who accepts part of the dominant message, but also interprets part of the content according to his or her own experience and preferences. An *oppositional reading* is an active stance in which the media consumer consciously interprets the content in a way that fits with his or her own experience, preferences, and world view. These three positions depend largely on the experience, knowledge, and critical tools of the audience.

All in the Family, which aired from 1971 to 1983, was one of the all-time most popular television series. It illustrated the possibilities of these various forms of interpretation or readings. The creator of this series, Norman Lear, developed the character of Archie Bunker to reflect bigotry and political conservatism and as a symbol of the resistance to the movements for social and political change occurring in 1960s and 1970s.

So the *dominant* reading, as put forth by the show's producer, would be that Archie Bunker was a conservative bigot; his wife, Edith, a sweet simple soul; and his daughter, Gloria, and son-in-law, Mike, laughable but politically correct liberals. In fact, a large segment of the television audience agreed with the ideology put forth by Archie Bunker and revised Archie as something of a folk hero—a gruff but lovable character who held on to traditional American values. This would be considered an oppositional reading of the program.

Another central tenet of cultural studies is its foundation in politically radical theories that explain dominance and oppression. Cultural studies has used Marxist theories of economics and class to explain media as one of many institutions that control individual freedom via dominant structures and hegemony. This analysis offers a way to understand political and ideological positions and how dominance and resistance to these positions are reflected in the media (Kellner 1995, 56).

What this means is that a program such as *All in the Family* could be analyzed in terms of feminist theories about gender. Through this lens, Archie's wife, Edith, represents the old gender order. Edith defers to Archie, cooks for him, waits on him, and runs back and forth to the kitchen as Archie sits comfortably in his easy chair pontificating about the troubles of the world. Edith is a warm and likable character. Their daughter, Gloria, is a quintessential 1960s woman. She believes that women should be independent and often criticizes her father's demands and expectations of her mother. Yet as a character, Gloria is shrill, sometimes strident, and not nearly as warm or likable as Edith. Based on the contradictions between character likeability and political ideology, the audience would be drawn to mixed conclusions about the role of women. While Gloria's political views of gender are presented as palatable, it is ultimately Edith's likeability to which the audience is drawn. According to this cultural studies analysis, *All in the Family* would ultimately underscore a dominant ideology about gender. This ideology would say that women like Edith who go out of their way to wait on everyone, particularly their husbands, are the "good women." This is a *negotiated* reading of the program, which uses feminist ideology as a lens.

Cultural studies take an activist position in its outright criticism of the reflection of dominant ideology in media. It positions itself as an advocate and ally of oppressed groups whose alternate stories and ideologies need to be heard (Kellner 1995, 57). This aspect of cultural studies is compatible with liberation theory and the fabric and cycle of oppression in that its goal is transformation of the media and the dismantling of oppression.

Cultural studies theorists and activists regard entertainment media as a battleground in which dominant themes and ideologies are challenged by oppositional readings as well as themes and ideologies of resistance. This theory of criticism involves developing an alternative norm as a vantage point for criticism. This norm takes a particular political stand that includes the values of resistance, empowerment, democracy, and freedom used to criticize forms of oppression and domination.

Analysis of Media Production and Economy

The *analysis of media production and economy* is another set of theories used to examine entertainment media. This analysis is often used in tandem with other methods that ascribe meaning to content. In the last half of the twentieth century there has been increasing concentration of ownership of the media. By 1992 only twenty national and international corporations dominated the mass communications industry. Media integration has occurred in these conglomerates in which ownership of production of multiple types of media as well as distribution structures have become increasingly concentrated (Bagdikian 1997, 7).

As media consumers, we are often unaware that the many different production companies whose programs we might enjoy in a given week are actually all owned by a single conglomerate. If in one week you see a film from Miramax and a film from Buena Vista, rent videos from Blockbuster that were produced by Touchstone and Hollywood Pictures, watch ABC-TV, and turn to cable for ESPN and specials on Arts and Entertainment and Lifetime, you have actually spent a week watching programs from just one source: Disney.

As of 1996, Disney holdings included film, television, radio, and cable television. In addition to the companies mentioned above, Disney holdings also included Walt Disney Pictures, Caravan Pictures, Buena Vista Pictures, eleven TV stations, Walt Disney Records, ABC Radio networks, and the Disney Channel (Croteau and Hoynes 1997, 35). How does this concentrated form of media ownership and control affect program content?

> When the same corporations expand their control over many different kinds of media, they speak glowingly of providing richer public choices in news and entertainment. But the experience has been that the common control of different media makes those media more alike than ever. Movies become more like television series. Cable, once thought to be a fundamental alternative to programs on commercial television but now under control of companies also in television and other media, is increasingly an imitation of commercial television. (Bagdikian 1997, 9)

Ben Bagdikian has conducted important research in this area and does not see this concentration of ownership as a conspiracy. Rather, Bagdikian asserts that the level of wealth, ownership, and experience of individuals who run these conglomerates results in a high degree of shared values. These corporate decision makers become primary shapers of how we see the world and interpret its meaning. Their shared values translate into an ideology that is consistently conveyed in the media. The power to "treat some subjects briefly and obscurely but others repetitively and in depth" is where the power of concentrated ownership is most apparent. And as in social learning theory, "Continuous repetition and emphasis create high priorities in the public mind and in government . . ." (Bagdikian 1997, 16).

Concentration of media ownership makes it difficult for alternate voices to be heard because the bottom line profit motive affects programming decisions. According to media analyst Todd Gitlin, "One consequence of the profit-driven logic of safety is the general tendency to avoid controversy, even though it might bring high ratings" (Gitlin 1983, 50). This approach makes television, music, and film more formulaic and predictable. It certainly drives the enormous numbers of sequels that we see in films such as *Home Alone 3*. The profit motive also links advertising and music videos such that most "video versions of songs . . . are the result of marketing decisions made by record companies, not the artistic expression of the musicians" (Gitlin 1983, 50).

The motive for profit and the goals of advertisers have an enormous impact on the content of television as well. Sex and violence are used extensively because they are formulaic, easily produced, and attract a large audience, which in turn sells more products. According to Bagdikian, advertisers kill even successful serious dramas because they remind audiences that their problems cannot be easily solved by "switching to a new deodorant" (Bagdikian 1997, 160). The resulting narrowness of content limits ideas and information that are presented to the American public, thus limiting independence of thought and choice. "If a nation has narrowly controlled information, it will soon have narrowly controlled politics. . . . In the end, no small group, certainly no group with as much uniformity of outlook and as concentrated in power as the current media corporations, can be sufficiently open and flexible to reflect the full richness and variety of society's values and needs" (Bagdikian 1997, 223).

We, the consumers of television programming, focus on the programs and its content as central. The producers/owners of television programming view television's advertising time as central. Most TV is not a public service offering, but a business, a vehicle for profit. For network executives, the shows are often high-visibility couriers that deliver the real moneymakers: the commercials! In 1998, ABC sold thirty-second spots during the final episode of *Seinfeld* for a record $1.7 to $1.8 million each (Haber and Edelson 1998, 11).

This relationship between advertisers and program producers affects the content of prime time television. Networks want advertisers; advertisers want programs with audience demographics that match the products being advertised. From the network point of view, then, it is not surprising that segments of the population who are outside desirable demographic target groups find themselves marginalized or excluded from vast stretches of prime time TV. If we do not have the necessary discretionary income and the cheerful willingness to spend it, then in strictly financial terms we are not worth courting.

Cultural Indicators Analysis

Another method of analyzing entertainment media is the *cultural indicators approach,* a comprehensive system originated and utilized by George Gerbner in his many years of studying and analyzing entertainment television. This approach has three components: institutional process analysis, message system analysis, and cultivation analysis (Gerbner et al. 1986, 22).

Institutional process analysis examines the formation of policies directing media messages. The work of Bagdikian, Gitlin, and Croteau and Hoynes that evaluates the economics of media production fits into this category of analysis. Federal Communications Commission (FCC) regulations and policies, production codes, censorship, and ratings all are subject to examination in order to further the understanding of media messages. For example, when the technology of television became available, there were many options for how it could have operated as an industry. It could have been primarily government owned and operated as in England, or it could have been a commercial enterprise as it ended up being in the United States. Because TV has always been a profit-making endeavor in the United States, we assume this to be a natural attribute of the industry. Its commercial nature has meant that program content is largely dictated by economic forces and desires for profit. But suppose the government, a quasi-governmental agency, or an independent nonprofit organization such as PBS operated television. The motivation for programming and the content itself would vary according to whether it was meeting needs for profit, propaganda, or art.

Message system analysis is a quantitative assessment of the content in entertainment television. The Cultural Indicators Project, headed by Gerbner, annually collects a large sample of prime time television. The research team uses *content analysis* to assess this content in measurable units that describe characters, themes, and plots. The data are summarized and the messages are analyzed. Message system analysis refers to the overall messages that are gleaned from this broad sample and does not focus on particular messages in single programs.

According to Gerbner's long-term studies, television's messages are homogeneous across the board and create an effect he calls "mainstreaming" in which audiences are flooded with the same repetitive messages (Gerbner et al. 1986, 31). In 1997 Gerbner examined 1,755 prime time characters from ABC, CBS, NBC, and Fox, as well as WB and UPN. Some of his major findings were:

- Poor people are nearly invisible on television.
- African American men are surprisingly over-represented on television and portrayed as wealthier than their white counterparts. This does not square with current demographics and thus misrepresents the actual situation.
- Children and older adults, particularly women, are grossly under-represented.
- Women, Latinos, and Asian American characters are significantly under-represented (Gerbner 1997, 1).

The third component of the cultural indicators approach is *cultivation analysis,* which assesses audience impact. Cultivation analysis utilizes the content and messages gathered from message system analysis. Depending on the number of hours an individual views television per week, he or she is categorized as a light or heavy viewer. Subsequently, light and heavy television viewers are questioned about their beliefs and worldviews, and a determination is made as to whether their beliefs conform to the overwhelmingly consistent "TV reality." Given the homogeneous and repetitive messages on prime time television, the exact programs viewed are not particularly relevant to this analysis. For example, Gerbner has repeatedly found that the violence on television is far more extreme and prevalent than in reality. Heavy television viewers, however, tend to believe the "TV reality" over the documented reality of crime statistics or even their own experience (Gerbner et al. 1986, 22).

During the summer of 1996, I took my then nine-year-old son to see the hot film of the season, *Independence Day.* While the critic in me found weaknesses and flaws, the consumer in me loved it. Never mind that most of the women still had their blouses tucked in, high heels on, and impeccable lipstick after hours and days of grueling battle—it was engaging, visually dazzling, and fun. We got what we paid for—a few hours of entertainment. So why go through the tedious process of analyzing something that is clearly not designed to inform or educate?

The producers of entertainment media are the "storytellers" of the twentieth and twenty-first centuries (Gerbner 1998b, 1). Before the middle of the twentieth century, children heard stories and were taught values primarily from parents, grandparents, members of their extended family, religious institutions, and other trusted adults in their community. The socialization process continued with the "stories" learned in school and from peers. From these sources and stories, children learned what it meant to be male or female, rich or poor, American, right or wrong, and so forth. These are the stories we will explore as we investigate experience and reconstructing knowledge.

After the advent of television, while many families have continued these traditions of conveying what they believe to their children, they now face stiff competition from a little box that lives in and can tell stories straight from their home. What are these stories and what impact do they have on children and adults alike? What are the messages conveyed from popular film and music? Are there consistent messages that children and adults receive from these various forms of entertainment media? What are we learning about what is right and wrong, and what are we learning about people who are different from us?

The theories and methods above provide important background for critical analysis of entertainment media and will be used throughout this book to interpret the meaning of selected samples of popular media. However, some of these methodologies are beyond the scope of what one individual can do in his or her daily life to discern the messages in film, television, and music. In the next section of this chapter, we will look at accessible entertainment assessment tools that are designed with the individual in mind. While these tools do not provide us with the generalized conclusions that media researchers can determine from large samples, they will help students of media, media producers, and consumers of media to think critically about media culture and to recognize and understand its underlying ideology and values.

Entertainment Assessment Tools

Entertainment assessment tools examine how diversity by race, gender, sexual orientation, and socioeconomic class appear and are treated in popular film, prime time television, and popular music. We can investigate trends, patterns, messages, and assess images and stereotypes. We can compare one program, song, or film to another. Researchers, using larger and more random samples, can determine whether a particular program is unique in the messages it sends or whether it is part of a broader trend that conveys homogeneous content and meaning. Whether the investigation is on a small or large scale, we can begin to unravel some of the explicit and implicit values in media texts and to search for their underlying meaning and ideology.

Character Investigation

Central to the application of entertainment assessment tools to social groups is the understanding of stereotypes. A *stereotype* is a preconceived and oversimplified generalization about a particular social group. Generalizations are one way that people organize information so that we do not have to rethink everything every day. When we are babies and toddlers, our parents may tell us daily, "Don't touch the stove—it's hot!" Every day is a new day for toddlers who are intrigued by this tempting stove and the meaning of the word "hot." When the child succumbs to temptation and touches the stove, he or she learns quickly what that particular meaning of hot is and is unlikely to touch the stove again. This is a generalization that works for us.

Another example of generalizations or stereotypes involves hair color. As a young child I may meet someone with red hair who is very funny. As an elementary school student, I may meet another red head with an engaging sense of humor. My mind organizes that information to say that redheads are hilarious: a fairly benign stereotype. But suppose the first two redheads I meet have made a strong impression on me because they are mean or lazy or not so smart. This creates a negative expectation or fear every time I encounter someone with red hair. If these images are also conveyed in the media with any regularity or repetition, I will believe that they are true.

Stereotypes operate most effectively in entertainment media in three ways. The first is by limited exposure. So, for example, if there are few American Indian characters depicted in film, television, and popular music, the images that are there take on added significance and have a more powerful impact on audiences. The second way in which stereotypes operate in media is through the range of characters portrayed. If there are a limited number of American Indians in media, it is unlikely that there will be a wide range of different character types. And if one or two character types are consistently repeated, a stereotype will be created or reinforced.

Finally, stereotypes work best in media because they are conveyed through simple characters. Complex characters, whether heroes or villains, have many different layers and contradictions. They more closely resemble real people and their depth and intricacy defy easy categorization. Simple characters generally convey one or two strong elements of their personality or behavior and have little texture, complexity, or depth.

There are several ways to detect *character stereotypes* in a particular media text. The first is to ask simple questions about the social group we are investigating. We will focus on Asian Americans as the social group to investigate for now; but we could also replace this group in the questions below with any other race, ethnic group, gender, sexual orientation, or class. Follow the instructions in Media Activity 1.1 below to see how this works.

This is a simple tool to use while watching prime time television. Try it over the course of a week to investigate images of Asian Americans in the prime time television programs that you normally watch. Determine the actual number of images that appear and ascertain whether the characters are simple, complex, or a mix. Remember, simple characters are one-dimensional and unrealistic. Complex characters are multilayered, perhaps contradictory, and seem like real people. Either simple or complex characters can be heroes or villains. Most likely you will find very few or perhaps no Asian American characters. This provides an important piece of information. If you live in a community with few Asian Americans, where and what will you learn about this group? And if you live in a community with many Asian Americans, what are the implications of the disparity you note between the Asian American population on television and that within your own community?

Another form of character investigation builds on the simple schema of Media Activity 1.1 and provides specific character types to investigate, which are described in Media Activity 1.2.

This kind of assessment provides a crude analysis of characters from which some conclusions can be drawn. It allows the investigator another way to determine which characters are simple and which are complex. Mimetic characters are complex and romantic and ironic characters are simple. Superheroes can be either. And as discussed before, it is the simple characters that tend to create or perpetuate stereotypes.

Again, use this character analysis to examine the prime time television programs you ordinarily watch in a week. If you are not a TV consumer, pick a night and watch a few hours of television. Be sure that what you watch is narrative fiction and not a special movie, news program, or "infotainment." This time look at the portrayal of low-income characters with speaking parts and classify them according to the character types listed above. What do you find? How many low-income characters are there? How many are mimetic, ironic, romantic, or superheroes? Are there any patterns or trends? What messages do you think are conveyed?

Another layer of analysis that can be used in both types of character investigation described is to distinguish between major and minor characters. Major characters are those without whom the plot makes no sense; they are essential to what

---

Media Activity 1.1
Detecting Character Stereotypes in Entertainment Media

Instructions

Select an entertainment television program or film that you have recently seen, or a current popular song, and answer the following questions:

---

1. Are there any Asian Americans portrayed in the film, TV program, or song?

2. If so, how many Asian Americans are speaking characters? List the names of these characters.

3. For each Asian American character identified, determine the following:
    a. Is the character simple or complex?
    b. Is there a range of simple and complex characters?
    c. Is there a range of different types of characters?

---

unfolds. Minor characters are all other characters with speaking parts. If you look back at the two character investigations you conducted, you can distinguish between major and minor characters and see if there are any other patterns. For example, if there are no major characters in the social group you are investigating, that provides some messages about the conveyed significance of the group.

As you conduct these mini research projects, it is important to thoroughly understand that the results suggest some messages and perhaps ideology about the particular programs you have observed, but without a larger sample and more thorough investigation we cannot generalize about prime time television as a rule.

Another method that can be used for character investigation is *content analysis*. As described earlier, content analysis is the quantification of information contained in media that allows researchers and consumers alike to identify patterns and meaning in the media studied. Content analysis can only describe and summarize messages. From the messages, meaning can be extracted, but content analysis does not measure influence. In conducting content analysis, it is tempting to assume audience impact. While we can speculate that recurring messages may have a particular effect on the audience, it is important to remember that these conclusions cannot be drawn exclusively from the data gathered from content analysis. We will be using content analysis as an important tool to ascertain messages in popular media.

To examine women's physical appearance in prime time television you can apply the survey below to another small sample of narrative fiction television. You may select three dramas or comedies from prime time television. Prime time tele-

Media Activity 1.2
Identification of Character Types in Entertainment Media

Instructions:

Select a character from an entertainment television program or a film you have recently seen and identify him/her based on the following:

Mimetic:

Does the character seem like a "real" person? Is he or she complex and/or realistic in behavior and appearance? Does it seem plausible that a person such as this could exist? These characters are not simple. They demonstrate depth, contradictions, and ambiguity. Television characters such as Roseanne in the program of the same name and Andy Sipowicz in *NYPD Blue* are examples of mimetic characters.

Ironic:

Does the character seem overly simplistic and/or laughable? If the character does not appear intelligent, that does not mean the character is unrealistic or ironic. The key question here is does the character seem more like a caricature than an authentic person? Does the character lack depth, texture, and complexity? TV characters such as Al Bundy on *Married with Children* and Homer Simpson in *The Simpsons* are examples of ironic characters.

Romantic:

Does the character seem somewhat realistic, yet too good or too evil to be true? In this context, the term romantic does not necessarily involve love and affection. Rather, this character may appear real in personality yet walks through life unscathed. The female characters in the film *Independence Day* are good examples of romantic characters as they wander through the post-battle portion of the film in full make-up and heels. Another example of the evil side of romantic characters would be the characters who appear on soap operas as beautiful, rich, and consistently and predictably evil.

Superhero:

Does the character possess superhuman powers such as Bionic Woman, Superman, and so forth? This category can also apply to aliens such as "Alf" or the characters from *Third Rock from the Sun.*

Source: Chesebro (1987, 25–37).

vision is defined as regular programming that occurs Sunday through Friday from 8:00 P.M. to 11:00 P.M. Eastern Standard Time. This programming does not include news, infotainment, sports, variety programs, or special broadcasts. This time investigate only the major characters and answer the questions in the survey.

This form can be copied and each of the major female characters coded on a separate survey form. The results should then be tallied and added. For example, if you are investigating six major female characters—how many of them are plain, glamorous, and so on? To take the analysis one step further, you may figure the percentage for each category. Are most of the women average, attractive, or glamorous? Are most of them thin, average, voluptuous, or overweight? What messages do you think are conveyed by the results? To carry this particular content analysis one step further, you could investigate the major male characters and see if there are any differences in the numbers of major characters and their physical appearance and perhaps draw some conclusions from the comparison. There are other kinds of character investigations that will be introduced throughout the text to examine particular social groups.

Examination of Themes

Still another way to analyze entertainment media is to observe the occurrence of various themes. *Themes* are subjects that are introduced in the media text and can be minor, significant, or central to the unfolding of the story. For example, themes can involve crime, health and medicine, friendship, or sexual orientation. Analyzing themes is another method of understanding messages and ideologies. The types of themes that occur in popular media convey what is important in society and suggest appropriate values and norms.

To understand how themes convey messages, examine the last few feature films you have seen at the theater or viewed on video. Using Media Activity 1.4, determine which of the themes listed were present in the film and to what degree. Again, you may copy the survey and apply it to each film investigated.

After completing one survey form for each film, tally the results and provide the following totals:

- How many times did various themes appear as major?
- How many times did various themes appear as significant?
- How many times did various themes appear as minor?
- In how many of the films were various themes nonexistent?
- Which themes were most and least prevalent?

As you review the appearance and relative significance of these themes in films you have seen, you can begin to ascribe meaning to their presence or absence, keeping in mind that without a larger and more random sample you will not be able to make broad generalizations and conclusions. However, you can understand messages in the particular films that you investigate.

Media Activity 1.3
Analysis of Women's Appearance in Small Sample of Prime Time Television

Instructions

Choose a minimum of three prime time television programs that offer a fictional narrative. This can be drama or comedy but not news, variety or award shows, or news magazine programs. Major characters are defined as those characters without whom the plot makes no sense in the particular episode selected. As you determine the attractiveness of the character, rely on U.S. norms and conventional standards of beauty rather than your personal preferences. Answer questions 6–8 for each major female character.

Name of Program _____Date viewed_____

1. Summary of basic plot

2. Number of major characters:
3. Number of major male characters: _____
4. Number of major female characters: _____
5. Name of major female character #1: _____
6. Is the character: _____
     0 = cannot code
     1 = very thin
     2 = slim
     3 = average weight
     4 = voluptuous
     5 = overweight
7. Is the character: _____
     0 = cannot code
     1 = blond
     2 = brunette
     3 = red hair
     4 = other
8. Is the character's appearance: _____
     0 = cannot code
     1 = homely
     2 = plain
     3 = average
     4 = attractive
     5 = glamorous
     6 = other

Media Activity 1.4
Analysis of Social Group Themes in Feature Films

Instructions

Select a minimum of three feature films that you have recently seen in the theater or on video. Answer the questions below separately for each of the films you saw using the codes below (0–3).

0 = the topic was not present
1 = the topic was present but minor or incidental to story
2 = the topic was significant to the story
3 = the topic is the outstanding issue or is central to the story

1. _____ Folk culture
2. _____ Race
3. _____ Ethnicity/nationality
4. _____ Sexual Orientation
5. _____ Gender
6. _____ Social or economic class
7. _____ Physical or mental disability
8. _____ Other (please describe)

Source: Gerbner (1995).

This survey investigated only themes that involve targeted groups, groups that tend to be disempowered in our culture. In a large sample, this kind of research can determine how these groups are treated in film. In our small sample, we can begin to see if these groups appear at all in the films we watch and if they are significant to the development of the plot. If there are never themes regarding physical and mental disability in the films we view, we can draw at least one conclusion: the message conveyed is that issues involving disabilities are not important. If there are few or no themes about disabilities in film or television, where do we learn about life's challenges and rewards for people living with disabilities? If our personal experiences do not involve people with disabilities and we are not taught in school about disabilities, the media becomes an important conveyor of information. As we note the absence of certain themes in entertainment media, we may then begin to question what our source of information is about disabilities or other topics. This questioning increases our independent thinking. We may determine that we have learned a great deal about disabilities from school or our own personal experiences and the absence of media themes makes little difference. We may decide that we have had almost no exposure to the issues facing people with disabilities and decide to learn more. If we are a person living with a disability, we may feel invisible or be angry that issues and topics that effect us are rarely conveyed in media.

In this exercise, themes were assessed simply in terms of their occurrence. Themes can also be investigated with more depth to determine underlying ideology in the way that a theme is conveyed. Further analysis can be conducted regarding plot and interactions between characters. These, in combination with the character and theme analyses above, can be used to evaluate messages in various forms of entertainment media.

Chapter Summary

This chapter describes a three-part process of how we learn about individuals and groups that are different from us. We learn about diversity from direct experience with our families, our neighbors, our friends, our classmates and the people who attend our place of worship. This informal kind of learning through exposure to and interaction with different people is called *personal experience.* When there are many groups missing from this direct experience, there are gaps and voids in our informal learning. Some of the gaps and voids may be filled through what we learn about groups that are different from us in our formal education. In the schools we attend, our teachers and textbooks are sources of information. *Reconstructing knowledge* is a method of reviewing this formal education to detect what is accurate and where there are gaps, misinformation, and distortion. This will be used as a basis to consider and evaluate information we may not have learned. Finally, we receive indirect or mediated information from entertainment media in the form of popular film and music and prime time television. The messages and ideology in media may fill in some of the gaps in our personal experience and formal education or it may reinforce or challenge what we have learned elsewhere. *Entertainment assessment theories and tools* provide us with methods to determine, understand, and evaluate the messages we receive as well as their accuracy.

As we employ this process of assessing entertainment media, we can review media messages in the context of what we know about our personal experience and through reconstructing knowledge as we examine what we have been formally taught. This is not an exercise in political correctness, but rather an exploration of a multitude of possibilities of how to see and interpret the world. After we consider the many ways available to understand diversity, we may choose to change how we understand difference or we may choose to maintain our original values, beliefs, and perspectives.

As we investigate and assess and perhaps revise what we have learned, we will be building a warehouse of tools. These tools allow us to consciously and independently choose and construct our own identity, beliefs, and values and a deeper understanding of diversity in our culture.

Bibliography

Adams, Maurianne; Bell, Lee Anne; and Griffin, Pat, eds. 1997. *Teaching for Diversity and Social Justice: A Sourcebook.* New York: Routledge.

Andersen, Margaret L., and Collins, Patricia Hill, eds. 1995. *Race, Class, and Gender: An Anthology.* Belmont, CA: Wadsworth.

Bagdikian, Ben H. 1997. *The Media Monopoly.* Boston: Beacon Press.

Cader, Michael, ed. 1994. *Saturday Night Live: The First Twenty Years.* Boston: Houghton Mifflin.

Chesebro, James W. 1987. "Communication, Values, and Popular Television Series: A Four Year Assessment." In *Television: The Critical View*, ed. Horace Newcomb, 25–37. New York: New York University Press.

Croteau, David, and Hoynes, William. 1997. *Media/Society: Industries, Images, and Audiences.* Thousand Oaks, CA: Pine Forge Press.

Dines, Gail, and Humez, Jean M., eds. 1995. *Gender, Race and Class in Media.* Thousand Oaks, CA: Sage.

Gerbner, George. 1998a. "Casting and Fate in '98: Fairness and Diversity in Television: An Update and Trends Since the 1993 SAG Report." A Cultural Indicators Project Report to the Screen Actors' Guild.

———. 1998b. "Why the Cultural Environment Movement?" Unpublished manuscript.

———. 1997. "Television Demography: What's Wrong With this Picture?" Unpublished manuscript.

———. 1995. "Cultural Indicators Survey." Unpublished survey.

Gerbner, George; Gross, Larry; Morgan, Michael; and Signiorelli, Nancy. 1986. "Living with Television: The Dynamics of the Cultivation Process." In *Perspectives on Media Effects,* ed. Jennings Bryant and Dolf Zillman Lawrence, 17–31. Hillsdale, NJ: Erlbaum Associates.

Gitlin, Todd. 1983. *Inside Prime Time.* New York: Pantheon Books.

Gonzales, Anthony; Laurie, Byron; McDowell, Brigit; Tymrak, Kristin. 1993. *Baby X.* Presented as part of the President's Peace Commission Fall 1993 program, "Identity in the 90s: Individual, Family and Community." Video.

Grusec, Joan E. 1992. "Social Learning Theory and Developmental Psychology: The Legacies of Robert Sears and Albert Bandura." *Developmental Psychology* 28: 776–86.

Haber, Holly, and Edelson, Sharon. 1998. "Retail Ads: Upping the Ante." In *Women's Wear Daily*, May 15, 11.

Hall, Stuart. 1993. "The Whites of Their Eyes: Racist Ideologies and the Media." In *Gender, Race, and Class in Media*, ed. Gail Dines and Jean M. Humez, 18–19. Thousand Oaks, CA: Sage.

Hamamoto, Darrell Y. 1994. *Monitored Peril: Asian Americans and the Politics of TV Representation.* Minneapolis: University of Minnesota Press.

Hochschild, Jennifer. 1995. *Facing Up to the American Dream: Race, Class and the Soul of the Nation.* Princeton: Princeton University Press.

Institute for Public Media Arts. 1997. "-(N)ISM Toolkit." Unpublished manuscript.

Internet Movie Database. 1999. http://us.imdb.com.

Jhally, Sut, and Lewis, Justin, 1992. *Enlightened Racism: The Cosby Show, Audiences and the Myth of the American Dream.* Boulder, CO: Westview Press.

Kellner, Douglas. 1995. *Media Culture: Cultural Studies, Identity and Politics Between the Modern and the Postmodern.* London: Routledge.

Love, Barbara. 1989. From unpublished lecture at "Parallels and Intersections" Conference, University of Iowa.

McIntosh, Peggy. 1995. "White Privilege and Male Privilege: A Personal Account of Coming to See Correspondences Through Work in Women's Studies." In *Race, Class and Gender: An Anthology*, ed. Margaret L. Andersen and Patricia Hill Collins, 76–86. Belmont, CA: Wadsworth.

McNeil, Alex, 1996. *Total Television: The Comprehensive Guide to Programming from 1948 to the Present*. New York: Penguin Books USA.

Marcuse, Ricky Sherover. From undated, unpublished manuscript.

Mead, George Herbert. 1995. *Mind, Self, and Society from the Standpoint of a Social Behaviorist*. Chicago: University of Chicago Press.

Morgan, Michael, and Signiorelli, Nancy, eds. 1990. *Cultivation Analysis: New Directions in Media Effect Research*. Newbury Park, CA: Sage.

National Conference on Community and Justice. 1994. Unpublished manuscript, St. Louis.

Olsen, Joan. Handouts from "Cultural Bridges" workshop.

Postman, Neil, and Weingartner, Charles. 1969. *Teaching as a Subversive Activity*. New York: Delacorte.

Salzman, Jack; Smith, David Lionel; and West, Cornel, eds. 1996. *Encyclopedia of African-American Culture and History*. New York: Macmillan Library Reference USA, Simon and Schuster.

Silverblatt, Art. 1995. *Media Literacy: Keys to Interpreting Media Messages*. Westport, CT: Praeger.

Takaki, Ronald. 1993. *A Different Mirror: A History of Multicultural America*. Boston: Little, Brown.

Zinn, Howard. 1995. *A People's History of the United States: 1492–Present*. New York: Harper Perennial.

"Father Knows Best" (August 1955). The fictional Anderson family was also the fictional American norm [*top left to right:* Jane Wyatt, Robert Young; *bottom:* Billy Gray, Lauren Chapin, Elinor Donahue]. © Bettmann/CORBIS.

"I Love Lucy" (1950s). Lucy literally gets tied up as a result of her antics [*left to right:* Desi Arnaz, Lucille Ball, Vivian Vance]. © Bettmann/CORBIS.

Pillow Talk (1959). Doris Day and Rock Hudson toast in this fluffy, romantic comedy. © American Film Institute.

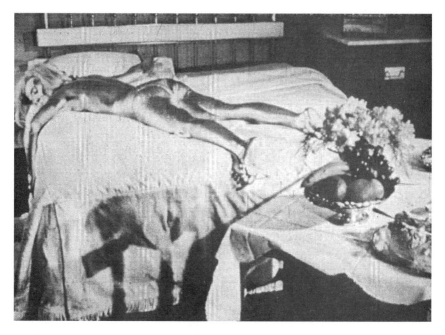

Goldfinger (1964). The villain kills Shirley Eaton's character by painting her in gold. © American Film Institute.

Norma Rae (1979). Sally Field as Norma Rae passionately urges fellow factory workers to join the union and fight unfair conditions.
© American Film Institute.

Turning Point (1978). When they meet later in life, two women second guess their respective life decisions [*left to right:* Shirley MacLaine, Anne Bancroft, Tom Skerritt]. © American Film Institute.

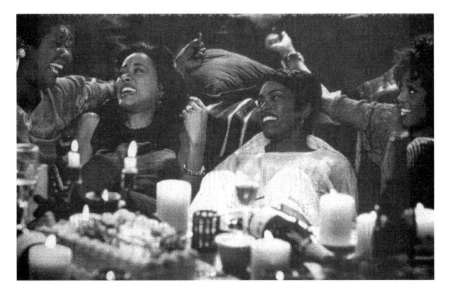

Waiting to Exhale (1995). A rare depiction of the diversity of African-American women in this ensemble cast [*left to right:* Loretta Devine, Lela Rochon, Angela Bassett, Whitney Houston]. © American Film Institute.

"The Honeymooners" (1950s). Audrey Meadows and Jackie Gleason play the working class characters Alice and Ralph Kramden. © CORBIS.

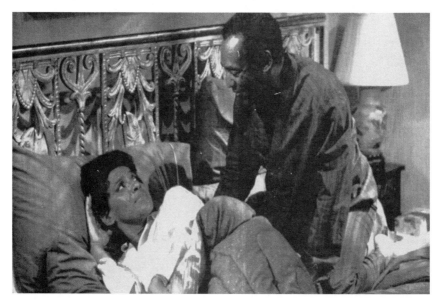

"The Cosby Show" (1985). Cliff and Clair Huxtable [Bill Cosby and Phylicia Ayers-Allen] represent the African-American realization of the American Dream. © Jacques M. Chenet/CORBIS.

"Roseanne" (1990). The living room set was ordered from the Sears catalog to establish working class authenticity [*left to right:* Lecy Goranson, Roseanne, John Goodman, Michael Fishman, Sara Gilbert]. © Lynn Goldsmith/CORBIS.

Working Girl (1988). The story of Tess McGill's rise from secretary to executive is the familiar story of the American Dream. © American Film Institute.

West Side Story (1961). Love and class similarities are not enough to conquer the battle for turf between two gangs [*left to right:* Richard Beymer, Russ Tamblyn, George Chakiris, Natalie Wood]. © American Film Institute.

Aladdin (1993). The love between Aladdin and Princess Jasmine overcomes their class differences. © Disney.

"Lone Ranger" (date unknown). Tonto is a classical American Indian stereotype with broken English and buckskin and serving as a faithful side-kick [*left to right:* Clayton Moore, Jay Silverheels]. © Bettman/CORBIS.

Thunderheart (1992). The good guys and bad guys shift as this film takes a hard look at conditions on reservations, the role of the FBI, and Indian activism [*left to right:* Graham Greene, Val Kilmer]. © American Film Institute.

Pocahontas (1995). The Disney animated image of Pocahontas (looking remarkably like the Disney animated Princess Jasmine in *Aladdin*) was a supermodel composite. © Disney.

The World of Suzie Wong (1960). Suzie Wong is depicted as exotic and ultimately tragic as her love with a white man is thwarted [Nancy Kwan and William Holden]. © American Film Institute.

The Killing Fields (1984). A complex telling of war in Southeast Asia and the development of a friendship between men of two very different cultures [*left to right:* Haing S. Ngor, Sam Waterston]. © American Film Institute.

The Karate Kid (1984). Pat Morita as the wise, Asian karate expert [*left to right:* Ralph Macchio, Pat Morita]. © American Film Institute.

Mississippi Burning (1988). The FBI are the heroes, the Ku Klux Klan the villains, and most of the black people are frightened and passive [*left to right:* Gene Hackman, Willem Dafoe]. © American Film Institute.

The Little Colonel (1935). Bill Robinson plays the happy dancing servant to Shirley Temple. © Bettman/CORBIS.

Superfly (1972). Superfly [played by Ron O'Neal] was considered one of the "Blaxploitation" era films. © American Film Institute.

Boys on the Side (1994). Whoopi Goldberg plays an African-American lesbian who is the hero of this otherwise white cast [*left to right:* Whoopi Goldberg, Drew Barrymore, Mary-Louis Parker]. © American Film Institute.

Boyz 'N the Hood (1991). Lawrence Fishburne as a strong black man fighting for his and his son's survival in a relentlessly racist and violent atmosphere [*left to right:* Morris Chestnut, Lawrence Fishburne, Ice Cube]. © American Film Institute.

"Amos and Andy" on the Radio (1935). White actors Freeman Gosden *[left]* and Charles Correll *[right]* do their version of black dialect in the radio version of the program. © Bettmann/CORBIS.

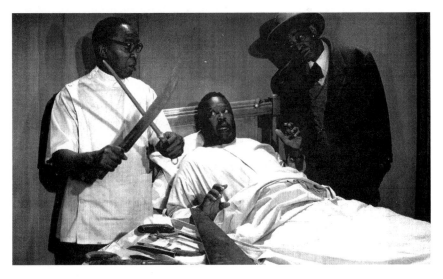

"Amos and Andy" on Television (early 1950s). One of the first television shows to feature an all-black cast; the NAACP fought its depiction of stereotyped characters [*right to left :* Tim Moore as George "Kingfish" Stevens, Spencer Williams as Andy, and unidentified actor as the doctor]. © Bettmann/CORBIS.

"Ellen" (April 2000). The public uproar surrounding the coming out episode of "Ellen" blurred the lines between Ellen the character and Ellen the person [Ellen DeGeneres, *left*, Anne Heche, *right*, and Ellen's mother, *second from left,* attend a gay rights rally]. © AFP/CORBIS.

"Will and Grace" (May 17, 1999). Characters, Jack [played by Sean Hayes, *left]* and Will [played by Eric McCormack, *right]* offer a rare view of humor, complexity, and diversity among gay men. © Mitchell Gerber/ CORBIS.

Marlene Dietrich (1930s). Marlene Dietrich's portrayal suggested bisexuality of characters in films such as *Morocco.* © Hulton-Deutsch Collection/CORBIS.

Boys in the Band (1970). The scriptwriter looks back at this ensemble of gay male characters as a reflection of the internalized homophobia of the times. © American Film Institute.

Torch Song Trilogy (1988). Harvey Fierstein and Matthew Broderick create a sense of love, dignity, and humor in their committed relationship. © American Film Institute.

Go Fish (1994). *Go Fish* provided a snapshot of a diverse lesbian community. © American Film Institute.

Philadelphia (1993). Denzel Washington, Tom Hanks, Antonio Banderas, and Jason Robards star in this commercially successful portrayal of a gay man's battle against AIDS and discrimination. © American Film Institute.

Chapter 2

Gender: In Pink and Blue and Vivid Color

> To see that all knowledge is a construction and that truth is a
> matter of the context in which it is embedded is to greatly expand
> the possibilities of how to think about anything, even those things
> we consider to be the most elementary and obvious.
>
> —*Field Belenky*

Personal Experience and Gender

As we explore what it means to be male or female, feminine or masculine, pay close attention to your reaction to the information. Are you nodding in agreement, are you rejecting various elements, are you confused? In order to resolve any dissonance between past beliefs and "knowledge," and current information, you will need to actively decide what blend you believe to be accurate and true. The first experiential step to explore what you have come to understand about gender in both your thoughts and your behavior is the Gender Journey in Personal Inventory 2.1 (Orenstein 1994, xii). As you analyze your two journeys as a girl and as a boy, it will begin to be clear that some of your experiences represent clear choice, some have been explicitly chosen for you, and some have been subtly suggested to you. Examples of a relatively independent or gender neutral choice may be the food you eat or the type of music you listen to. Expressions of your gender that were most likely directed by your parents and perhaps the media include the clothes, toys, and room decorations of babyhood and early childhood.

Consider another scenario. After having three boys in a row, Jennifer's parents were thrilled when she was born. Her parents and grandparents, aunts, and uncles lavished her with gifts—lacy pink dresses, tiny pearl necklaces, china tea sets, and delicate dolls. After years of wearing pink dresses and bows as a baby, toddler, and young girl, Jennifer *decided* that this is what girls wear to be feminine and beautiful. She decorated her room in lavender and pink and *chose* ruffles on the bedspread with lots of dolls and stuffed animals piled on the bed. By the time she was in high school, her old jewelry box with the musical ballerina was crammed with

51

Personal Inventory 2.1
The Gender Journey

Transport yourself to the time when you were a junior in high school. Picture yourself in one of your classes. Pay attention to where you are sitting and the way you are sitting. Then think about the following questions:

1. What were you wearing and how was your hair styled?
2. What kind of shoes, jewelry, or makeup were you wearing?
3. How was your bedroom at home decorated? What were the colors? What was on the walls?
4. Who were your friends outside of class?
5. What kinds of activities did you participate in outside of school?
6. What clubs or organizations did you belong to?
7. What did you do for fun?

Now picture yourself in seventh grade. Again, situate yourself in one of your classes and ask these same questions.

Next, imagine yourself in second grade and once again ask the questions above.

Finally, take one more step back in time to the day you were born. Imagine the excitement of your family and answer the questions below:

8. Were your parents expecting a boy or a girl?
9. What do you imagine your parents and other relatives might have said when they discovered what sex you were?
10. What kind of clothes and stuffed animals and toys do you think people bought for you?

Now pause for a moment. Take a breath. Imagine that same instant of your birth, but this time envision that you were born the opposite sex. With this new identity take the journey back through time. Visualize yourself, again, at the moment of your birth and ask the same questions as if your sex had been different. Go back to second grade, then seventh grade, and finally to a junior year in high school. Ask all of the same questions you asked the first time.

When you complete this journey forward through time as the opposite sex, take a moment and write down all of the things that were the same and all of the things that were different depending on what sex you were born as. Were you dressed in pink or blue as a baby? Did you wear dresses or pants to school? Did your friends play baseball, dolls, or both? Did you sit with your legs crossed or wide open? Did you curl or blow dry your hair or just let it hang after washing? Did your bedroom have pictures of dancers, animals, race cars, or athletes hanging on the walls?

Source: Peggy Orenstein (1994).

earrings and necklaces that she sorted through daily to find the right match for her outfit. Her parents and girlfriends commented on how sweet and pretty and feminine she was and her teachers complimented Jennifer on her quiet well-mannered behavior. By junior high school, boys began calling Jennifer and noticed the same things her friends, teachers and parents had been telling her for years. While Jennifer may have felt that she was making independent choices, the early choices made for her and the support and reinforcement she received for their continuation constituted a perhaps unintentional, but subtle, way of leading her to a particular set of characteristics that defined her femininity, her gender identity.

However, boys and girls can also be raised to make their own choices early on. They may be presented with Legos or easy-bake ovens from which to choose. Their rooms may be decorated in yellow or red with gender-neutral pictures on the walls. Girls and boys may also rebel against the gender expression that was chosen for them as young children. A girl might decide that she hates dresses and pink and dolls and prefers trucks and football. A boy may decide he hates sports and mud and prefers dolls and playing house. These options have become increasingly acceptable in some subcultures in the United States, but in many communities girls who make nontraditional gender choices are called "tomboys" and boys who make these choices are called "sissies."

Later in the chapter, the issues of gender identification and socialization will be systematically explored and analyzed. But for now, focus on your own experience as a boy or a girl, working to trace and describe your childhood without judging, defending, or criticizing it. To continue the process of understanding your experience of gender, take the quiz in Personal Inventory 2.2. This quiz analyzes a set of elements in your life that serve as indicators of how you were raised to express your "masculinity" or "femininity" and what choices you made in that context.

- If you scored 12–15 points, your gender socialization as a child tended to match the culture's definition of traditionally masculine.
- If you scored 5–8 points, you were socialized to express your gender as more traditionally feminine.
- If you scored 9–11 points, your gender socialization as a child tended to be mixed or neutral.

As you examine your score, resist again the pull to judge and evaluate your experience. Instead, use these rough indicators as a means to understand what you were told and how you behaved according to standard definitions of masculinity and femininity. Understand that there are no right or wrong answers, but rather descriptions that will serve as a foundation, an underpinning to analyze and reconstruct what you have learned explicitly and implicitly about what it means to be male or female in U.S. society.

Try one more exercise in Personal Inventory 2.3 to investigate your current

Personal Inventory 2.2
Childhood and Gender Quiz

Instructions

Mark those answers that come closest to matching elements of your life. Select an answer if even one part of the item listed is correct and write the number of points in the blank in front of the correct answer. Select the one answer that comes closest to matching your experience. When you have completed the quiz, total your score.

1. Which of the toys or games below were your favorites to play with as a young child?
   a. ____ dolls, paper dolls, tea sets, or play kitchen toys (1 point)
   b. ____ Candyland, Chutes and Ladders, Monopoly, Yahtzee, Checkers, Chess (2 points)
   c. ____ action figures, toy guns, toy cars and trucks, toy tools (3 points)

2. What kind of interactive play with other children was your favorite?
   a. ____ playing dolls, house, or hopscotch (1 point)
   b. ____ playing board games, riding bicycles (2 points)
   c. ____ softball, football, baseball, play war or forts (3 points)

3. As a young child, what did you want to be when you grew up?
   a. ____ a mother or father, a model, teacher, dancer, nurse, secretary (1 point)
   b. ____ a musician, salesperson (2 points)
   c. ____ a firefighter, police officer, truck driver, doctor, lawyer, architect, athlete (3 points)

4. What household chores were you given as a child?
   a. ____ setting or clearing the table, helping with cooking, dusting, washing dishes (1 point)
   b. ____ cleaning bathrooms, sweeping, making your bed, keeping your own room clean (2 points)
   c. ____ taking out the trash, raking leaves, mowing the lawn, shoveling snow (3 points)

5. Which of the statements below comes closest to what you were told (or what you learned by observing) as a child about what you were supposed to do if your body or feelings were hurt?
   a. ____ "Oh, sweetheart, I'm so sorry that happened. Go ahead and cry. I know that hurts." (1 point)
   b. ____ "If you're hurt really badly, go ahead and cry if you have to. But don't make such a big deal out of things." (2 points)
   c. ____ "Buck up. You're big now. Big boys (or girls) don't cry. Be a little man (or little woman)." (3 points)

experience as a male or female. This is most useful when a group of five or more people of eighteen years or older works simultaneously and compares answers.

After answering the questions, compare your total products and hours of preparation to the totals of other men and women and see if you detect any patterns. Generally, this activity reveals that there is somewhat of a continuum based on whether you are male or female. People who report spending two hours or more preparing for a special event are principally women. There is somewhat of a gender mix in the one-hour range. But those people who jump in and out of the shower and run a comb through their hair are most frequently men.

Are these preparations biologically hardwired? Probably not. Does our culture socialize us in such a way that primping and pampering seems more feminine? Probably so. There are some clear implications for traditional masculine and feminine socialization. "[T]o fail at the feminine difference is to appear not to care about men, and to risk the loss of their attention and approval. To be insufficiently feminine is viewed as a failure in core sexual identity" (Brownmiller 1984, 15).

According to a study conducted by the American Association of University Women (AAUW), girls emerge from their teen years with reduced expectations and less confidence than boys. In fact, this drop in self-esteem is reflected in lowered scores on standardized tests (AAUW 1995, 62). Gender socialization has profound consequences that are emotional and financial and impact the experience of success for both men and women.

In the next section of this chapter, the *reconstructing knowledge* approach will be used to build a framework for analysis of the experiences you have reported above.

Reconstructing Knowledge and Gender

Gender socialization is a universal experience. Even if parents work very hard to raise their children with gender neutrality, input from grandparents and other adults, peers, and the media provides daily cues and information about what it means to be a boy or a girl. When my daughter was born, she had almost no hair. Yet in spite of that, and without my consent, the hospital allowed a photographer to tape a pink bow on her bald head and try to sell us the photographs.

My daughter and son are fifteen months apart and were both in diapers at the same time. It was just at that time, 1987, that major diaper companies began decorating their diapers and plain disposable diapers became unfashionable and difficult to find. There were blue diapers (for boys) with drawings of trucks and cars and baseball bats, and pink diapers (for girls) with pictures of teddy bears and ballerinas. According to the manufacturers, these diapers were designed anatomically to specifically fit boys or girls. Had I wanted to switch diapers I may have reduced stereotypes and increased wetness. There are not many choices under these circumstances.

Sex is determined biologically. When you are born, the doctor informs your

Personal Inventory 2.3
Gender and the Fine Art of Preening

Instructions

Think of an extremely special and somewhat formal occasion that you are preparing to attend. You want to look and feel exceptionally good. The occasion could be a prom, a dance, a wedding, or some other formal event. Think of all of the items you need and activities you plan to prepare yourself for this event. Mark everything that you would use and do on the list below and add anything else you that is not on the list.

Preparation Activities (Indicate the amount of time in hours that each activity will take and then add the total of all of the activities.)

shopping for clothes	___
ironing	___
going to the cleaners	___
going to the hairdresser or barber	___
taking a nap	___
taking a bath or shower	___
shaving	___
manicure or pedicure	___
any other preparation activities	___
Other activities _____	
_____	___

TOTAL HOURS ____

Products (Write the number beside each product you use; be sure to indicate separate numbers for each product. So if you use 5 different kinds of lotion, write 5 in the blank. Then add the total number of products.)

toothpaste	___
deodorant	___
shampoo	___
conditioner	___
hair products	___
lotion	___
soap	___
body gel	___
perfume, cologne or aftershave	___
bubble bath	___
facial masque or lotion	___
make-up	___
any other products you would use to prepare _____	
_____	___

TOTAL PRODUCTS ____

parents that you are a boy or a girl according to your genitals. Other characteristics that are determined by your sex and hormones are breasts, menstruation, relative hairiness, and to some degree bone and muscle structure. It is important to note that there are some babies who are born with ambiguous genitalia. These families and children have difficult decisions to make and a whole set of issues to face that are beyond the scope of this book.

But gender is something entirely different. Gender is constructed socially, culturally, and psychologically. In fact, many studies have demonstrated that roles of males and females vary in different cultures. Anthropologist Margaret Mead conducted studies with three different tribes in New Guinea and found that in one tribe both sexes behaved in ways that were considered traditionally feminine in the United States: nurturing, passive, peaceful, and deferential. In a second tribe, men and women assumed gender roles that are regarded in the United States as traditional: the men were aggressive hunter-gatherers, with most of their work occurring outside the home and hearth, while the women were peaceful nurturers who took care of the children and worked inside the home. In a third tribe, the roles were reversed and the women played the U.S. version of traditionally masculine roles while the men assumed traditionally feminine roles (Mead 1935). "What we do know with confidence is that however strong the influence of biology may be, it seldom, if ever, determines behavior. It *influences* behavior in greater or lesser amounts, but it doesn't determine behavior, personality, and so on" (Wood 1994, 20–21).

As you read this information on gender socialization, reflect on the experiences you explored in the first section of this chapter. Look closely at whether you were socialized and behaved according to traditional codes of gender to a more gender neutral code of behavior, or one that was oppositional to a traditional gender identification. As you observe your response to the data and theories discussed in this chapter, note whether you find your own beliefs challenged or reinforced by the material and determine whether there is any connection between your reactions and your own gender socialization.

Gender Theory

While biology and interpersonal dynamics clearly have an important impact on the development of gender identity, many theorists believe that culture is the most critical determinant. Three key elements contributing to gender development are described below.

Biological research has demonstrated that higher levels of the male hormone testosterone may predict more aggressive behavior. There is also research indicating that men may have greater development of the left side of the brain, which impacts linear thinking, while women seem to have greater development of the right side of the brain, which governs holistic and intuitive thinking. There is also some research indicating that women may have greater ability to cross from one side of the brain to the other, thus blending linear and intuitive thinking (Wood 1994, 37).

Theories of *interpersonal* relationships and dynamics also explain elements of gender development. These theories focus on the impact that family dynamics and social learning have on personality development and gender identification. According to social learning theory, individuals learn to be masculine or feminine according to what they see and observe. In Chapter One we discussed social learning theory, which explained that if children mimic behavior they are told is appropriate to their gender and receive reinforcement, they are likely to repeat it (Wood 1994, 37).

Jean Piaget and Carol Gilligan are major contributors to cognitive development theories that contend that children play an active role in the development of their own gender identity. According to these theorists, by age five or six, children begin to see their gender definition as permanent and seek role models to pattern themselves after (Wood 1994, 44–45).

Cultural explanations of gender development include both interpersonal and biological theories and research. Anthropological studies suggest that

> the more technologically complex and advanced a culture is, the more stratification it creates to divide people by gender, as well as by other factors such as race and class. With technological advancement comes competition, and this lays a foundation for inequality, since some people will have more than others of whatever is valued in a culture. One of the arrangements that capitalism encourages is a division between public and private realms of life and the placement of women in the private or domestic sphere. Because public life is considered more important, this arrangement fosters subordination of women. (Wood 1994, 47)

In other words, according to cultural explanations of gender, traits such as aggressiveness and nurturing exist in both boys and girls. It is the way the culture fosters and encourages the assignment of these characteristics to males or females that determines which characteristics are acceptable for each gender to cultivate. This reinforcement of traits assigned according to gender is the work of parents, peers, schools, and the media.

Cultural theories regarding gender development are often constructed in a political context and analyzed according to which gender wields more power. This political analysis conforms closely to the fabric of oppression as described in Chapter One. You may recall the definition of targeted groups as those with less access to resources, privileges, and power. In the United States, according to these definitions, men constitute the dominant group and women constitute the targeted group. This does not mean that all men have great power and wealth, nor does it mean that all women are powerless or impoverished. Rather, this theory addresses structural access to the factors that lead to success. U.S. culture tends to value traits that are considered traditionally masculine and that lead to the kind of success defined as economic wealth and professional status. This is often a less than visible cultural norm.

The Relative Status of Men and Women

By 1997, the percentage of women working full time and earning wages had increased from 29 percent in 1967 to 41 percent. Until 1987, there was a trend for men to earn more real wages than their fathers. This has continued to be true for college-educated men, but the median income for all other groups of men actually fell. The real income for women increased during this time period because of the increase of the percentage of women working. But in 1998, despite this growth in employment and income for women, they continued to earn only 74 percent of what men earned (Weinberg 1998, 1).

While the education gap between men and women had closed significantly by 1993, the income gap had not. Women with high school diplomas made $19,163 to men's $26,820, and women with bachelor's degrees earned $32,291 to men's $45,987. Some of this wage gap was due to men and women being paid different amounts for the same work and some was due to the kinds of jobs that were considered gender specific for men or women. There were more female heads of household in 1993, a status that has become a strong predictor of poverty. Married couples with children had a poverty rate of 9 percent while female headed households with children had a poverty rate of 46 percent (U.S. Bureau of Census 1995).

Another indicator of authority and power is that of positions held in government and private industry. A record 55 women were members of the House of Representatives, and 9 women were senators in 1998. While these numbers represent all-time highs, it is sobering to note that there were 380 men in the House and 91 men in the Senate (Associated Press, May 4, 1998).

A 1996 analysis of Fortune 500 companies revealed that there were only two women who were chief executive officers (CEOs). When the analysis was expanded to include the top 1000 companies, the numbers increased to five women (Elliot 1997, 50).

In 1950, 28 percent of married women with children worked outside the home, and by 1986 this percentage increased to 68 percent. But despite this shift in labor, the "second shift" of work at home still fell largely to women. Arlie Hochschild has documented that housework and the work to care for children remain the domain of women and that, in fact, women work the equivalent of an extra month each year at home performing these domestic chores. "But for men, the situation differed in one fundamental way. By tradition, the second shift did not fall to them. In contrast to their wives, it was not a 'new idea' that they should work. In the eyes of the world, they felt judged by their capacity to support the family and earn status at work. They got little credit for helping at home" (Hochschild 1989, 200).

The AAUW has documented sharp differences in self-esteem and scores on standardized tests for boys and girls as they move through puberty and adolescence. "Large-scale empirical studies, public-opinion polls, and in-depth clinical studies following individual girls through school all report significant declines in girls' self-esteem and self-confidence as they move from childhood to early adolescence. . . . A nationwide survey commissioned by the AAUW in 1990 found that on average 69 percent of elementary school boys and 60 percent of elementary school girls reported that they were 'happy the way I am'; among high school students the percentages were 46% for boys and only 29% for girls" (AAUW 1995, 19). While the study found that these percentages held steady for white middle class girls, they found interesting differences for African American girls and young Latinas. Girls of color demonstrated higher levels of personal self-esteem, yet significantly lower levels of self-esteem related to academics (AAUW 1995,19–21).

The AAUW study documented the gender socialization process that begins with the use of the terms *boy* and *girl* as "simple labels rather than conceptual categories" (AAUW 1995, 17). By age four, children begin to see certain activities and toys as appropriate exclusively for girls or boys and by age five, sex roles seem to be more rigidly defined with clearly understood rules. There is evidence that by ages six and seven, boys and girls internalize these rules and are strongly inclined to play in sex-segregated groups. Yet eight to ten year olds continue to exhibit flexibility regarding sex stereotyped behavior and many girls move back and forth from the rules for boys' and girls' behavior (AAUW 1995, 17).

By early adolescence this flexibility begins to disappear in girls: "Early adolescence is a significant transition period of both sexes, but research reveals it to be a particularly difficult time for girls. Moving from 'young girl' to' young woman' involves meeting unique demands in a culture that both idealizes and exploits the sexuality of young women while assigning them roles that are clearly less valued than male roles" (AAUW 1995, 18).

There have been some challenges, however, to the AAUW report. Other studies have observed the negative results of gender socialization in boys. Boys have a greater tendency to repeat a grade in school, to drop out of school, to be diagnosed with learning disabilities, to be placed in special education, and to be suspended or expelled from school. These reports do not necessarily contradict those of gender socialization and its consequences for girls. Rather, they point out that extreme gender socialization has different but often negative consequences for boys *and* girls (Lewin 1998, 3).

One final bit of information that provides another layer to the issue of self-esteem involves how women regard their appearance. I graduated from high school in 1967. There were at least ten girls in my graduating class who had had cosmetic surgery on their noses, what we referred to as "nose jobs." This was at least 5 percent of the females in my graduating class. These girls underwent surgery in which their noses were broken and reshaped. I remember visiting them in the hospital and shuddering from the enormously bruised eyes resulting from the break and the huge white bandage on the nose. These girls all began as attractive. Yet with the permission and encouragement of their parents, they were willing to undergo this ordeal to more closely match societal norms. In fact, from 1981 to 1984, women increased elective cosmetic surgery by 30 percent, changing their eyes and noses, lifting their faces, and enlarging their breasts (Franck and Brownstone 1993). By 1997 plastic surgeons performed close to 2 million cosmetic procedures to reduce the size of noses, enlarge the size of breasts, and to suck the fat out of women's thighs. This figure was up 50 percent since 1992, and procedures such as breast augmentation and liposuction had more than tripled (Hamilton and Weingarden 1998, 14).

Gender and American History

Think carefully about the people in American history you were taught were significant, the ones you were told made key contributions to the development of the United States. Who were they? My list, which comes from the mid to late 1960s, includes George Washington, Thomas Jefferson, Benjamin Franklin, Ulysses S. Grant, Robert E. Lee, Abraham Lincoln, John D. Rockefeller, John Smith, Teddy Roosevelt, and Franklin Roosevelt. The only women who I remember learning about as historical figures were minor players in the texts—a pre-Disney Pocahontas and Betsy Ross of American flag fame. Perhaps those of you who are younger have more women on your list, but by and large, our U.S. history books are the story of men's contributions, literally *his* story.

Consider the women described below and their contributions to American history. How many of them have you studied? How many even sound familiar to you? How do you think your perspective on American historical figures and history itself would have been different had you learned about these women?

In 1539, Francesca Hinestrosa was the first European woman to reach the New World alive (Rappaport 1990, 6). In 1634, Anne Hutchinson was the first American woman to challenge the unequal status of women. She defied the Puritan clergy and held meetings that ran against the rules and norms of society. These meetings, held in her home, were attended by men and women together to discuss religious and political ideas contrary to the dominant ones of the time. In 1683 Hutchinson was found guilty of religious and civil slander and improper behavior. As a result she was excommunicated and banished (Rappaport 1990, 37). It is not commonly known that many woman who were brought to the American shores as indentured servants and slaves fought for their freedom. "In 1781, in an unusual act of defiance, Elizabeth Freeman protested her enslavement by going to court and argued that the Massachusetts Bill of Rights had ended slavery. She won her case and her freedom" (Rappaport 1990, 28). These are bits and pieces of American history rarely found in history textbooks.

In the first decades of the nineteenth century, one impact of the Industrial Revolution was a dramatic change in the gender assignment of work and labor. Tasks that had previously belonged to women were taken over by factories. Ironically, as white middle class women became revered as mothers, wives, and "ladies," their position in the family became less productive and began to be regarded as inferior. "The world of business, trade, and government was seen as the right place for men, whom society viewed as competitive, aggressive, and materialistic. Women were thought of as gentle, spiritual, and nurturing. The idea of a woman's sphere, separate and different from the man's sphere, was accepted as an eternal truth" (Rappaport 1990, 50). The woman's domestic sphere was not only separate but unequal as well.

Most high school history books address the development and consequences of the Industrial Revolution with little mention of how this phenomenon impacted the organization of labor inside and outside the home and how earning money became more highly valued. More importantly, there is rarely any mention of how the assignment of labor was done along gender lines—with the highly valued paid labor in the public sphere assigned to men and the unpaid and devalued home labor assigned to women.

The untold stories above are predominantly about white women, particularly white women of middle class and above. A story that is even more deeply hidden from accessible and common history is the story of women of color. While there are many stories of immigration, discrimination, and valor, the story of African American women is a quintessential American story rarely told in general American history books.

"Judged by the evolving nineteenth century ideology of femininity, which emphasized women's roles as nurturing mothers and gentle companions and housekeepers for their husbands, Black women were practically anomalies" (Davis 1981, 5). African women, brought to the United States as slaves, were first valued according to the amount of labor they could do. Contrary to myths established in such films as *Gone with the Wind,* seven out of eight black women were field workers rather than housekeepers or nursemaids (Davis 1981, 5).

One former slave described her situation:

> We had ragged huts made out of poles, and some of the cracks chinked up with mud and moss, and some of them wasn't [weren't]. We didn't have no [any] good beds, just scaffolds nailed up to the wall out of poles and the old ragged bedding throwed [thrown] on them. That sure was hard sleeping, but even that felt good to our weary bones after them [those] long hard days' work in the field. I tended to the children when I was a little gal and tried to clean house jus[t] like Old Miss tells me to. Then as soon as I was ten years old, Old Master, he says, "Git [get] this here nigger to that cotton patch." (Watkins and David 1970, 16)

While motherhood was revered in white middle class society in the nineteenth century, after the abolition of the international slave trade black women were instead valued for their ability to reproduce as many offspring as possible to continue to "supply" free labor in the form of more slaves. Black women were therefore prized either as laborers or as "breeders," depending on which function they could perform best.

The central place that work occupies in contemporary black women's lives and the features of relationships between black women and men were established during slavery. Because black women's labor was measured the same as that of black men, "the economic arrangements of slavery contradicted the hierarchical sexual roles incorporated in the new [post–Industrial Revolution] ideology. Male-female relations within the slave community could not, therefore, conform to the dominant ideological pattern" (Davis 1981, 18).

The tragic irony of slavery for women was that while post–Industrial Revolution white women's work was taken over by factories and their status thus reduced, black women were performing the same work as black men. In the limited domestic life of slaves, the work black women and men performed for themselves was characterized by equality. "Within the confines of their family and community life, therefore, Black people managed to accomplish a magnificent feat. They transformed the negative equality which emanated from the equal oppression they suffered as slaves into a positive quality: the egalitarianism characterizing their social relations" (Davis 1981, 18).

The Nat Turner rebellion against slavery in 1831 marked the beginning of the abolitionist movement. At the same time strikes in the textile factories by working class white women in the northeast began, and groups of wealthier white women began fighting for the right to education and careers outside the home. These women used the language of "slavery" to describe their oppression in factories and in marriage, and while the comparison was often exaggerated, the stage was set for the affinity of the first phase of the women's movement and the antislavery movement.

Some of these women began to engage in acts of courage and heroism, important elements of history that are rarely documented in our common education. For example, in 1833 Prudence Crandall, a white teacher in Canterbury, Connecticut, accepted a black girl into her school. She remained steadfast as the parents of the white girls boycotted the school. She ultimately recruited more black girls and eventually operated an all-black school in defiance of the white people of the town (Davis 1981, 34–35).

Sarah and Angelina Grimké were white women born in South Carolina to a slave-holding family. They moved to the North and became outspoken abolitionists and the first to explicitly link women's rights to black rights. "More than any other women in the campaign against slavery, the Grimkés urged the constant inclusion of the issue of women's rights. At the same time they argued that women could never achieve their freedom independently of Black people" (Davis 1981, 44).

While Sojourner Truth's "Ain't I a Woman" speech has attained some recognition and acclaim, few people are aware of this ex-slave's contribution to the fight for freedom of women and slaves. She had to struggle simply for the right to speak at women's conventions and said, "I know that it feels a kind of hissing and tickling like to see a colored woman get up and tell you about things and Woman's Rights. We have all been thrown down so low that nobody thought we'd ever get up again, but we have been long enough trodden now, we will come up again, and now I am here." (Davis 1981, 59).

"Meanwhile, large numbers of Black women were manifesting their commitment to freedom and equality in ways that were less closely connected with the newly organized women's movement" (Davis 1981, 64). African American women from the North were prominent in the Underground Railroad and took enormous risks to illegally transport slaves to freedom. This work was separate from the newly organized women's movement. There was Jane Lewis from Ohio, who rescued slaves through hundreds of crossings of the Ohio River. There was Frances E.W. Harper, a poet and antislavery lecturer, and there was Charlotte Forten, an important black educator and abolitionist. There was Sarah Remond, who brought her antislavery lectures to England and helped dissuade the British from intervening on the side of the Confederacy (Davis 1981, 64).

The Grimkés, Crandall, Sojourner Truth, Lewis, Harper, Forten, and Remond are just a few examples of courageous women, white and black, who took strong antiracist steps to change their own lives and to contribute to changing history. The omission of their stories and historical significance frames what we think of as important historical information and what we think of as tangential or trivial.

The women you have just read about made enormous contributions and changes in history, yet they are rarely mentioned in American history. This gap in important information contributes to how boys and girls construct the meaning of the importance of each gender. These voids in the story of America have a subtle, but enormous, impact on how boys and girls see themselves in the context of history as well as their own relative value.

The Women's Movement and Feminism

> She is dissatisfied with a lot that women of other lands can only dream of. Her discontent is deep, pervasive, and impervious to the superficial remedies which are offered at every hand. . . . From the beginning of time, the female cycle has defined and confined woman's role. As Freud was credited with saying: "Anatomy is destiny." Though no group of women has ever pushed these natural restrictions as far as the American wife, it seems that she still cannot accept them with good grace. A young mother with a beautiful family, charm, talent and brains is apt to dismiss her role apologetically, "What do I do?" you hear her say. "Why nothing; I'm just a housewife." (*Newsweek* 1960, 57–60)

There are several interesting elements embedded in this 1960 quote from a *Newsweek* magazine article titled "Young Wives." The first, and most obvious, is that women are identified, even in the title, in their relationship to their husbands. They are young wives, not young women. A second embedded belief is that a woman's menstrual cycle and her body dictate the kind of person she is to be and the work she is destined to perform. The third is the scorn with which the dissatisfaction of middle class women is treated, as if to say, "How dare they be unhappy and apologetic when they have so much?" The fourth, and perhaps most subtle, is the acceptance of the "natural restrictions" imposed upon women's lives and the implication that women who reject these restrictions are by extension "unnatural." Forty years later, most of us would find this analysis of women silly or even outrageous. However, it is important to recognize that these statements, which now seem painfully outdated, were regarded by and large as "truth" in the 1950s and 1960s. Women and men who were raised in this time period internalized these "facts" about gender. Part of the process of reconstructing knowledge is to lift these "truths" to a conscious level and analyze them. What are the invisible "truths" about gender that we hold onto today?

It was in 1963 that Betty Friedan first published *The Feminine Mystique,* which began the public challenge to these "natural restrictions" (Friedan 1963). The feminine mystique is the belief that middle class women with cars and garages, dishwashers and garbage disposals, children and car pools, husbands and products that got the ring out of the collar should be pleased with their lives. Dissatisfied women knew that either something was wrong with them as individuals or that their lives and marriages were not living up to a well-known and well-accepted ideal. During this time period, there was little thinking that perhaps this ideal was a myth. Until the 1950s and 1960s, few women discussed their sense of dissatisfaction. Many believed their unhappiness to be an individual problem or failure rather than a collective or political issue. It was in the late 1950s that women began to communicate with each other about the problem with no name, the dissatisfaction, the lack of fulfillment, the emptiness, the invisibility, the sense of no identity independent of their husbands or children.

In some ways, the 1950s repeated societal conditions that were similar to those during the period following the Industrial Revolution. New technology meant less housework for middle class women and more pressure to be the constantly available wife and mom. The division between the private and public spheres, female and male, became increasingly sharp. Women were told that being a wife and mother should be all they needed for fulfillment. And for those who were not filled up by those roles there was often anguish and guilt. By 1962 the plight of the trapped housewife was a popular topic in articles and conversation.

Again, middle class women found their way to political organization, this time in the form of the civil rights movement of the 1950s and 1960s and the antiwar movement of the 1960s and 1970s. Many of these women were organizing behind the scenes and marching in the streets in these struggles for justice for other groups.

During the 1960s, as the women's movement began to form, some women organized consciousness raising (CR) groups in which they began speaking to each other about issues such as the shortage of good quality options for child care, about rape and incest, body image, about the need for greater access to choices in education and work, and abortion. CR groups differed from therapy sessions in that while part of their intent and outcome was therapeutic, they were organized primarily so that women could begin to understand the collective and political nature of their problems. The CR groups were not led by professionals. Rather, women in the groups shared leadership, avoiding the kind of permanent hierarchy that they believed had elevated men and damaged women. When the topic for a CR session was child care and individual women spoke of their inability to work or go to school because of few good choices for their children, it became increasingly clear that this was a collective problem, not an individual one, and women began to organize for legislation and increased funding for quality day care centers.

It was from this perspective that a central slogan of the women's movement emerged: "The personal is political." This meant that while women were programmed to keep their problems to themselves because they were private and individual, the more they spoke to each other, the more they realized that what had been contained in the woman-occupied private sphere was neither neutral, natural, nor apolitical (Shreve 1989).

Parallel to the development of CR groups and the embryonic women's movement was women's involvement in the burgeoning student group Students for a Democratic Society (SDS). SDS was participating in sit-ins for the rights of black people in the south and organizing demonstrations to protest the Vietnam War. While women were in the thick of this planning and these activities, it was men who occupied the formal leadership positions. And when women demanded that issues of day care and rape awareness and assistance be made a part of the SDS platform, once again they were scorned. Yet this time the scorn did not emanate from the middle class establishment or sources like *Newsweek,* but rather from the political left that was trying to create a more just world.

Women's participation in the consciousness raising movement, the civil rights movement, the New Left, and the emerging counterculture provided them with important lessons that translated to the women's movement of the 1960s and 1970s. These lessons included nontraditional political experiences, radical ideas about the individual and society, alternative institutions, and an awareness of the discrepancies between egalitarian ideals and sexist practices. While there were radical and liberal branches of the women's movement that wanted society restructured in different ways, the essential feminist ideals were the importance of equality and equity and the need to change the quality and the economics of human relationships and institutions.

Yet, by the late 1970s through the present, feminism was often regarded as a dirty word conjuring images of strident male-haters and often derided as led by unattractive hairy-legged women unable to attract men. How did this revision and distortion happen? The news media often reported on the women's movement's work to change the norms of social interaction with derision and negativity. For example, women who were part of a guerrilla theater protest at a 1960s Miss America pageant burned artifacts to symbolize how beauty and cosmetics served as instruments of women's oppression. This event was reported not as the symbolic protest it was, but rather as women scandalously burning their bras. As late as 1970, West Virginia Senator Jennings Randolph was quoted by ABC's Howard K. Smith as referring to the women's movement as "a small band of bra-less bubbleheads" (Douglas 1994, 163).

Table 2.1

The Roles of Men and Women in Education

	Teachers		Principals/Presidents	
	% Male	% Female	% Male	% Female
Elementary schools	14	86	82	18
Junior high schools	39	61	97	3
High schools	53	47	98	2
Colleges	93	7	90	10

Source: Julia Wood, *Gendered Lives*, 1994.

The news media also regularly reported that the women's movement was about women opening their own car doors, lighting their own cigarettes, and paying for themselves on dates. The shift in these norms of interaction between men and women was certainly an important element of feminism. But what went largely underreported was the women's movement focus on the fundamental issues of equality in relationships, pay equity, child care, a wider array of choices for women, and women's rights to make decisions about their bodies (Faludi 1991).

Education—What You Know and How You Know It

The snapshots of missing history described above tell us what content was typically missing from our common American history. They tell us of women who made important contributions in their lives, careers, and their work for equality. This information is a small portion of the story of American women, but it begins to paint a picture of the partial nature of what children learn and do not learn in the formative years of their lives. While the specific content of early history books may not always stick in the minds of young children, the subtle message about the relative importance of men and the relative unimportance of women becomes an essential element of what Peggy Orenstein calls the "hidden curriculum" (Orenstein 1994, 5) and what Julia T. Wood calls "gendered education" (Wood 1994, 206).

Young girls are often boisterously androgynous, barreling through their lives with enthusiasm and little regard for sexual stereotyping. Yet something dramatic happens in early adolescence, including the dropping of IQ scores and the plummeting of math and science grades (AAUW 1995). Simone de Beauvoir says that part of what happens to teenage girls is that they realize that men have power and that the largest part of their power as girls comes from agreeing to be submissive adored objects. "All girls, from the most servile to the haughtiest, learn in time that to please they must abdicate" (McPhee and Fitzgerald 1979).

Schools are powerful agents of socialization, a central source of learning about gender identity. The organization of education, the information that is taught, and the roles that adult males and females play in schools convey a sense of standards to children about what is normal and who holds power. The lower status of women is reflected in school structures in which the majority of people in positions of power are men, while teachers and staff are largely women. At the higher levels of education where the status and compensation increase, the numbers of women in teaching positions decrease (see Table 2.1). This limits the kind of role models available for both boys and girls and becomes a part of the hidden curriculum in which there are many ways to tell students which sex is more important in the world.

From elementary school on, the explicit curriculum continues to reinforce the image of men as more important than women. A 1990 study documented pervasive gender stereotypes in elementary school reading primers. They found that while the numbers of male and female characters in primer stories had evened out, that males were still represented in two-thirds of the pictures and photographs. In addition, the study demonstrated that the male characters were more likely to be depicted as adventurous risk-takers, while the female characters were portrayed as more dependent on males for help (Purcell and Stewart 1990, 177–185).

As discussed earlier in the chapter, history books also chronicle primarily male involvement in discoveries, politics, inventions, war, and social change. "Women virtually disappear in historical accounts of our country and the world . . . when education makes women invisible and distorts their experiences by using male standards, social life as a whole is distorted" (Wood 1994, 212).

The AAUW study documented that girls are less likely to reach their full academic potential than boys. AAUW observations of even the most well-meaning teachers indicated that they were more likely to recognize and affirm the participation of boys than of girls. Some of the teacher attitudes documented in the study reflected praise and reinforcement for quiet girls while allowing and encouraging more boisterous and aggressive behavior for boys. Schools, in fact, often contribute to the socialization of boys and girls into traditional gender roles by encouraging boys to be competitive and assertive and girls to build relationships and be nurturing (AAUW 1995). "People who have learned to use communication to build relationships and collaborate with others find it uncomfortable to compete, to assert themselves over others and to speak in absolute terms that don't invite others to participate. This may explain why many women students in coeducational institutions speak up less often in the classrooms" (Wood 1994, 220).

This educational socialization of boys and girls does not end when they complete high school but continues into higher education. Another study indicated that verbal and nonverbal practices by college and university teachers provide more recognition to males than females. Faculty members are more likely to know male students' names, ask more challenging questions of males, and call on male students more often. According to the study, female students' responses are dismissed more often than those of males (Wood, 1994, 232).

So far, we have considered the gendered content of education and the gendered information we receive through the organization of education and teacher behavior. But, have you ever thought about *how* you know things? How do you *know* or how did you learn who Christopher Columbus was? How do you *know* what it means to be polite, kind, or courteous? How do you *know* whom to believe when different people give you conflicting information or perspectives? It is not just what we learn but how we learn it and the way we express it that has relative value. "Nowhere is the pattern of using male experience to define the human experience seen more clearly than in models of intellectual development. The mental processes that are involved in considering the abstract and the impersonal have been labeled 'thinking' and are attributed primarily to men, while those that deal with the personal and interpersonal fall under the rubric of 'emotions' and are largely relegated to women" (Field Belenky et al. 1988, 7).

A 1986 study interviewed 135 women, documenting distinct ways in which people learn or "know" things. The study found that while there was some gender overlap, particularly in the way that formally educated men and women know things, overall there were distinct patterns of learning that fell along gender lines. According to this study, the kind of knowledge that is most revered in education is received knowledge, which comes primarily from outside sources or authorities. This kind of knowing is largely the domain of men who have been socialized to believe this is the proper or only way to learn as well as women who have learned that received knowledge is the way to successfully navigate academia. Those men and women who succeed academically have *mastered* (a gendered word, you may notice) the ability to take in and analyze received knowledge. Subjective knowledge, which values personal and internal sources of information, is often regarded as soft and invalid in the academy. Yet, as we have learned, many women are socialized to learn about personal relationships and life experiences in this way (Field Belenky et al. 1988, 54). The authors of the study propose a third way of knowing, constructed knowledge, which allows for the blend of information that comes from both inside and outside the self, recognizing both as valid authorities (Field Belenky et al. 1988, 119).

When education is modeled predominantly along the lines of received knowledge, all authority exists outside the self. Paulo Freire refers to this kind of teaching as the banking model, in which the teacher fills the student by making deposits of information and the student regularly returns the same deposits to the teacher (Freire 1989). When models of learning are used that are predominantly male, both boys and girls receive messages about which kind of knowing is superior. If boys and girls are successfully socialized to believe that internal knowledge is inferior, they may be unnecessarily and destructively cut off from an important source of information—themselves.

"To see that all knowledge is a construction and that truth is a matter of the context in which it is embedded is to greatly expand the possibilities of how to think about anything, even those things we consider to be the most elementary and obvious" (Field Belenky et al. 1988, 138). When we learn about our history and our place in it as men and women, when we learn about what it means to be feminine or masculine, we are only receiving knowledge. We are relying on other authorities —parents, school, or the culture at large—to tell us who we are and what we should think. In order to transcend and expand a one-way receipt of knowledge, it is essential to understand that all knowledge and information is limited by perspective, context, experience, and time. As you read this book, it is important to recognize that even as the author or expert in the field, I cannot tell you what I do not know, have not been told, have not learned, have not experienced, or do not see.

Gender, Oppression, and Liberation

Looking back to Chapter One, you will recall that social groups are groups of people who share a common social identity such as gender. Social power accrues to those social groups who have greater access to resources that increase the chances of getting what one wants and influencing others. Oppression is the structural arrangement by which resources, privilege, and power are allocated in such a way that some social groups have more access to these and some have less. As what we know about gender and how we know it is carefully analyzed, it becomes increasingly clear that women as a social group have significantly less social power than men.

It is important to reiterate that women can be targeted by oppression without consciously ever experiencing a hateful act. As you review who holds the seats of power in the public and private sectors, you will see that the vast majority of these positions are held by men and that women have less access to power. As you ponder the post–Industrial Revolution division of labor into public and private spheres, with women assigned primarily to the lower status of the private sphere, you can see that women have less access to privileges and resources. As you contemplate what happens in schools and how I.Q. points for girls drop in early adolescence, you can see that women and men are socialized to take certain assigned places in society.

Remember again the definition of hegemony, the process by which those in power secure the consent or social submission of those who are not in power. Hegemony is secured not through force, but rather through the way that values are taught in religious, educational, and media institutions; in other words—through socialization. Remember the story of the little girl, Jennifer, who learned that to be feminine meant pink and ruffles and makeup and jewelry, and that admiration from boys and girls and parents and grandparents for prettiness and sweetness was the core of what was important. Jennifer was socialized in a particular way, not representative of all women, but rather a sharp and dramatic symbol of the impact of socialization. Jennifer may experience a good life, but hegemony has established a limit to her choices. Given what she has learned so well, she is unlikely to choose to be a corporate executive or a chemical engineer.

Understanding how oppression and hegemony operate with regard to gender is not fatalistic, nor does it carry a predictable life sentence. Rather, it describes the obstacles to making independent choices and the structural barriers to power, privileges, and resources. Certainly, there are women engineers and attorneys, doctors and corporate executives who have found a way to resist complete gender socialization. Understanding oppression is understanding the big picture; it does not explain everyone's individual story.

For women to have greater access to the power and the resources to get what they want in life does not necessitate that every woman aggressively seek positions of great stature and power. Rather, what is needed is for women and men to have information about:

- women's role in history;
- the disparity in income and employment;
- the way that socialization happens;
- the role that parents and the educational system play in grooming girls to be women and boys to be men; and
- an understanding of how different ways of knowing are assigned with higher status to men and lower status to women.

What is needed is not to dictate and prescribe what one must do to be masculine and feminine, but rather an understanding of the role that individuals and groups have played and can play in order to offer girls and boys, women and men a wider array of choices for their lives.

Liberation theory, as applied to gender, presumes that women and men have infinite capacities to be successful, and yet boys and girls are bombarded from birth with messages and misinformation about what it means to be male and what it means to be female. As young boys and girls, we learn these lessons well. Yet liberation theory maintains that the possibility of reaching full potential is innate, while misinformation that is oppressive is learned. Therefore, all of the misinformation about status and femininity and position that is oppressive can be unlearned. Liberation is the group and individual process by which people and institutions can observe, recognize, rethink, and interrupt the negative messages and change how we see ourselves and others.

Gender and Entertainment Media

This next section will guide you as you begin to connect the dots between what you learned through your personal experience, through your formal education, and the messages received through entertainment media. Your challenge is to evaluate and integrate new information on gender and reevaluate what you have learned to be true in the past. It will be important to determine whether the messages about gender in entertainment media challenge or reinforce what you have been taught in school and in your life.

Entertainment media is a central source of gender socialization. Consider these differences in the way that men and women are portrayed in television and film:

- Women are portrayed in all media as being primarily involved in relationships and men are more often portrayed in the context of their careers.
- Women are portrayed in both television and film as seeking romance 35 percent of the time, while men are portrayed seeking romance only 20 percent of the time.
- Women's appearance is more than twice as likely to elicit comments in television and film than men's appearance.
- Women are shown to groom or preen three times more than men in television and film.
- Across all media, 46 percent of women are portrayed as thin as compared to 16 percent of men (Media Awareness 1997).

There are several key questions to consider as we analyze media images and their impact on our understanding of gender:

- What images of men and women do prime time television, feature films, and popular music convey?
- How does media ownership and production impact the images of men and women that we see and hear in these popular media forms?
- What are the underlying messages and ideologies about gender that are represented in the various forms of entertainment media?
- Do the images, ownership, messages, and ideology contribute to the standard socialization of men and women or do they challenge this status quo?

These questions will be analyzed in several different ways including the use of simple content analysis to examine characters and themes, a review of research and analysis about gender in popular media forms as well as media ownership and gender, and finally, an analysis of the particular and overall messages and ideology about gender in entertainment media. Content analysis, message system analysis, media literacy, and cultural studies will all be employed to examine these questions.

As you analyze fictional characters and themes in popular film, music, and television, it is critical to keep in mind a fundamental concept about *stereotypes*. A stereotype organizes information in such a way that it signals repetitive and often negative images based on an individual's membership in a particular group. As you recall, stereotypes are reinforced in entertainment media by maintaining simplicity. The simpler the character or theme, the more likely it is to be stereotyped. The more complex the character or theme, the less likely stereotyping is to occur and the more likely is the emergence of richness and complexity that defy easy categorization.

Prime Time Television

Content Analysis

It is your turn to conduct a content analysis that will assess gender images on prime time television when you were a child. Think of yourself from age four to age twelve. Imagine what you did when you got up in the morning, when you came home from school, and during and after dinner. How much television did you watch in the average day? Did you watch television during meals? Record the approximate number of hours of television you watched weekly and note where and when you watched it. Next think hard and make a list of your ten favorite television programs during the eight years from four to twelve. You can list cartoons, dramas, comedies, children's programs, and adult programs that are designed to entertain. For the purposes of this exercise, list only programs that have a cohesive narrative and are not variety shows. This rules out programs such as *Sesame Street, MTV, Saturday Night Live*, and *Entertainment Tonight*. As you make your list, think of all of the programs that you begged your parents to let you watch during dinner or to allow you to stay up past your bedtime to watch. Remember those programs (do *Teenage Mutant Ninja Turtles* or *Saved by the Bell* ring any particular bells for you?) that you loved to watch, discuss with your friends, and even act out when you were hanging out with your friends. When you finish your list, conduct the content analysis outlined in Media Activity 2.1.

After you have completed the questions in the activity, answer the following questions:

- What were the total numbers of males and females in starring roles in the programs you watched as a child?
- Were men or women more numerous in their employment outside of the home?
- Were men or women more likely to work at home or be a homemaker?
- Of those who were employed, were men or women more numerous in lower and higher paid positions?
- Were men or women more likely to be victims or heroes?
- Were men or women more likely to be beautiful, fit, and thin?
- Were men or women more responsible for taking care of children?
- Do you observe any patterns by gender in these characteristics and roles?
- Are there some roles in which men are in the clear majority? What are they?
- Are there some in which women are in the clear majority? Which characteristics and roles are those?
- What do these numbers signal about who is important in U.S. culture?

To get a larger sample, you can do this exercise with a group or class, ensuring that each program is only listed or analyzed one time.

Media Activity 2.1
Men and Women's Roles in Prime Time Television

Instructions

List the television programs that were your favorite as a child. These programs should all be narrative fiction and not news, variety shows (such as *Sesame Street*), infotainment, movies, or specials. Then answer the following questions.

1. Determine how many men and how many women in each program had starring roles. Starring roles are those for which you can bank on the actors making the biggest salaries of the cast. If a character is on the program regularly but only featured occasionally as a major character, do not count him or her. Now total the numbers of men and women in starring roles in all of the programs you listed.

    a. Total number of male characters in starring roles   _____
    b. Total number of female characters in starring roles   _____
    c. Total number of all characters in starring roles   _____

2. Take a closer look at the list of men and women in starring roles and note, by gender, how many of them played the following roles in the programs:

	men	women
a. homemakers	_____	_____
b. worked outside home	_____	_____

    (cont'd)

As you think through the patterns that emerge through this crude content analysis, begin to think about what kind of information is conveyed about the appropriate roles, work, and appearance for men and women. Are they about the same, slightly different, or significantly different for each sex? If you watched a minimum of ten hours of television per week as a child, the messages about gender that were conveyed from the programs you watched had an impact on you. What did you learn about being a boy or a girl, a man or a woman, from the entertainment television you watched?

Popular television has an enormous impact on children and teenagers. These programs play a key role in shaping a sense of self, gender identification and roles, and beliefs about what we can do as well as what we want to be and do as both children and adults. The roles and characteristics of men and women on television signal a sense of norms to the audience and can either confirm or challenge what we learn about gender roles and identification at home, in school, and from our peers. In fact, studies by George Gerbner, among others, have indicated that people who watch fifteen hours or more of television weekly tend to believe

c. professionals   _____ _____
d. secretaries/clerical workers   _____ _____
e. law enforcement   _____ _____
f. doctors   _____ _____
g. victims/martyrs   _____ _____
h heroes   _____ _____
i. took major responsibility for children   _____ _____

Totals   _____ _____
(add the column for men for one total and the column for women for a second total)

3. Look at the starring roles by gender once again and add up the totals of males and females that exhibited the characteristics of appearance as follows:

	men	women
a. average in appearance	_____	_____
b. attractive in appearance	_____	_____
c. glamorous in appearance	_____	_____
d. thin in size	_____	_____
e. average in size	_____	_____
f. overweight	_____	_____
g. physically fit	_____	_____
h. voluptuous or sexy body	_____	_____

Totals   _____ _____

the "TV reality" over their own experience and observations in the world (Gerbner 1997, 1).

From 1965 to 1985, the percentage of male characters on prime time television was 71 percent and that of female characters was 29 percent. While more women were portrayed as workers by the 1990s, overall women were still under-represented, held lower status, and were chiefly focused on domestic issues (Elasmar et al. 1999, 21–26).

Sally Steenland examined eighty television entertainment programs during the spring 1990 season and found the following:

- most men and women were portrayed in their twenties and thirties; women's age drops off at forty, men's age drops off at fifty;
- the most common job for women on television was clerical;
- the most common job for men was law enforcement;
- the number of full-time female homemakers on television had increased;
- almost twice as many men as women were portrayed in the workplace;

- women of color were largely segregated to situation comedies; and
- as a rule men wore more clothes and kept them on longer than women (Steenland 1995, 180–187).

Despite Steenland's findings that the most common job on television for women was clerical, she also determined that television characters, including women, were likely to have more money than their real-life counterparts. Advertisers are seeking attractive surroundings for their thirty-second commercials. They want programs featuring affluent characters who can afford to buy their products.

Approximately 50 percent of the U.S. population are women, but only one-third of all characters on prime time television are women. In children's programming, only 18 percent of all characters are women (Gerbner 1997, 1).

In this section, we have used content analysis to examine gender roles in prime time television. Another method of analyzing gender in television is by recording and observing the number of interactions between characters according to gender. Media Activity 2.2 provides a method for tabulating and evaluating these interactions.

Which interactions occur the most frequently and which occur least frequently? If you are skeptical about your results, try another ten scenes from another program or get together with others who are tallying the same kinds of interactions from different programs. If there are sizable differences in who interacts with whom, it conveys still another set of messages about gender. This analysis goes beyond the assessment of characters and their roles, jobs, and personalities. Most of these analyses indicate that interactions between men and women are the most frequent, that those between men occur second in frequency, and that interactions between women are by far the least frequent. This signals to the audience a ranking of gender importance in conversation.

In her 1990 study, Steenland found that

> It's the norm for men to talk more, give orders, solve problems, and run things. Society's bias is so commonplace that it seems normal. Even though few of us notice the gender imbalance in TV programs, an imprint is made. Girls grow up with fewer role modes. Their choices are smaller (Steenland 1995, 187).

Television as a Tool of Culture

Television interacts with gender in two critical ways. It reflects cultural values and it serves as a trusted conveyor of information and images (Wood 1994, 231). A 1986 study determined that children who watch television had more stereotyped views of the sexes than children who did not (Kimball 1986, 265–301).

Prime time television provides girls and women with a series of mixed and confusing messages:

> American women today are a bundle of contradictions because much of the media imagery we grew up with was itself filled with mixed messages about what

Media Activity 2.2
Interactions in Prime Time Television by Gender

Instructions

Choose a contemporary television program that is narrative fiction, either comedy or drama. You will need to record this program in order to view it several times. Select ten scenes from the program you choose. These scenes can be consecutive or at random. For the purpose of this analysis, a scene is defined as the time frame and dialogue in which the same characters are in the same physical space. Any time a character enters or departs or the physical setting changes, it constitutes another scene. Determine the number of conversational interactions there are in each scene between men and men, men and women, and women and women. Using the chart below, total these raw scores and determine their percentage of the total.

	% of interactions	% of total interactions
male/male interactions	————	————
female/female interactions	————	————
female/male interactions	————	————
Total interactions	————	100%

Source: Gerbner (1997).

women should and should not do, what women could and could not be. This was true in the 1960s, and it is true today. The media, of course, urges us to be pliant, cute, sexually available, thin, blond, poreless, wrinkle-free and deferential to men. But it is easy to forget that the media also suggested we could be rebellious, tough, enterprising and shrewd. (Douglas 1994, 9)

The 1951 debut of *I Love Lucy* (1951–57) featured a woman who although dizzy and troublesome was the central character of the program. Producers tried to emulate this success with other programs such as *I Married Joan* (1952–55) and *My Little Margie* (1952), but few of the copies were successful. The early 1950s to the mid 1960s were filled with situation comedies in which women were house-wives and played the support role and men were the workers and often the prob-lem solvers. Programs such as *Father Knows Best* (1954–63), *Leave It to Beaver*

(1957–63), and the *Donna Reed Show* (1958–66) represent this genre. This television depiction was a good match for what was happening in post–World War II U.S. culture. After the war, women were largely taken out of the job market and remained at home while their husbands went back to work. Women's role as homemaker became central to the postwar economy and the ongoing division of the public and private spheres (Lout 1995, 169).

Despite the rigid gender roles on prime time programs, even the 1950s offered choices, complexities, and ambiguities for women. Douglas examines the interplay of prime time television with news coverage in the 1950s and 1960s. Along with *Leave It to Beaver*, there was the news coverage of the civil rights movement, the Nixon–Kennedy debates, and rocket launches. Girls got the impression that to be an American was to be tough, individualistic, brave, and smart, while to be a girl was to be nurturing and passive (Douglas 1994, 26). Since girls were both female and American, this meant some confusing choices amid the contradictions. I can remember a dilemma of this sort when I was about thirteen years old. My family had a pool table in the basement and I became quite proficient at pool. My friends would come over on the weekends and I could clobber most of the boys in pool. But my teen magazines warned me to never beat a boy at a game because it was not feminine and because their egos could not take it.

By the 1970s there was an increase in programs that centered around female characters. There were working women depicted on shows ranging from *Mary Tyler Moore* (1970–77) to *Rhoda* (1974–81) to *Charlie's Angels* (1976–81). By the mid-1970s, beautiful women cops emerged in *Police Woman* (1974–78) and *Get Christie Love* (1974–75). By the mid-1970s to early 1980s, more roles for black women emerged in *Good Times* (1974–79) and *What's Happening* (1976–78). Yet in each of these shows the central black women, Florida and Shirley, respectively, played the role of the good-natured "mammy" (Lout 1995).

Although the 1970s featured more women characters in prime time television, studies also revealed that there were more males in evening television than females, more diverse roles were available to males, and female characters appeared less competent than male characters. From 1972 to 1981 only 44 percent of female prime time characters worked outside the home as compared to over 60 percent of women in reality (Steenland 1990).

The CBS series *Cagney and Lacey* (1982–88) broke some of these tried and true portrayals and omissions of women characters on television. This story of two female police officers who solved their own cases without relying on men was the first TV drama to star two women. In the series, Christine Cagney was single with an active sex life, and Mary Beth Lacey was the primary breadwinner of her family and often shown as the partner to initiate sex with her husband. *Cagney and Lacey* was first made as a TV movie; it received high ratings and moved on to become a series starring Meg Foster as Cagney and Tyne Daley as Lacey. After a few episodes, CBS said the women were too tough and aggressive, "too women's lib," and said they would only continue the series if Foster were replaced. Meg Foster was subsequently replaced by Sharon Gless (D'Acci 1995, 454–459).

"The quest for the working women's market in the late 1970s and 1980s led to women oriented programs and feminist subject matter in prime time. But as we have seen, when these representations deviated too much from the acceptable conventions of the industry, they were quickly brought back in line"(D'Acci 1995, 465). Because so many women viewers hungered for alternative female images, they persisted in using oppositional viewing modes in order to identify with Cagney and Lacey as nontraditional women despite the changes to soften the characters and make them more traditionally feminine (D'Acci 1995, 460).

A new image in the 1980s was women as "superwomen." Women who held professional jobs, were raising families, had fun at home, and resolved problems gracefully within thirty to sixty minutes were seen on *Family Ties* (1982–89) and *The Cosby Show* (1984–92). There were also increasingly diverse roles available for women in such 1980s programs as *Murder She Wrote* (1984–96), *Frank's Place* (1987–88), *Cheers* (1982–93), and *Murphy Brown* (1988–98). "Prior to the late 1980s, men were more likely to interact with other men, whereas women were more likely to interact with men, thus reinforcing the ideas that women compete with one another and prefer to be with men. In the mid-1980s groups of women were shown as friends and family to one another in such programs as *Designing Women* [1986–93] and *Golden Girls* [1985–92]" (Lout 1995, 171).

Another 1980s television phenomenon was the meteoric rise of the single dad as character in programs such as *Full House (*1987–95), *My Two Dads* (1987–90), and *Who's the Boss?* (1984–93). While in the real world the vast majority of single parents were and continue to be women, in TV land single parents were predominantly men.

The 1990s offered a wider array of female characters in continuing programs such as *Murphy Brown* and newer programs such as *Roseanne* (1988–97) and *Northern Exposure* (1990–95). But these less traditional female characters continued to be more the exception than the rule (Lout 1995, 171).

Soap operas are still another television genre that offers a unique perspective on gender. Evening soaps, in particular, often present strong female characters and address issues from a point of view that is sympathetic to women. For example, evening soaps present an unusually high number of middle aged women and women with access to great power. The characters of Alexis and Angelica from *Dynasty* (1981–89) and *Dallas* (1978–91) represent unusual television examples of the successful, independent career woman (Geraghty 1991, 43).

According to British author Christine Geraghty, the structure and characterization in soap operas offers an oppositional point of view with regard to gender. In the first place, daytime soaps are slow paced in the development of action, which Geraghty maintains reflects the drudgery in the lives of housewives. In the second place, these daytime soaps present women characters as the glue that holds the family together (Geraghty 1991, 43).

Perhaps most importantly, Geraghty provides an analysis of soap operas that reinforces the feminist notion that the personal is political: "Soaps overturn a deeply entrenched value structure which is based on the traditional opposition of masculinity and femininity. . . . Instead, the essence of soaps is the reflection on personal problems and the emphasis is on talk not on action, on slow development rather than the immediate response, on delayed retribution rather than instant effect" (Geraghty 1991, 41). The action in soap operas is strongly rooted in the personal sphere of life.

Prime Time Television—Employment and Economics

Sally Steenland's 1990 study also revealed the gender gap in employment in prime time television production. In 1990, only 15 percent of all producers were women, 25 percent of all writers were women, and 9 percent of directors were women. In addition, two-thirds of entertainment network executives at the vice president level and above were men.

The conglomerate ownership of media described in Chapter One and the prevalence of males in charge in entertainment media tend to proscribe and limit the roles and personality traits of women characters on television. As emphasized by Ben Bagdikian in *The Media Monopoly,* this does not indicate a conspiracy or a plot. Rather, the level of wealth, ownership, and experience of the individuals who own and run entertainment television results in a high degree of shared values, which are conveyed in programming (Bagdikian 1992, 16). If men dominate the writing, production, and direction of prime time television, it is likely that their collective life experiences and world view will be reflected.

As it emerged in the 1960s, feminism was and continues to be a concept that challenges the conventional place of women by criticizing and proposing to change traditional roles in order to allow women a wider array of life choices. Feminism invites women to question the narrowly defined, exclusive, and prescribed roles as homemaker and primary nurturer, as secretary and waitress, as nurse and teacher. Feminism does not criticize the value of these jobs and roles, but rather raises questions about why they offer such low pay and low status and are occupied predominantly by women. Feminism also asks women to consider what they put on and do to their faces and bodies to conform to an image of beauty that is almost universally inaccessible.

"One of the reasons why television is resistant to the messages of feminism, then, is that they [sponsors] view those messages as conflicting with women's desire to consume. Women buy products, it is thought, to please their families and to make themselves more attractive. Feminism, which argues that women should not base their self-image on the approval of others, inhibits women's desire to consume" (Dow 1995, 200). It is critical to remember that in addition to its explicit function to entertain and what we have discovered to be its implicit function to socialize, entertainment television is a vehicle for advertising. It would not be in

Media Activity 2.3
Gender Ideology in Prime Time Television

Instructions

Select three prime time television programs that are narrative fiction and family-based. These programs can be from the past and/or present (e.g., *Leave It to Beaver, Father Knows Best, Silverspoon, The Simpsons, Roseanne, The Cosby Show, Fresh Prince of Bel Air, Home Improvement*). Write the names of the male and female characters that you recall from each of these programs.

Program 1	Program 2	Program 3
_____	_____	_____
_____	_____	_____
_____	_____	_____
_____	_____	_____
_____	_____	_____

Place a check beside each of the male (adult and children) characters that conform to the traditional ideology that says boys are rough-and-tumble and love sports and that men are tough, work outside of the home, and take care of their families financially. Place a check beside each of the female (adult and children) characters that conform to the traditional ideology that says girls are sweet and pretty and women are soft and nurturing and take care of the family.

prime time television's self-interest to promote characters and themes that discourage women from buying products that pay for a program's survival.

Gender Ideology in Entertainment Media

This is hegemony, socialization without the use of force, at its subtle best. TV entertainment executives, directors, producers, and advertisers do not participate in hegemony because they are evil, bad guys. They participate in perpetuating stereotypical images of women because it is in their economic best interest and because it is the world they live in and from which they benefit. But the most compelling aspect of this hegemony is that it is held by men and women alike who are accustomed to and often see traditional gender roles as so standard and normal that hegemonic structures, limits, and barriers are all but invisible.

One way to examine the operation of hegemony and to make the invisible visible is to go directly to prime time television and use a simple content analysis in a small sample to understand how it works. Chapter One describes ideology as "a system of meaning that helps define and explain the world and that makes value judgments about the world" (Croteau and Hoynes 1997, 163). Ideology in entertainment media works best when it operates at a less than conscious and less than visible level and is applied to aspects of the social order that are considered the norm and rarely questioned. Some examples of traditional ideology about gender are:

- real boys are rough-and-tumble and love sports;
- real girls are sweet and pretty;
- real men are tough and work and take care of the family financially; and
- real women are soft and nurturing.

Can you find any examples in contemporary entertainment television that support this simple ideology about gender? Can you think of any examples of entertainment television from the past that support this ideology? Complete the survey in Media Activity 2.3 for a better understanding of how gender ideology operates in prime time television.

If more than half of the characters listed display these traditional traits, the program is likely to reflect a dominant gender ideology. If less than half of the characters display these traditional traits, the program most likely offers a different gender ideology. If half of the characters display these traits and half do not, it is most likely that the program conveys a mixed gender ideology. While this sample is neither large nor representative, it does give an indication of an often invisible framework that exists on prime time television.

From your analysis, what do you conclude about the way that gender within the family and the family itself are represented in your sample? Do you see any consistent or repeated patterns in the programs you reviewed? Is there a framework or a somewhat uniform story that is being told about men and women in the family? Is there a norm that is repeated about the configuration of the family? As you uncover and understand these messages about the family on prime time television, you will begin to make your own independent judgments about whether and to what extent television serves as a force to socialize boys and girls, and men and women, to play their assigned roles in the family and society.

Film

Not surprisingly, the history of the depiction of women in film often runs parallel to the history of women's treatment in American society. In the early 1900s, industrialization produced leisure time and the split into public/private spheres of labor for those in the middle classes and above. During this time, it was an important societal norm for the middle class woman to be traditionally feminine and run a smooth household. Yet there were also women in the labor force in 1900. Eighteen percent of the working population was female. Working class women were employed in sweatshops and factories 48 to 60 hours per week and earned $3 to $6 per week (Rosen 1973, 19). "The birth of the movies coincided with—and has-tened—the genesis of modern woman" (Rosen 1973, 23).

The sweetheart of the early 1900s film was Mary Pickford. Her specialty was the winsome waif, the sweet ragamuffin who appealed to Victorian audiences. During the 1920s several genres of film developed that portrayed women in clear and concrete roles. There was the continuation of the good girl as originated by Mary Pickford. There was the flapper who was in danger of becoming a bad girl, and there was the chorus girl often portrayed by Gloria Swanson or Joan Crawford (Rosen, 1973, 99).

By the end of 1941, the Japanese had bombed Pearl Harbor and the United States had officially entered World War II. Women entered the work force with a bang. The previous call to middle class femininity, which involved sustaining the hearth and home, switched to a call for patriotic women to support their men at war by going to work. With men off to war, the movie audience changed and for the first time there were a preponderance of films made that were dubbed "women's pictures." Some of these films such as *Spellbound* (1945) and *Mildred Pierce* (1945) explored women's lives and emotions and careers while others such as the Katharine Hepburn/Spencer Tracy classics *Adam's Rib* (1949) and *Woman of the Year* (1942) explored a new version of a woman who could be simultaneously feminine and independent (Rosen 1973, 190).

"Had Hollywood built on its image of the career woman, films might have acted as a more positive force in shaping the role of women in years to come. But as the men returned home from the war, box-office—and social—demands changed. Slowly heroines moved into the background, becoming less aggressive or inca-pable of working out their own fates" (Rosen 1973, 201). By the late 1940s more than 3 million women had resigned or been fired from their wartime jobs (Douglas 1994, 47). And film, rather than reflecting this phenomenal change in the roles of men and women, reverted to women's role as playful, as love object, or as stead-fast companion. *The Best Years of Our Lives,* starring Fredric March and Myrna Loy, won the Academy Award for Best Picture in 1947 and was a powerful por-trayal of men coming home from war, and their joy, agony, and ambivalence. The film, however, demonstrated no parallel transition or difficulty for women, but rather depicted women as remaining constant throughout and after the war, lov-ingly, patiently, and unambivalently supporting their men.

Over the years, film has inaccurately reflected working women. In 1930, over one-third of American films reviewed by the *New York Times* featured working women in the leading female role. In 1975, just over one-fourth of these films featured working women. "Compare this decline in Hollywood representations with the extraordinary growth in the percentage of actual adult women who work, from less than 20 percent in 1930 to 56 percent in 1975" (Galerstein 1989, xviii).

During the 1950s, 75 percent of women were married by the time they were nineteen (Rosen 1973, 245). During this Eisenhower era, there were signs of con-formity in suburbia contrasted by the development of the Beat Generation and the seeds of the civil rights and women's movements. During this era, there were few representations of powerful, independent or career minded women in film. Women were catching their men in *How to Marry a Millionaire* (1953) and *Seven Brides for Seven Brothers* (1954). They were preparing for marriage in *Father of the Bride* (1950) and *High Society* (1956). They were discontented wives and lovers in *From Here to Eternity* (1953). Many films featured no women at all, such as *Twelve Angry Men* (1957) and *Mister Roberts* (1965). There were the lovelorn and perky women in rock and roll–influenced films such as *April Love* (1957), *Tammy and the Bachelor* (1957), and *Gidget* (1959). By the late 1950s Doris Day had emerged as the symbol of the struggle of the virginal woman (in which the virgin always won) in *Pillow Talk* (1959) and *That Touch of Mink* (1962) (Rosen 1973, 205–305). By contrast, the 1950s was also the decade of Marilyn Monroe as the ultimate sex symbol.

In 1962 Helen Gurley Brown wrote *Sex and the Single Girl,* which advised women on romance and sex for its own sake; birth control pills began to be widely prescribed. In 1963 Betty Friedan wrote *The Feminine Mystique,* which analyzed the dissatisfaction of the trapped middle class housewife. Yet the early 1960s were dominated by films such as those in the James Bond series, which treated women as sex objects and made intelligent women invisible. Barbra Streisand dominated the roles of strong women that were available in films such as *Funny Girl* (1968) and *What's Up Doc?* (1972) (Lout 1995, 226).

By 1964, Beatlemania was in full swing. The youth and drug culture emerged in Haight Ashbury, college dormitories, and concerts. Yet the mid-1960s film industry chose to depict teenage angst with such films as *Bikini Beach* (1964), *Beach Party* (1963), and *Muscle Beach Party* (1964) (Rosen, 1973, 317). "The most astonishing aspect of Hollywood in the mid-1960s was its total inability to reflect the tapestry of youth culture—and perhaps its unwillingness to do so. During these years of turmoil, the industry opted out of making meaningful contributions in interpreting the role of the new young woman" (Rosen 1973, 317). Instead we got *Mary Poppins* (1964), *The Sound of Music* (1965), and *My Fair Lady* (1964); all were period pieces—the lead characters were all women: an ideal nanny with magic powers, a nun struggling with her own identity, and a street urchin turned lady through the will of a man.

By the mid-1960s, the youth culture began to be explored as Hollywood's awareness of the market potential of the youth audience was awakened with the popularity of *The Graduate* in 1967. By 1969 films such as *Easy Rider, Midnight Cowboy,* and *Alice's Restaurant* focused attention on the emerging alternative youth culture. Yet, few of these youth films depicted strong women or reflected the struggle with identity, role, and sexuality that young women were facing.

While the early 1970s continued by and large to lock women in stereotypical roles, there were some breakthrough films such *An Unmarried Woman* (1978) in which a married woman who has played her part as wife well is divorced, struggles with and finds her independent identity. Other strong female characters were depicted by Jane Fonda in *Klute* (1971), *Julia* (1977), and *China Syndrome* (1979). Sally Field depicted a complex working class woman who becomes a hero in the film *Norma Rae* (1979). *Diary of a Mad Housewife* (1970) depicted the most horrible manifestations of the feminine mystique, the trapped middle class housewife. *Turning Point* (1977) provided a complex portrait of two strong women who were dancers—one of whom chose a dance career and the other of whom chose to raise a family.

The top box office films in the 1980s were:

- *E.T.: The Extraterrestrial*
- *Return of the Jedi*
- *The Empire Strikes Back*
- *Raiders of the Lost Ark*
- *Ghostbusters*
- *Indiana Jones and the Last Crusade*
- *Indiana Jones and the Temple of Doom*
- *Beverly Hills Cop*
- *Back to the Future* (Internet Movie Database 1999).

Other than the fact that Harrison Ford appeared in five of these films, what do these popular films convey about gender? (Ford also was cast as the school principal in a sixth film, *E.T.,* but received no credit for this role because the scene was deleted from the final production.) Of the nine films, eight were categorized as either action or adventure. In all of these action and adventure films, male actors received top billing, and only Karen Allen in *Raiders of the Lost Ark* and Kate Capshaw in *Indiana Jones and the Temple of Doom* received as high as second billing. Despite her higher billing, Allen's role was that of a shrill female victim clad in a long white dress and heels who shrieked as Harrison Ford's Indiana Jones saved her from snakes and Nazis. All nine of the action films were dominated by male characters and actors. *Ghostbusters,* the one film that was typed as a comedy, was also overwhelmingly male.

The top money-making films in the 1990s were:

- *Jurassic Park*
- *Independence Day*
- *The Lion King*
- *Forrest Gump*
- *Terminator 2: Judgment Day*
- *Ghost*
- *Twister*
- *Titanic*
- *Pretty Woman*
- *Mrs. Doubtfire*

Media Activity 2.4
Gender and This Year's Top Box Office Films

Instructions

Follow the steps below to find and analyze gender in the top box office hits for the current year.

Step One: Log on to the All-Time Box Office Leaders website at http://www.filmsite.org.boxoffice.html. The site is organized according to two lists. The first list is the top 100 box office hits throughout film history and the second list is by decade.

Step Two: Scroll down to the current decade and year.

Step Three: List the top money-making films for the current year.

Step Four: Log on to the Internet Movie Database at http://us.imdb.com.

Step Five: Find each of the films you identified in Step Three in the Internet Movie Database and review the plot summary and the acting credits for each film.

Step Six: Answer the questions below for each film.
- What genre were these films? (action, adventure, comedy, drama, romance)
- List the major characters for each film. (Remember that major characters are those without whom the plot would make no sense.)
- List the first two actors in the billing order on the credits and indicate whether they are male or female.

Step Seven: Complete the chart below with the information you obtained in Step Six.

Name of Film	Genre	Major female characters	Major male character	1st billing (male or female)	2nd billing (male or female)
TOTALS		_____	_____	_____	_____

- *Men in Black*
- *Saving Private Ryan*
- *Armageddon*
- *The Fugitive*
- *Toy Story* (Internet Movie Database 1999).

These hits reflect more diversity in genre than the 1980s. Fifty-five percent of the films were action or adventure, 15 percent were children's animation, 15 percent were comedies, and 15 percent were romance. It was only in *Twister* that a woman, Helen Hunt, received top billing. Women received second billing in *Terminator 2: Judgment Day* (Linda Hamilton as a human action figure), *Forrest Gump* (Robin Wright as the misguided and on-again, off-again girlfriend of Forest), *Mrs. Doubtfire* (Sally Field as the uptight, shrill ex-wife), *Titanic* (Kate Winslet as the rich young woman who falls in love with a poor, handsome artist), and *Pretty Woman* (Julia Roberts as the prostitute with a big heart and a great flare for classy clothes). Male characters dominated a full 76 percent of these films.

Even the few major female characters in these popular 1980s and 1990s films were frequently simple and one-dimensional objects of romance or foils for the main character who, with one exception, was always male. Most of these films depicted important relationships or conflicts between men. A few depicted romance and romantic conflict between men and women; but none of these box office hits portrayed women's relationships.

The top money making-films rarely overlap with the films that are listed by critics as the top one hundred films, or with those that receive the Academy Awards' Best Picture recognition. Some of these critically acclaimed films feature major female characters who defy simplification and stereotypes. Academy Award winners such as *Driving Miss Daisy* (1989), *The English Patient* (1996), *Silence of the Lambs* (1991), *Out of Africa* (1985), and *Ordinary People* (1980) portrayed women who were strong, obstinate, mysterious, and filled with the contradictions that occur in real people. But these characters are the exception. Among the eighteen films awarded Best Picture by the Academy from 1980 to 1987, ten were dominated by male characters. The 1995 film *Waiting to Exhale,* based on the book by Terry McMillan, was one of the first mainstream popular films to feature an ensemble cast of African-American women. While the characters were only somewhat complex, there was diversity among them.

Roles for women in film have expanded and changed since the early twentieth century when waifs and chorus girls, virgins and whores dominated the scene. Yet male characters are still featured in most films. This underscores messages learned in school and in life about which gender is most interesting and important.

To determine some of the contemporary gender messages in high-earning films for the year in which you are reading, conduct your own research by following the steps in Media Activity 2.4.

After you conduct the research in Media Activity 2.4, answer the following questions:

What different genres were represented in your sample? How many major male characters and how many major female characters were there in the films you identified? What were the total numbers of male and female actors that received first and second billing? Overall, do men or women seem to dominate the money-making films of this year, or is their representation fairly even? What messages do these films convey about the relative significance of men and women?

You could proceed further and design a content analysis that examines physical appearance and personality similar to the one we conducted about prime time television in Media Activity 2.1. Through the decades of women in film, there have been more complex and independent women characters who are defined in broader terms than chorus girl or wife. Yet, the studies we have reviewed, as well as our own content analysis, reveal that women are still under-represented and stereotyped in many films. The top box office hits are those that are obviously the most widely viewed; these are the films in which women are most notably absent and stereotyped. This is another piece of the puzzle that contributes to socialization regarding gender.

Gender and Popular Music

Follow the instructions in Media Activity 2.5 to investigate some of the gender messages in popular music. Once again, a word of caution as we begin to analyze these images of gender. This content analysis utilizes an extremely small sample so that your results will simply help you to better understand how messages about gender and romance are portrayed in popular music and what kind of messages are conveyed in this particular limited sample.

When you complete the questions in the activity, the next step is to summarize each of the nine items both in raw numbers and percentages. For example, in number 9, if of the five relationships in the songs there was one that engaged in everyday conversation and four that did not, that would mean that "yes" would be 20 percent and "no" would be 80 percent. As you review the summary of each item, what have you found? Is there an indication of whether men or women are the aggressors, the most romantic, and the most sexual? What does this small sample tell you about roles of men and women in popular music? To what degree are the relationships featured intense, dramatic, romantic, conversational? What messages are conveyed about the nature of romantic relationships? The dominant ideology of gender roles in romance consists of the man as pursuer and most interested in sex and the woman as the pursued and most interested in romance. To what extent did your sample reinforce or challenge the dominant ideology of the gender roles in romantic relationships and the nature of the relationship itself? Are the relationships in this sample similar or different to the relationships you have had?

Popular music has traditionally featured romance as its central theme with lyrics sung by both men and women, proclaiming the joy of love and the agony of its loss. In the 1930s and 1940s Frank Sinatra, Ella Fitzgerald, and others rhapsodized and idealized love and romance in melodic ballads. In the 1950s when rock and roll began, the popular music scene exploded, however, and control of the industry and reflection of gender in the music became more highly contested.

In the 1950s, the emergence of the first "girl groups" began with the Shirelles' top ten song, "Will You Still Love Me Tomorrow?" Written by Carol King, this was the first song by a group of women to make it to the top ten (Lout 1995, 321). "The most important thing about this music and the reason it spoke to us so powerfully, was that it gave voice to all the warring selves inside us struggling blindly and with a crushing sense of insecurity, to force something resembling a coherent identity. Even though the girl groups were produced and managed by men, it was in their music that the contradictory messages about female sexuality and rebelliousness were most poignantly and authentically expressed" (Douglas 1994, 87). These groups sang about dependence on men, rebellion, sexuality, resistance, and compliance.

More than film or television, these songs of the 1950s reflected the struggle and upheaval in the changing lives and roles of young men and women. The lyrics of "I Will Follow Him" sung by Little Peggy March demonstrate the traditional compliant girl who goes to the ends of the earth for the man she loves. "Sweet Talking Guy" by the Chiffons demonstrates the sexual pull of a "sweet talking guy" and the struggle of the girl to sort out love and sex. By the mid-1960s the "girl" singer replaced the "girl group" and more women entered the musical scene singing a wide range of songs with a variety of gender representations. By and large these soloists and groups depicted girls with a single purpose—finding and keeping their true love.

Before continuing the analysis of the next round of female singers, it is interesting to note the language that is used for the women and young women who sang popular songs in the 1950s and 1960s. Male singers were called "singers" or "rock and roll groups" or "recording artists," but female singers were called "girl groups" or "girl singers." This language difference is significant in two ways. First, the terms for men are generic and assume that male singers are the norm; second, the term for females is the diminutive, childlike "girl."

From 1963 to 1965 there were a total of sixty-nine songs that made it to the number one spot on the popular music chart. Of these songs, only fifteen were recorded by women. Some examples of these songs are the 1963 "He's So Fine" by the Chiffons in which the woman sings lyrics such as "If I were a queen and he asked me to leave my throne, I'd do anything that he asked, anything to make him my own.' Cause he's so fine." Then there is the classic 1964 Mary Wells hit "My Guy," in which she praises her guy and all of the things she would pass by for him. The 1965 Supremes song "Stop in the Name of Love" begs the man to stop seeing another woman for sex and to stay with his woman for real love.

During the mid-1960s Lulu sang "To Sir with Love," while Leslie Gore poured out her heart with such romantic sorrows and triumphs as "It's My Party" and "It's

Media Activity 2.5
Gender and Popular Music

Instructions

Select a minimum of five songs that are currently among the top ten on the music charts. You may choose songs that are on the Top 40, Country, or Rhythm and Blues charts. Select songs that depict a romantic or sexual relationship. For each song, answer the questions below. Do not make any assumptions about the relationship. Take all information strictly from the lyrics.

Role of Men and Women

1. Who initiates or pursues the relationship?
   a. male _____
   b. female _____
   c. both _____
   d. neither _____
   e. cannot tell _____

2. Who waits for someone to initiate or pursue the relationship?
   a. male _____
   b. female _____
   c. both _____
   d. neither _____
   e. cannot tell _____

3. Who appears most interested in the sexual part of the relationship?
   a. male _____
   b. female _____
   c. both _____
   d. neither _____
   e. cannot tell _____

4. Who appears least interested in or ambivalent about the sexual part of the relationship?
   a. male _____
   b. female _____

(cont'd)

Judy's Turn to Cry." Yet in "You Don't Own Me," Gore deviates from the schoolgirl dependence on her guy to declare independence and the unwillingness to change for a boy. Then there was Tina Turner belting out strong songs full of female lust and desire and Aretha Franklin insisting on "Respect." While Turner wanted lust and Franklin wanted respect, their songs and styles shared a strength and an assertion of their rights and needs vis-à-vis men.

c. both   ___
d. neither   ___
e. cannot tell   ___

5. Who seems to romanticize the relationship the most?
   a. male   ___
   b. female   ___
   c. both   ___
   d. neither   ___
   e. cannot tell   ___

6. Who seems to romanticize the relationship the least?
   a. male   ___
   b. female   ___
   c. both   ___
   d. neither   ___
   e. cannot tell   ___

Nature of the Relationship

7. Which of these words most closely describes the relationship?
   a. unromantic   ___
   b. somewhat romantic   ___
   c. romantic   ___
   e. cannot tell   ___

8. Which of these words most closely describes the relationship?
   a. light   ___
   b. moderate   ___
   c. a mix of light and intense   ___
   d. intense, dramatic   ___
   e. cannot tell   ___

9. Is there everyday conversation in the relationship?
   a. yes   ___
   b. no   ___
   c. cannot tell   ___

By the mid-1960s the so-called "British invasion" by the Beatles and their many clones dominated the American music scene and white female soloists lost much of their audience. During this time, the only American music with a substantial audience was Motown, which included a second wave of the "girl groups," including the Supremes, Martha and the Vandellas, and the Marvelettes. While not as conventionally popular as the others, another female phenomenon hit the music scene of the 1960s and that was political folk music as sung by artists such as Joni Mitchell, Judy Collins, and Joan Baez (Lout 1995, 322). These women were singing of peace and the environment as well as love and romance. But there were still few images of strong independent girls and women, or women struggling with their own gender identities in a rapidly shifting society.

"Music is perhaps one of the most powerful tools for the conveyance of ideas and emotions. It is also a great vehicle for propaganda. Lyrics in music reinforce a culture's values. Rock music, as part of the youth culture, always sent out strong messages, picked up by listeners, consciously or unconsciously. Embedded with the messages are female and male portrayals" (Lout 1995, 324). And it appears that both the singers and the lyrics reinforced traditional expectations of the roles of males and females in U.S. society.

By the 1970s rock was a central component of the cultural revolution and most rock bands were male. Tina Turner and Janis Joplin were early exceptions, followed soon by women musicians, such as Bonnie Raitt, Joan Armatrading, and Joan Jett, who began to play electric instruments. A study conducted in 1970–79 revealed that fewer than 12 of more than 260 prominent musical acts featured individual women or women in a band. "Females growing up in the 1960s and 1970s were offered narrow roles to emulate. As teenagers, they listened to chirpies, love-crazed girl groups, folk madonnas, or sexy Black singers. When rock became popular, teenage girls could be 'groovy chicks' or 'uptight.' In general, women's roles in rock music were prescribed by men and handed to women to fulfill. Real problems (being different, peer pressure, abuse, homosexuality) were rarely discussed. Yet, there was little room for growth or diversity" (Lout 1995, 325). Janis Ian's song "Society's Child" was a notable exception, telling the poignant and politically charged story of a girl's family's rejection of an interracial relationship.

By the 1980s the number of female bands had increased and 1981 ushered in a new era—that of music television or MTV. In the early days of television broadcast, producers saw audiences as largely homogeneous, undifferentiated. As cable developed the idea of capturing a more narrow audience with buying power, the television industry began to make programming decisions based on the results of demographic research and its potential to attract sponsors. Fred Silverman at NBC made broadcast history by perfecting this concept, using market research to determine program content. This research said that young adults ages 18 to 29, mostly female, were the main buyers of television goods. Bob Pittman followed this marketing strategy to create an audience of buyers for MTV (Lewis 1990, 17).

MTV's target audience was 12 to 34 year olds whom Pittman defined as a cultural group that grew up on two dominant forms of media—television and rock and roll. The goal of MTV was to combine these two entertainment phenomena. MTV established another strategy that began as a financial consideration and ultimately dictated programmatic decisions. Pittman decided to replicate the standard radio format, which utilized free demos on the air, by using free video demos promoted by the companies that produced them (Lewis 1990, 21). "What had begun as a practical approach to securing cheap (free) programming within the parameters of MTV's concept ended up being a factor that determined MTV's program content. By getting record companies to supply videos, MTV ensured that the videos would look like advertisements for record companies" (Lewis 1990, 24).

Prior to the advent of MTV, the musical and ideological foundations of rock music and popular music had been quite different. Some musicians, audiences, and music critics saw pop music as simple, "bubblegum" and formulaic while viewing rock as the "people's" music—more complex and cutting edge in both music and lyrics. Prior to MTV, hard rock had taken a more anticommercial stance—which MTV turned upside down (Lewis 1990, 28–35).

The commercially driven MTV became a central cultural phenomenon for American adolescents and its depiction of gender has had a strong impact. Teenagers developed their own fashion and style based on popular music videos. Girls assumed the dark roots with blonde hair and clothing style of Madonna in the 1980s and in the 1990s young boys wore the scarves and goggles of 'N Sync. Adolescence has assumed an important role in U.S. culture. It is often a life phase in which young people are given or take some freedom and permission to explore sexuality and rebel against authority. Yet this has been a largely masculine tradition in American culture in which the construct of femininity restricts how girls participate in this rebellion and exploration (Lewis 1990, 28–35).

"Adolescence and masculinity are united ideologically to support a social system of male privilege. . . . Toward this end, boys learn to feel comfortable in public space, adjust to competitive pressures, network with their male peers, build a familial support system, and to prepare for risk-taking in future work endeavors. However, the social authorization given to such practices is directed specifically to boys, and does not extend as fully to girls" (Lewis 1990, 35). The videos in MTV "were united by a central focus on articulating adolescence within the context of male-adolescent experience and sexual desire" (Lewis 1990, 53).

A 1987 study of MTV music videos found that men were more likely to be aggressive, violent, or dominant while women were more likely to wear revealing clothing, show affection, and pursue sex (Seidman 1992, 209). By 1989, the increasing presence of female singers seemed to have changed those numbers. In 63 percent of female or mostly female groups, women were treated in the same way as men (Lout 1995, 335).

The careers of Tina Turner, Cyndi Lauper, and Madonna represent the contradictions in MTV gender ideology and the opportunity for women to succeed. These women exerted some creative control over their music and its production, and their careers and personal stories offered inspiration and served as role models to adolescent girls. While Turner's and Madonna's images were hard and sexual, their lives told a different story of rising above abuse and dependence and creating and controlling their own music and images. "The emergence of female-adolescent discourse on MTV is important politically because it has provided a vehicle for girls to speak about their experiences as female adolescents. But it is also important because it has expanded the reconsideration of gender inequality to include adolescence, thus beginning the much needed work of acknowledging the fact that oppressed women begin their lives as oppressed girls" (Lewis 1990, 234).

As in other forms of entertainment media and popular culture, the impact of popular music is measured primarily through repetitive images. To understand the role of women, men, and romance in popular music it is critical to determine if there is any range, diversity, and complexity in the images or if these images of men, women, and romance reinforce the dominant ideology of gender in the United States.

What are some images of love, romance, and sex in popular music as conveyed in lyrics, music videos, CD covers? What kind of gender roles do these images of love, romance, and sex convey? In what ways do these images reinforce or challenge conventional gender ideology?

It is useful to first examine what constitutes dominant ideology in the interaction of gender with love, sex, and romance. The first aspect of a traditional ideology involves the roles played by men and women in heterosexual romance. The conventional role of men in romance and sex is that of the initiator or the aggressor, the one most interested in sex, the detached partner, the one least interested in romance. The conventional role of women is that of the pursued, uninterested, or torn about sex, the involved partner, the one engrossed in romance. The dominant ideology involves a dramatization of love as intense, highly romanticized and/or tragic as opposed to a relationship of intermittent and perhaps more moderate passion, conversation, conflict, and resolution. Of course, one could easily argue that a song that lyricizes moderation and mundane conversation would not ignite the audience or record sales. But given the impact that popular music has on its young listeners, it is critical to understand the messages that are being offered.

Chapter Summary

When my daughter was four years old, she took her first dance class with seven or eight other little girls. The dance teacher chose the music, choreographed a piece, and designed costumes for their first recital performance. The girls and the parents were very excited and exuberant about the process and the experience. When I learned what the selected song was, my heart sank. It was "Chapel of Love" by the Dixiecups. The lyrics were traditionally romantic and centered around going to the chapel of love to get married. The costumes were white leotards with silver sparkles and a headband with material made to look like a wedding veil. All of the other moms were cooing over the cuteness of the music, the dance, and the costume. I knew this event by itself would not damage or finish off the socialization of these girls permanently. But this was only one event in many that would teach them that cuteness, relationships to men, and being brides were at the core of what it meant to be a girl. However, my own socialization got in the way of intervening. I thought that if I protested the content, no matter how politely, I would be viewed as a curmudgeon at best and a spoiler at worst. Socialized as I was to be a woman who was polite, easy to get along with, and pleasing to others, I chose not to raise my concerns.

But the more individuals understand how each of these events in the life of children adds up to limit their ultimate choices and independence, the more people and institutions will have the wherewithal to intervene and interrupt. Schools can examine the policies and practices that value only received and separate knowing. They can provide information and strategies for change to teachers about what contributes to lowering I.Q. points in adolescent girls. Parents can offer more choices to children early in their lives so that their boys and girls can decide whether to play with dolls or trucks or both. Institutions can analyze employment and salaries according to gender and promote changes that are more equitable. Individuals can read more about gender history and socialization and can find ways to interrupt gender oppression when they see it. Film, television, and music can portray girls and women as complex characters with a range of personalities and roles in life.

The connections between personal experience, formal knowledge, and entertainment media are key to an understanding of U.S. gender socialization in general and your own gender experience and expression in particular. This chapter guides you through the discovery of what you were taught formally and informally about what it means to be male or female in this society. We are born a particular sex and taught how to be a particular gender. The concepts of dominant, alternative, and mixed gender ideology are fundamental to the understanding of what we were taught about gender and what other ways of being male and female are available. Entertainment media in the forms of popular music, film, and television are central tools of socialization and send strong messages about what it means to be a boy or a girl, a man or a woman. Entertainment assessment tools are a means to uncover these messages and to determine whether a particular song, film, program, or an entire genre reinforces or challenges dominant gender ideology. The ability to understand how our personal gender values and behavior are formed is the foundation to making independent choices about how and who we want to be.

Bibliography

All Time Box-Office Leaders. 1999. http://www.filmsite.org.boxoffice.html.

American Association of University Women (AAUW). 1995. *How Schools Shortchange Girls, the AAUW Report.* New York: Marlowe.

Associated Press. May 4, 1998. *http://lexis-nexis.com.*

Bagdikian, Ben H. 1992. *The Media Monopoly.* Boston: Beacon Press.

Brownmiller, Susan. 1984. *Femininity.* New York: Ballantine Books.

Connell, R.W. 1987. *Gender and Power: Society, the Person, and Sexual Politics.* Stanford: Stanford University Press.

Croteau, David, and Hoynes, William. 1997. *Media/Society: Industries, Images, and Audiences.* Thousand Oaks, CA: Pine Forge Press.

D'Acci, Julie. 1995. "Defining Women: The Case of Cagney and Lacey." In *Gender, Race and Class in Media—A Text Reader,* ed. Gail Dines and Jean M. Humez, 454–59. Thousand Oaks, CA: Sage.

Davis, Angela Y. 1981. *Women, Race, and Class.* New York: Random House.

Douglas, Susan. 1994. *Where the Girls Are: Growing Up Female with the Mass Media.* New York: Times Books.

Dow, Bonnie J. 1995. "Prime-Time Feminism: Entertainment and Women's Progress." In *Women and Media: Content/ Careers/Criticism,* ed. Cynthia Lout, 200. Belmont, CA: Wadsworth.

Elasmar, Michael; Hasegawa, Kazumi; and Brain, Mary. 1999. "The Portrayal of Women in U.S. Prime Time Television." *Journal of Broadcasting and Electronic Media* 3 (Winter): 20–26.

Elliot, Heidi. 1997. *Electronic Business Today,* September, p. 50.

Faludi, Susan. 1991. *Backlash: The Undeclared War Against American Women.* New York: Putnam.

Field Belenky, Mary; McVicker Clinchy, Blythe; Rule Goldberger, Nancy; and Mattuck Tarule, Jill. 1988. *Women's Ways of Knowing—The Development of Self, Voice, and Mind.* New York: Basic Books.

Franck, Irene, and Brownstone, David. 1993. *The Women's Desk Reference.* New York: Viking Penguin.

Freire, Paulo. 1989. *Pedagogy of the Oppressed.* New York: Continuum.

Friedan, Betty. 1963. *The Feminine Mystique.* New York: Dell.

Galerstein, Carolyn L. 1989. *Working Women on the Hollywood Screen: A Filmography.* New York and London: Garland.

Geraghty, Christine. 1991. *Women and Soap Opera: A Study of Prime Time Soaps.* Cambridge, England: Polity Press.

Gerbner, George. 1997. "Television Demography: What's Wrong with This Picture?" Unpublished manuscript.

Gilligan, Carol. 1993. "Joining the Resistance: Psychology, Politics, and Women." In *Beyond Silenced Voices: Class, Race, and Gender in the United States Schools,* ed. Lois Weis and Michelle Fine. Albany: State University of New York Press.

Hamilton, Kendall, and Weingarden, Julie. 1998. "Lifts, Lasers, and Liposuctions: The Cosmetic Surgery Boom," *Newsweek* 131, no. 24: 14.

Hochschild, Arlie, with Machung, Anne. 1989. *The Second Shift.* New York: Avon Books.

Internet Movie Database 1999. http://us.imdb.com.

Kimball, M. 1986. "Television and Sex-Role Attitudes." In *The Impact of Television: A Natural Experiment in Three Communities,* ed. Tannis M. Williams, 265–301. Orlando: Academic Press.

Lewin, Tamar. 1998. "How Boys Lost Out to Girl Power," *New York Times,* December 13, p. 3.

Lewis, Lisa A. 1990. *Gender Politics and MTV: Voicing the Difference.* Philadelphia: Temple University Press.

Lout, Cynthia. 1995. *Women and Media: Content/Careers/Criticism.* Belmont, CA: Wadsworth.

McPhee, Carol, and Fitzgerald, Ann. 1979. *Voices of Rebels, Reformers, and Visionaries.* New York: Thomas Y. Crowell, 17.

Mead, Margaret. 1935. *Sex and Temperament in Three Primitive Societies.* New York: Dell.

Media Awareness. 1997. http://www.media-awareness.ca/eng/issues/STATS/issgen. html.

Orenstein, Peggy. 1994. *Schoolgirls: Young Women, Self-Esteem, and the Confidence Gap.* New York: Doubleday.

Pipher, Mary. 1994. *Reviving Ophelia: Saving the Selves of Adolescent Girls.* New York: Putnam.

Purcell, Piper, and Stewart, Lara. 1990. "Dick and Jane in 1989." *Sex Roles: A Journal of Research* 22: 177–85.

Rappaport, Doreen. 1990. *American Women: Their Lives in Their Words.* New York: HarperCollins.

Ries, Paula, and Stone, Anne J., eds. 1992. *The American Woman: 1992–93: A Status Report.* New York: W.W. Norton.

Rosen, Marjorie. 1973. *Popcorn Venus: Women, Movies and the American Dream.* New York: Coward, McCann, and Geoghegan.

Seidman, Stephen A. 1992. "An Investigation of Sex-r\Role Stereotyping in Music Videos." *Journal of Broadcasting and Electronic Media* 36, no. 2: 209.

Shreve, Anita. 1989. *Women Together, Women Alone: The Legacy of the Consciousness Raising Movement.* New York: Viking.

Steenland, Sally. 1995. "Content Analysis of the Image of Women on Television." In *Women and Media: Content/Careers/Criticism,* ed. Cynthia Lout, 180–87. Belmont, CA: Wadsworth.

———. 1990. "Women and Television in the Eighties." *Television Quarterly* 24, no. 3 (Summer).

U.S. Bureau of Census. 1995. *Statistical Abstract of the United States* (115th ed.). Washington, DC: U.S. Government Printing Office.

Watkins, Mel, and David, Jay, eds. 1970. *To Be a Black Woman: Portraits in Fact and Fiction.* New York: William Morrow.

Weinberg, Daniel H. 1998. "Press Briefing on Measuring 50 Years of Economic Change." Washington, DC: U.S. Census Bureau.

Wood, Julia T. 1994. *Gendered Lives: Communication, Gender, and Culture.* Belmont, CA: Wadsworth.

Chapter 3

Is the United States a Classless Society?

> [A]s a result of the class you are born into and raised in, class is
> your understanding of the world and where you fit in; it's
> composed of ideas, behavior, attitudes, values, and language;
> class is how you think, feel, act, look, dress, talk, move, walk;
> class is what stores you shop at, restaurants you eat in; class is the
> schools you attend, the education you attain; class is the very jobs
> you will work at throughout your adult life.
>
> —*Langston*

> In the absence of real contact of communication, stereotypes
> march on unchallenged; prejudices easily substitute for
> knowledge.
>
> —*Ehrenreich*

Personal Experience and Class

Many of us who grew up in the United States were taught that we were a "classless" society and that distinct classes and castes were characteristic of England and India and feudalism. In this chapter we will examine and reconstruct this information and our beliefs. To begin the exploration of your personal experience and social and economic class answer the questions in Personal Inventory 3.1. The highest possible score is 18 and the lowest possible score is negative 15. If you scored between 16 and 18 points, chances are you and your family lived in a fairly to extremely high economic bracket. If you scored between −13 and −15, you and your family most likely lived in very difficult economic circumstances. If you scored between −12 and +15 points, your family was somewhere in the vast working or middle class.

What thoughts did you have as you were answering the questions? What memories did it evoke? Were you surprised to discover where you and your family fit in the economic scheme of things?

The exercise you have just completed is designed to help you begin to examine the economics of your family and to guide you in beginning to think about how your family's economic status impacted your sense of self, your world view, and your opportunities in life. According to your comfort level, I encourage you to invite others to do this exercise and to compare your score, experiences, and memories with classmates, family members, or friends. Then, through discussion with others who have completed the exercise or through the continuation of your autobiographical journal, answer the questions in Personal Inventory 3.2.

Open discussion of income is often considered impolite in the United States. In fact, it is quite common for children to be unaware of their parents' income and to be chastised if they inquire. While these unspoken rules and norms may make it difficult to get precise answers to these questions, I encourage you to probe when you can and estimate if you need to. As you consider your score on the Level Playing Field exercise in Personal Inventory 3.1 as well as your answers to the autobiographical questions in Personal Inventory 3.2, where do you think you and your family sit economically? Are you above, below, or in the middle of most Americans?

Class is a word that is rarely used in American households or schools and is therefore difficult for us to conceptualize and hold concretely in our hands. In fact, we are often told that the United States is a "classless" society. But *class*—the understanding of our socioeconomic place and life chances—is exactly what we are addressing here. Later in the chapter, we will examine various sociological and economic definitions of class. For now, we will explore and analyze personal and family experiences that have been driven by family income. You are invited to begin to sort out how these experiences have influenced your values, beliefs, and behavior.

Personal Inventory 3.3 provides a quiz that helps assess your family's expectations and assumptions and their connection to social and economic class. Sometimes these expectations are spoken and sometimes they are unspoken, but nevertheless, they are remarkably present.

As you review your responses to these statements, be sure to distinguish between family *expectations* and family *goals, dreams,* or *hopes* for the future. How did your family's income and/or wealth contribute to these expectations? How did the history of generations of your family's income and/or wealth contribute to these expectations? Examine those statements that accurately describe your family's expectations. Do you think these expectations are more characteristic of people with low income, middle income, or high income?

As we investigate our own family's socioeconomic position and class and look at those of others, it is fairly easy to see that there is great wealth in the United States, just as there is dire poverty and a middle ground of income. It is also plain to see that the higher the income, the higher the access to better education, health care, housing, travel, employment, and all of the other factors that heighten opportunities for success. While we may all see the same things around us, our own class

---

Personal Inventory 3.1
The Level Playing Field

Instructions

Answer the questions below based on your personal experience.
There are no right or wrong answers.

---

1. If you were raised in a two parent family, score 1 point   ____
2. If you had your own car as a teenager, score 1 point   ____
3. If you had a phone in your room as a teenager, score 1 point   ____
4. If you had a separate telephone line as a teenager, score 1 point   ____
5. If you had to work for economic necessity as a teenager,
   subtract 1 point   ____
6. If your family ever experienced economic difficulty, setback,
   or crisis, subtract 1 point   ____
7. If due to finances, you ever had to forego camp or extracurricular activities that your friends participated in, subtract
   1 point   ____
8. If your parents are paying for or paid for your entire college
   education, add 1 point   ____
9. If you receive or received need-based financial aid for college,
   subtract 1 point   ____
10. If you had all the clothes you wanted as a teenager, add 1 point   ____
11. If your family frequently had dinner at restaurants (other than
    fast food), add 1 point   ____
12. If your family had a children's library of 50 or more books, add
    1 point   ____
13. If your family had an adult library of 50 or more books, add
    1 point   ____
14. If your family went on regular vacations, add 1 point   ____
15. If your family took you to museums, libraries, or other
    enrichment activities, add 1 point   ____
16. If either of your parents completed college, add 1 point   ____

(cont'd)

---

position and experiences deeply influence how we interpret the distribution of wealth and opportunity. Key to this interpretation is our understanding of the "American Dream."

Take a look at four definitions of the American Dream described below:

Definition 1: "What I want to see above all is that this country remains a country where someone can always get rich. That's the one thing we have and that must be preserved" (Hochschild 1995, x).

Definition 2: "[The American Dream] simply states that the playing field is

17. If you ever needed to or currently need to rely on public transportation to get around, subtract 1 point ___

18. If either of your parents did not complete high school, subtract 1 point ___

19. If there was a period of time in which either of your parents was involuntarily unemployed, subtract 1 point ___

20. If, as a child, you often wore hand-me-down clothes, subtract 1 point ___

21. If your family shopped primarily at discount stores, subtract 1 point ___

22. If either of your parents worked as a clerical worker, domestic worker, laborer, or service worker, subtract 1 point ___

23. If your parents or grandparents were immigrants to the U.S., subtract 1 point ___

24. If your family owned their own home, add 1 point ___

25. If your family rented an apartment or home, subtract 1 point ___

26. If your family had major credit cards, add 1 point ___

27. Add one point for each of your parents who graduated from college ___

28. If you are the first generation of your family to attend college, subtract 1 point ___

29. If supermarkets, cleaners, drug stores, and other amenities were easily accessible in your neighborhood, add 1 point ___

30. If you attended private school for elementary, middle, or high school, add 1 point ___

31. If you lived in a high crime neighborhood, subtract 1 point ___

32. If your family did not have a checking or savings account, subtract 1 point ___

Add all of your plus 1 points and subtract all of your minus 1 points for a TOTAL ___

Source: Based on an unpublished manuscript and workshop exercise by Joan Olsen, 1995.

level, that although everyone may not start with the same income and wealth, everyone has the same chance to reach the top of the income hierarchy because a person's class background does not limit a person's chances of economic success . . . this belief is a significant framework within which we think about our society. Although everyone knows and accepts that there is no equality of income, it is also accepted that there is equality of opportunity" (Jhally and Lewis 1992, 89).

Definition 3: "The American dream that we were all raised on is a simple but

---

Personal Inventory 3.2
Autobiography on Class

Instructions

Answer the questions below in writing or on a tape recording to explore your experiences with socioeconomic class.

---

1. As you were growing up, how did you dress? Where did you shop? What kind of restaurants did you frequent? How did your family's income affect these choices?

2. What kind of social or athletic activities did your family most frequently participate in (e.g., bowling, golf, tennis, watching television, playing cards)? How did your family's income affect these choices?

3. Describe the neighborhood(s) in which you grew up. Were there houses, apartments, or both? Were the streets and sidewalks well maintained? Were supermarkets easily accessible? What would you say the average income level was for most of the people in your neighborhood? What kind of jobs did people have? Did many young people go to college? How did your family's income affect these choices?

4. How many generations ago did your family come to the United States? Did they come voluntarily or as slaves, indentured servants, or refugees, or were they part of a conquered people? How many generations back can you identify the kinds of jobs your grandparents and parents had? Were the jobs and income similar or different from generation to generation? Did the income from generation to generation go up, down, or stay the same?

---

powerful one—if you work hard and play by the rules you should be given a chance to go as far as your God-given ability will take you" (Hochschild 1995, 18).

Definition 4: "By the American dream, I mean not merely the right to get rich, but rather the promise that all Americans have a reasonable chance to achieve success as they define it—material or otherwise—through their own efforts, and to attain virtue and fulfillment through success" (Hochschild 1995, 32).

Now, for each definition ask yourself these questions:

1. Does this make sense to you? Do you believe this to be true?
2. Has this been true for you? For your family? For how many generations has this definition been accurate or inaccurate for your family?

Personal Inventory 3.3
Class and Values Quiz

Instructions

Read the statements below and circle the response that most closely matches the expectations your family had for their circumstances and your future as you were growing up. Mark "a" if the statement reflects an accurate account of your family's expectation in life. Mark "b" if your family expected more from life than the statement reveals. Mark "c" if your family expected less from life than the statement reveals, and mark "d" if this statement was never even a consideration in your family.

Responses

- a. accurate expectation
- b. expected more
- c. expected less
- d. not even a consideration

Statements

1. Getting by   ___
2. Making a moderate living   ___
3. Making a good living   ___
4. Gaining social status or prominence   ___
5. Working out psychological issues through therapy   ___
6. Community service   ___
7. Saving money   ___
8. Making your money work for you   ___
9. Getting a high school degree   ___
10. Getting a college degree   ___
12. Getting an advanced or professional degree   ___
13. Learning a trade   ___
14. Being an entrepreneur   ___
15. Owning a home   ___
16. Going to private school   ___
17. Being a professional   ___

Source: Based on material from Adams, Bell, and Griffin (1997).

3. From your observations, do you believe most Americans regard the dream in this way?

for each definition ask yourself these questions:

1. Does this make sense to you? Do you believe this to be true?

2. Has this been true for you? For your family? For how many generations has this definition been accurate or in accurate for your family?
3. From your observations, does this definition seem to apply to most Americans?

Later in the chapter, we will discuss the meaning and significance of the American Dream both currently and throughout American history. But for now, as you examine your personal beliefs—do not criticize or evaluate—pay attention to and notice what you have come to believe about the American Dream and how it flavors your hopes and visions and beliefs about your own life chances and the life chances for other Americans. Definitions two and four are reflections by scholars, definition one was proclaimed by President Ronald Reagan in 1983, and definition three by President Bill Clinton in 1993. The fact that at least two recent U.S. presidents have incorporated the American Dream into their rhetoric is an indication of the pervasiveness of this concept.

This is just a beginning of understanding our personal experience of class and how our relative position and economic privilege impacts our values, beliefs, and behavior. Class identity differs significantly from racial and gender identity. From very early ages most of us knew whether we were male or female, African American, European American, Asian American, Native American, Latino, or biracial. While our life experiences dictated how we perceived those gender or racial identities, the identities themselves were generally clearly expressed to us. It is different with class identity. It is rare that Grandma or Grandpa take little Johnny on their knee and say, "Now, Johnny, you know we're working class—have been for many generations and that's something you can be proud of," or "Susie, you will inherit great wealth some day. Our family is owning class and that means that you have more money, clothes, and better education and health care than most Americans."

Because our income dictates where we live, Americans often settle in communities surrounded by other families of their same means and class. These communities seem "normal" to us. In fact, many people report as adults that they did not know they were "poor" because everybody else was just like them. The purpose of this chapter is to help make sense of the concept of class and the American Dream, its reflection in entertainment media, and how these ideas and messages influence our lives. Much of the literature on socioeconomic class is highly politicized and characterized by strong convictions. As the reader, it will be your task to sort out how your own personal experiences around class have shaped you and how you see the world. You will also be invited to take in new information and it will be your challenge to think critically about this new information and ultimately make independent decisions about what you choose to believe.

Reconstructing Knowledge About Class

"*Class* is about money and it is about more than money. As a result of the class you are born into and raised in, class is your understanding of the world and where you fit in, it's composed of ideas, behavior, attitudes, values, and language; class is how you think, feel, act, look, dress, talk, move, walk; class is what stores you shop at, restaurants you eat in; class is the schools you attend, the education you attain; class is the very jobs you will work at throughout your adult life"(Langston 1995, 101–102). Some sociologists define class as "the relative location of a person or group within a larger society, based on wealth, power, prestige, or other valued resources" (Kendall 1999, 73). Other sociologists define class according to category of occupation. Some economists define class by income and economic status, while others define it by ownership, power, and control (Adams et al. 1997, 233). According to the fabric of oppression, class is defined as the structural arrangement by which income and wealth are distributed unevenly through various layers of society.

One effective working definition of class is "a relative social ranking based on income, wealth, status, and/or power" (Adams et al. 1997, 233). *Classism*, then, is a set of individual and institutional beliefs, systems, and practices that assigns value to people according to their class ranking and creates an economic inequality affording economic privilege to some while targeting others for oppression.

One way of understanding class identity is by type of occupation. Using this categorization, the working class is composed of white collar clerical workers, technicians, salespersons, craftsworkers, laborers, factory workers, and others who do not attain control over other workers or their own lives. Members of the middle class work as professionals, managers, self-employed storekeepers, and independent farmers and other jobs that give them some degree of economic autonomy or control over other workers. Those in the owning class have extreme wealth and are owners of major corporations and international businesses; they are characterized by the control they have over their own lives and those of others. Members of the owning class need not work to earn the means to support themselves and often are the beneficiaries of inherited wealth (Vanneman and Cannon 1987, 11).

Because class is discussed so little in the United States, its definitions and measurement and our own class identity are often unclear. At the top of the distribution of wealth is a tiny percentage of people—the owning class—who own and control an enormous amount of resources and wealth. At the bottom of the income and wealth distribution are people who have extremely low incomes or none at all, commonly labeled as poor. But the lines between poor, working class, and middle class people are blurred. Some say that anyone who is not owning class is working class. Others say that the distinctions in income mark the difference in the remaining classes. Still others say that it is the difference in the nature of work; the degree of autonomy, physical labor, and danger of work; and the degree in control over one's labor that distinguishes the middle class from the working class (Zandy 1995, 9).

Of all of the issues discussed in this book, class is the least visible, the most disguised, and in some ways the most challenging concept to grasp and attribute common meaning. "The ability of average Americans to analyze and understand the current situation is thwarted by prevailing myths about class and classism and a version of history in which class and classism have been largely invisible" (Adams et al. 1997, 231).

History books and school courses have been designed primarily by people who are middle class and above, and information in these sources has typically been from this perspective. Yet class difference and class struggle have been integral in the combination of stories that comprise American history. Some of this struggle has been violent and its telling contradicts the more simple stories and myths of the United States as a class-free and economically mobile society. "Part of the problem of visibility is a problem of knowledge—how knowledge is constructed, layer after layer, generation after generation. Working-class people have not had much to say how school knowledge is constructed" (Zandy 1995, 13).

A study of high school textbooks reveals that there is virtually no information about class inequalities or structural barriers to class mobility. Rather, most high school textbooks focus on the openness of opportunity and the fluid nature of social mobility. Yet social class is arguably one of the most important predictors of accessibility to resources and to success in U.S. society. Consider some of these facts:

- Affluent expectant mothers are more likely to get good prenatal care than poor and working-class mothers who often see their doctor for the first time in the last month of their pregnancies.
- Wealthy suburban schools spend two to three times more money per student than poor urban and rural schools.
- Poor children often have more than 50 percent larger classes than do wealthier children.
- Wealthy high school students are more likely to take courses to prepare them for the Scholastic Aptitude Test (SAT), and social class is a strong predictor of SAT scores.
- Social class is the strongest predictor of both the rate of college attendance and the type of college attended.
- Wealthier people have longer life expectancies than poor and working class people (Loewen 1995, 204–5).

There are clear consequences for the lack of information about the structural barriers of social class. Without an understanding of how opportunities for people in the United States have been organized according to income and social standing, many people, both rich and poor, come to blame the poor for being poor and credit the rich for being rich. When working class people come to understand issues of social class, they often find this information liberating. "If to understand is to pardon, for working-class children to understand how stratification works is to pardon themselves and their families" (Loewen 1995, 207). When wealthier students come to understand issues of social class, they are less likely to blame the victims for their circumstances.

As you consider the supposed invisibility of class in U.S. society, recall how hegemony works by securing the consent of those who are not in power—not by force but through socialization of values that get taught at home, in school, and through the media. Hegemony is neither conspiratorial nor visible. For countless new immigrants as well as for families who have been in the United States for many generations, belief in the American Dream is virtually synonymous with the belief in democracy and freedom. For many of us it seems that if we identify and recognize a class system in the United States, we are challenging and questioning the very fiber of democracy. To some of us it may even seem unpatriotic to consider an American class system.

As we discussed gender in an earlier chapter, it became clear that there is little disagreement that males and females exist, possessing different biological and character traits. While theories diverge as to which character traits are biological and which are socialized according to culture, most of us share a common recognition of the existence of men and women. This shared recognition does not exist regarding the concept of class.

As you take the journey through your own personal experience and begin to reconstruct formal knowledge you may experience resistance to and disagreement with some of the theories, concepts, and information introduced. When you notice resistance or acceptance of information that is introduced, ask yourself what relationship this has to your own class background. As you study class, it is important to remember that a primary objective of this book is to encourage independent thinking on these difficult and controversial issues. You are never required to change your beliefs about any topic. You are invited and encouraged, however, to take the journey whether it leads you to a different place of understanding or takes you back to where you began. The journey of reconstructing knowledge regarding class will include studying American history in relation to class; the status of employment, wealth, and income in the contemporary United States; and analysis of the American Dream.

American History and Class

The word *history* encompasses the word *story* and is a collection of stories that comprise what we are taught in school and learn to call American history. The "stories" you are about to read have been culled from primary sources and scholarly works of historians, sociologists, and economists. Most of these stories of American history are not among those included in most high school textbooks or curriculum.

Early American History

"What has replaced the earlier happy picture of pervasive fluidity is not a grim picture but a mixed one. In many new communities in colonial America, opportunities for poor men were far better than in England. But not everywhere. Seventeenth-century Salem's rich had had 'considerable wealth' to start with" (Pessen 1974, 2). A study of over one thousand Massachusetts immigrants in 1637 indicated that their economic fate in America was largely determined by their social and economic status upon arrival. Yet there were those who benefited from "shipboard mobility," improving their economic status simply by coming to the New World. During the time period of 1637–1676, the population of Maryland grew from 200 to 20,000, and by 1676 "class was settled and to achieve upward mobility mean moving south or west" (Pessen 1974, 3).

During the seventeenth century, over half of English immigrants were indentured servants who worked for five to ten years to repay their passage to America. In Virginia, over two-thirds of these indentured servants died before their contracts were repaid (Adams et al. 1997, 259). In Maryland over 40 percent of indentured servants died during this same time period. For those who survived, there were many opportunities to move upward in economics and in status.

A study of the mobility of indentured servants in Maryland indicated that many of these young men worked 10–14 hours a day, six days a week, and went on to become small planters on leased land. Less than 10 percent of the survivors went on to be prominent in politics by virtue of education or marriage (Menard 1974, 20–27). "It seems probable that Maryland continued to offer ambitious immigrants without capital a good prospect of advancement throughout the 1640s and 1650s. But there is evidence to suggest that opportunities declined sharply after 1660" (Menard 1974, 28).

So while most of us learned that early American history was characterized by vast opportunity for advancement and economic mobility, these studies indicate that in at least some areas of the United States, the chances for upward mobility dropped sharply as early as the seventeenth century in colonial America. These chances, slim though they were, were available only to white men. Women of any race and African American and American Indian men had little political recourse to change or improve their lives (Adams et al. 1997, 259).

There were four main avenues to create wealth in eighteenth- and nineteenth-century America. Typically, these capital-producing strategies placed enormous wealth in the hands of a few, gave some income boost to the middle, and created poverty for the vast numbers of Americans. These four wealth-creating strategies were:

- slavery;
- immigrant labor during industrialization;
- land grabs from American Indians, French, and Mexicans; and
- tenant farming, sharecropping, and farm mortgages (Adams et al. 1997, 259).

There were some organized groups and movements that resisted this accumulation of wealth in the hands of the few. The anti-renter movement (1840s to 1860s) in New York organized tenants to reduce the power of landowners. The populist movement of the 1880s and 1890s organized farmers in the South and West to work together to protect their land rights.

Yet despite these efforts to seek economic equity and protection, difficult and rigid economic distinctions existed in early America. The United States lacked the European history of feudalism and formally defined class hierarchy and structure, but separations between the economic classes were often hardened and opportunities for mobility were bleak. European observers such as Alexis de Tocqueville commented on the vast differences between the Old World and New World class structure and hierarchy and interpreted these as the indicators of an egalitarian society. But as de Tocqueville and others wrote glowingly about American opportunities for mobility, early America was becoming increasingly stratified. "It was the children and grandchildren of the colonial elite who alone were able to brush off the financial panics of 1819, 1837, and 1839, and who had the necessary capital to participate in the great financial, commercial, and entrepreneurial ventures that beckoned. . . . The evidence indicates that the typical man was a farmer or artisan of little or no property and with modest to bleak prospects. The man on the make was a man who to a large extent was already made" (Main 1974, 57).

By the mid-1800s, 95 percent of New York City's 100 wealthiest persons had been born into families of wealth or high status and occupation. "[T]he age of egalitarianism appears to have been an age of increasing social rigidity" (Pessen 1974, 114).

The early Industrial Era (1860–1900) was an era of big business that marked the completion of the railroad network and the rise of giant corporations. During this time most Americans still lived in small towns or rural communities. In the early days of manufacturing, some of the men who rose to success in industry may have depended on the skills and knowledge they gained from working in the field (Gutman 1974, 125). A study of working class upward mobility during the mid-1800s examined 287 people in one town and revealed, "The contrast between the literal claims of the rags-to-riches mythology and the actual social experiences of these families thus appears glaring: a few dozen farmers, small shopkeepers, and clerks, a large body of home-owning families unable to escape a grinding regimen of manual labor; this was the sum of social mobility achieved by Newburyport's unskilled laborers by 1880" (Thernstrom 1974, 163).

Throughout the nineteenth century only 2 percent of American industrialists rose from the ranks of the working class. Yet most high school textbooks focus on the legendary exceptions, such as Joseph Pulitzer and Andrew Carnegie. "By concentrating on the inspiring exceptions, textbooks present immigrant history as another heartening confirmation of America as the land of unparalleled opportunity" (Loewen 1995, 209).

The Early Twentieth Century

By 1913, forty-four American families had incomes of over $50 million a year while most adult workers earned $10–20 per week. By 1933, over one-fourth of the labor force was unemployed (Adams et al. 1997, 260). How did these vast gaps and changes come about?

World War I had multiple effects on class mobility and the norms for national values. During the war, President Woodrow Wilson called on Americans to express their patriotism by making personal economic sacrifices to support a larger and more important cause—freedom and democracy. Most U.S. citizens did this quite willingly, but in the prosperity of the postwar twenties were ready to return to a self-centered norm characterized by individualism, materialism, and hedonism (McElvaine 1993, 10).

The 1920s were prosperous times for the owning class and for the working and middle classes as well. The late-nineteenth-century values of thrift and savings were replaced with a consumer ethic that encouraged self-indulgence. For the first time, massive advertising was used to convince working and middle class people to use credit, to buy products on installment that they could not otherwise afford. The United States was becoming increasingly industrialized and urbanized. In the past, people lived primarily in relatively small, rural communities in which their survival was more dependent on the family, the farm, and the community than on the job. With the rapid rise in industry and the move to the cities, an increasing number of people were in positions that were dependent on their jobs in industry, which were in turn dependent on market forces (McElvaine 1993, 17).

While workers seemed prosperous on the surface, a deeper analysis discloses that in 1929, Americans' workweek was longer than that of any other industrial country and they had no protection against unemployment. The United States, China, and India were the only countries that continued to allow children to work at night (McElvaine 1993, 222).

Economist Adam Smith's concept of laissez faire—allowing market forces to evolve "naturally" of their own accord—was based on the nineteenth century U.S. economy in which there were many competing smaller private businesses and enterprises. Laissez faire was based on the belief that the market was characterized by a "level playing field" between these businesses, thus making competition fair. With the assumption of fairness and equality at its core, the economic wins and losses of a laissez faire economy were set in what was believed to be a context of morality.

Despite the flaws in the analysis of the equal starting point of businesses in a pre-industrial United States, Smith's concept applied even less in the 1920s. By the end of the 1920s, two-thirds of industrial wealth in the United States went from individual ownership to publicly financed corporations. By 1929, 200 corporations controlled almost half of American industry and roughly 2,000 men dominated U.S. economic life (McElvaine 1993, 37).

Another by-product of World War I was a fanatical rise in patriotism and the valuing of everything American. The sense of who was the "other" was on the rise, as was membership in the Ku Klux Klan and hate crimes directed at Jews, blacks, immigrants, and Catholics (McElvaine 1993, 12).

Concurrent to these changes in business, industry, culture, and the economy, President Calvin Coolidge and his cabinet believed that catering to big business and promoting production would mean continued prosperity for everyone. Business leaders instituted a form of welfare capitalism in which they devised programs to keep the workers happy as a way of increasing productivity. Some of these production incentives included immigrant Americanization programs and citizenship classes. These industries saw their contribution to immigrant socialization and assimilation as part of their service to the workers. Giving up the language, clothing, food, and culture of one's country of origin was considered a positive step toward becoming an American.

Coolidge's Secretary of Treasury, Andrew Mellon, was explicit about his goals for government to serve the interests of the wealthy. Mellon said that his major goal was to reduce the tax burden on the rich and shift it to poor and working class people. In 1926, he initiated legislation that was ultimately passed by Congress in which a person with $1 million in income went from paying $600,000 to $200,000 in taxes. Between 1921 and 1929, $3.5 billion was granted to corporations and friends of the Republican party. Along with other cabinet members, Mellon devised another tax shift scheme that did not materialize during the Coolidge years, but nevertheless reflects some of the thinking of the owning class. This strategy was to repeal prohibition, make beer legal, and tax it heavily. Mellon's thinking was that since beer was the working man's drink, this tactic would significantly shift the burden of taxes in still another way (McElvaine 1993, 23).

By 1929, the upper 0.1 percent of American families had a combined income equal to that of the lower 42 percent, and 80 percent of all families had no savings (McElvaine 1993, 24). For the economy to remain stable the supply of goods had to equal the demand. During this time period productivity was increasing at a faster rate than worker income, and the supply was exceeding the demand. This wide gap in income meant that for economic stability to succeed, new ways to increase demand were necessary. Working families needed to continue to buy on credit and wealthy families needed to continue to consume luxury items and investment at ever increasing rates to keep up with the increased productivity.

The Depression

With few government regulations and controls on big business, mergers, real estate, and stock speculation continued to climb. This speculation meant that buyers and sellers continued to jack up stock market and real estate prices with the idea that they would get out before prices sank. "Once a sizable number of important investors decided the boom had ended, it had ended. It had all been built on expectations of rising prices. As soon as those expectations were reversed, the market had to fail" (McElvaine 1993, 47).

But the stock market crash did not of its own accord necessitate a massive economic depression. According to many economists and historians, while the causes of the Great Depression were complex and multiple, one of its main causes was the unequal distribution of wealth, which led to overconsumption and the instigation of stock speculation. The stock market crash and the depression began in 1929 and ended on December 7, 1941, when the Japanese bombed Pearl Harbor.

From 1929 to 1933, the gross national product dropped by 29 percent and consumer spending dropped by 18 percent. Construction and investment fell a whopping 78 percent and 98 percent respectively. Unemployment rose from 3.2 percent in 1929 to 24.9 percent in 1933. The American Dream had turned into the American nightmare. "Glad to believe themselves responsible for whatever success they had enjoyed in the twenties, many 'ordinary' people found themselves during the early Depression in a position similar to that of businessmen and Republicans. Having taken credit for the good, they had little choice but to accept responsibility for the bad" (McElvaine 1993, 75).

Job discrimination became increasingly serious for African Americans and women. Among African Americans, unemployment was closer to 50 percent. Jobs that had previously been held by blacks and viewed as "negro occupations," such as elevator operators, bellhops, street cleaners, and so forth, were claimed by many whites. The dominant thinking of the times was that no black person should be working while white men were still out of work. A group of whites in Atlanta adopted the slogan, "No Jobs for Niggers Until Every White Man Has a Job." Lynchings increased from 8 in 1932 to 28 in 1935. Black workers who were primarily tenant farmers during the depression had an average annual income of less than $200 (McElvaine 1993, 187).

The dominant public perception was that women were taking jobs from men who needed to support their families. In fact, most working women were also attempting to support their families and did so from jobs that had been considered traditionally women's domain, such as domestic and clerical work. Interestingly, throughout the depression these jobs continued to be considered women's jobs and were neither desired nor filled by men (McElvaine 1993, 183).

The government sanctioned gender employment discrimination with their public works programs that paid men $5 and women $3 a week. The 1935 passage of the Social Security Act under Roosevelt's New Deal was significant in its protection of older adults, people with disabilities, and the unemployed and poor people—it was also significant in that it excluded protection for many job categories such as farm and domestic work, which tended to be the domain of blacks or women (McElvaine 1993, 256).

By late 1941, when Pearl Harbor was bombed and the United States entered World War II, the economic cycle had turned again. Spending and investment in the defense industry boosted the economy back to prosperity. The American public was once again asked to make sacrifices in the name of patriotism during the war. And by the 1950s, with World War II and a decade of depression behind them, Americans wanted a return to materialism and prosperity. This prosperity became available to many in the 1950s. Many Americans also wanted a return to the traditional family roles that had been upset by both the depression and the war. They achieved this goal temporarily as well.

Americans' values are in part dictated by their class interest. It is in the interest of the owning class to be individualistic and acquisitive and to run business in a way that is amoral, rather than moral or immoral. It is in the interest of the working class to be individualistic, as well, but in a different way from the wealthy. The working class tends to measure policies and actions according to their impact on individual human beings rather than their effect on production or profit. The middle class has been pulled either up to be in accord with the interests of the owning class, or down to be in accord with the interests of the working class in a way that corresponds to specific historical economic circumstances.

During the Great Depression, middle class interests and values were aligned with the working class and poor and in the twenties and 1950s their interests were aligned with the wealthier classes. "The interplay between the egoistical, amoral individualism of the owning class and the ethical individualism of most workers is essential to understanding many facets of American history" (McElvaine 1993, 201). But owning class values have often been parlayed in the form of the American Dream and have pushed working and middle class people to consume more, borrow more, and use more credit. This somewhat invisible logic goes something like this for working and middle class people: "Someday I will have the real possibility of economic success. For now, while I am waiting for this success, I can borrow and use credit to have the material things I want and so others will see me as successful."

Post–World War II

The 1950s and 1960s in America were characterized by a booming economy and a sudden burst in opportunities for social mobility. "The U.S. came out of World War II the only intact industrial economy in the world. Tremendous economic growth from exports to the rest of the world created a large middle class and stable working class. Skilled and/or unionized working-class people began to own homes and have pensions; the children and grandchildren of poor immigrants and African Americans went to college in large numbers and populated the new sprawling middle-class suburbs" (Adams et al. 1997, 260).

This boom represents a time in American history when class lines became more permeable. Structural boundaries, by virtue of race and gender, still prohibited many people from moving upward from poor and working classes; but many Americans were able to move into the growing middle class. Unemployment was relatively low, businesses were growing, and the G.I. Bill offered unprecedented educational and home-buying opportunities for World War II veterans.

This was the "bootstrap" period in America in which postwar economic growth and opportunities created and structured by the government temporarily removed some of the hardened barriers to class mobility. While many of the people who "made it" worked hard, it was the combination of this hard work and the structural changes in society that provided a shift in life chances. Through a combination of personal experience, the absence of information, and the presence of myth, many Americans began to understand this period of growth, individual success, and some class mobility exclusively as the result of individual industriousness and merit. By this interpretation, those worthy and virtuous individuals pulled themselves up by their own bootstraps to achieve class mobility and some measure of economic success. The logical counterpart to this interpretation of the 1950s and 1960s is that those who did not succeed lacked virtue and industriousness and the willingness to use their own bootstraps. By this argument, their economic failure was exclusively a personal failure. As we begin to analyze the myth and reality of the American Dream, we will look at economic success and the Dream in terms of both individual effort and structured opportunities and barriers.

Contemporary Indicators of Class in the United States

The 1970s through the 1990s were a time of deindustrialization characterized by the loss of manufacturing growth and jobs. This shift threatened the relative prosperity that the working class gained in the 1950s and 1960s. From 1979 to 84, 11.5 million Americans lost their jobs due to plant shutdowns or the closing of related industries. Over 60 percent of these workers were able to find other jobs. But half of these new jobs were at lower pay. Beginning in 1979, a highly inflated housing market made it difficult for middle class families to afford to buy homes (Hochschild 1995, 107).

During the 1980s, under Ronald Reagan's presidency, two significant changes affected poor, working poor, and working class Americans. The first change was in the tax structure, which, as in Coolidge's presidency, shifted benefits to the wealthy. In addition, there were massive changes in the federal budget that increased military spending and simultaneously made huge cuts in domestic spending and programs that had previously benefited low income families and children.

From 1979 to 1984 the working poor, who earned under $20,000 for a family of four, comprised 40 percent of the population over the age of fourteen. In the 1980s, the after-tax median income was $20,000— not enough to support the kind of life-style typically attributed to the middle class (U.S. Bureau of Census 1990). Two cars, annual vacations, regular dinners at restaurants, and other middle-class indicators increasingly became the domain of higher income families. Real wages, corrected for inflation, had fallen more than 11 percent from 1972 to 1986 (Adams et al. 1997, 260).

In 1982, the average wealth for U.S. families was measured. This wealth was measured by assets or inherited resources that were distinct from income or money earned. The study revealed that the lowest 20 percent of Americans were in debt for an average of $14,000, which meant that their "wealth" was in the negative column. On the other hand, the top 20 percent of Americans had an average wealth that ranged from $243,000 to $12,482,000 (Mishel and Bernstein 1993, 79). The disparity between the top and bottom 20 percent is staggering. Below are just some of the economic realities that have characterized contemporary American society:

- From 1977 to 1988 the average income of the poorest American families decreased while that of the highest 20 percent increased.
- By 1990 chief executive officers of U.S. manufacturing corporations were paid 120 times higher than the average worker (Phillips 1990, 28).
- By 1992, the poorest 20 percent of Americans earned an average family income of $8,130, while the wealthiest 20 percent earned an average range of $65,700–$676,000 (U.S. Bureau of Census 1992).

By the late 1990s, the most accurate predictor of one's income was the occupation of one's father (DeLone 1979, 74). This points to some stagnancy in income mobility from generation to generation.

While these factors of income and wealth are devastating simply on the face of the information, there are further consequences for lower income people and people of color in the United States:

- In 1992, 32.1 people per thousand were victims of violent crime. For poor blacks this number was 60.1 per thousand and for poor whites it was 44.7 per thousand. Higher income blacks were victims of violent crime at a rate of 35.0 per thousand, while the number for well-off whites was 20.7 per thousand (Hochschild 1995, 37).
- In 1994, 37 million Americans were without health care coverage and an equal number were underinsured (Barlett and Steele 1992, 29).
- In 1994, poor people and people of color were more likely to live in areas of toxic waste sites (Bullard 1993, 33).

As you consider the information in this section of the chapter, think back to your own personal experiences regarding class. As you recall your own family's income and assets, place yourself in the demographic scenario above. Does your economic position impact how you understand, resist, or accept this information? If your family was relatively wealthy, was it difficult to believe that so many Americans have had such low income? If your family was poor or working class, was there any comfort in understanding the structural ways this was determined? If your family was middle income, where did you find yourself in these various scenarios?

As we begin to consider the American Dream, it is this process of reconstructing knowledge that helps us to understand our relationship to the Dream. What were you taught about opportunity in the United States? How did your family's economic position impact what you believed to be possible? What were you taught in school and at home about disparity in the United States in income, education, health care, employment, and housing? What did you believe about responsibility for poverty or wealth? Were poor people to blame for their lack of resources? Were wealthy people to be credited for their economic status?

The American Dream

Recall our earlier personal exploration of our beliefs and experiences with the American Dream, the promise and the belief in the level playing field, and the conviction that there is equal opportunity for all Americans. This Dream includes the ability to move ahead, to move up, to succeed. The four elements of the American Dream are:

1. The belief that everyone can participate equally and can always start over.
2. The belief that it is reasonable to anticipate success.
3. The belief that success is a result of individual characteristics and that actions are under one's control.
4. The belief that success is associated with virtue and merit (Hochschild 1995, 3–30).

"Recent historical studies of popular thought demonstrate that the 'rags-to-riches' myth and variations on it have been a central theme of the American dream from the seventeenth century to the present" (Pessen 1974, xi). The Horatio Alger stories of the late nineteenth century were an integral part of the development of the American Dream. Alger wrote fictional accounts of young boys and men with nothing who rose to great heights in industry and politics by their individual determination, hard work, and merit. "The hundreds of novels that seemed to fly off Alger's pen popularized as never before the rags-to-riches theme. Many contemporaries mistook fiction for fact" (Pessen 1974, 124).

The rags-to-riches stories used to teach the American Dream focus on individuals and their potential and possibilities for success. But the Dream requires a relatively high income to begin with in order to have access to opportunities. These privileges include access to books, health care, education (both public and private), professional jobs, travel, cultural events and institutions, and the resources and wherewithal to do more than simply financially survive in the world. The Dream also ignores structural barriers to success. In fact, working class white people and most people of color face systemic obstacles in employment, housing, education, health care, and so on by virtue of their income and race—not according to their individual effort or merit. The figures above also indicate that lower income people of any race and African American people live with the prospect of violence occurring in their lives at a strikingly higher rate than people who are well off.

The American history outlined in this chapter indicates that there were critical times in both the early seventeenth and mid-twentieth centuries in which there

were structural openings for upward mobility created by economic conditions and/
or government constructed opportunities for pursuing and attaining the American
Dream. While these opportunities were certainly impacted by individual industriousness, there were still gender and race barriers that locked out other individuals
regardless of their hard work and merit. Further, there were other times in American history, the late 1660s as well as the early twentieth century, in which class
barriers were hard and virtually impermeable, so that chances for mobility were
bleak and for most people the American Dream was just that—a dream.

Our history teaches us that while there have been times when opportunity is
available and hard work and virtue pay off, there are many more times when it is
the rare individual who is able to pierce the barriers of gender, race, and class and
attain the American Dream. One purpose of the American Dream is to give us
hope; yet one outcome of belief in the American Dream is that the structural barriers that keep many of us from moving ahead are rendered invisible. If the American Dream is made up of half-truths and myths, what does this mean for Americans
as individuals and as a society?

If we review the American Dream and its four elements, we can begin to see the
parts of each that inform, the parts that misinform and distort, and then we can
form some sort of analysis of the dream and rethink and reconstruct its place in our
lives and society.

Despite all of the structural barriers to success and the myth of the application
of the American Dream, there continue to be individuals in the United States who
burst through the barriers to enormous economic success and recognition. Are
these individuals the exceptions that prove the rule, or are they the exception that
is used to support the myth of the American Dream? As you ponder this question,
it is important to factor in your own class position and experience, the American
history you have learned in school, and the brief history you have read in this
chapter to weed out information from misinformation, distortion from truth. The
answers are not always simple or easy or consistent.

If the American Dream has served to sustain many immigrants and people with
hard lives through four centuries of American history and has also served to cru-
elly deceive many into false hope, what are the alternatives? Is it possible to offer
hope with a more complex and realistic set of beliefs attached to it? Consider these
alternatives to the four tenets of the American Dream described above:

- *The American Dream has historically been available largely to white men
  from the middle classes and above.*
  Others have found success, but the obstacles have been much greater for all
  women, men of color, and poor and working class men and women. As you
  work toward your dream, it is important to understand that your starting point
  has a strong impact on the barriers to achieving the American Dream.
- *Your starting point and standing point by virtue of class, race, gender, sexual
  orientation, and disability have an enormous effect on how much economic*

success you can reasonably anticipate exclusively through your own individual effort.

While it is important to hang on to your dream and hopes, it is also important to learn the history of opportunity and success for the group(s) you belong to and learn how groups have worked together to widen opportunities. As you learn about the efforts for change by labor unions or civil rights groups, you may have a better understanding of the connection between individual success or failure, structural obstacles, and mobilization for change.

- *Your economic success depends on a combination of your own individual efforts, the economy, the openness of society to the group or groups to which you belong, and the history of movements for change.*

  While your actions and hard work and attitude are critical to walking into the doors of success, it is important to understand that opening those doors is not always exclusively within your individual control and power.

- *Finally, your virtue and merit are dependent on your values and beliefs, and how you choose to lead your life to match these ethics.*

  You are not measured according to the heights you attain in your field nor by the money and objects you accumulate, but rather by the kind of person you choose to be.

You may want to revise either version of the American Dream in a way that matches your sense of the connection of hope to realistic expectations. As you assess your own class position and experiences and the history of economic class and mobility, you can draw your own conclusions about the availability of the American Dream. As we move into considering how entertainment media reflects social and economic classes, we will be questioning what messages about class are conveyed through characters, themes, plot, and lyrics. As we examine entertainment media it is important to keep making the connections between your own life experiences and your understanding of concepts, theories, and history about class.

Entertainment Media and Class

Although some of us raised in the United States are aware of class divisions, others have little understanding about social and economic class. We have had personal experiences and formal education that have taught us that there are no class divisions or class barriers in the United States. The concept of class is one that we associate with other countries, other cultures, other societies and the concept of a U.S. class system seems out of reach. In short, to some of us class is invisible.

In the first two sections of this chapter we have examined personal experience and have reconstructed knowledge in a way that lifts up and explains some theories of the existence of class in the U.S and how it operates. In this section we will take a close look at entertainment media's depiction of class and the messages that we, the media audience and consumers, receive. We will examine the answers to several questions about the relationship of entertainment media and class, including:

- How do television, film, and popular music depict characters in various occupations and different levels of income?
- What kinds of themes and messages about social and economic status are conveyed in popular media?
- How do the media images of occupation, income, and status compare to U.S. demographic realities regarding occupation, income, and status?
- How do media ownership and control and the organization of entertainment media impact the depiction of class?

These issues will be analyzed in several different ways:

- simple content analysis about class depiction in popular media to analyze characters and themes;
- review of available research about entertainment media and class;
- the media industry and class; and
- the overall messages conveyed about class and their impact on audiences.

Content analysis, message system analysis, media literacy, and cultural studies will be the entertainment assessment theories and tools used to examine these issues.

As we investigate fictional characters and themes in popular film, television, and music, it is important to keep in mind the ways that entertainment media serve to socialize us and reinforce cultural beliefs and norms. As we tease out images and messages about class, remember that we will often be going against the grain of what we have been explicitly taught and what we have internalized as fact and truth. When our analysis is over, it will be your task to determine how to integrate this new information into what you already "know."

Prime Time Television and Class

It is your turn again. Use the content analysis in Media Activity 3.1 to observe some of the ways in which class is conveyed in prime time television. When you have completed it, total the data you have collected. Total the numbers in each category for all of the major characters you analyzed and write these numbers in the appropriate place in Media Activities 3.2 and 3.3. When you have figured all of the totals, calculate the percentage in each category.

When you complete the content analysis, ask the following questions:

- Did most of the characters hold higher-level occupations, lower-level occupations, or mid level occupations?

Media Activity 3.1
Content Analysis of Character Occupation and Income in Prime Time Television

Instructions

Choose a minimum of three current fictional narrative television programs. These programs can be dramas or comedies. Answer the questions below about the major characters in these programs. Remember that major characters are those characters without whom the plot makes little or no sense. The larger the sample of prime time television reviewed, the more revealing the results will be. You may either choose a larger sample for your individual analysis or work with a class or a group to review more programs. If you work with a group, be sure that no television program is analyzed twice and that the sample is comprised of all currently aired programs.

Name of Program _____

I. Major Character #1 Name _____

  1. Occupation:

    a. unemployed   ____

    b. clerical worker, technician, salesperson, craftsworker   ____

    c. store or shop owner, lower ranking professional (nurse, police officer, teacher, social worker) middle manager, independent farm owner   ____

    d. business executive, upper manager, or higher ranking professional (lawyer, doctor, architect)   ____

    e. owner of major business   ____

    f. unknown   ____

    g. other (please indicate) _____

  2. Income:

    a. clearly very poor or no income   ____

    b. clearly lower income, struggling to make ends meet   ____

    c. clearly middle income, not wealthy but comfortable   ____

    d. business executive, upper manager, or higher ranking professional (lawyer, doctor, architect)   ____

    e. owner of major business   ____

    f. unknown   ____

    g. other (please indicate) _____

II. Major Character #2 Name _____

  1. Occupation:

    a. unemployed   ____

    b. clerical worker, technician, salesperson, craftsworker   ____

    c. store or shop owner, lower ranking professional (nurse, police officer, teacher, social worker) middle manager, independent farm owner   ____

    d. business executive, upper manager, or higher ranking professional (lawyer, doctor, architect)   ____

    e. owner of major business   ____

    f. unknown   ____

    g. other (please indicate) _____

(cont'd)

2. Income:
    a. clearly very poor or no income   ____
    b. clearly lower income, struggling to make ends meet   ____
    c. clearly middle income, not wealthy but comfortable   ____
    d. business executive, upper manager, or higher ranking
       professional (lawyer, doctor, architect)   ____
    e. owner of major business   ____
    f. unknown   ____
    g. other (please indicate) _____

III. Major Character #3 Name _____
  1. Occupation:
    a. unemployed   ____
    b. clerical worker, technician, salesperson, craftsworker   ____
    c. store or shop owner, lower ranking professional (nurse, police
       officer, teacher, social worker) middle manager, independent
       farm owner   ____
    d. business executive, upper manager, or higher ranking
       professional (lawyer, doctor, architect)   ____
    e. owner of major business   ____
    f. unknown   ____
    g. other (please indicate) _____
  2. Income:
    a. clearly very poor or no income   ____
    b. clearly lower income, struggling to make ends meet   ____
    c. clearly middle income, not wealthy but comfortable   ____
    d. business executive, upper manager, or higher ranking
       professional (lawyer, doctor, architect)   ____
    e. owner of major business   ____
    f. unknown   ____
    g. other (please indicate) _____

IV. Major Character #4 Name _____
  1. Occupation:
    a. unemployed   ____
    b. clerical worker, technician, salesperson, craftsworker   ____
    c. store or shop owner, lower ranking professional (nurse, police
       officer, teacher, social worker) middle manager, independent
       farm owner   ____
    d. business executive, upper manager, or higher ranking
       professional (lawyer, doctor, architect)   ____
    e. owner of major business   ____
    f. unknown   ____
    g. other (please indicate) _____
  2. Income:
    a. clearly very poor or no income   ____
    b. clearly lower income, struggling to make ends meet   ____
    c. clearly middle income, not wealthy but comfortable   ____
    d. business executive, upper manager, or higher ranking
       professional (lawyer, doctor, architect)   ____
    e. owner of major business   ____
    f. unknown   ____
    g. other (please indicate) _____

Media Activity 3.2
Summary of Major Character's Occupation in Prime Time Sample

	Total numbers	Percentage of total
Unemployed		
Clerical, etc.		
Store owner, etc.		
Business executive, etc.		
Business owner, etc.		
Total		100%

Media Activity 3.3
Summary of Major Character's Income in Prime Time Sample

	Total numbers	Percentage of total
Poor		
Lower income		
Upper income		
Total		100%

- Was there more than 50 percent in any one of these categories?
- Did most of the major categories have low income or no income, middle income, or upper income?

If most of the characters were in low level occupations (1, a or b) with lower incomes (2, a or b), the characters can be characterized largely as working class. If most of the characters were in mid-level occupations (1, c or d) with middle income (2, c) they can be characterized as largely middle class. If most of the characters had high level occupations (1, e) and high incomes (2, d) they can be characterized as largely upper income or owning class. What messages do you think your sample conveys about economic status and class? To investigate further, you can begin to ask the question, To what degree does this class depiction reinforce or challenge the American Dream?

One study analyzed 262 family-based situation comedies from 1946 to 1990. This study revealed that 11 percent of the heads of households were blue collar, clerical, or service workers—plainly working class—and that 70 percent of the heads of households were clearly middle class. In 1992 professionals comprised only 15 percent of the U.S. workforce but on television, 44.5 percent of the families were headed by professionals (Butsch 1992, 387). Another study of the 1992–93 television season demonstrated that 25 percent of all characters were in lower status occupations. These characters served "neutral plot functions" and were "usually relegated to the sidelines of the story." The researchers found that doctors and lawyers and other people holding executive or professional jobs populate prime time television at a significantly higher level than in real life (Lichter et al. 1994, 186).

In order to understand this phenomenon of overrepresentation of the wealthy and underrepresentation of the working class and poor we will take a journey through the years of prime time television's portrayal of economic class and examine the characters, the depiction of the American Dream, and other economic themes, and analyze the impact of the industry's organization and economy on these messages.

In the early 1950s, there were some working class people in situation comedies that continued some of the traditions begun in radio. These characters were primarily defined by their ethnicity such as in *Mama* (1949–56), the family of a Norwegian carpenter; *The Life of Riley* (1949–50), an Irish American airplane riveter; and *The Goldbergs* (1949–54), a Jewish tailor. But even the Goldbergs moved to the suburbs and began to buy appliances on time (Marc 1997, 105). "As these shows came to the ends of their long production runs in the late 1950s, blue-collar ethnic families disappeared from prime time. The only remaining working-class characters were typically treated as honorary members of bourgeois families: Hazel, Grindl, Mr. French of *Family Affair*, and so on. . . . From the mid-1950s until the end of the 1960s, domestic situation comedy narrative was thoroughly dominated by professional, college-educated WASPs [*sic*, White Anglo Saxon Protestants]" (Marc 1997,147).

Early situation comedies of the 1950s and 1960s such as *The Adventures of Ozzie and Harriet* (1954–60), *Father Knows Best* (1954–60), *Leave it to Beaver* (1957–63), and *My Three Sons* (1960–72) demonstrated clear signs of middle class. They were all suburban families who were "upscale, socially conservative, politically inactive, and essentially kind to one another and their neighbors" (Himmelstein 1994, 122).

Urban situation comedies of the same time period were distinct from these suburban sitcoms, including such classics as *The Honeymooners* (1955–56), *I Love Lucy* (1951–57), *Make Room for Daddy* (1953–65), *The Dick Van Dyke Show* (1961–66), and *The Mary Tyler Moore Show* (1970–77). *The Honeymooners*, main characters—Ralph Kramden, bus driver, and Ed Norton, sewer worker—were clearly working class characters. Nevertheless, all of these urban comedies reinforced the same class themes as their suburban middle class counterparts. "Whether mildly cynical or bordering on euphoria, at the core of all these comedic works is the myth of eternal progress. From the New York City bus driver Ralph Kramden and his sewer-worker sidekick Ed Norton of the *Honeymooners,* to the Ph.D. level psychologist Bob Hartley of *The Bob Newhart Show*, and the dry-cleaning entrepreneur and social climber George Jefferson of *The Jeffersons,* the social construct of the good life is manifest in these works—an urban American vision framed by the achievements of commerce and the ideology of equal opportunity" (Himmelstein 1994, 135). These examples of early prime time television represent strong reinforcement of the American Dream.

You will recall that ideology is a constructed belief system that explains a version of reality. Television conveys the dominant cultural ideology through the establishment of myths. "Myths occur primarily through the telling of stories and serve to underscore understandings of power, about the fundamental order of things which work against any alternative understandings or ideologies" (Himmelstein 1994, 5). The establishment of the "myth" of equal opportunity disguises and camouflages the reality of the inequities present in U.S. society.

The research regarding television's role in the creation and perpetuation of myth and ideology is steeped in the tradition of cultural studies, which takes an explicit liberal or left political perspective. These theories criticize entertainment media because it reinforces the dominant culture and leaves little room for alternative ideologies. While other researchers challenge the observations and analyses of cultural studies analysts, they still maintain that "television has transcended its role as mere entertainment to become a potent force shaping everyday life" (Lichter et al. 1994, 12), and that "the most innocuous sitcom carries messages about how our society works and how its citizens should behave" (Lichter et al. 1994, 12).

Norman Lear's *All in the Family* (1971–79) brought the Bunkers, a white working class family of unknown ethnicity, into the living rooms of America. As we learned in Chapter One, Lear's character Archie Bunker was intended to reflect the resistance to the movements for social change in the 1960s and 1970s. Archie was clearly a bigot—he disliked people of color, "ethnic" people, he was against "women's lib" and any other movement for liberation. While according to researcher Richard Butsch, Archie Bunker stood among Ralph Kramden, Fred Flintstone, and Homer Simpson as a "white male working class buffoon" (Butsch 1995, 403), many audiences read him differently.

To liberal audiences, Archie was just what Norman Lear intended—a symbol of the barriers to movements for equality. To more conservative and some working class audiences Archie was neither a buffoon nor a bigot, but a hero of the working class. "Archie's animus is mitigated by the fact the he is the sole breadwinner in a house of four adults, a relevant reminder to any high-minded, middle-class viewers who may be watching that a contempt for hardhatism does not change the fact that workers like Archie are the people who make civilization and culture possible" (Marc 1997, 151).

We will take another look at contemporary prime time television by analyzing themes as described in Media Activity 3.4. This exercise lends itself to working in teams or small groups.

Now we will summarize the results and determine if there are any consistent messages or patterns in these programs about economic class. Remember that this is a small sample and that you cannot generalize from these results. However, it is possible to make some observations about this particular evening of television.

Complete the charts in Media Activity 3.5 with the information you have gathered.

In each of the charts in Media Activity 3.5, the first column (a) represents lower income characteristics and themes, the second column (b) represents middle income characteristics or themes, and the third column (c) represents higher income or themes. Answer the questions below to begin to make sense of the messages about class in this analysis.

- In which column in each of the charts were there the highest numbers and percentages?
- Were most of the adults lower, middle, or higher income?
- Were most of the adults portrayed as lacking economic success, moderately successful economically, or highly successful economically?
- Were most of the adult possessions inexpensive, moderately expensive, or luxury level?
- What level of income and economic comfort did their discussions reveal?
- Overall, what economic class or classes were represented most often in the sample you studied?
- What kind of messages does this sample convey about which class or classes are "typical," "normal," and "acceptable"?

According to many researchers, *The Cosby Show* (1984–92) marked a critical shift in how prime time television portrayed class and the relationship between class and the American Dream. One team of researchers conducted an extensive study of content, audience impact, and ideology of *The Cosby Show*. They used content analysis, focus groups, and a cultural studies approach to analyze the phenomenon of this successful series. As you read and assess the conclusions of their study, you may bristle at the criticism of such a popular and highly regarded television series. It will be interesting to take into account that Bill and Camille Cosby funded and supported this critical research.

Different economic classes had very different readings of *The Cosby Show*. Middle and upper middle class viewers, whether white or black, saw the show as being about people like them. Working and lower middle class viewers read the program as universal and classless—again about people like them. Both groups interpreted *The Cosby Show* as evidence that anyone in the United States could make it economically (Jhally and Lewis 1992, 28–29).

Media Activity 3.4
Analysis of Themes of Economic Class and Success in Prime Time Television

---

Instructions

View an evening of network prime time television from 7 P.M. to 10 P.M. central time. Choose an evening and a network in which there are no news specials, infotainment, or movies. Each program observed may be a drama or comedy but it must be narrative fiction. Once again, major characters are those that are essential to the plot of the particular episode viewed. For each of the programs count the following.

Name of Program _____

Date and time aired _____ Network_____

1. Number of major adult characters   ___
2. Number of major adult characters with the following categories of occupation:
   a. Working class or low income (service workers, factory workers, clerical, police officers, nurses, unemployed, underemployed, recipients of federal aid)   ___
   b. Professional (doctors, lawyers, teachers, architects, etc.)   ___
   c. Owning class (extremely wealthy by virtue of inheritance or position)   ___
   d. Other (please list) _____

(cont'd)

The intent of the creators of *The Cosby Show* was to convey a positive image of a successful African American family. But like *All in the Family* before it, there was an unanticipated audience impact:

> [T]elevision envisages class not as a series of barriers but as a series of hurdles that can be overcome. That view promotes the idea of the American dream. Although the American dream was not invented for television, television appears to nourish and sustain it. We see countless examples of people making it, but few examples of people (apart from the lazy, deviant, or generally undeserving) prevented from making it. This makes it easy for us to think of the individual enterprise that defines the American dream as the organizing principle of the social structure—and difficult for us to conceive or articulate the idea of inequality of opportunity." (Jhally and Lewis 1992, 73)

According to this study, *The Cosby Show* was significant in that it marked a time in which television began to portray few, if any, barriers to the American

3. Of these adult major characters determine how the program portrays their economic and career success and indicate how many of the major adult characters are in each of the following categories:
   a. not very successful _____
   b. moderately successful _____
   c. very successful _____
4. How many of the major characters' homes are portrayed in the program? _____
5. Of the homes portrayed indicate how many meet the following descriptions:
   a. inexpensive, shabby, or nonexistent furniture, decorations, and appliances _____
   b. moderately priced furniture, decorations, and appliances _____
   c. expensive furniture, decorations, and appliances _____
6. Observe the plot of the program and determine if any of the following themes are present. Write the number of programs in which these themes appear:
   a. individuals or families depicted struggling financially (e.g., difficulty paying bills, difficulty finding a job, etc.) _____
   b. individuals or families discussing financial matters, choices, and decisions characteristic of middle income (e.g., should we buy a new car or go on vacation this year?) _____
   c. individuals or families discussing financial matters, choices and decisions characteristic of higher incomes (European trips, swimming pools, stock market, boats, charter planes, and other luxury items) _____

Dream—particularly for African Americans. The ease of economic success depicted has had an impact on audiences.

The researchers concluded that *The Cosby Show* conveyed an unintended and unanticipated conservative ideology. This conservative ideology says that neither class nor race is a barrier to personal and economic success in the United States. If people work hard and are virtuous, like the fictitious Huxtables, success is theirs. The politically conservative message, according to Jhally and Lewis, is that since achievement and success are based on individual merit and hard work, there is no need for compensatory funds or programs that address structural barriers to success (Jhally and Lewis 1992).

The Cosby Show was ground breaking in both its success and its portrayal of an upper income African American family. Its audience impact was significant for two reasons. First, its enormous viewing audience demonstrated the potential wide appeal of African American characters and themes. Second, since African American characters and programs were so rare, there was little range in characters and

Media Activity 3.5
Results of Analysis of Class Themes in Prime Time Television

Question	Total numbers	Percentage of total
1. Total adult characters by income in the sample (question #2)		
a. low income		
b. middle income		
c. high income		
d. totals		
2. Economic success of adult characters in the sample (question #3)		
a. not very successful		
b. moderately successful		
c. very successful		
d. totals		
3. Description of the homes of adult characters in the sample (question #5)		
a. inexpensive		
b. moderate		
c. expensive		
d. totals		
4. Financial themes in the sample (question #6)		
a. low income themes		
b. middle income themes		
c. high income themes		
d. totals		

Note: These results correspond to the questions in Media Activity 3.4.

their income and success. Thus, the Huxtables took on a supercharged meaning in conveying the "black experience" and its possibilities. If *The Cosby Show* had been alongside five other television series with African American families from different income levels, its significance and impact would have been less dramatic.

While there are distinct patterns that portray Americans as middle class and above on prime time television there are notable exceptions. We will examine *Laverne and Shirley* (1981–83), *Roseanne* (1988–97), *The Simpsons* (1989–), and *Married with*

Children (1987–97) to assess television series that have portrayed the working class as the centerpiece of the program and were commercially successful.

Laverne and Shirley was distinct from the standard middle class sitcom formula. The main characters were both working class and single. The two women worked in a factory and struggled to survive economically. These facts alone distinguished the program from most situation comedies. But what set *Laverne and Shirley* apart from the rest most clearly was that they talked about, bemoaned, and joked about being working class and their conversations rang true.

> *The Fonz, Laverne and Shirley* are different [from previous portrayals of the working class]. They have their self-mockeries, but these are leavening features, not the point. They are aware of class and of how it functions in their lives. And they can summon values, which, though not reserved exclusively to their own class, seem securely rooted in a sense of class experience. (Sklar 1980, 16)

Both *The Simpsons* and *Married with Children* clearly feature working class families who regularly lament their lack of money; they also share many parallels in reinforcing working class stereotypes. The children in both series are irreverent and often disrespectful to their parents. Neither Marge Simpson nor Peg Bundy works outside the home. Both Homer Simpson, the father in *The Simpsons*, and Al Bundy, the father in *Married with Children,* play the role of the buffoon. "In most middle-class series, there is no buffoon. More typically, both parents are wise and work cooperatively to raise their children in practically perfect families, as in *Father Knows Best, The Brady Bunch* and the *Bill Cosby Show*. In the few middle-class series featuring a buffoon, it is the dizzy wife, such as Lucy. The professional/managerial husband is the sensible, mature, partner—thus inverting gender status in working-class but not middle-class" (Butsch 1992, 404). The working class characters in these series do little to challenge the dominant ideology and the myth of the American Dream. Homer and Al are foolish and dumb, lacking the initiative and virtue that are prerequisites to the American Dream. The audience does not expect them to succeed, and because they are not particularly admirable people, we believe they get what they deserve.

Roseanne was an interesting departure from the stereotypical or invisible ways that working class people have been portrayed on prime time television. Even the set of *Roseanne* was carefully constructed with furniture ordered from the Sears catalog, inexpensive knickknacks, and clutter that seemed familiar to many working families. The creators of *Roseanne,* including Roseanne Barr herself, insisted on authenticity in appearance of the set, the characters, and the plot. All of these creative decisions in *Roseanne* marked a deviation from the conventional formulas of family-based situation comedies before it (Mayerle 1994, 102).

> Although its blue-collar setting is not shared by all of its viewers, the problems of surviving in post-Reagan America (e.g., with a mortgage, three children, two wage-earners, and employment problems) has a broad appeal. . . . Roseanne and Dan Conner, as well as others with whom they interact in the series, experience feelings

of anxiety and depression in their lives, but they do not have the time or desire to really dwell on them. Their response is not to become more introspective, but to go bowling on a Friday night, to share a six-pack of beer with friends while pretending to fix the truck, to go to the mall even though they cannot afford to buy anything.

Roseanne thus flies in the face of pop culture establishment by its irreverent and candid putdowns, as well as in the face of the series' sponsors, most of whose products the Conner family cannot afford to buy (Mayerle 1994, 113).

While it is clear that Roseanne is top dog in the series, the character of her husband Dan is an unusual male working class character. Dan has many business failures and is constantly struggling along with Roseanne to support their family. As a couple, they fight, laugh, make love, and torment each other with sarcastic humor. Dan and Roseanne work together, and as a man Dan is portrayed as neither a failure nor a buffoon.

Given the successful long run of *Roseanne,* an obvious question is, why was this program so unique? Why hasn't it been copied like so many other television series? These questions can be analyzed by exploring three contributing factors: the role of the network, the organization of decision making, and the culture of the creative team (Butsch 1992, 405).

The cost of producing prime time television has become exorbitant, and only large corporations can afford this kind of production. The competition for ratings and the advertising dollar is steep between the networks. Advertisers want prime time to feature characters who are likely to buy their products. The need to please advertisers and the competition between networks contributes to the push to minimize risks, which in turn drives content decisions and the hiring of creative personnel. All of this pushes decision-makers to stick with the formulas and the personnel that have proven track records. "This proven talent then self-censor their work on the basis of a product image their previous experience tells them the networks will tolerate; creating an imaginary feedback loop' between producers and network executives" (Butsch 1992, 406).

This analysis echoes that of Ben Bagdikian's that we studied in Chapters One and Two. It is not that there is an evil television conspiracy set up to ignore and stereotype working class people, but rather a combination of several factors that add up to this result:

- Most of the people who create prime time television are middle class and above.
- There is great competition between networks for advertising dollars.
- Advertisers want programs and characters that will promote the products they want to sell.
- Creative talent needs to comply with these demands in order to work.

These factors add up to a prime time television industry and culture that will occasionally create a *Laverne and Shirley* or *Roseanne*, but largely sticks with the safer formulas that have worked over the years.

Popular Film

It is your turn again. This time you will need to take a trip to the local video store and rent the film *Working Girl,* directed by Mike Nichols and starring Melanie Griffith, Harrison Ford, and Sigourney Weaver, and featuring Joan Cusack and a young Alec Baldwin. As you view the film, keep the questions in Media Activity 3.6 in mind and answer them at the end of the film.

The film *Working Girl* was made in 1988 and was a popular box office hit. It had everything. It was the Cinderella story of Tess, a woman (or "girl") struggling to succeed in her career and her personal life who moved from a verbally abusive, cheating, working class boyfriend and a secretarial job to a high-powered career and a middle class, supportive, enlightened boyfriend. While the first boyfriend, Mick (Alec Baldwin) bought her only Frederick's of Hollywood style underwear, the second boyfriend, Jack (Harrison Ford) bought her a leather briefcase. The audience is also delivered an evil, successful career woman, Catherine (Sigourney Weaver), who demonstrates just what happens to women when they climb all over people to make it in the business world. And of course, there are several gratuitous, audience-pleasing scenes with the working girl herself, Melanie Griffith, in her underwear. On one level, *Working Girl* is a light romantic comedy. But on another level it provides an important, yet largely invisible, commentary about class.

The working class characters of Mick and Cyn (Tess's friend, played by Joan Cusack) are depicted as simple. Cyn is comically sympathetic, somewhat streetwise, and as a friend to Tess believes it is her duty to warn her of the dangers of moving up in the world. She tells her that romance with Jack is a fantasy and encourages her to go back to the abusive Mick. Mick reads auto magazines in bed, cheats on Tess in her own bedroom, curses at her, and expects her to continue to make him the center of her life. Neither Cyn nor Mick are portrayed as particularly intelligent or successful. While we, the audience, are coaxed to laugh with Cyn and snarl at Mick, we also are steered to find their working class lives difficult at best and pathetic at worst. The ultimate sign of their miserable status in life is their total ignorance of the symbols and joys of middle class life. In one scene in a working class bar where Cyn's engagement is being celebrated, Tess arrives late wearing clothes she has "borrowed" from Catherine. Mick looks at her and comments on how good she looks and says, "What, d'ja [did you] have to go to traffic court?"

Tess and Jack are more complex characters. The audience is led to root for their business success as well as the success of their romantic relationship. We are encouraged to see Tess and Jack as hard working people who deserve good things in the world. If there is any true villain in the film it is the evil Catherine (please remember to boo whenever her name is mentioned). Catherine is the epitome of the nightmare of the successful woman who has lost her feminine softness and turned into a hardened, calculating "bitch."

Yet it is interesting to compare Jack to Mick and Tess to Catherine. Both Jack and Mick cheat on their girlfriends; Mick with Doreen and Jack with Tess. Both

Media Activity 3.6
Analyzing Class in the Film *Working Girl*

Instructions

After viewing the 1988 film *Working Girl,* answer the following questions. Support all of your answers with examples from the film. Pay close attention to the way the film leads or manipulates the audience to a particular point of view about the characters, class, success, and the "American Dream."

For questions 1–3 examine the characters Tess, Jack, Catherine, Cyn, Mick, and Orrin. For clarity, define *working class* characters as those whose jobs are likely to leave them one or two paychecks from poverty; *owning class* as those characters who by virtue of their own position or inherited wealth have no need to work for income; and the *middle class* as those in between.

1. Which of the characters were working class? Which of the characters were middle class? Which of the characters were owning class?
2. What specific cues did the film give you about each of the characters' class (e.g., clothes, job, language, leisure activities, education, residence, etc.)?
3. Which characters were simple or one-dimensional and which were complex?
4. Which characters are the audience led to like and admire and which characters are the audience led to dislike? Be sure to give examples to support your opinions.
5. How does the film characterize working class life? Is it an acceptable place to be or something to strive to escape? Separate *your* views on working class life from the *film's* perspective.

For questions 6 and 7 review the characters Jack, Tess, and Catherine.

6. What are the goals in the film of the major characters?
7. How would you characterize these goals (e.g., are they about financial success, romantic success, happiness, etc.)? What do these goals say about the characters' values? Are their values and goals personal, materialistic, etc.? What are the film's overall messages regarding what it means to be successful?
8. What is the "American Dream" as defined in Chapter Three? What does the film say about the desirability of the "American Dream"? Does the film characterize the "American Dream" as realistic or unrealistic?
9. What overall messages does the film convey about class, success, and the "American Dream?" How do these messages compare to your own views?

Catherine and Tess engage in deceit; Catherine in stealing Tess's idea and Tess in stealing Catherine's clothes and professional identity. Tess also deceives Jack about her identity.

By the end of the film, the secretaries and the audience are celebrating Tess's achievement of the American Dream. Her hard work and her necessary, but forgivable, deceit have bought her a piece of the Dream and proven to the rest of us that individuals with the drive to succeed can escape the working class. On the side, we receive the subtle message that "losers" like Cyn and Mick are destined to remain in the tedious working class because they fall short of the intelligence, industriousness, and merit needed to move up in the world and lack even the awareness of how deficient their lives truly are.

As we have reconstructed what we were taught about class through formal and informal means, it becomes increasingly clear that many, if not most, of us raised in the United States have understood or misunderstood that we live in a classless society. This broad understanding of American self-identity as largely middle class is a twentieth-century phenomenon. While films such as *Working Girl* are the norm in the last half of the twentieth century, these messages about class were not always prevalent in film.

In the nineteenth century, many North Americans viewed themselves as workers or part of the working class. How did this class identity change and what role did film play in this shift? (Ross 1998,1).

In early twentieth-century silent films, class was a central theme. In 1910, 26 million people, or 30 percent of the population, went to the movies each week (Ross 1998, 11). At that point in history popular film had not yet evolved to the strictly fictional, narrative entertainment format that we became accustomed to by the 1930s. Rather, many early silent films were unabashedly political, often explicitly setting out to persuade audiences to think in a particular way. The low cost of producing films made it possible for many different organizations to express their political positions through this new medium.

Film audiences in the early twentieth century were largely working class and saw hundreds of silent films about strikes and union organizing. "Social realism and political commentary are not the hallmarks of the modern movie industry. Yet there was a time when entertainment and political engagement did not seem incompatible, and when movies and Hollywood were not synonymous in the minds of most Americans. The movie industry began as a small-scale business with small Spartan theaters spread throughout the country and production facilities centered largely in New York, Philadelphia, and Chicago" (Ross 1998, 5).

The composition of the audience and the content of films changed after World War I for two key reasons (Ross 1998, 13). First, government authorities feared that radical ideas on the screen might trigger radical activities among workers. These concerns lead to a movement for censorship to keep strike films and other films that featured worker exploitation off the screen. The second major factor in the shift in film content and audience was that after World War I elaborate, ornate, and expensive movie palaces were constructed, the price of admission went up, and the audience became largely middle class. The content of films began to shift from class exploitation to "fantasies of love and harmony among the classes" (Ross 1998, 18).

By the early 1920s, a small group of entrepreneurs transformed film production into a well-financed studio system with which the small-scale producers could not compete. This new system was now based more squarely on building audience and profit. Its new target audience was the middle class, a group with a larger disposable income. The newer, larger-scale producers made a judgment that more money could be made if the content of film was less controversial and addressed more marketable topics such as "the delights of the new consumer society" (Ross 1998, 11). Thus, class conflict virtually disappeared from the big screen.

From 1920 to 1929, romance and fantasy films outnumbered labor films 308 to 67. "Dreams of wealth, mobility, respect, and luxury could all be found on the screen, but love between the classes remained the cornerstone of these films. All problems, both personal and societal, could be solved through love; and true love was strong enough to break down any class barriers. After all, class was an artificial construct, love was real" (Ross 1998, 199).

The transformation of the film industry from an enterprise that supported small businesses with a wide array of agendas and political standpoints to a studio system whose main purpose was to entertain and be commercially successful was complete by the 1930s. This shift had an enormous impact on how class was portrayed in film. Much of popular film has continued to praise the American work ethic and the American Dream while depicting working class people and their organizations as worthy of contempt.

Since films began to talk and the Hollywood system began to prevail, there have been two dominant class themes in popular film. The first of these themes is that of cross-class romance in which true love conquers all. This is depicted in films such as *Pretty Woman* (1990), in which a successful but hardened executive undergoes a humanizing transformation as he falls in love with a poor but good-hearted prostitute who teaches him how to love and gets a lot of expensive clothes in the process.

The second prevalent theme supports the American Dream by the portrayal of the industrious individual's successful struggle against difficult odds to achieve financial and personal success. The message embedded in this theme is that a good person faces no insurmountable structural barriers to success. This underscores one of the primary myths of the American Dream—that it is the virtue and hard work of the individual that is central to his or her success. Of course, the flip side of this myth is present as well—that failure is a result of an individual's lack of virtue and hard work. This is depicted, as we have seen, in *Working Girl*.

According to an article in the *National Review,* a conservative weekly magazine, "Movies are the leading art form of our popular culture, with a unique ability to move and enlighten a mass audience" (Warren 1994, 53). The article, entitled

"The 100 Best Conservative Movies," touts the thirties and forties as promoting important American ideals such as "God and country, tradition and family, freedom and resistance to tyranny, individual achievement and the American Dream," commending these "movies that celebrate the creativity of business achievement, [and] depict the evils of Communism and collectivism." According to the *National Review* these American ideals were derailed in the 1970s as counterculture themes were expressed in "nihilistic themes and chaotic styles" in films such as *Midnight Cowboy* and *Easy Rider.* These ideals then made a comeback in the late 1970s as the Star Wars Trilogy once again portrayed the triumph of good over evil as the individual overcame great and even cosmic odds (Warren 1994, 53).

While critics on the left disagree with the politics of the *National Review,* they are in agreement about the power of visual images in film. Many popular films on labor and class have presented the subjects negatively, but there are less mainstream films that have shown them in a more balanced manner. "Yet, because we live in a culture that receives so much of its information (and ultimately derives so many of its opinions) from visual media, it is especially important to see, to understand and to study a variety of media images" (Zaniello 1996, 19).

This, then, is our next task—to see, understand, and study a variety of film images about class. There are many critical analyses in the form of articles and books on the depiction of gender and race and sexual orientation in film, but very few on the portrayal of class in film. To see and understand some of the patterns, trends, and exceptions in this depiction, we will examine some key films that contain central images of class. We will examine trends over the last fifty years and review mainstream box office draws as well as less financially successful and independently produced films about class. Most of these are available for rental so that you can read the analysis, see the film, and decide for yourself what you believe the messages about class to be.

Of the 100 films that are rated as the top box office hits in the United States (tdirks@filmsite.org), there are nine films, or 9 percent, that have major themes explicitly involving social and economic class. These films are *Gone with the Wind* (1939), *Titanic* (1997), *Love Story* (1970), *My Fair Lady* (1964), *West Side Story* (1961), *Rocky* (1976), *Aladdin* (1992), *Funny Girl* (1968), and *Pretty Woman* (1990).

How do these films rate according to the two trends in themes about class involving cross-class romance and/or the American Dream? Seven of these films *(Gone with the Wind, Titanic, Love Story, My Fair Lady, Aladdin, Funny Girl,* and *Pretty Woman)* tell the story of love across the classes, two have themes that involve the American Dream *(Rocky* and *Funny Girl),* and one has a theme that addresses class with somewhat more complexity *(West Side Story).*

Gone with the Wind tells a personal story, set in the historical context of the Civil War, of the financial, material, and class losses of a southern white woman, Scarlett O'Hara, and her family. Scarlett's determination, hard work, and scheming pay off as she finds ways to build back her family's money, rebuild the family home, and at the same time demonstrate one tenet of the American Dream—that one can always start over and be successful again. The racial messages in *Gone with the Wind* will be discussed in Chapter Five.

In *Titanic*, a wealthy, engaged young woman falls hopelessly in love with a poor young man who is a struggling artist. While their love transcends their class differences, it also underscores the other story, that of the real *Titanic,* in which the upper classes had greater access to the lifeboats and survival.

In *Love Story,* an owning class Harvard student, Oliver, falls in love with and marries a brilliant but poor Radcliffe student, Jenny. After their marriage, his family disowns him because they believe he has married beneath his class. But they return to him when Jenny becomes ill and eventually dies.

Professor Henry Higgins is challenged by Colonel Pickering to transform some poor unfortunate "girl" into a lady. Higgins picks Eliza Doolittle, a cockney accented, crude flower girl and whisks her to his London home to work on changing her accent, manners, and appearance. And of course, he is so successful that he eventually falls in love with her. The film? *My Fair Lady,* based on George Bernard Shaw's *Pygmalion.*

Even in the animated Disney film, *Aladdin,* we are treated to near tragic love across the classes. Aladdin, a poor boy who is a thief with integrity, falls in love with Princess Jasmine, the daughter of the sultan. Aladdin first poses as a prince, but after many mishaps and adventures, Jasmine loves him regardless of whether he is of high or low birth.

Funny Girl offers the audience both cross-class love and the American Dream. Fanny is a poor Jewish girl, the daughter of immigrants, whose talent brings her to the top of her career and leads her to fall in love with a handsome, non-Jewish man. *Rocky* offers the classic American Dream of the poor boy who makes it big, albeit in boxing, because of his hard work, perseverance, and virtue.

West Side Story is a twentieth-century, musical *Romeo and Juliet* in which the lovers are separated not by class but by nationality. Tony was born in the United States, and Maria was born in Puerto Rico. It is their respective cultures and bigoted families and peers that separate them. Yet, there remain some interesting themes about class because both sides live together in poverty in New York City, and Maria's brother, as well as Tony, is ultimately killed because of the hatred between the two groups. While the lyrical nature of the film removes it from gritty reality, part of its message is that these warring gangs have more in common than they understand. What divides them is their ethnicity. But what should unite them is their class, as both groups struggle to survive the streets and poverty and discrimination. Even though *West Side Story* offers a different look at class than the other eight films, it is important to recognize that the characters are simply drawn, much of the interaction is musical, and the concluding message about class is a reach.

Of these nine films about class, three are musicals, one is animated, and only in *Gone with the Wind* and *Funny Girl* are any of the characters remotely complex. These are the films that Americans have rushed to see over the last sixty years, and if both the political left and political right are correct, these are the films that have left an indelible mark on the viewers.

As discussed in Chapter One, images and stereotypes of groups and concepts can be investigated in several ways. The first is to determine the availability of images. This fits with the fact that only nine of these one hundred box office hits feature themes about class, which demonstrates how popular film images that address class are rarely available to movie-going audiences. A second investigative strategy is to determine whether the characters and themes are simple or complex. We have seen that of the nine films featuring class, only one addresses class thematically with any level of complexity, and only two have characters with any complexity. This simplicity tends to support the perpetuation of stereotypes. A third strategy of analysis looks for repetition of similar characters and themes. With little range or complexity in the nine films, the themes regarding romance across classes and the achievement of the American Dream become the core messages conveyed to film audiences.

Other important American films have featured themes of class and working class characters with greater complexity and range, however, and while they have not made the top 100 list, several of them have won Academy Awards. Award winners such as *The Best Years of Our Lives* (1946), *Midnight Cowboy* (1969), and *The Deerhunter* (1978), and the American classics *On the Waterfront* (1954) and *A Streetcar Named Desire* (1951) offer an alternative look at class. The critically acclaimed *Norma Rae* (1979), the controversial *Blue Collar* (1978), and the independently produced *Matewan* (1987) present an even more in-depth view of working class life and labor unions. Brief descriptions of these films demonstrate the possibilities for feature films to examine serious subjects without serving as propaganda for the unions, as in the early silent films, nor of promoting the dual myths of the American Dream and love conquers all. These are each interesting and compelling films and, again, I encourage you to rent them and judge their messages for yourself.

The 1946 Academy Award winner for Best Picture was *The Best Years of Our Lives,* starring Fredric March, Myrna Loy, Dana Andrews, and Teresa Wright. The film follows the lives of three men from three different economic classes as they return from active service in World War II. It does not flinch from the difficult issues of reentry for these men and how economic class and the competition for jobs impacts them. Dana Andrews plays a working class man who was a pilot with some glamour and stature during the war. When he returns, the only job he can find is as a soda jerk, which he finds demeaning and demoralizing. This film does not push a strong political agenda; it nevertheless drives home the message that the availability of opportunities and resources is not equal, that class weighs heavily on one's fortunes.

A Streetcar Named Desire, written by Tennessee Williams, was released as a film in 1951. Among its many themes was one of class. Stella (Kim Hunter) and her sister Blanche (Vivien Leigh) were raised in a wealthy, elite family in the South, a family that lost its fortune. Blanche derided Stella for marrying beneath her by choosing the working class, Polish Stanley Kowalski (Marlon Brando). Amidst Stanley's drinking and physical abuse of Stella is the presence of a powerful lust and a sweet tenderness between the couple. However, the film rarely follows the love-conquers-all theme. If anything, *Streetcar* depicts the American Dream gone sour. As much as Blanche wishes to pretend that nothing has changed while scheming to rebuild her fortune, she is not able to start over and find financial success once again.

On the Waterfront is the story of Terry Malloy (Marlon Brando) and the stand that he takes against racketeering and mob connections in the longshoremen's union. The film takes a hard look at how this corruption exploits the working men in the union. In spite of promises, bribes, and direct threats of violence, Malloy stands up to his brother, to the union, and, by extension, to evil in the world. He says to Edie (Eva Marie Saint), "They always said I was a bum. I ain't a bum, Edie." The film is a complexity of messages. The labor union represents corruption and evil, and Terry represents integrity and morality. Terry Malloy is a multilayered character that defies easy stereotypes of working class men.

Another level of complexity in the film involves its director, Elia Kazan. Kazan had originally refused to testify before the House Un-American Activities Committee, but in the middle of the 1952 filming of *On the Waterfront* changed his mind. He gave names of fellow communists, causing a sense of shock and betrayal among friends and fans. Some critics said that *Waterfront* was an attempt on the part of director Kazan and writer Budd Schulberg to use Terry Malloy to exonerate themselves. The film was listed as one of the top 100 conservative films by the *National Review* (Koehler 1999, 98).

In the Academy Award–winning *Midnight Cowboy* (1969), the young Texan Joe Buck (Jon Voight) is a handsome, uneducated dishwasher who naively heads to New York City to become rich by prostituting himself to wealthy older women. When a series of encounters fail, the disillusioned and broke Buck meets Ratso Rizzo (Dustin Hoffman), a down-on-his-luck hustler. The *National Review* finds *Midnight Cowboy* to be an example of the "nihilism and chaotic styles" of the 1970s that rejects the ideals of Western civilization (Warren 1994, 1). Certainly the film is a dark and grim view of life among the underclasses in New York City. But in many ways it offers a view of the complexity and humanity of the characters that more privileged folks find invisible in large urban areas.

Rizzo and Buck originally start out simply using each other to expand their respective hustles, but end up forming a bond, a friendship that eventually finds Joe Buck nurturing a fatally ill Ratso Rizzo. It is not a happy story about poverty—but it sends a message about the reality of its grimness and of the possibilities of human kindness amid darkness.

The 1978 film *Blue Collar* offers both complex themes and characters that revolve around class and race. The film is set in working class Detroit and most of the action takes place inside an auto factory. The three main characters (played by Harvey Keitel, Yaphet Kotto, and Richard Pryor) are workers in the factory, good friends who are portrayed as basically good guys. But they are not perfect. They all drink and do drugs occasionally, two of them cheat on their wives, and the third is an ex-convict. They are all struggling to survive financially, and the two family men are shown to love their wives and children. None of these three characters can easily be confined to a standard stereotype. Their friendship bonds are strong and cross racial boundaries. While all three men do things that are illegal and that audiences may view as immoral, we are nevertheless pulling for them to overcome the corruption they discover in their union.

Some critics have chided the film for portraying and stereotyping the thinly disguised United Auto Workers union as financially corrupt and lacking commitment to workers' rights; this is a fair criticism. But the film's unflinching look at the struggles of the working poor to fight the IRS and the union, pay for braces for the children, and so forth, paints an important and complex picture. Each of the three men faces the corruption and its seductive pull in different ways. One is destroyed by it, one succumbs to it and takes a job offer from the union as a payoff, and the third discloses the details of the corruption to the FBI. Ultimately, *Blue Collar* analyzes power, its impact, and its staggering ability to divide people.

Norma Rae is still another portrait of the working class and organized labor. In this film, organized labor is the hero, management is the villain, and the workers are caught in between. The main character, Norma Rae (Sally Field), works in a textile factory in Alabama. She is a single mother, a woman with fire and ardor who is imperfect and complex. She becomes outraged by the treatment of the workers and the conditions of the factories and passionately teams up with the labor organizer, Reuben (Ron Leibman), sent from New York to unionize the workers. Again, it is the film's resistance to glamorizing the lead characters, the factory workers, or working class life that sets it apart from other films about class. The film also resists the cheap shot of creating a relationship in which Norma Rae and Reuben might fall in love, whisking her away from her hard life. While Norma Rae the character and *Norma Rae* the film convey hope, there is no zealous or unquestioned portrayal of the American Dream, or even a hint that love conquers all.

Finally, the 1987 *Matewan*, directed by independent filmmaker John Sayles, tells another story of organized labor, workers, poverty, class, and race. This time the scene is the West Virginia coal mines, the struggle to unionize, and union busting. There is integrity and corruption everywhere—in management, workers, and in the union itself. There is the hint of love and attraction, but it never emerges as a central theme nor does it suggest that somehow romance will solve the problems of workers owned by the company or the violence that emerges when the black and white workers join forces to unionize. "Swathed in the trappings and pioneer themes of such classic models as *The Godfather* and *Once Upon a Time in America,* it tells of a different American Dream—of the unemployed and exploited" (Howe 1987, 1).

Entertainment film is a powerful force. It can reflect the realities or illusions of class, it can reinforce our beliefs and myths, and it can challenge us to question the invisibility of class in the United States. As we have seen, images of class are few in popular film and it is their absence that reinforces the notion of a classless society. The tools to tease out hidden themes and messages of class and to analyze the meaning in a character's class are critical to independent judgments about any particular film. But these tools play a far more important role—they give us the information and resources that allow us to determine the influence of entertainment media on our values and understanding about class and if we so choose, to rethink and reconstruct our beliefs.

Music and Class

In the 1962 top forty song "Patches," singer Dickey Lee plaintively describes the broken down house where his love Patches lives in an old shanty town. He painfully sings of his parents' refusal to let him marry her because they say she will bring him disgrace. The narrator discovers that Patches has killed herself and ends the song with "It may not be right, but I'll join you tonight. Patches, I'm coming to you" (Lyrics World 1999).

In the case of this song, love does not conquer all for these young lovers. Their economic differences and the class prejudices of the boy's parents keep them apart, and the couple decides to die rather than live without each other. While this song may be more extreme and melodramatic in its ending, it is indicative of how the messages about class in music differ from those in popular film and prime time television. Though class is not prevalent in all forms of contemporary music, it plays a significant role both in the definition of musical genres and in the expression of divisions by class. Contemporary music does not typically reflect class invisibility, the American Dream, or the love-conquers-all themes we found in prime time television and popular film.

In this section, we will look at the intersection of class with targeted music audiences and analyze the presence of class themes in contemporary and popular music. We will consider-twentieth century music to be contemporary music and will focus on music that has either been generated from the United States or has made a mark on U.S. culture by virtue of its popularity or impact.

Radio Audience Segmentation

The distribution of music through segmented radio is one explanation for popular music's depiction of class. Contemporary music is typically distributed first through popular radio stations, which are formatted according to their listening audience. In 1998, some of the standard radio formats were news, classical, easy listening, top forty, rhythm and blues (R & B), jazz, country, rock, oldies, and alternative. Rap music can be found on both top forty and R & B stations. The segmentation of radio audiences typically occurs according to some combination of age, race, and class. Older listeners, for example, tend to be the dominant audience for news, classical, and easy listening while younger audiences listen to R & B, top forty, rock, and alternative stations.

The segmentation of radio audiences according to race intersects with class and age as well. "Many stations reflect a class style, with some stations wooing urban contemporary listeners with jazz, soul, and traditional R & B while other stations woo black youth with hip-hop influenced R & B and rap music" (Dates and Barlow 1990). Country stations draw a broad white audience with significant working class representation.

Musical audiences change and evolve, and there is often "crossover music." LeAnn Rimes songs are played on country stations and top forty. Puff Daddy's (Sean "Puffy" Combs) songs are played on R & B stations and top forty. The audience for rap has evolved from primarily young, working class African American males to middle class white teens and young men (Samuels 1991, 24). Yet while the class divisions may often be muddy, the segmentation of the radio listening audiences more often corresponds to economic distinctions than those audiences for prime time television and popular film. Perhaps it is because of this that there have been musical genres that directly address themes of class.

Musical Genres

It is in the musical genres of rap and country where the most explicit themes of class can be found in the lyrics. "Rap and country lyrics implicate underclass reality. . . . Though both genres are based on somewhat different social realities, they both share a rhetoric of violence. Analyses of press coverage of country and rap have found that while the genres share a tendency towards machismo, they are not treated the same way by the press" (Croteau and Hoynes 1997, 227). "When rapper Ice Cube says, 'Let the suburbs see a nigga invasion,' many whites interpret that as an incitement to violence. But when Johnny Cash sings, 'Shot a man in Reno/just to watch him die,' the public taps its feet and hums" (Noe 1995, 20).

Racism clearly plays a key role in the differential press reaction to expressions of violence in rap and in country. We will explore this further in the Chapter Five. For now, it is interesting to note that two very different musical genres have emerged as the primary musical categories that focus on class. Although top forty, rock, and alternative music have far fewer songs that are reflective of class, they nevertheless share similar themes to rap and country songs. These themes do not generally support the dominant ideology of the American Dream, the invisibility of class, or love conquers all. Rather they focus on the anguish of poverty, violence and poverty, love that cannot overcome the barriers of class differences, and political analyses of power and poverty.

Popular Music

Examine the music charts that reflect the top popular songs of today. Many music stores encourage customers to listen to these songs. Do you find much explicit mention of economic class in contemporary popular music? Probably not. Like the top box office hits in film and successful prime time television, there are few examples of popular music that rhapsodize about or criticize economic divisions. But while these numbers are small, their messages are distinctly different from film and television.

A content analysis that examined themes about class in top forty songs during the years 1955, 1965, 1975, 1985, and 1995 revealed some interesting messages and trends (Holtzman 1998). As you recall, stereotypes of class were prevalent in prime time television and film partially because there were so few themes about class in these popular forms of entertainment. This same phenomenon holds true for popular music.

There were 1,095 songs that made it to the top forty lists of the five years in the study (Lyrics World 1998). Of these songs only forty-one, or 4 percent, had themes or characters that explicitly involved economics or class. As stereotypes work, this means that the messages in these few songs take on a hypersignificance, especially if the same themes are repeated over and over (see Table 3.1).

Despite the low occurrence of class themes, the study demonstrated themes that were surprisingly distinct from the other forms of popular entertainment media. In popular film and television the themes of class were largely reflective of the belief in the American Dream and that love conquers all. By and large they sent messages that underscored the dominant ideology. In these 1,000 plus top forty songs, the themes were far more diverse (see Table 3.2).

The 1955 songs about class are strikingly different from each other. "Band of Gold" and "My Boy Flat-Top" are love songs with lyrics such as, "Don't want the world to have and hold, For fame is not my line. Just want a little band of gold to prove that you are mine." "The Shifting, Whispering Sand" is a sort of mystical story of how the sands reveal the truth of the life of a miner. "Sixteen Tons" is the only one of these 1955 songs about class to tell the story of a poor man's destiny tied to his physical labor and lack of hope for financial success. The lyrics of the chorus repeat the theme of hard labor and deep debt and the hopelessness of the cycle characterized by "I owe my soul to the company store" (Lyrics World 1998).

By 1965, a few patterns about ideology in popular music begin to emerge. Sixty percent of the songs that had themes about class involved the dominant ideology of the American Dream or love conquers all. But all of these songs also had some themes that challenged the dominant ideology by criticizing class or economic disparity, describing the personal sorrows caused by money, or by describing complex stories or characters impacted by class. Of these thirteen hits, there were three Bob Dylan songs, two Roger Miller songs, as well as an assortment by Barbra Streisand, Sam Cooke, Sonny and Cher, and Billy Joe Royal.

Some of the songs that reflected love conquers all were "Hang On, Sloopy" by the McCoys, "I Got You Babe" by Sonny and Cher, and "Down in the Boondocks" by Billy Joe Royal. In "Hang On, Sloopy" the narrator is male and sings of his love "Sloopy" who, like Patches before her, lives on the wrong side of town. But this time, the narrator defies the people who try to put her down and says, "Sloopy, I don't care what your daddy do" because their love will conquer all (Lyrics World

Table 3.1

Percentage of Top Forty Songs with Themes About Class

	Total number of top 40 songs	Number	Percentage
1955	149	4	3
1965	323	13	4
1975	266	14	5
1985	215	4	4
1995	142	6	4
Totals	1,095	41	4

Source: Lyrics World Web site (1998).

Table 3.2

Themes About Class in Top Forty Songs

		Themes				
Year	Total no. of themes about class	Support the American dream No. (%)	Love conquers all No. (%)	Personal sorrows of money No. (%)	Complex story or character No. (%)	Criticism economic disparity No. (%)
1955	4		2 (50)	1 (25)	2 (50)	1 (25)
1965	13	3 (23)	5 (38)	3 (23)	6 (46)	5 (38)
1975	14	3 (21)		4 (29)	6 (43)	9 (64)
1985	4				3 (75)	4 (100)
1995	6	1 (17)			5 (83)	5 (83)
Totals	41	7 (17)	7 (17)	8 (20)	22 (54)	24 (59)

Source: Lyrics World Web site (1998).

Note: Many of the songs contained multiple themes and therefore the percentages do not add up to 100 for each year.

1998). "Down in the Boondocks" reiterates the same theme, but this time the male narrator is the person who lives on the wrong side, and he bemoans that their love cannot work since he is the boy from the boondocks (Lyrics World 1998).

Roger Miller's songs have more of a country than pop sound and each tells a story of a man; in "King of the Road" he is a traveler or vagabond, and in "Kansas City Star" he announces the local cartoons on television. In both of these songs, the man is happy with his status and the implication is that he has chosen his life with no implied criticism of the economic system (Lyrics World 1998).

An interesting song from 1965 was "May the Bird of Paradise Fly Up Your Nose," sung by Little Jimmy Dickens. While this song was clearly designed to be humorous, the humor was based on class distinctions made visible in the song. The narrator is a middle or upper middle class man who has interactions with taxi drivers, beggars, and laundry men. His insensitivity to these individuals from the working class causes them to wish him misfortune, albeit with silly curses. When he gives a penny to the "beggar man," the man mutters as he leaves that he hopes a bird of paradise flies up his nose and that an elephant steps on his toes and that the man's wife have runs in her hose (Lyrics World 1998). This certainly does not represent serious social criticism, but even within its silly lyrics, it makes class differences visible.

Other songs from 1965 were more explicitly critical of the dominant culture and were regarded during the time as protest songs. Bob Dylan had three top forty songs during this year, including "Like a Rolling Stone," "Subterranean Homesick Blues," and "Positively Fourth Street." While these songs are each distinct, their similarity is that they tell complex stories about individuals and their fall from high to low places or they explore the grimness of poverty and despair (Lyrics World 1998).

In 1975, the numbers shifted dramatically. Only 21 percent of the songs about class were about the American Dream and none revolved around love conquering all. All of the other songs challenged, criticized, or expressed sorrow about poverty or the emptiness of economic wealth. Interestingly, the three songs that expressed hope in the American Dream or pride in one's status were all country style songs by either Glen Campbell or John Denver. Campbell's "Rhinestone Cowboy" is the story of a man who is down on his luck but holds out great hope for economic success, and even though he has had to make compromises, he is certain he will make it to the top (Lyrics World 1998).

The other eleven top hits that feature themes about class are all over the place in content and style. There are songs that are clearly of the protest genre or social criticism by Bob Dylan, Joni Mitchell, Simon and Garfunkel, Janis Ian, and Bruce Springsteen. But there are also songs performed by more standard pop or rock or rhythm and blues or country singers that criticize or lament economic disparity. These are songs by such diverse artists as Harold Melvin and the Blue Notes, David Bowie, the Marshall Tucker Band, Chicago, and Neil Sedaka. Chicago's hit "Harry Truman" invokes the spirit of this former president in saving the United States from the corruption of materialism and corporate power (Lyrics World 1998).

Harold Melvin criticizes the president in "Bad Luck" as he sings about reading the newspaper, "Guess what I saw, Huh? Saw the president of the United States, huh. The man said he was gonna give it up. He's giving us high hopes. But he still turned around and left all us poor folks behind" (Lyrics World 1998). Janis Ian sings of the plight of homely, unpopular girls in "At Seventeen" and ties the success of the beauty queens to their "rich relations" and guarantee of marrying into wealth. Springsteen's "Born to Run" uses rock to explicitly criticize the American

Dream. In the first line of the song he refers to the runaway American Dream (Lyrics World 1998).

By 1985, there were only four songs with themes about class, and none of these had lyrics that supported the dominant ideology. These songs were sung by Madonna, Bruce Springsteen, Tina Turner, and Dire Straits. Madonna and Turner's songs, "Material Girl" and "Private Dancer," respectively, were snapshots of particular women who do whatever they need to do to make money, including sexual favors or prostitution. Dire Straits' song, "Money for Nothing" is the flip side of these last two. While in "Material Girl" and "Private Dancer" there is a cynicism about material success, "Money for Nothing" speaks of the cynicism of economic failure and the easy road of the musicians who make it on MTV. Springsteen's "Glory Days" speaks of the fall in happiness for some and in prosperity for others. He sings of his father's layoff from the Ford plant and his inability to find work because everyone said he was too old (Lyrics World 1998).

In 1995, there were 142 songs that made it to number one on the pop charts throughout the year. Of these hits, there were six that directly addressed class or economics. It is interesting to note that four of these songs were rap, one was rhythm and blues, and one could be considered alternative or pop.

"Gangsta's Paradise" is a lament on how poverty, racism, and street violence lock young African American men into lives of hopelessness. "I'm living life do or die, what can I say. I'm 23 never will I live to see 24 the way things is going I don't know" (Lyrics World 1998). The lament also combines with somewhat of a political analysis of how power and economics and the lack of role models and education keep young African American men trapped in a "Gangsta's Paradise" (Lyrics World 1998).

"This Is How We Do It" is about "making it" in two ways. Montell Jordan speaks in the first person, using his first name, about how he has made it out of South Central L.A. with his music and his big money. But he makes it clear that he still makes it sexually the same way they do in the old neighborhood or the "'hood." At first glance, the song seems to be about the American Dream and how money and success can take someone away from poverty and distress. But Jordan is clear that his roots are still in South Central (Lyrics World 1998).

Remember that some of the tools to assess entertainment media revolve around the prevalence of the presence of various characters and themes, the range of images and messages, and the repetition of these messages. Messages about class do not prevail in hit songs from the year 1995. However, of the songs that do address class 83 percent question the dominant culture and the meaning of the divisions according to class and the human consequences of poverty.

From the 1950s to the 1990s, images of class in top forty hits stay under 5 percent. But those images are not cookie cutter replicas of each other. They offer the kind of range and diversity in themes that defy stereotypes and make economic distinctions visible. Perhaps this is because the audience demographics of top forty music is much younger than those of film or prime time television. Or perhaps because it is cheaper to produce one song or CD than it is to produce a film or TV series, more risks can be taken. In any case, this form of entertainment media is an example of the possibilities of the expression of diverse themes coupled with the economic success of the media.

Chapter Summary

Many of us were taught through formal education and personal experience that the United States is a classless society in which the American Dream of economic success is available to all those who work hard and demonstrate virtue. Most of us learned little about the history of labor and the history of structural barriers to economic success. In our informal education, many of us were also taught that it is impolite to discuss money or income or economic status. Most prime time television and film reinforced these themes about economic class, social mobility, and the possibilities for economic success. For the most part, popular music does not address themes of class. But in the few hit songs that do, the audience is invited to think critically about the existence of economic divisions and how they hurt individuals and groups in the United States. Much of the information in this chapter is different from what we have been taught and from what most of us have learned. As you read it, you may find yourself resistant to the material or have difficulty reconciling it to what you already "know." This is part of the process of reconstructing knowledge. It is your work to weigh what you have learned in the past with how it is challenged through this chapter, rethinking your perspective on economic class.

Bibliography

Adams, Maurianne; Bell, Lee Anne; and Griffin, Pat, eds. 1997. *Teaching for Diversity and Social Justice: A Sourcebook.* New York: Routledge.

Barlett , D.L., and Steele, J.B. 1992. *America: What Went Wrong?* Kansas City, MO: Andrews and McMeel.

Bullard, R., ed. 1993. *Confronting Environmental Racism.* Boston: South End Press

Butsch, Richard. 1992. "Class and Gender in Four Decades of Television Situation Comedy." *Critical Studies in Mass Communications* 9, no. 4 (December): 387–406.

———. 1995. "Ralph, Fred, Archie, and Homer: Why Television Keeps Recreating the White Male Working-Class Buffoon." In *Gender, Race, and Class in Media,* ed. Gail Dines and Jean M. Humez, 403. Thousand Oaks, CA: Sage.

Croteau, David, and Hoynes, William. 1997. *Media/Society: Industries, Images and Audiences.* Thousand Oaks, CA: Pine Forge Press.

Dates, Jannette L., and Barlow, William, eds. 1990. *Split Image: African Americans and the Mass Media.* Washington, DC: Howard University Press.

DeLone, Richard D. 1979. *Small Futures: Children, Inequality, and the Limits of Liberal Reform.* New York: Harcourt Brace Jovanovich.

Dirks, Tim, 1996. © by Tim Dirks. All rights reserved. tdirks@filmsite.org.

Ehrenreich, Barbara. 1995. "The Silenced Majority: Why the Average Working Person Has Disappeared from American Media and Culture." In *Gender, Race, and Class in Media,* ed. Gail Dines and Jean M. Humez, 41. Thousand Oaks, CA: Sage.

Gutman, Herbert G. 1974. "The Social Backgrounds of Entrepreneurs in Paterson, New Jersey." In *Three Centuries of Social Mobility in America,* ed. Edward Pessen, 125. Lexington, MA: Heath.

Himmelstein, Hal. 1994. *Television Myth and the American Mind.* Westport, CT: Praeger.

Hochschild, Jennifer L. 1995. *Facing Up to the American Dream: Race, Class and the Soul of the Nation.* Princeton: Princeton University Press.

Holtzman, Linda. 1998. Unpublished content analysis of class in popular music.

Howe, Desson. October 16, 1987. "Matewan." Washingtonpost.com.

Internet Movie Database, Ltd. 1999–2000. www/http://us.imdb.com.

Jhally, Sut, and Lewis, Justin. 1992. *Enlightened Racism: The Cosby Show, Audience, and the Myth of the American Dream.* Boulder, CO: Westview Press.

Kendall, Diana. 1999. *Sociology in Our Times.* Belmont, CA: Wadsworth.

Koehler, Robert. 1999. "Kazan's HUAC Testimony a Permanent Black Mark." *Variety* 374: 48.

Langston, Donna. 1995. "Tired of Playing Monopoly?" In *Race, Class and Gender.* ed. Margaret L. Andersen and Patricia Hill Collins, 101–2. Belmont, CA: Wadsworth.

Lichter, Robert S.; Lichter, Linda S.; and Rothman, Stanley. 1994. *Prime Time: How TV Portrays American Culture.* Washington, DC: Regnery.

Loewen, James W. 1995. *Lies My Teacher Told Me: Everything Your American History Textbook Got Wrong.* New York: Touchstone.

Lyrics World. 1998–2000. http://lyrics.natalnet.com.br.

McElvaine, Robert S. 1993. *The Great Depression.* New York: Times Books.

Main, Jackson T. 1974. "Social Mobility in Revolutionary America." In *Three Centuries of Social Mobility in America,* ed. Edward Pessen, 57. Lexington, MA: Heath.

Marc, David. 1997. *Comic Visions: Television Comedy and American Culture.* Malden, MS: Blackwell.

Mayerle, Judine. 1994. "Roseanne—How Did You Get Inside My House? A Case Study of a Hit Blue-Collar Situation Comedy." In *Television: The Critical View,* 5th ed., ed. Horace Newcomb, 102–13. New York: Oxford University Press.

Menard, Russell. 1974. "The Social Mobility of Indentured Servants." In *Three Centuries of Social Mobility in America,* ed. Edward Pessen, 20–28. Lexington, MA: Heath.

Mishel, L.R., and Bernstein, J. 1993. *The State of Working America.* Armonk, NY: M.E. Sharpe.

Noe, Denise. 1995. "Parallel Worlds: The Surprising Similarities and Differences in Country-and-Western and Rap." *The Humanist* 55: 20–23.

Olsen, Joan. 1995. "The Horatio Algier Exercise." Unpublished manuscript.

Pessen, Edward, ed. 1974. *Three Centuries of Social Mobility in America.* Lexington, MA: Heath.

Phillips, Kevin. 1990. *The Politics of Rich and Poor.* New York: Harper.

Ross, Steven J. 1998. *Working-Class Hollywood.* Princeton: Princeton University Press.

Samuels, David. 1991. "The Rap on Rap: 'Black Music' That Isn't Either." *The New Republic* 205: 24–29.

Sklar, Robert. 1980. *Prime-Time America: Life On and Behind the Television Screen.* New York: Oxford University Press.

Takaki, Ronald. 1993. *A Different Mirror, A History of Multicultural America.* Boston: Little, Brown.

Thernstrom, Stephan. 1974. "Working-Class Upward Mobility in Newburyport." In *Three Centuries of Social Mobility in America,* ed. Edward Pessen, 63. Lexington, MA: Heath.

U.S. Bureau of Census. 1990. *Statistical Abstract of the United States.* Washington, DC: U.S. Government Printing Office.

————. 1992. *Statistical Abstract of the United States.* Washington, DC: U.S. Government Printing Office.

Vanneman, Reeve, and Cannon, Lynn Weber. 1987. *The American Perception of Class.* Philadelphia: Temple University Press.

Warren, Spencer. October 1994. "The 100 Best Conservative Movies." *National Review* 46, no. 20 (October): 53.

Wolff, Edward. 1995. *Top Heavy: The Study of Increasing Inequality of Wealth in America.* New York: The Twentieth Century Fund Press.

Zandy, Janet. 1995. "Decloaking Class: Why Class Identity and Consciousness Count." *Race, Gender, and Class* 4, no. 1: 9–13.

Zaniello, Tom. 1996. *Working Stiffs, Union Maids, Reds, and Riffraff—An Organized Guide to Films About Labor.* Ithaca, NY: ILR Press, an Imprint of Cornell University Press.

Chapter 4

Racing in America—Fact or Fiction?

> [B]eing the other means feeling different. It means being outside the game, outside the circle, outside the set. It means being on the edges, on the margins on the periphery. Otherness means feeling excluded, closed out, precluded, even disdained and scorned. It produces a sense of isolation, of apartness, and disconnectedness, of alienation.
>
> —*Madrid*

> [W]as your ethnic or cultural group ever considered not white? When they arrived in the United States, what did members of your family have to do to be accepted as white? What did they have to give up?
>
> —*Kivel*

Personal Experience and Race

In Chapter One you took a multicultural quiz that asked you to examine your experiences in the context of race, religion, sexual orientation, and economic and social class. This time the questions in Personal Inventory 4.1 will ask you to focus exclusively on race.

Once you have completed the inventory, tally your score. If you scored 6–11 points on this quiz, you are similar to the majority of U.S. residents and have lived in a very racially isolated world as you have grown up. You have been around people that are primarily your race and have had limited contact with people who are racially different from you.

If you scored 12–17 points, you have had some contact with people who are racially different from you. Perhaps you went to school with young people of other races or perhaps you belonged to clubs with people of other races. Your daily and regular contact with people of other races was still quite limited.

If you scored 18–23 points, you have had contact with a few racial groups that

149

Personal Inventory 4.1
Racing in America

Instructions

Answer the questions below with the response that comes closest to your experience. If you have moved frequently, answer the questions with your combined experiences. As you answer these questions determine in each instance whether you were in the racial majority or minority. Score 1 point for answers "a," "b," "c," "d," or "e." Score 2 points for any "f," 3 points for responses with "g," 4 points for "h," and 5 points for "i."

1. Describe the racial composition of the neighborhood in which you grew up:
   a. mostly European American (white)   _____
   b. mostly African American   _____
   c. mostly Asian American/Pacific Islander   _____
   d. mostly Latino   _____
   e. mostly American Indian   _____
   f. a strong mix of 2 of the groups listed in a–e _____
   g. a strong mix of 3 of the groups listed in a–e _____
   h. a strong mix of 4 of the groups listed in a–e _____
   i. a strong mix of 5 groups listed in a–e   _____

2. Describe the racial composition of your friends from grade school through high school:
   a. mostly European American (white)   _____
   b. mostly African American   _____
   c. mostly Asian American/Pacific Islander   _____
   d. mostly Latino   _____
   e. mostly American Indian   _____
   f. a strong mix of 2 of the groups listed in a–e _____
   g. a strong mix of 3 of the groups listed in a–e _____
   h. a strong mix of 4 of the groups listed in a–e _____
   i. a strong mix of 5 groups listed in a–e   _____

3. Describe the racial composition of your parents' friends:
   a. mostly European American (white)   _____
   b. mostly African American   _____
   c. mostly Asian American/Pacific Islander   _____

(cont'd)

are different from your own racial group. If you are Asian American, perhaps you went to school with other students who were Latino or African American but had limited contact with American Indians or European Americans.

If you scored 24–30 points, you have had a rare experience living in the United

d. mostly Latino _____
e. mostly American Indian _____
f. a strong mix of 2 of the groups listed in a–e _____
g. a strong mix of 3 of the groups listed in a–e _____
h. a strong mix of 4 of the groups listed in a–e _____
i. a strong mix of 5 groups listed in a–e _____

4. Describe the racial composition of the school(s) you attended:
   a. mostly European American (white) _____
   b. mostly African American _____
   c. mostly Asian American/Pacific Islander _____
   d. mostly Latino _____
   e. mostly American Indian _____
   f. a strong mix of 2 of the groups listed in a–e _____
   g. a strong mix of 3 of the groups listed in a–e _____
   h. a strong mix of 4 of the groups listed in a–e _____
   i. a strong mix of 5 groups listed in a–e _____

5. Describe the racial composition of the religious institution you attended:
   a. mostly European American (white) _____
   b. mostly African American _____
   c. mostly Asian American/Pacific Islander _____
   d. mostly Latino _____
   e. mostly American Indian _____
   f. a strong mix of 2 of the groups listed in a–e _____
   g. a strong mix of 3 of the groups listed in a–e _____
   h. a strong mix of 4 of the groups listed in a–e _____
   i. a strong mix of 5 groups listed in a–e _____

6. Describe the racial composition of the extracurricular activities in which you participated (clubs, athletics, dance, bowling, debate, etc.):
   a. mostly European American (white) _____
   b. mostly African American _____
   c. mostly Asian American/Pacific Islander _____
   d. mostly Latino _____
   e. mostly American Indian _____
   f. a strong mix of 2 of the groups listed in a–e _____
   g. a strong mix of 3 of the groups listed in a–e _____
   h. a strong mix of 4 of the groups listed in a–e _____
   i. a strong mix of 5 groups listed in a–e _____
   TOTAL SCORE _____

States. You have had extensive contact and interaction with people of many other races where you lived, in school, and socially.

Most of us who have grown up in the United States will score 15 points or under on this quiz. Despite laws and programs regarding school desegregation and open housing, most U.S. neighborhoods and schools are still racially isolated. Even those communities that have been intentional in their goals to be multiracial are still limited. I live in an inner ring suburb of St. Louis called University City. The population of the community is approximately 50 percent European American and 50 percent African American with a negligible percentage of any other race. The public school population is closer to 80 percent African American. This is partially because the white population is older than the black population, and it is partially because a significant number of white families send their school-age children to private schools. Those black and white children who do go to the public schools have the opportunity to interact with each other, but have virtually no opportunity to come into contact with young people who are American Indian, Asian American, or Latino. Despite their parents' efforts to live in a racially mixed community, their experiences are still limited.

In the previous exercise we investigated our exposure to racial groups that are different from ours. In the exercise in Personal Inventory 4.2 below we will begin to consider what we were told about race. The answers to the eight questions in the inventory will vary greatly across urban, rural, and suburban communities. They will be influenced by whether you grew up in the racial majority or minority in your community. They will be influenced by what region of the United States you lived in. They will be influenced by your age and generation and when and under what circumstances your family came to this country. They will be influenced by the beliefs and values of your family and friends. And most significantly, your answers will be influenced by whether your racial group is regarded as the dominant group in the United States (white) or your group has been targeted by racism in the United States (Latino, Asian American, African American, American Indian, multiracial, and forth).

Reading is a private and often anonymous experience. Unless the author is famous, we, the readers, generally do not know the author's race or ethnicity. And certainly, your race, as the reader, is not known to the author nor are you always conscious of your race and ethnicity as you read fiction and nonfiction, newspapers and magazines. We will change that tradition for this chapter.

My name is Linda Holtzman. I am a white, Jewish woman. Three of my four grandparents were Russian Jews who immigrated to the United States during the first decade of the twentieth century. My fourth grandparent was born in the United States of Russian Jewish immigrant parents. My grandparents' primary language was Yiddish, a combination of Hebrew and German. They spoke little Russian since that was the official language of the land and Jews were not welcome in Russia at that time. Jewish families were targeted by violent pogroms that destroyed their small villages and few possessions.

I do not know the details of what happened to my particular family. I do know that Jews in Russia could only live in certain areas and practice certain jobs and professions. I know that they were generally poor. I know that they wanted to come to "America," where they could be free to practice their religion and support

Personal Inventory 4.2
Sticks and Stones

Instructions

Answer the questions below in written or oral form to add to your developing autobiography. Exchange your experiences and comments with another person. If you grew up hearing or experiencing hateful things about your race or other races, this may be difficult for you. But if you stay with the answers, you will learn an enormous amount about your informal learning about race.

1. What did your parents tell you about your race? What word(s) did they use to describe your race? What did your parents tell you about other racial groups? What word(s) did they use to describe other races?

2. What did your grandparents and other extended family tell you about your race? What word(s) did they use to describe your race? What did your parents tell you about other racial groups? What word(s) did they use to describe other races?

3. Was there ever a time that any of your family members engaged in conflict with each other or people outside of the family regarding race? Describe the situation.

4. What did your friends and classmates say about your race? What kinds of things did they say about racial groups that were different from yours? What words did they use to describe various racial groups?

5. Did you ever see your friends engage in any conflict regarding race? Describe the situation.

6. Have you ever made a derogatory remark about your race or the race of other people? Have you ever called someone a racial name either to their face or behind their backs?

7. Have you ever engaged in any conflict regarding race? Describe the situation.

8. How do you feel about the race you are? What are you most proud of about your race? What is most difficult about being the race you are?

their families. I know that when they moved to St. Louis, they lived in Russian Jewish enclaves where many people spoke Yiddish and lit candles on Friday night for Shabbes (the Jewish sabbath) and cooked brisket and rolled meat and cabbage and knishes. They lived in places where they did not feel so different from their neighbors.

I know that my paternal grandfather had a small retail store called "Holtzman

Furniture, Clothing and Appliances" in a poor neighborhood in which his customers were primarily African American. As a young girl, I remember "collecting"
with my uncle, who would visit customers' homes to secure their monthly pay-
ments. My uncle was very nice to the customers, but I noticed that he changed his
accent to match theirs when he went to collect. Twenty years later, my first job out of
college was teaching elementary school in an African American community. One
day, one of my students came running into the classroom and said to me with great
excitement, "Miss Holtzman, Miss Holtzman, I found your name on my couch!"

Many of the Jewish families I knew hired someone to clean their houses every
week. Their cleaning ladies were always African American, and they were generally personally kind to the women who cleaned their houses. They called them by
their first names and referred to them among each other as "the girl" or "the
schvartze," which in Yiddish means black. The women who cleaned made hourly
or daily wages and generally did not receive benefits or health insurance.

My parents were born in the United States and learned English as their first language and today know only a few expressions of Yiddish. My mother can cook some
of the traditional Jewish foods, and I can too. I have my grandmother's silver candle-
sticks, which I light on Shabbes with my family. But I do not know Yiddish and I do
not know in what town in Russia my family lived. I do not know what kind of work
they did nor the exact circumstances under which they left Russia. My grandparents
never said anything to me about Russia and there were no records, only a few photos
after they died. In their heavily accented English they were determined to be American and were proud at how American their children and grandchildren were.

My parents, like many second generation white Americans, pursued the American Dream. My father fought as a U.S. soldier in World War II and was one of the
first soldiers present when Allied forces liberated the German concentration camp
at Buchenwald. A strong memory from my childhood was my father's story of
having captured a German SS guard. My father was holding the German soldier as
a prisoner at gunpoint and said to him in German, "I am a Jew," and the man
turned and spit into my father's face. Equally strong are the memories my father
told my brothers and me about anti-Semitism in the U.S. Army and other soldiers
who taunted and tortured him because he was a Jew. He came home from the war
to help my grandfather with his small retail business. Neither my parents nor any
of my aunts and uncles went to college. They all carved out middle class incomes
through retail businesses they owned or in which they were employed. My mom
stayed home to raise the kids. We lived in a middle class white suburb in a house
with a lawn and a two-car garage. There were no people of color in my neighborhood. There was one African American girl in my high school graduating class.

When I was five years old, I remember that while I was walking to kindergar-
ten, a little girl who had just moved in up the street hid behind a tree and threw
rocks at me and called me "kike" and "sheeny." I did not know what those words
meant, but they sounded mean and hurt my feelings and I told my parents. The
girl's father was in the military. My dad told me that he had her father transferred

to Okinawa. My dad was in the furniture business with his father at the time and did not have the power to do such a thing. But I believed him and felt protected.

When I was in high school, there were dozens of Jewish girls and a handful of Jewish boys who had cosmetic surgery on their noses to "improve their appearance." Now that our families lived in neighborhoods that were Jewish and Christian, we looked and seemed more different. They wanted to look more like their friends and neighbors.

My teachers, doctors, and neighbors were white, and a few were Jewish. The store clerks and managers were almost all white and Christian. There was one African American woman named Nan who was a clerk at the drugstore near our house. All of the elected officials were white, and none of them were Jewish. The people who owned the big companies around us were white and Christian. The people who owned one of the regional department store chains were Jewish. The milkman was white and Christian. The soda deliveryman was white and Jewish. The man who delivered the dry cleaning was white and Christian. I do not remember seeing anyone who was Asian or Latino or American Indian.

The African American adults I saw in my community cleaned houses and did yard work or hauled trash or bought what was called "low-end" furniture from Holtzman Furniture.

Today, I think of myself as white and Jewish, not Russian American. While I choose to live in a multiracial, multiethnic community and do antiracist work, I am also a product of my story, my history, and my racial legacy. My family's journey to the United States is both a story of being the "other" as Jews and one of becoming "white" in America.

Now it is your turn to tell your story. Write or record your story and exchange it with at least one other person. As you discuss your stories, ask each other questions and let more details and greater understanding emerge. If you do not know the answers to some of the questions, talk to family members or dig around in family scrapbooks, photo albums, or other formal or informal family archives. If you still cannot find the answers to some of the questions, think and write about how your family's race or ethnicity may have contributed to the gaps and voids. For example, given the anti-Semitism in Russia, my grandparents were forced to leave at time of great danger to them and brought almost nothing with them. Their strong desire to be American and the cultural imperative for assimilation meant they talked very little about the "old country," and as a child, it never occurred to me to ask questions. Consider the questions in Personal Inventory 4.3 as you develop your racial and ethnic autobiography.

This autobiographical exploration is intended to dig deeply into each of our personal and family histories regarding race and ethnicity, to delve into what we know of our racial history, and to document our experiences regarding race. Our individual and family stories about race are each uniquely American and add up to what we know as U.S. history. Finding our place in this anthology of stories is critical to understanding the larger story of race in the United States.

Personal Inventory 4.3
Autobiography on Race and Ethnicity

1. How many generations has your family been in the United States?

2. What continent and/or country did your ancestors come from?

3. Under what circumstances did your ancestors come to the United States? Were they voluntary immigrants, were they refugees, or were they forced to come as slaves? Were your ancestors part of a group or country that was conquered by the United States such as American Indians or Mexicans?

4. Were your ancestors welcomed when they arrived in the United States? If your ancestors were in the United States before Europeans arrived, were they greeted with friendliness or hostility? Were they considered white or nonwhite? (Please note that if your family was Irish, Jewish, German, Polish, or Finnish and arrived in the United States some time before the early twentieth century they were most likely considered nonwhite).

5. Were there any restrictions as to where your ancestors could live or work when they or others arrived in the United States?

6. What do you know of their customs and culture? Discuss what you know of their food, clothing, language, beliefs, religion. How much of these customs and culture do you and your contemporary family still know about and practice?

7. What kind of work did your ancestors do? Were they laborers, merchants, professionals? What was the race and ethnicity of the people they worked for, their supervisors or bosses, or of the people who worked for them? Did the kind of work they did change and improve through subsequent generations or did it remain basically the same?

(cont'd)

If, like me, you are a second-generation Jewish American, you may know the experience of being both other and white in this country. If you are American Indian, you may know how many generations of your family had their land taken by whites, lived on government controlled poverty-stricken reservations, or were forced to give up their native language at Indian boarding schools. If you are Irish American you may know that your grandparents faced signs in New York that said "No Dogs and No Irish" and that their generation was considered nonwhite. You also probably know that by the second and third and fourth generation, your Irish American family had the same job and housing opportunities as other white people in the United States. If you are Mexican American you may know that in 1847 what was now Texas belonged to Mexico and that Mexico declared slavery illegal and stopped immigration of people from the United States. You may not know that

8. Was your family able to improve their economic situation over the generations since they first came to the United States? What racial or ethnic factors fostered this improvement or acted as barriers to this improvement?

9. Did your ancestors and subsequent generations live in neighborhoods with primarily one race and ethnicity, or were these neighborhoods racially and ethnically mixed? Did they live in these neighborhoods by choice?

10. How were your ancestors and subsequent generations treated by people who were racially and ethnically different from them? Did that change over time, and if so, in what way?

11. What race and ethnicity were the adults you knew growing up? Think of teachers, doctors, lawyers, store clerks, laborers, service people. What was the race and ethnicity of people who owned the businesses and stores in your community? What about the elected officials?

12. What experiences did you have or observe as you were growing up about race or ethnic discrimination? How were you or your parents involved in this? Were you and your family the target or agent of racial or ethnic discrimination? Or perhaps, were you and your family both the target and the agent?

13. How connected do you feel to your family's country of origin today? Is the connection strong, blurry, or nonexistent? Does your own sense of identity include your race, ethnicity, family background? How much are you aware of the history, culture, customs and traditions of your ancestors? Are these a strong part of how you see yourself and your interactions with others today?

thousands of U.S. citizens moved into Texas as "illegal aliens" and fought a war that "annexed" Texas as part of the United States and then made it increasingly difficult for your ancestors to get work that was anything above the most menial. If you are Chinese American, you may know that when the Chinese first came to the United States during the gold rush and began working on the railroads, only men were allowed to come here from China, and families were torn apart out of financial necessity. And if you are African American, you may know that even after slavery was over, those Europeans who immigrated to the United States after the Civil War benefited from the discrimination your ancestors endured. These European immigrants were hired in the factories that would not hire your grandparents and lived in the neighborhoods that would not rent to your families.

We will explore the details of these historical facts later in the chapter. For now, we can begin to see how each of our stories is a thread that intertwines with all the other stories and that the threads together weave an intricate American tapestry of race that is complex, interdependent, and interwoven with discrimination and assimilation.

As you have reflected upon your personal experiences with race, you may experience a wide range of emotions. Race in this country is a highly charged topic, loaded with strong beliefs, opinions, and feelings. Uncovering old memories and family history may also uncover strong emotions. These exercises may elicit intensity. I encourage you to continue to write about your thoughts and experiences and to talk to others in your community who are thinking about race or teaching or conducting training about race. As you examine your own experiences regarding race there are two central questions for reflection. Where is your place in the racialized history and atmosphere of this country? In other words, how has your particular story formed how you see race in your world? The second question is, what is the informal learning that you have gained from your experiences about race and how has this learning shaped your views and opinions and feelings about race?

Our stories have shaped us and have formed a unique and particular frame to the window from which we see the world of race and ethnicity and discrimination. People of other races and histories have frames and windows that are remarkably different. As we each look out our particular racial window, what we see is also different from what others see. Recognizing and acknowledging this difference is the first step toward a larger, broader, and deeper understanding of race in America. As you read the next section, some of it may challenge what you have been taught and some of it may reinforce your beliefs about race. It will be important to track your reactions to the information in the context of your own experiences and personal history about race.

Reconstructing Knowledge

Just a few moments ago, you were reflecting on your personal experiences with race. You answered questions about your race and your family's racial history. You examined how what you learned informally about race has shaped you and your world view. Although I did not define race in the previous section, most of you knew what I meant. You are African American or Asian American or Latino or American Indian or European American or multiracial. What exactly does race mean?

In 1848, California debated over the status of the Chinese and Mexicans and decided that Mexicans would be considered white and that the Chinese would have the same status as African Americans (Kivel 1996, 18). In 1860 three races were acknowledged in the United States: whites, blacks, and mulattoes (1 black and 1 white parent). By 1890 these three races had been joined by 5 more: quadroon (3 white grandparents and 1 black grandparent), octoroon (7 white great grandparents and 1 black great grandparent), Chinese, Japanese, and Indian. In the 1930s and 1940s in Germany, the two races acknowledged were Aryan and Jewish. For the purposes of the census, the racial groups in 1990 were white; black or African American; Asian or Pacific Islander; American Indian, Eskimo, or Aleutian; and one of two ethnicities—Hispanic or non-Hispanic (Moraga 1995, 61). Up to the mid-twentieth century many American schoolchildren were taught a "biological" explanation of race. This description said that the three races were Caucasoid, Negroid, and Mongoloid, based on skin color, skull size, and other physiological characteristics.

Wars have been fought in which race has been central to the conflict. Groups of people have been denied citizenship, the vote, housing, and jobs because of race. Some people have died trying to vote or helping other people register to vote because of race. This is U.S. history. How can so much national tragedy have happened that revolves around a concept of race that is so fluid? How can we attain clarity about our own racial identity when the definitions keep changing? How can we understand the impact of race in the United States when it keeps getting redefined?

Theories and Constructs of Race

The shifting meaning of race throughout U.S. history provides important clues to its definition. It is not biological, nor is it based primarily on skin color. As we look at history we will see that it is not necessarily based on ethnicity or one's country of origin. Rather, race is constructed socially, politically, and economically. "Various racial categories have been created or changed to meet the emerging economic and social needs of white United States culture. Racial categories artificially emphasize the relatively small external physical differences among people and leave room for the creation of false notions of mental, emotional, and intellectual differences as well" (Adams et al. 1997, 83).

Racism is built on this artificial foundation of race. While race itself is fiction, the consequences of racism have become historical fact. "Racism is based on the concept of whiteness—a powerful fiction enforced by power and violence. Whiteness is a constantly shifting boundary separating those who are entitled to have certain privileges from those whose exploitation and vulnerability to violence is justified by their not being white" (Kivel 1996, 17).

As U.S. history has unfolded there are at least two things about race that are clear. The first is that the definition of who is white and who is "minority" is constantly shifting. The second is that being nonwhite in the United States has been dangerous, both emotionally and physically. The history that we will review has often been deleted from our formal education. We have, by and large, been underinformed and misinformed about the impact of race and racism in our history. As we learned in the first chapter, misinformation is the foundation of oppression. When applied to race, it has meant that during various times in our history, U.S. citizens who have considered themselves white have operated from the misinformation that people of color are inferior to them. This misinformation has turned into public and private, collective and individual laws, policies, attitudes, and behaviors that have excluded, discriminated against, injured, and killed people considered nonwhite.

"Nearly all sociologists and anthropologists now recognize that 'race' is a socially constructed concept whose meaning has evolved over time. There is no biologically valid difference in the genetic makeup of different 'races.' However, racial distinctions have powerful social meaning with profound real-world consequences" (Croteau and Hoynes 1997, 138). As a result of this misinformation about superiority of one group of people over others, various aspects of racism have emerged.

Some individual white people have been cruel, hateful, and at times violent to people of color. This is *individual racism* in which the source and the impact are from one person to another. Yet, as you will see, there have been official policies and laws and practices in the United States that have eliminated and discriminated against whole groups of people.

As you learn about the Indian Removal Policy, the "separate but equal doctrine" of education, the "annexation" of Texas, and the internment of Japanese Americans, you will be learning about *institutional racism* in which public and private entities have built race discrimination into their very fiber.

Individual racism and institutional racism are always based on the misinformation that one group is superior to another. The instances described above are examples of *overt racism* in which the hatred and discrimination are outright and on the surface. Name-calling and personal violence are examples of individual acts of overt racism. Examples of overt institutionalized racism are the Jim Crow laws (segregation of public and private facilities) or the practice of red lining (refusing to offer mortgages or insurance to whole communities of color).

However, racism can also operate on a less blatant, subtler level and this mutation of racism is *covert racism*. It is important to note that the results of covert racism are often as discriminatory as those of overt racism. Observe large public and private employers (corporations, hospitals, universities, etc.) in your community. Do their workforces reflect the racial composition of your community? Are there any or many people of color in upper management positions? It is possible for unequal treatment by race to exist in housing, employment, education, and health care without any overt hateful act or explicit law or policy.

Central to the understanding of racism in the United States is the understanding of how power operates on an individual and institutional level. It is the power to name and describe races in textbooks and the census, to make laws, declare war, enforce discrimination, deny education or housing, to hurt and kill that is on the surface or just below the surface in racism.

Misinformation about race impacts people of color and white people in different ways. White people in the United States are socialized to see their race not simply as dominant, but as the norm, the standard for behavior, and the benchmark for what it means to be American. While there certainly remain many white individuals and groups who are overtly racist, there are millions of other white people who benefit from racism in ways that are often invisible to them. This is the way that misinformation about race insinuates itself into a way of thinking and behaving that remains unquestioned. This is *white privilege.*

When I wrote earlier of my personal story, I discussed the anti-Semitism my grandparents faced in Russia and as new immigrants to the United States. But because they and their descendants would ultimately be considered white, they were allowed to find work and housing and education from which African Americans and Japanese Americans were prohibited. Without ever initiating or participating in one overtly hateful act, they benefited from racism.

The same misinformation received by whites is also part of the socialization of people of color in the United States. The myth of white superiority also penetrates the minds and hearts of people who have been targeted by racism. This taking in of the negative messages of overt and covert racism, superiority and inferiority, and white privilege constitutes *internalized racism.* Internalized racism is always involuntary and is a direct by-product of racism that works in many ways. It may operate as a survival mechanism. In the post–Civil War South, it was a matter of survival for an African American man to avert his eyes and step off the sidewalk when a white woman passed him, perhaps uttering a quiet and deferential "Good morning, ma'am." Even something as simple as direct eye contact or speaking to a white woman as an equal could be used as an excuse for lynching. A tactic that was needed to survive in the nineteenth century can become internalized racism in the twenty-first century. Internalized racism can also have the effect of lowering self-esteem. If an individual or group is told long enough that they are not smart or beautiful or equal to others, without intervening information and interruption of that process, they will often believe this misinformation and act upon it. Acting upon this information can result in depression, low achievement in school, or violence turned on one's own community. The key to understanding internalized racism is that it is a reaction to the power and poison of racism that can only be healed as racism itself is healed.

The definitions of race and racism described above focus on whiteness as the location of power and privilege and indicate that it has often been the protection of whiteness that has led to exploitation and violence in this country. This is not what most of us were taught in school. This is not what many of us learned from our parents. As you read this section keep two things in mind: first, remember your own racial history and its impact on your beliefs; and second, remember that you are never required to change what you believe to be true. Consider the information in this section and then draw your own independent conclusions.

The landing of Christopher Columbus began hundreds of years of violence toward American Indians: "Thus began the history, five hundred years ago, of the European invasion of the Indian settlements in the Americas. That beginning . . . is conquest, slavery, death. When we read history books given to children in the United States, it all starts with heroic adventure—there is no bloodshed—and

Columbus Day is a celebration" (Zinn 1995, 7). There is much to be learned by studying these hard facts of conflict and oppression and violence spurred by race and racism. We can learn from the parts of our history when average people and leaders resisted racism and showed compassion. We can learn that neither race nor racism is "natural" but rather the result of historical conditions. When we understand our history, we can change the impact of racism.

Many of us were taught that history is factual, objective, and indisputable. History is what we read in textbooks and were told by teachers of what happened in the past. We base our knowledge of equality and fairness in the United States on the "facts" and "stories" that we learned.

> [T]he easy acceptance of atrocities as a deplorable but necessary price to pay for our progress (Hiroshima and Vietnam, to save Western civilization . . . to save us all)—that is still with us. One reason these atrocities are still with us is that we have learned to bury them in a mass of other facts, as radioactive wastes are buried in containers in the earth. We have learned to give them exactly the same proportion of attention that teachers and writers often give them in the most respectable of classrooms and textbooks. This learned sense of moral proportion, coming from the apparent objectivity of the scholar, is accepted more easily than when it comes from politicians at press conferences. It is therefore more deadly. (Zinn 1995, 8–9)

Some important stories were omitted from our education. Some of these stories will be retold in this section. Some may challenge your concept of the United States as a nation of justice and equality. Some may make you angry. Some may trigger disbelief. But disillusion is as safe a haven as illusion in our history of race and racism. Understanding how the construct of race and the practice of racism evolved is using history as empowerment. As long as we understand only part of our history, we are prone to perpetuate racial myths and to act upon them as if they are true.

Within these stories are people who took small and mighty stands against racism, changing their lives and making a dent in history—moving it closer to the ideals of justice and equality. With full information, we have the foundation, the tools, and the options to make changes both in our own actions and in those of our nation.

Contemporary U.S. Population by Race

The 1990 census indicated that the U.S. population consisted of 199.6 million whites (77 percent), 29.9 million blacks (11 percent), 22.3 million Hispanics or Latinos (8 percent), 7.2 million Asian or Pacific Islanders (3 percent), and 1.9 million Native Americans (1 percent). The overall U.S. population growth from 1980 to 1990 was 9.8 percent. This rate of growth varied widely according to race with white growth 6 percent, Latino growth 53 percent, Asian growth 107.8 percent, black growth 13.2 percent, and Native American growth 37 percent. Population predictions project that by the year 2013 the Latino population will surpass the black population with Latinos projected at 42.1 million and blacks at 42 million. The Asian and Pacific Islander population is projected to grow by five times its current population so that from 1990 to 2005 it will grow from 24 million to 81 million (Wilson and Gutierrez 1995, 7).

History of Race in the United States

The telling of personal stories can be liberating. We can suddenly remember something wonderful that happened in our childhood and the telling of it can bring great joy. We can uncover a painful memory or family secret and the telling of it can bring healing and emotional recovery. As we share these memories with other people we often find common bonds and connections. Those are the human connections that bind us with understanding and compassion. The same process occurs in the telling of the collective stories, the history of a nation. This can be liberating and healing and can forge connections between disparate groups.

Since this is not exclusively a history book, and there are only a few selected stories in this section, the focus is primarily on the stories that have been left out of traditional American history. The citations and references will point you to more complete historical accounts of the many faces of race in the United States.

American Indians

In the late 1990s, only 22 percent of American Indians lived on reservations, more than 50 percent lived in urban areas, and the rest lived in rural areas. The 1990 U.S. median income was $35,225, and the median income for American Indians was $21,619. Twenty-seven percent of American Indians lived below the poverty line in 1990 as compared to 10 percent of the entire American population. Only 2.1 percent of the American Indian population had earned four-year college degrees during this same year (U.S. Bureau of the Census 1990, CP-3–7). What is it in the history of the United States that caused this disparity and these economic and educational difficulties for American Indians? The information in this section will provide some insight into contemporary conditions for American Indians.

Generalizing about cultural norms can contribute to stereotypes and racism, but there are nevertheless some shared cultural values that distinguish the deep and surface culture of many American Indians. Deep in American Indian culture is the belief that extended family and kinship bonds are extremely important. Traditionally, American Indians have considered group needs to be more important than individual needs and have made communal decision making and sharing an integral part of life. There is also a traditional and often spiritual belief that all living things are connected and should be treated with care and respect (Tatum 1997, 143–44). Many American Indian tribes have believed that owning land or "real estate" contradicts a basic understanding of nature and spirit. It is not hard to imagine how these traditional beliefs and the practices that grew out of them would be in conflict with the emphasis that European settlers placed on individualism, materialism, and the acquisition of land.

In the fifteenth century Columbus wrote of his encounters with the indigenous people whom he called Indians because he thought he had reached India:

> They . . . brought us parrots and balls of cotton and spears and many other things, which they exchanged for the glass beads and hawks' bells. They willingly traded everything they owned. . . . They were well-built, with good bodies and handsome features. . . . They do not bear arms, and do not know them, for I showed them a sword; they took it by the edge and cut themselves out of ignorance. They have no iron. Their spears are made of cane. . . . They would make fine servants. . . . With fifty men we could subjugate them all and make them do whatever we want. (Zinn 1995, 1)

In 1607, the English established a settlement at Jamestown, Virginia, and encountered the Powhatan Indians. They dubbed the father of Pocahontas, King Powhatan. But after his death, the Powhatans tried to drive the English back to the sea, and the English retaliated. The 8,000 Powhatan Indians were reduced to less than a thousand (Brown 1970, 2).

In 1620 the Pilgrims encountered the Wampanoag Indians, a farming community with a representative political system and a specialized system of labor. The Wampanoags helped the Pilgrims through the winter by giving them food and helping them learn how to cultivate the land. "However, many colonists in New England disregarded this reality and invented their own representations of Indians. What emerged to justify dispossessing them was the racialization of Indian 'savagery,' Indian heathenism and alleged laziness that came to be viewed as inborn group traits that rendered them naturally incapable of civilization" (Takaki 1993, 37).

More than three centuries after Columbus arrived and two centuries after the English colonists first landed in the United States the results for the American Indians were:

- The friendly Taino Indians that greeted Columbus had been obliterated.
- The Wampanoag, the Chesapeake, the Chicahominy, and the Potomac of the great Powhatan confederacy had vanished.
- Thirteen more eastern and southern tribes had been scattered or significantly reduced (Brown 1970, 7).

When young people conduct research about American Indians, they often begin with an encyclopedia. *Compton's Encyclopedia Online* offers information for these student papers including, "Because of European colonization of North and South American since 1500, *Native Americans* have been greatly reduced in numbers and largely displaced," and "*Native Americans* belong to the *American* Indian geographic race. Characteristics include medium skin pigmentation, straight black hair, sparse body hair, and a very low frequency of male pattern balding. In addition to a marked absence of blood type B and the Rh-negative blood type among Native Americans, several other characteristics of their blood types set them apart from the Mongoloid peoples, with whom they were sometimes classed in the past" (*Compton's Encyclopedia Online* 1999, 1).

Notice certain words employed in this brief description of American Indians. The terms "greatly reduced in numbers" and "displaced" make the history of bloodshed seem clean and antiseptic. That the "reduction" and "displacement" are attributed to "colonization" reiterates the theme of the "necessary price to pay for our progress" (Zinn 1995, 8). The notion that American Indians belong to the "Indian geographic race" that was sometimes confused with "Mongoloid peoples" presumes a geographic, physical, and biological construct of race. Anthropologists have rejected the notion of races divided into Caucasian, Negroid and Mongoloid. Nowhere in this brief description is there any mention of how the so-called race of the Indians was constructed by the European colonists to justify taking their land and killing off their people. There is no mention of how setting a group of people apart as "the other" and naming them as a race that is savage, brutal, and ignorant might be connected to colonization, reduction, and displacement.

An eighth grade social studies textbook probes more deeply into this history. It says that the Indians were here before Columbus, and they fought many bloody wars to protect their land but were eventually pushed west into land that was not conducive to their way of life. But ultimately, the text ignores the weight of history and puts the responsibility of contemporary poverty and poor education squarely on the shoulders of American Indians by stating, "Many Native Americans realize that to prepare themselves for the future, they must overcome the handicaps of poverty and lack of education" (Davis and Fernlund 1996, 8). It is interesting to note that this text is a civics book that addresses the Constitution and other laws of the land, yet there is no mention of the way that laws were used by the U.S. government for what was called "Indian Removal."

In 1829, Andrew Jackson, called "Sharp Knife" by the Indians, came to office and proposed a massive program of Indian Removal in which all Indians were to be moved west of the Mississippi (Brown 1970, 5). The policy of Indian Removal, in fact, cleared the land from the Appalachians and the Mississippi for growing cotton in the South and grains in the North and for expansion of the U.S. boundaries and the building of railroads and new cities.

In 1838, 17,000 Cherokees were rounded up into stockades and sent on foot from Georgia to "resettle" in Oklahoma. During this march, known as the "Trail of Tears," approximately 4,000 Cherokees died. The purchase of Florida was not simply a land deal. In Florida, this "purchase" meant that Andrew Jackson ordered the burning of Seminole villages in which whole communities were killed. Yet President Jackson is depicted in high school and elementary school textbooks as a "frontiersman, soldier, democrat, man of the people—not Jackson the slaveholder, land speculator, executioner of dissident soldiers, exterminator of Indians" (Zinn 1995, 124–146). In 1820, 120,000 American Indians lived east of the Mississippi and by 1844, fewer than 30,000 remained (Zinn 1995, 124).

As one example of the many acts of Indian resistance, the Florida Seminoles refused to relocate. Under Chief Osceola and joined by hundreds of escaped slaves, a guerrilla campaign known as the Seminole War was launched against Jackson's troops. This resistance and the Indian–African American alliance are little known in U.S. history (Segrest 1994, 201).

Many other U.S. policies and laws contributed to the fate of American Indians. Some of these are described briefly below:

1. The *Reservation System* was invented in the 1870s by James Amasa Walker, who had visited Indian communities once and learned everything he knew from reading James Fenimore Cooper's *The Last of the Mohicans*. Walker believed that the reservation system would give Indians the support they needed for transition. The transition he referred to was that of being removed from their land and the livelihood of hunting and farming. Walker believed that the Indians were like children who needed structure and discipline to succeed and he strongly advocated assimilation (Takaki 1993, 231–232).

2. There were many *treaties* signed by the U.S. government with various Indian tribes. The Treaty of 1851 was with the Cheyenne, Arapaho, Sioux, Crow, and other tribes. It permitted European Americans to establish roads and military posts across Indian territories. Within ten years, wagon trains, stagecoaches, forts, pony-express riders, and telegraph wires had been driven through Indian territories. This was exacerbated by the 1858 gold rush in which thousands of white miners dug for gold on Indian land (Brown 1970, 68).

3. The *Treaty of 1868* guaranteed the Indians absolute and undisturbed use of the Great Sioux Reservation. This could only be changed if three-fourths of the adult males on the reservation agreed. In 1861 Congress had established the U.S. Territory of Dakota for the use of European Americans. This land was virtually the same as the reservation. This treaty became the source of major dispute and conflict between the Sioux and the U.S. government at two critical times in our history.

4. The 1887 *Dawes Act* was another move toward Indian assimilation. This piece of legislation was based on the belief that the Indians had been shortchanged by the reservation system, which displaced them onto nonproductive land. The intent of the Dawes Act was to convert American Indians from their nomadic, tribal, "savage" ways to become individual landowners. It broke up reservations and gave land to some Indian families for twenty-five years and granted them citizenship if they would give up their tribal ways and become "civilized." The Dawes Act also authorized the federal government to seek tribal consent to sell some of the land to whites. This move to individual ownership destroyed a tradition of generosity and sharing for the common good. It was a sacred tradition that people could not "own" land. Indians had no experience of the white economy

and had enormous difficulty adjusting to this new system. "[M]ost of those who tried to adjust to the new system were sooner or later relieved of their land due to innocence, drink, inability to pay off mortgages and taxes, and finally the hard exigencies of starvation. . . ." (Matthiessen 1983, 18).

5. Concurrent to the passage of the Dawes Act was another piece of legislation that granted the right of way to railroads through six Indian reservations. By 1891, Indian land was reduced by 17,400,000 acres. This process continued in 1902 when a new law was passed stating that all land that had been allotted to the Indians could be sold when the original owner died (Takaki 1993, 231–232).

6. By the late 1800s the Lakota (Sioux) were legally forced to *assimilate* into white culture. They were told that they would be jailed if they continued their traditional spiritual ceremonies. They were forbidden to wear Indian clothing or engage in Indian crafts, their language was discouraged (Matthiessen 1993, 21). From 1890 to 1930 many Indian children were forcibly taken to boarding schools where their hair was cut, their language and traditions were forbidden, and they were socialized into white American culture (Segrest 1994, 222).

7. It was not until 1924 that Congress gave full *citizenship* to American Indians (Segrest 1994, 222). The 1934 *Indian Reorganization Act* rescinded the allotment program and gave Indians the right to vote to maintain communal land. It also gave power for economic planning to tribal councils, which established leadership that would ultimately cooperate with corporate and government efforts to gain rights to profitable mining on Indian land (Segrest 1994, 223).

There are two stories that dramatically illustrate the complexities of the past and the present and of conflict and bloodshed and resistance. Ironically, both of these events occurred on the Pine Ridge Reservation at Wounded Knee in South Dakota. These stories are not isolated Indian stories; rather, they are an integral component of American History.

In 1883, Sitting Bull was a strong independent leader of the Sioux who had been jailed in Canada for many years. This was during the time of the Dawes Act in which Indians had become aware that the U.S. government had told many lies to encourage the Sioux to give up their land. U.S. officials were concerned that the release of Sitting Bull could give rise to armed resistance and conflict between the Sioux and U.S. forces and as a result attempted to marginalize him at every opportunity.

But in 1883, the Northern Pacific Railroad celebrated its completion by inviting President Benjamin Harrison and asking Sitting Bull to welcome the president. The old Indian wrote a flowery speech that was read and reviewed by his interpreter. However, when it came time to deliver the speech, Sitting Bull said instead, "I hate all the white people. You are thieves and liars. You have taken away our land and made us outcasts." Since Sitting Bull knew that the interpreter was the only one who could understand him, he smiled and bowed and paused for applause as he spoke (Brown 1970, 426–427).

This act of resistance came just a few short years before Sitting Bull was killed by U.S. troops on the Pine Ridge Reservation, which was followed by the Massacre at Wounded Knee. A bizarre series of events lead to this massacre. In 1890 Kicking Bear came to the Sioux to tell of the Messiah, Wovoka, who had started the religion of the Ghost Dance. The religion was a combination of Christianity and Indian tradition. The belief was that Jesus Christ would return to earth as an Indian and that all dead Indians would live again and all whites would disappear or die. The Ghost Dance spread to almost every reservation and the U.S. army adopted an official policy to stop it (Brown 1970, 431–435).

Indian Bureau agent James McLaughlin wired Washington to send military protection to arrest the Ghost Dancers. It was in the violence that ensued during this arrest that Sitting Bull was killed. The others that were arrested were taken to a camp called Wounded Knee near a frozen creek. There were 120 Indian men and 230 women and children and 500 soldiers. The Indians were ordered to give up their weapons, which they did. But some of the Indians began to resume dancing the Ghost Dance, and the soldiers began to fire. Some of the Indians were killed or wounded by gunfire; some of the wounded froze to death. At the end, some 300 Indians and 25 soldiers were dead (Takaki 1993, 228). This was the last nineteenth-century battle between the U.S. army and American Indians.

Some eighty years later, in the 1970s, another drama unfolded at Wounded Knee Creek on the Pine Ridge Reservation. After the repeal of the land allotment of the Dawes Act, the Bureau of Indian Affairs (BIA) established tribal councils that were largely beholden to the BIA. On Pine Ridge, the tribal council families were mostly biracial (Indian and white) Christians whose administrations were often filled with nepotism and corruption (Matthiessen 1983, 46). Many of these tribal leaders had been assimilated through the process of boarding schools, land allotment, subsequent land deals, and generations of Indian culture being subject to either punishment or ostracism. It is not so much of a stretch to see that this group of corrupt leaders exemplified internalized racism in which misinformation about Indians, negative stereotypes, and hatred became part of their own identity and how they saw the world.

Dick Wilson was tribal president on the Pine Ridge Reservation during the 1970s. Wilson was a heavy drinker who gave tribal jobs to his family and outfitted and armed a special tribal force, "Guardians of the Oglala Nation," known as GOONs (Matthiessen 1983, 62–63).

Parallel to the development of the tribal councils was the development of another Indian organization, the American Indian Movement (AIM). It is important to understand the context of AIM's evolution. During the 1960s and 1970s there were many liberation movements working for individual and collective human rights and equality. There was the civil rights movement, the women's rights movement, the antiwar (Vietnam) movement, and the student rights movement among others. There was much conflict in the United States between these political and social movements on the left that called for drastic change and those on the right that resisted these changes.

It was in this climate of change and conflict that AIM developed a cultural and political agenda. AIM leaders observed the poverty and dependence of both reservation and city Indians and analyzed the historical reasons for this. They became a civil rights organization that focused on jobs, housing, and education, and received funding from President Lyndon Johnson's War on Poverty program. AIM advocated the principle of Indian sovereignty and reclaimed the identity of Indians as warriors. The atmosphere on many reservations and for many city Indians was one of crime and danger, and some AIM members saw this as war and began to carry arms (Matthiessen 1983, 36).

In addition to the delivery of social service programs, AIM began to plan and carry out political demonstrations. In 1970 they occupied Alcatraz to publicize the lack of education, jobs, and housing for Indians. In 1972, AIM participated in the Trail of Broken Treaties march in Washington, D.C., in an effort to improve U.S.–Indian relations.

The U.S. government saw AIM as a threat and took two actions. First, the FBI classified AIM as an extremist organization. Counterintelligence tactics of monitoring and disrupting AIM were carried out through COINTELPRO (the FBI's counterintelligence program). The second government action was to withdraw funding from AIM's programs for education, housing, and employment because of the group's political positions and strategies (Matthiessen 1983, 38–46).

In the meantime there were developments on the Pine Ridge Reservation. The BIA Indian police began to receive training in paramilitary tactics. In 1972, a young Indian from Pine Ridge, Raymond Yellow Thunder was killed by two white men who were charged only with second degree manslaughter. AIM leaders went to Pine Ridge to help organize the people and were able to secure more serious charges against the killers and to have the police chief fired. This earned AIM great respect among the Pine Ridge traditionalists. The U.S. military and the FBI began to provide what appeared to be unusual support for the Tribal Council and police. Later, it emerged that valuable uranium had been found on the reservation and the government was protecting these interests.

In 1973 another young Indian on the Pine Ridge Reservation was killed by a white man, who was subsequently charged with involuntary manslaughter. This time 200 AIM supporters arrived, and the police beat the young man's mother, claiming she had shouted obscenities at them. Police used tear gas on the demonstrating AIM members, who then overturned police cars and set an abandoned building on fire. This was the first outbreak of violence between Indians and white authorities since the Massacre at Wounded Knee in 1890 (Matthiessen 1983, 64).

As a symbolic act, AIM took over the trading post at Wounded Knee, which was soon surrounded by FBI and BIA police. "For seventy-one days, a few hundred men, women, and children—supplied by volunteer airlifts and by sympathizers who slipped in and out during the night—had challenged a large paramilitary force abetted by hundreds of short-haired vigilantes, red and white, who were eager to wipe out the 'long-hair troublemakers.'" Through the course of the occupation there were outbursts of gunfire on both sides; two Indians were killed, and a U.S. marshal was seriously wounded (Matthiessen 1983, 81).

When the siege ended, there was an agreement for AIM leaders to turn themselves in to authorities and for U.S.–Indian negotiations to proceed about two major issues. The first was a commitment to review the 1868 treaty that was to have protected the Pine Ridge Reservation. The government agreed to work with AIM to determine if there were violations of the treaty and to correct any that existed. The government also made a second commitment to investigate the corruption of the BIA and tribal councils. In the end, over 100 Indians who participated in the occupation were indicted, and neither of these issues was agreed upon nor were the issues that they were protesting discussed with the government (Matthiessen 1983, 85).

The nineteenth-century conflict at Wounded Knee was an overwhelming demonstration of U.S. power in which hundreds of unarmed Indians were killed because of the perceived threat represented by the Ghost Dance. In 1890, the Indians willingly gave up their arms and danced the Ghost Dance as a nonviolent symbol of their spiritual beliefs and of resistance. In the twentieth-century conflict at Wounded Knee, AIM and its supporters recognized the combined power of the U.S. forces and their supporters in the Tribal Council. They saw the corruption in the laws that took land from the Pine Ridge Indians and saw that the Tribal Council and its supporters had been co-opted to see their self-interest aligned with the U.S. military and FBI. They looked at Indian history and they saw the conditions under which most reservation and city Indians lived and they chose to be warriors. The circumstances that had plagued American Indians for hundreds of years were present again in the twentieth century at Wounded Knee. This time the ore was uranium instead of gold, the military was the U.S. Army, and the FBI was involved rather than the cavalry. And it was the militant AIM that resisted the government rather than the Ghost Dancers.

One AIM supporter who was inside the trading post spoke of the night she saw her nephew killed by sniper fire: "I remember back on days when they had unarmed our ancestors, killed them and let them freeze to death; there was no mercy for our children, there was no mercy for women. That's the very first thing that had come to my mind during that firefight" (Matthiessen 1983, 81).

As you reflect on these pieces of history, remember that this is not *Indian* history, but United States history. I am not advocating any of the violence that occurred, but rather retelling stories that have often been omitted. How much of this history have you learned as a student? Does this information confirm or contradict what you have already learned? Where were your ancestors and family in 1890 and 1973? What is the history of the land you live on now? Was it transferred from communal Indian guardianship to private ownership? Did you learn about this transfer when you studied your state's history? Who were you taught to see as the "good guys" in the historical violence between Indians and U.S. forces? How does your best independent thinking reconcile what you have learned (or not learned) in the past with the information you have just read?

African Americans

Anyone who has taken social studies or American History in the United States knows something about slavery. Most of the texts and lessons from these classes tell us how wrong slavery was and how it ended with the Civil War. Many of us were taught that Abraham Lincoln was a quintessential American hero who ended slavery with the Emancipation Proclamation.

A few passages from *Compton's Encyclopedia Online* and a sixth grade social studies textbook illustrate the kind of information that students receive about slavery. These passages are standard for much of American education. On closer examination, there are important values and messages encoded by what they directly say, what they imply, and what they omit:

Passage 1: "American blacks are largely the descendants of slaves, people who were brought from African homelands to work for whites in the New World" (*Compton's Encyclopedia Online*, "Black Americans, or African Americans," 1).

Message 1: The passage assumes that slavery was a negative part of American history. But saying that Africans were "brought . . . to work for whites" completely omits the violence of slavery, the dehumanization of a whole group of people, and the painful separation and destruction of families both in Africa and in the United States. It is a simple declaration of "fact" that allows the reader to glide easily over the sentence and the horrors and legacy of this part of our history.

Passage 2: "Black slaves played a major, though unwilling and generally unrewarded, role in laying the economic foundation of the United States, especially in the South" (*Compton's Encyclopedia Online*, "Black Americans, or African Americans," 2).

Message 2: According to the encyclopedia, African Americans were not willing slaves but they were sometimes rewarded for their work. The message here is that their biggest reward was the satisfaction of the knowledge of essential contributions to the development of the U.S. economy. There is no mention of the legacy of enslavement and work without compensation and life without freedom. There is no indication that these two hundred years have had an impact on contemporary African Americans and their access to the rewards of the contemporary U.S. economy.

Passage 3: A sixth grade social studies text says that enslaved Africans were one group of immigrants that did not come to America by choice. This textbook says that by 1808, when importing slaves became illegal, about 700,000 Africans had been brought to America against their will. "Individuals suffered terribly, but as a group they managed to persevere and contribute greatly to the nation" (Bednarz et al. 1997, 660).

Message 3: While the text acknowledges the suffering of slaves, the overriding message is the same as message 2: survival and contribution. What has it meant for African Americans to "persevere" in the United States and how have 200 years of the work and "contributions" of slaves measured up to the rewards of groups that immigrated voluntarily?

Passage 4: In a section of the sixth grade text called "Upholding Our Rights" the focus is on the civil rights provided for in the Constitution for all people. This section indicates that blacks suffered discrimination even 100 years after the Civil War. However, it goes on to say that in the historic case of *Brown v. Board of Education* (in which it was decided that "separate but equal" in education was unconstitutional) the Supreme Court ruled against discrimination. "The civil rights movement of the 1950s and 1960s assured African Americans the rights they were guaranteed under the Constitution" (Bednarz et al. 1997, 663).

Message 4: The message of this excerpt from the text follows logically from the first three messages. Slavery was bad and its legacy continued even after slavery, but *Brown v. Board of Education* and the civil rights movement fixed all of that, and now everything is equal and fine. If you believe this message, you have learned that the injustices of slavery, segregation, and discrimination were fortunately resolved and ended by the Supreme Court and the civil rights movement. Without additional information that supplements and contradicts these glib statements, that is exactly what many Americans believe.

Young students who read these passages and others like them can conclude that slavery was a horrible chapter in U.S. history. But they can also feel relieved at its outcome and be spared disillusion with U.S. justice if they can be led to conclude that not only was slavery eventually abolished, but African Americans were given their rightful entitlements to equality and justice. What are the logical conclusions of thinking and policy that can be drawn from these messages?

According to this line of thinking: All's well that ends well. For many people who receive these messages without intervening experiences or contradicting information, there is a progression that leads to certain conclusions. These conclusions, grounded in partial and distorted information, assert that it is time for blacks to stop complaining about the consequences of slavery and racism and take charge of their lives. This leads to thinking that any failure of African Americans is a failure of individuals, not a failure of racist history, laws, policies, or institutions. This thinking leads to policies that are based on the belief that the playing field is level and there is no longer any necessity for laws or resources to assist African Americans or compensate for past injustices. This logic says that the past is past— it is time to move on for all Americans.

Perhaps you have heard someone say something like this. Or perhaps you have had thoughts like these or agreed with policies that terminate compensation for African Americans. Of course, you are entitled to your own thoughts and politics. What is critical in the assessment of your thoughts and politics about slavery and its relationship to the contemporary situation of African Americans is the availability of informational resources to allow you to arrive at conclusions after careful consideration of history and conditions that may have been omitted from your education.

As you read this section, begin to trace the sources of your thoughts and beliefs and political perspective and join it with your personal experiences with African Americans or as an African American. Carefully observe your thoughts and experience as you take the next journey into American history. "To engage in a serious discussion of race—we need to begin with the flaws of American society rooted in historic inequalities and longstanding cultural stereotypes" (West 1995, 557).

Volumes have been written about slavery in the United States, its impact, and its legacies in the contemporary circumstances of African Americans. This comprehensiveness is beyond the scope of this book. This next section will examine some of the conditions of the slave trade, the impact of slavery on the family, and the legacy of slavery for all Americans.

The Slave Trade

When Africans were captured as slaves, they were pulled from their families and communities and catapulted into intolerable situations. "The marches to the coast, sometimes for 1,000 miles, with people shackled around the neck, under whip and gun, were death marches, in which two of every five blacks died. On the coast they were kept in cages until they were picked and sold. . . . Then they were packed aboard the slave ships, in spaces not much bigger than coffins, chained together in the dark, wet slime on the ship's bottom, choking in the stench of their own excrement" (Zinn 1995, 28). One of three Africans died aboard these ships, but according to the slave traders, there was still profit to be made.

By 1800, 10–15 million Africans had been kidnapped and uprooted from their homes and families and transported to North and South America for the purposes of slavery. While this number of enslaved people is staggering, it is important to remember that it represents only the one-third of Africans who survived the journey on foot to the coasts of Africa and the sea voyage known as the Middle Passage. "It is roughly estimated that Africa lost 50 million human beings to death and slavery in those centuries we call the beginning of modern Western civilization, at the hands of slave traders and plantation owners in Western Europe and America, the countries deemed the most advanced in the world" (Zinn 1995, 29).

How could a country that was considered so advanced take the lead in so insidious a trade that profited from the sale of and indifference to human life? How could a country that was founded by people seeking a life free of religious persecution participate in slavery? The founding documents of the United States—the Declaration of Independence and the Constitution—were based on freedom and equality and yet slavery contradicted all of the basic rights that were guaranteed. How could herding, transporting, selling, and owning human beings for profit possibly be explained?

Such inhumanity cannot have a reasonable explanation that could cause us to say, "Oh yes, now I understand, that's fine." However, understanding what could lead an entire group of people to enslave another entire group of people can give us enormous insight into the strange workings of racism.

The Europeans and Americans who were involved in the slave trade as ship captains and crew, high ranking officials in the trading companies, plantation owners, and small farmers had two things in common. They understood their race as white and as the epitome of humanity, and they understood people with different color skin (American Indians, Africans) as either inferior humans or subhuman. "When these Englishmen met Africans for the first time, one of the most fair-skinned people on the globe came into contact with one of the darkest, a difference reinforced by the existing dichotomy between dark and light in British culture. It led the English to see the Africans as both 'black' and 'heathen' and to link them immediately with barbarity, animalistic behavior and the devil. . . ." (Segrest 1994, 191). Once they made this leap to dehumanize an entire group of people and to see them as fundamentally different, this peculiar and insidious logic could and did lead to the human horror of slavery. Once the steps are taken to see other humans as inferior, all of the potential for racism and subsequent dehumanization and violence becomes possible.

Sometimes Americans ask why it is necessary to study in depth the most horrible and inhuman chapters of our history. There are many reasons for this endeavor. One reason is the intrinsic value of knowing the truth, no matter how grim. Another reason is to analyze and understand the faulty premises that such inhumane logic is based on so that it can never happen again. Still another reason is to see the ways in which constructing groups as the "other"—even through jokes or offhanded comments—can build step by step and brick by brick into monumental and destructive hate that becomes violent racism.

As discussed earlier in the chapter, racism is built on the erroneous assumption that skin color and other physical characteristics can make one group of people superior to another group of people. As we can see in the institution of slavery, racism can be grounded both in individual hatred and in a collective belief in superiority/inferiority that can be institutionalized for hundreds of years. The institutionalized racism that was slavery became embedded in commerce, education, housing, labor, the family, and religion, and has affected the distribution of power, privilege, land, and material goods for over two hundred years. Throughout much of the time that African Americans were enslaved, it was illegal for slaves to learn to read. The institutionalization of slavery impacted the rights to basic human freedom, independence, and privacy.

For 200 years slavery captured the bodies and the minds of African Americans. As slavery continued from generation to generation, the memories of freedom in Africa grew dimmer and more distant. To be considered property and treated as such had a devastating impact on the external and internal lives of slaves. In this atmosphere of unrelenting racism, the messages of inferiority that so many whites believed became the same messages that many blacks internalized and came to believe.

The subhuman physical treatment combined with the internalized belief in one's own deficiencies is crushing of both the body and the spirit.

> The system was psychological and physical at the same time. The slaves were taught discipline, were impressed again and again with the idea of their own

inferiority to "know their place," to see blackness as a sign of subordination, to be awed by the power of the master, to merge their interest with the master's, destroying their own individual needs. To accomplish this there was the discipline of hard labor, the breakup of the slave family, the lulling effect of religion ... the creation of disunity among slaves by separating them into field slaves and the more privileged house slaves, and finally the power of law and immediate power of the overseer to involve whipping, burning, mutilation and death. (Zinn 1995, 35)

In the mid-1600s the plight of black slaves and white indentured servants posed an opportunity for a common cause. In fact, there was evidence of the beginning of alliances along the lines of forced labor and across the color lines. In 1661, Virginia passed a law that increased the years of labor for any white indentured servant who collaborated with or ran away with any black slave (Zinn 1995, 39). In 1676, the Bacon Rebellion occurred, which was an uprising of African slaves and white indentured servants and unemployed workers. To preclude any further alliance across racial lines, colonial rulers began conferring to all European settlers rights that had previously been the exclusive domain of the English (Segrest 1994, 195). In 1680, the Virginia legislature permitted whites to abuse blacks physically with impunity (Takaki 1993, 67).

Ultimately the hierarchy of slavery evolved in such a way that the wealthier plantation owners hired poor white men to serve as overseers of the slaves. While poor southern whites were clearly distinct from black slaves in their freedom and right to their own labor, their conditions of housing, food, and income were often similar and the potential for alliance around class existed. But as long as poor whites could be socialized to see blacks as subhuman and to participate in the lower and middle rungs of overseeing slavery, the opportunities for alliance against a common oppressor were virtually nonexistent.

The Slave Family

One way to understand the impact of slavery is take a closer look at how the slave family was configured structurally and what kind of effect this had on family life. As we consider this information, it is important to remember that there was very little privacy for slaves in America and that the central feature of slavery was that a whole group of people was owned by another group and considered as property. Under this system, there was no understanding that slaves had a right to their families. During this same time period there were laws and social customs that protected white families. No such laws and customs were in place for African Americans.

As early as 1619, the London Company made provisions for young single white women to go to America to become the wives of settlers. At this point in history, women's labor was still considered essential to the family's survival. The nuclear family served as both a source of emotional support and a unit of labor and economics. In their settling of the "New World" white colonists were also encouraged to arrive together and stay together as families (Dill 1995, 237–241). As we learned in Chapter Two, the Industrial Revolution created a split between public and private labor in which, by and large, men worked outside the home and women were in charge of the domestic sphere. While this represents an important historical moment in the continued erosion of the rights of women, nevertheless the nuclear family was still protected by law and by tradition. In fact, white families in the United States were sacrosanct. "Thus, in its founding, American society initiated legal, economic, and social practices designed to promote the growth of family life among European colonists. The reception colonial families found in the United States contrasts sharply with the lack of attention given to the families of racial-ethnics" (Dill 1995, 241).

In contrast, as we also discussed in Chapter Two, one of the ironies of slavery was that it was not affected by the public/private labor division that so deeply influenced the work of men and women and thus that of family life for whites. There were few distinctions between the work of black men and women during slavery. This carried over into the limited domestic life, in which work was shared and rarely distributed along gender lines (Davis 1981, 18).

Forced labor was always at the center of slavery and black families during slavery. But when the international slave trade was prohibited in 1807, the only way to increase the number of slaves was to increase the number of offspring. Thus, another essential form of labor for black women became their reproductive labor. For slaves, reproduction was not like that of wealthy whites, whose purpose was primarily that of creating their own family and heirs. Nor was it similar to poor white families, who sometimes desired more children so they could increase their family's labor production and income. Rather, as with other aspects of their lives, slaves had no control over the creation of their own families. Reproduction was encouraged and insisted upon by slave owners in order to increase productivity and profits of the white family that owned the slaves (Dill 1995, 237–241).

While there were marriages among slaves, the organization and maintenance of the family was completely in the power of the white slave owner. Thirty-two percent of slave marriages were disrupted by the sale of one of the partners. African kinship practices, which extended central familial bonds beyond the nuclear family, became critical for the survival of families during slavery (Dill 1995, 246).

Another tragic irony of the family in slavery involves the gender norms that white society established during and after the Industrial Revolution. By these norms, the "good" man was the breadwinner and the "good" woman guarded the hearth. While clearly this system and its standards was based on female subordination, it provided white men with the rewards and resources of a patriarchal society. These privileges involved respect, access to jobs, access to political and economic power, and so forth.

None of this entitlement to respect or resources for white men was afforded to black men. The black man in slavery was not the breadwinner. In fact, the slave owners emphasized the mother–child relationship because it was the main source of labor (Dill 1995, 242). Within this context, the near egalitarian work relationship between black men and women was extraordinary. Yet ironically, according to what was valued by white society at the time, it was another example of the degradation of slaves.

"In addition to the lack of authority and economic authority experienced by the husband-father in the slave family, use of the rape of women slaves as a weapon of terror and control further undermined the integrity of the slave family" (Dill 1995, 242). The "one drop" rule established that any person with any percentage of black blood would be considered black and part of the "subordinate race." "This practice allowed plantation masters to have sexual access to Black women without jeopardizing the inheritance of white children; it also ensured that 'whites' would remain relatively 'pure,' while 'Blacks' became increasingly hybrid" (Segrest 1994, 193).

Remember that Africans were pulled violently from their homes and torn from their nuclear families and extended kinship networks. None of their familial ties or relationships were recognized or honored during slavery. There were no laws that held black families together, nor were there any of the traditions that honored white nuclear families. Men could not be breadwinners, and women could not stay home to raise the children. Men could not protect their wives and children from rape and abuse, and women could not protect their husbands or children from abuse or sale. These were the circumstances of the black family for two hundred years.

Contemporary Conditions for African Americans

In what way and to what degree does the legacy of slavery impact the contemporary lives of African Americans? After slavery, southern black labor revolved primarily around share-cropping and debt peonage. For the most part, blacks were shut out of labor unions, which were the source of the best working class jobs. Supreme Court rulings between 1873 and 1893 culminated with *Plessy v. Ferguson,* which established the separate but equal rule, the foundation of racial segregation in public schools. Racist violence escalated between 1882 and 1930. During this time there were 2,060 lynchings of blacks (Segrest 1994, 208–9). "By the turn of the century, the South was in the throes of a resurgent white supremacy" (Segrest 1994, 210). Southern legislators enacted segregation laws, prohibitive poll taxes for black voters, and other measures that ushered in the era of Jim Crow that was separate but anything but equal.

There are many indices in which the disparity between blacks and whites continues to be wide. These include housing, employment, health care, income, and education. Tracing some of the developments and consequences in education will provide one example of the legacies of slavery.

It is commonly taught in schools and widely known that the 1954 Supreme Court decision *Brown v. Board of Education* legally ended the law of separate but equal schools that was established in *Plessy v. Ferguson.* The belief embedded in this decision was that black children's education had not been equal to that received by white children and that integration in the schools was an essential step to remedy to inferior education.

According to one study, school desegregation has merely diminished isolation. Two-thirds of all African American students attend schools that are predominantly attended by students of color, particularly in isolated urban districts and areas with high concentrations of poverty. De facto racial isolation remains strong in U.S. schools and when combined with poverty continues to produce inferior educational opportunities for African Americans and other children of color.

Even in more integrated schools, in many instances children are resegregated through tracking at the classroom level (Mickelson and Smith 1995, 291). In the district where my children attend school, the racial population in the middle school is approximately 85 percent black and 15 percent white. When my daughter was in eighth grade, she was a student in a gifted reading program and an advanced math program. In the advanced math program there was one African American student and fourteen white students, and in the gifted reading program there were five African American students and twelve white students. The percentage of white students in these advanced classes has been consistently more than five times their percentage of the student population.

While many school districts have been legally forced to desegregate, most U.S. districts continue to be organized residentially according to neighborhoods and larger communities. Since most U.S. neighborhoods continue to be racially segregated, most neighborhood schools continue to be segregated as well. Studies demonstrate that white residents will stay in a neighborhood and some new white residents may move in if the black population does not exceed 8 percent of the neighborhood. But when the black population reaches 10–20 percent, the white population begins to move—even if the black residents have the same economic and social standing as the white residents (Hacker 1992, 37–38).

Those African Americans who attend college find that their earning potential is still affected by their race. Black men and women who attend one to three years of college earn $825 to white men and women's $1,000. Black men with college degrees end up just a few dollars ahead of white men with high school diplomas (Hacker 1992, 96).

Despite the lingering racial inequities in U.S. education, the African American community still supports public education. Seventy-six percent of blacks (as compared to 57 percent of whites) are likely to support increased government spending on schools (Feagin and Sikes 1994, 80). Black voters generally support school tax increases even when the black population's income is lower than that of the white population and will be more deeply impacted by tax hikes.

Discrimination and differential treatment by race often intersects with class. As we have noted, most schools whose populations are predominantly students of color are in lower income areas. These schools have lower tax bases and fewer resources. But what of middle class black children in middle class neighborhoods and schools? While they tend to fare better than their lower income counterparts, several studies show that black children in desegregated schools are more likely to be punished than white students and treated differently by white authorities. "At the heart of what Gunnar Myrdal called 'the American dilemma' is the contradiction between white American ideals and the reality of discriminatory actions. Black children often learn about this contradiction at an early age. In desegregated schools black children are taught 'The Star-Spangled Banner' and Pledge of Allegiance along with white children, and they read many stories about freedom, liberty, and justice. But degrading experiences with whites in the same schools doubtless raise serious questions about the meaning of these ideals" (Feagin and Sikes 1994, 91).

These same messages that are learned by African American children are also learned by white and Latino and Asian American and American Indian children. Differential treatment according to race contradicts the history lessons children learn about democracy and the American values of justice and equality. These contradictions are devastating to the psyches of children. Despite what young people may learn in the classroom about American justice and racial equality, if the treatment by the school does not reflect equality, the primary lesson learned is one of confusion, disappointment, cynicism, and/or hypocrisy.

How does this educational picture fit together with the legacies of slavery? Remember that throughout much of slavery, it was illegal for slaves to learn to read. Slave children did not have the same right to public education as white children. While many people defied this law, nevertheless there were two hundred years of the denial of formal education for African Americans. The absence of education is clearly not the same as inferior education. This was followed by another 60–80 years of legal segregation in housing and education. This segregation was not based on what lawmakers or voters thought was best for black children, but rather what white legislators and judges and parents thought was in the interest of white children. These laws were based on the construct of race, the misinformation that whites are superior to blacks and therefore they should not be schooled together. We have had barely fifty years of court-ordered school desegregation, yet the data show that the law in action has not eliminated school segregation or unequal treatment of black and white students, nor has it eliminated racism.

Our ability to understand how racism operates in education is central to moving toward a democratic society in which equality is substantive, not mythical and illusive. The legacy of slavery and segregation has created an institution characterized by self-perpetuating institutional racism. No superintendent or principal or teacher need take overtly racist action or make an openly racist remark in order to perpetuate this system. Rather, in order to make substantive changes, our history has taught us that it will require resistance and organization to reverse the lingering legacy of slavery and racism.

The fact of over 200 years of denial of education followed by so-called separate but equal education followed by only fifty years of court-ordered desegregation has a whole set of consequences. For example, since whites were accepted in medical schools for over one hundred years longer than African Americans, this means that in some white families there are many generations of doctors that may include mentors, resources, and a built-in medical practice waiting for the new physician—a set of advantages not typically available to most African Americans. African Americans who are in their forties and fifties and older still have strong memories of their experiences in segregated schools. These are the same segregated schools that were legally found to have provided unequal education for black children. The individuals who attended these schools received weaker education in writing, science, math, and so on. This has impacted their ability to attend and be successful in college and in the job market. By and large, *this does not reflect the personal difficulties or problems of the individual students.* Rather, the experiences of these individuals reflect the structural inequalities built into U.S. educational history for over 200 years. This does not mean individuals do not bear responsibility for studying hard in school. But it does mean that in the big picture of race in education there are institutional and historical reasons for differences in achievement.

It is true that many of us learned about *Plessy v. Ferguson* and *Brown v. Board of Education;* but that is often where the information we received in school stopped. Many of us learned that *Brown* and the civil rights movement "fixed" racism in the schools and that we now have a level playing field racially. As you consider what you learned in school and came to believe about African Americans, think about what policies that would lead you to now. Based on the belief that schools equally educate all students, how would you evaluate racial differences in academic achievement? Based on a belief that all is now equal, would you be for or against affirmative action? Would you be for or against educational programs that assist black children in public schools or black students in college? Would you call these programs preferential treatment or reparation?

Now consider the information you have just read about the current consequences of unequal education for African Americans and the continued inequality. Given this information and the belief that it is still not a level playing field for African Americans, what policies would you support? Would you be for or against affirmative action? Would you be for or against programs that assist black children in public schools or black students in college? Would you call these programs preferential treatment or reparation?

Contemporary high school U.S. history books have become increasingly strong in their in-depth study of the horrors of slavery and its impact on African Americans. However, a review of twelve history textbooks indicates that there is virtually nothing included about the role of European Americans and slavery's impact on whites. None of these textbooks makes the connection between racism and slavery, nor does any of them address white complicity; in fact there is the sense that slavery is "uncaused." We are in a relatively safe position to study the inhumanity of slavery because it is over. But the legacies of oppression and cultural racism continue (Loewen 1995, 142–143).

"To function adequately in civic life in our troubled times, students must learn what causes racism. Although it is a complicated historical issue, racism in the Western world stems primarily from two related historical processes: taking land from and destroying indigenous people and enslaving Africans to work that land. To teach this relationship, textbooks would have to show students the dynamic interplay between slavery as a socioeconomic system and racism as an idea system" (Loewen 1995, 143). To oversimplify slavery and its legacies is a disservice to students and is another way that distortions and misinformation about racism continue. If we do not know what happened and why, if we do not know what some people of all races did to try to end slavery and racism, and if we do not know what impact slavery and racism have today, then the beliefs we have and the decisions we make will be made on a wobbly foundation built from partial truths.

We have traced the legacies of slavery with regard to education. We could do parallel historical reviews and analyses of housing, employment, health care, and more. Ultimately, as you weigh what you have learned in the past and the information in this section, it will be your thoughtful and independent decision as to how you will make sense of it all and determine your own understanding and beliefs.

Latinos/Latinas or Hispanics

The current U.S. census lists five races: (1) white; (2) black or African American; (3) Asian or Pacific Islander; (4) American Indian, Eskimo, or Aleutian; and (5) one of two ethnicities—Hispanic or non-Hispanic. According to this categorization, Hispanics (or Latinos) can also identify as white, black, Asian, and so forth. Technically, the United States defines the term Hispanic as an ethnicity rather than a race, but the experience of Latino groups in the United States is more consistent with racial groups that have been treated differently than whites and are often characterized as the "other." The history of Latinos in the United States is often inaccessible and invisible.

Latinos are the second largest community of color and at 25 million are expected to grow larger than the African American population in the early twenty-first century. While each immigrant group has a distinct history with and in the United States, there are some commonalities. Researchers have found that Latinos tend to be more family oriented than white Americans, as demonstrated by emotional and material support provided by the family, a sense of obligation to support one's family, and the central role of the family (rather than peers) as a reference point. As an example of this difference, white U.S. teens cited independence and personal accomplishment as the main reasons to seek achievement in school, while Latino teens said that their main reason to succeed academically was to be able to support their families.

This kind of research into cultural norms has significant policy implications, particularly in public education. A program created for Latino students in a large urban high school used a simulated family setting to develop a sense of collective academic responsibility and significantly reduced the dropout rate and increased the college attendance rate among the Latino population (Tatum 1997, 137–138).

Another shared issue among Latinos is that of a common first or second language, Spanish. This, too, has public policy implications. In the Southwest and on the west coast of the United States where there are large Latino populations, bilingual education has become a lightning rod for anything from English ethnocentrism to cultural pride for Spanish-speaking communities. Part of the conservative backlash in the 1980s involved efforts to dismantle bilingual education based on the rationale that to refuse to assimilate to English was un-American.

Some studies have indicated that language is an integral component of a child's developing identity. If Spanish is a child's first language and it is rejected in school and in the larger English-speaking community, it can seriously damage a child's positive self-identity. In fact, it has been demonstrated that the more proficient a child is in his or her original language, the more likely he or she is to develop English-language proficiency. "Students who are encouraged to maintain their Spanish are able to maintain close family ties through their shared use of language and their parents feel more comfortable with the school environment, increasing the likelihood of parental involvement at school . . . bilingual language alone cannot completely reverse the history of school failure that Latino students have experienced. But it does challenge the alienating and emotionally disruptive idea that native language and culture need to be forgotten in order to be successful" (Tatum 1997, 143). This kind of information has enormous meaning for the development of policies that affect Latino communities

There are many examples of the exclusion of Latino culture and history. In a recent visit to Central Florida, I learned that Orlando is a multiracial community with diverse populations that are white, black, Latino (largely Cuban American and Puerto Rican), and Asian American (Chinese American, Vietnamese, and Indian). Despite this rich multiracial population, a 1970s court-mandated diversity curriculum omits any reference to history or issues facing Asian Americans or Latinos. A history of Central Florida published by the Orlando Historical Society and the daily newspaper in Orlando makes no mention of Asian or Latino immigrants nor their contribution to or treatment in Central Florida.

Some civics and history texts include mention of the history of Spanish speaking peoples in the United States, but they are often distorted. In the sixth grade textbook *We the People Discover Our Heritage,* there is a section regarding new immigrants and one mention of Latinos, "Some immigrants traveled from Mexico for economic opportunity and to escape political unrest there" (Bednarz et al. 1997, 661). An eighth grade civics textbook makes little reference to Latinos. It discusses U.S. expansion into Spanish-speaking territory: "As our nation expanded in the 1800s, it added areas that had been settled mostly by Spaniards, and later by people from Mexico, then a Spanish colony. The inhabitants of these regions—the present-day states of Florida, Louisiana, Texas, Arizona, New Mexico and California—became American citizens." The same text also refers to recent immigrants from Spanish-speaking countries in the following way, "Fleeing revolutions and political persecution at home they have come seeking better jobs and lives for themselves and their families" (Davis and Fernlund 1996, 11).

Assuming that this information is somewhat standard for social studies textbooks, let us examine what we have been told and what we may have learned. The first piece of information is that there were regions that are currently part of the United States that were once Spanish or Mexican. The passages from these texts imply that there was a smooth transition in which the Spanish or Mexicans became American citizens. We also are told that many Mexicans and other Spanish-speaking immigrants have continued to come to the United States to seek a better life than they had in their countries of origin. We are told of no historical or cultural distinctions between different Latino groups. Since we receive no further information, it is implicit that this search for a better life has been successful.

What has been omitted from these brief passages? What significant elements of history are overlooked? Review the questions listed below to see what you have been taught about Latinos in U.S. history:

- Under what circumstances were the Spanish or Mexican territories (now the states of Florida, Louisiana, Texas, Arizona, New Mexico, and California) annexed? Were there treaties, sales, compromises, wars, violence?
- What are the largest Latino populations in the United States? How are their histories of immigration, acceptance, and/or discrimination similar or different?
- What laws have affected the citizenship and treatment of Latinos in the United States?
- What are the current conditions in education, employment, housing, and health care for Latinos in the United States?

As we begin to consider the answers to some of these questions, think about what you have been taught, what has been omitted, and what partial truths or distortions you may have learned. Consider that the information omitted is not simply a reflection of incomplete education but rather an element in our socialization process. If you are Latino or live in an area with a substantial Latino community, you may have some additional information about Latino history and culture. However, if, like me, you grew up in a place with a very small Latino population, these tidbits of history taught in school (with some media thrown in here or there) may be your only source of information.

Mexican Americans or Chicanos

"[T]he nation's Latino barrios reflect a history of conquest, immigration, and a struggle to maintain cultural identity" (Moore and Pinderhughes 1995, 227). Cherie Moraga, a woman who identifies as Chicana (Mexican American) tells the personal story of how her family conveyed to her how much better it is to be light-skinned than dark-skinned in order to succeed in the United States: [T]o her [Moraga's mother], on a basic economic level, being Chicana meant being 'less.' It was through my mother's desire to protect her children from poverty and illiteracy that we became 'anglocized,' the more effectively we could pass in the white world, the better guaranteed our future" (Moraga 1995, 60). This is another powerful example of internalized racism in which the messages of inferiority are so potent that some people are convinced that the only way to survive is to deny their heritage, culture, and race—to try to appear white.

What was it in her personal experience or cultural history that would prod Moraga's mother to deny her heritage and encourage her children to identify as white? How have Mexican Americans and other Latino groups fared in the United States?

As of the 1990 census there were 22 million Latinos in the United States, 9 percent of the total population. Of these 22 million, 61 percent were Mexican, 12 percent Puerto Rican, 5 percent Cuban, and the remainder from Central and South America and other Spanish speaking countries. This population had increased by 53 percent from 1980 (Moore and Pinderhughes 1995, 227). We will examine some of the hidden history and contemporary conditions for Mexican Americans, Cuban Americans, and Puerto Ricans in order to broaden the base of what we understand as U.S. history.

It is important to recognize that the annexation of Texas from Mexico was not done on a handshake or a signing on the dotted line by U.S. and Mexican officials. It was not simply a land deal; it involved war and the loss of Mexican and U.S. lives. The connection between the annexation of Texas and slavery are little known, yet are nevertheless profound elements of our history.

In 1830, the Mexican government made slavery illegal and prohibited U.S. immigration into Mexico. Americans living in the Texas part of Mexico were slave owners and furious at these new Mexican laws. Americans continued to illegally cross into Mexican Texas until by 1835 their numbers were 20,000 compared to 4,000 Mexicans (Takaki 1993, 173–74). There is a certain irony to this information as by the twentieth and twenty-first centuries the issue of illegal immigration from Mexico to the United States has become quite controversial.

In 1846 Congress declared war on Mexico by using some border conflicts as justification. Many Congressmen had already determined that war with Mexico would be necessary in order to take over Texas. "[T]he Mexican War (1846–48), was again driven chiefly by Southern planters wanting to push the borders of the nearest free land farther from the slave states" (Loewen 1995, 150–51). While the majority of Congress voted for this declaration of war, there were strong clear voices for peace. These peace activists believed that the annexation of Texas was oppressive in two ways: first, in the killing of Mexicans for land, and second, in that the attempted annexation of Texas was an effort to extend slavery. Henry David Thoreau and Frederick Douglass refused to pay taxes to support the war. Horace Greeley, publisher and editor of the *New York Tribune*, wrote, "Who believes that a score of victories over Mexico, the 'annexation' of half her provinces, will give us more Liberty, a purer Morality, a more prosperous industry, than we now have?" (Zinn 1995, 154–157).

The U.S. victory and treaty that followed the war allowed thousands of Mexicans to remain in what became the United States. Initially, Mexicans were allowed to vote in both California and Texas. But by the 1890s in Texas, the legislature instituted the poll tax to disenfranchise Mexicans as well as blacks (Takaki 1993, 178–79).

Many of us were taught about the philosophy of Manifest Destiny. We learned that the United States was "destined" to expand from east to west in North America and as far north and south as they could. But Manifest Destiny had an enormous impact on the communities and people, primarily Mexicans and Indians, who already lived where the United States was intending or "destined" to go. "The doctrine of 'manifest destiny' embraced a belief in American Anglo-Saxon superiority—the expansion of Jefferson's homogeneous republic and Franklin's American of the 'the lovely white,' . . . Mexicans within this border were alienated, forced into becoming aliens in land that was once theirs, moving from being landholders to laborers" (Takaki 1993, 176). Manifest Destiny was a clear example of institutional racism in which the official policies and practices were based on the misinformed belief of white superiority.

Subsequent migration laws for Mexicans to the United States were dependent on the vacillating U.S. need for cheap labor. In the great migration of the early 1900s, many Mexicans came to the United States to escape the revolution and economic hardship and were predominantly young laborers. By 1918, 70 percent of Chicanos in Los Angeles were unskilled blue collar workers locked into the same low paying jobs from generation to generation.

The conditions in California and Texas prompted many Mexicans to move to the Midwest and to eastern cities where they worked in factories. In these new industrial locations, many Mexicans were recruited for factory work in order to drive the cost of labor down. Still others migrated to follow the crops; living in migrant camps in wretched housing and conditions (Takaki 1993, 324).

> Racial etiquette defined proper demeanor and behavior for Mexicans. In the presence of Anglos, they were expected to assume "a deferential body posture and respectful voice tone." They knew that public buildings were considered "Anglo territory," and they were permitted to shop in the Anglo business section of town only on Saturdays. They could patronize Anglo cafes, but only the counter and carry-out service. Schools were segregated. In Texas the schools were explicitly designed to keep Mexicans in their place as laborers. A Texas superintendent said, "You have doubtless heard that ignorance is bliss; it seems that is so when one has to transplant onions. . . . If a man has very much sense or education either, he is not going to stick to this kind of work. So you see, it is up to the white population to keep the Mexican on his knees in an onion patch." (Takaki 1993, 326)

In the 1900s, the large influx of Mexican immigrants to the United States created a racist backlash. The *New York Times* and the president of Harvard were among those pushing for Mexican exclusion from the United States. The AFL joined this movement because they believed that the influx of Mexicans was forcing wages into a downward spiral. Ultimately, 400,000 Mexicans were sent back to Mexico (Takaki 1993, 343).

The history of conquest, colonization, and relegation to second class citizenry has had far-reaching consequences for Mexican Americans. Even by the late twentieth century only 45 percent of Mexican Americans aged twenty-five or older had completed high school and 26 percent lived below the federal poverty line (Tatum 1997, 134).

Traditional Mexican family life relied heavily on the extended family. The rural, agricultural life that most Mexican families led was disrupted by war and a new set of laws and conditions of labor. While the 1848 Treaty of Guadalupe provided citizenship for Mexican Americans in the Southwest, it also displaced them from their land and forced them into a colonized labor force. The work that Mexican Americans found on the railroads and in the mines required the separation of families both through the nature of the work and the deaths that the work caused. For these reasons the number of female-headed households and the labor of women and children skyrocketed in the Mexican American community. Spanish was important to the integrity of the culture, but by 1880 there was enormous pressure for English-only public schools (Dill 1995, 249).

These are just a few stories of Mexican Americans and U.S. history. These stories examine the way in which the United States conquered Mexican territory and took control of the conquered people through war. Take another look at the questions that were asked at the beginning of this section: Under what circumstances were parts of Mexico annexed to the United States and what impact did this have on the people who lived there? What laws (immigration), policies (English-only education, poll taxes, etc.), and practices (employment in low-paying jobs) have affected Mexican Americans in the past and the present? Ultimately, how did the United States designate Mexican Americans as the "other" and thus justify discrimination?

Contemporary problems for Mexican Americans, including high levels of poverty and marginal employment, are based on structural and institutional discrimination that evolved from the bloody Mexican War in which the United States conquered and acquired part of Mexico over 150 years ago. The few sentences we learn in our history classes omit the devastating impact that Manifest Destiny, the 1846 war, the treatment of a conquered people, and subsequent policies had on the lives of real people. Most of us never learn that the impetus for Mexican War was intimately linked to slavery.

Let us take a second look at one of the quotes from a U.S. history book: "As our nation expanded in the 1800s, it added areas that had been settled mostly by Spaniards, and later by people from Mexico, then a Spanish colony. The inhabitants of these regions—the present-day states of Florida, Louisiana, Texas, Arizona, New Mexico and California—became American citizens." This quote literally whitewashes the long-lasting consequences triggered by our nation's "expansion" and gives the students who read this the impression that all was and is well in the transition from Mexican territory and citizenship to U.S. territory and citizenship.

As a student, it is easy to glide over these words in a textbook. It sounds like the issue is about land and property—not about real people. It makes it seem that this so-called expansion was natural and good and right. We are not guided to question this part of history or to look at the role that slavery played in the Mexican War or to consider the human costs of the patriotically depicted policy of Manifest Destiny. There are hidden lessons for all of us when history involving conquest and racism is depicted as progress and as a process that is almost organic in its development.

The misinformation and oversimplification that passes as history reinforce the subtle way that hegemony works to perpetuate a system that we are taught to believe is based solely on individual merit. Without a critical understanding of this part of our history, whether we are Latino or any other race, we will believe that economic success and academic achievement are based exclusively on our own hard work. We will also believe the obverse—that poverty and lower academic achievement are exclusively the results of our own failure. This thinking has pro-found effects on our sense of self, our beliefs about who is smart and successful and who is not, and on policies created by the government and businesses.

> How people think about the past is an important part of their consciousness. If members of the elite come to think that their privilege was historically justified and earned, it will be hard to persuade them to yield opportunity to others. If members of deprived groups come to think that their deprivation is their own fault, then there will be no need to use force or violence to keep them in their places. (Zinn 1995, 187)

Puerto Ricans

Puerto Rican immigration began in 1898 when the United States took possession of both Puerto Rico and Cuba during the Spanish American War. Puerto Rico became a commonwealth of the United States in 1952 and thereafter Puerto Ricans were automatically citizens of the U.S, not by choice but by conquest. The U.S. takeover of Puerto Rico had consequences for the island. "As a result of the U.S. invasion, the island's economy was transformed from a diversified, subsistence economy which emphasized tobacco, cattle, coffee, and sugar, to a one-crop sugar economy, of which more than 60 percent was controlled by absentee U.S. owners" (Moore and Pinderhughes 1995, 228).

Another consequence of Puerto Rico's status as a U.S. territory was the U.S. insistence on replacing Spanish with English in Puerto Rican schools. This policy, similar to the English-only policy in the newly conquered Mexican territories, was actively opposed by Puerto Rican students and teachers. In 1917, Congress passed the Jones Act, which required citizenship and military service for Puerto Ricans but denied the right to vote in national elections. In 1951, Puerto Ricans voted to become a commonwealth, which gave them more independence and control in the schools and restored Spanish as the language of instruction (Tatum 1997, 134–35).

From 1900 to 1945 the first wave of Puerto Rican immigration to the mainland was largely to New York. The second wave, from 1946 to 1964, found Puerto Ricans settling in other U.S. cities. What both waves of immigration had in common was a concentration of Puerto Ricans in low-skilled and low-paid jobs in urban areas. Of all Latino groups, Puerto Rican poverty in the continental United States is the greatest with almost 60 percent of the community below the federal poverty lines and 53 percent of Puerto Rican adults who have not graduated from high school (Tatum 1997, 135).

Cuban Americans

The pattern of Cuban immigration to the United States has been different from that of Mexican and Puerto Rican immigration. While the United States fought wars to annex Mexico and colonize Puerto Rico, Cuba became independent in 1902. The first wave of Cuban immigration to the United States occurred during the first days of the 1959 Fidel Castro revolution. These immigrants were predominantly lighter skinned, educated, wealthy professionals and business people who settled in Florida and New York and were welcomed by the U.S. government as political refugees.

The second wave of Cuban immigrants came to the United States within a few months of the Castro revolution, and these immigrants were middle income professionals and skilled workers. They, too, received U.S. government welcome and support.

But the third wave of Cuban immigrants was significantly different from the first two groups. They arrived beginning in 1980 having lived much of their lives in postcapitalist Cuba. As a group they were darker skinned, less educated and lower income (Tatum 1997, 136). This group was not embraced by the U.S. government in the same way as the first two waves of Cuban immigrants. Despite the fact that Cuban Americans have the highest family income of all Latino groups, in the 1990 census their poverty rate was still 16.9 percent (Moore and Pinderhughes 1995, 230).

As you examine these brief histories of various Latino groups, recall the questions you were asked to consider at the outset:

- Under what circumstances were the Spanish or Mexican territories (now the states of Florida, Louisiana, Texas, Arizona, New Mexico, and California) annexed? Were there treaties, sales, compromises? Was there war or violence?
- What are the largest Latino populations in the United States? How are their histories of immigration, acceptance, and/or discrimination similar or different?
- What laws, policies, and practices have affected the citizenship and treatment of Latinos in the United States?

- What are the current conditions in education, employment, housing, and health care for Latinos in the United States?

Are your answers different or the same after reading this material? As you consider that the current overall poverty rate for Latinos is 28 percent, do you find historical and structural reasons for these problems? Finally, as you reach for your own independent thinking and conclusions on the impact of war, conquest, language, and discrimination on Latinos, how do you now regard what you have been taught about this component of American history and culture?

Asian Americans

In the documentary film *Skin Deep,* a multiracial group of college students is brought together to discuss their experiences, beliefs, socialization, and hurt around race. In one segment of the film, students meet together in racial affiliation groups in which they discuss their experiences of discrimination among themselves and then proceed to share with the entire group what it is like to be the race they are. The report out of the Asian group was powerful. These students discussed the personal pressure they felt regarding the stereotype of Asians as the "model minority" in the United States. They stood together holding hands and told their peers that they wanted them to remember how many different countries they were from—China, Japan, Vietnam, India, Thailand, the Philippines, Sri Lanka, and so forth. One young man told of an elementary school experience in which he had had a crush on a little girl who was white. When she wrote in his yearbook, she told him that he was nice for an "ugly person." This same young man, whose name was Khan, told his peers, "I want you to remember my name" (Reid 1995).

As these students poignantly ask us to remember, Asian Americans come from many places and have many different histories, cultures, and experiences in the United States. The U.S. government includes in its definition of Asian, people from East Asia (e.g., Chinese, Japanese, Korean), from Southeast Asia (e.g., Vietnamese, Laotian, Burmese), from the Pacific Islands (e.g., Filipino, Samoan, Guamanian, Fijiian), from South Asia (e.g., Indian, Pakistani, Nepali), from West Asia (Iranian, Afghani, Turkish), and from the Middle East (e.g., Iraqi, Jordanian, Palestinian). The largest Asian American groups in the United States in the 1990s were Chinese (23 percent), Filipino (19 percent), Japanese (12 percent), Asian Indian (11 percent), Korean (11 percent), and Vietnamese (9 percent).

For now, our focus will be primarily on the immigration, history, and treatment of the Chinese, the Japanese, and the more recent immigrants, the Vietnamese. With the passage of the 1965 Immigration Act the flow of Asian immigrants increased to make Asians the fastest growing ethnic group in the United States. As the distinctions in these cultures and histories become increasingly clear, it will be important to keep in mind the myth of Asians as the so-called model minority, which cuts across various immigrant groups.

While various Asian immigrant groups have had distinct experiences as they have come to the United States, there are some common features as well. There are at least three U.S. policies and attitudes that have affected most Asian immigrants. First, the United States has typically been ambivalent about Asian labor. This has been reflected in U.S. immigration policy as well as discrimination toward Asian immigrants. "The simultaneous necessity and undesirability of Asian immigrant labor is a crucial political economic contradiction that informs much of the past and present experience of Asians in the United States" (Hamamoto 1994, 1).

Second, early Asian immigrant groups of the nineteenth century, Chinese and Japanese in particular, were targeted as the "yellow peril." Chinese immigrants were charged with being debased and clannish while Japanese immigrants were seen as loyal to the emperor of Japan, thus disloyal to the United States. Ironically, the third common experience has been the ambivalence in the late twentieth century of being held up as the minority group that has "made it" and achieved the American Dream.

As you will see below, there are vast distinctions between the immigration experiences and economic success of various Asian groups. While census data report that Asian American families have higher median family incomes than any other family group, significant information is often overlooked in this aggregate statistic. Asian Americans have more adults contributing to household income than whites, for example. This also breaks down according to specific countries of origin and immigration experiences. More than 25 percent of Vietnamese Americans, 35 percent of Laotians, and 43 percent of Cambodians live in poverty. While the overall Asian American high school completion rate is 82 percent, it is 35 percent for Cambodians, 36 percent for Laotians, and 58 percent for Vietnamese (Tatum 1997, 161).

Yet the concept of the model minority is monolithic. This myth has often been used as "proof" that there is no racism in the United States and that some groups just have what it takes to succeed and others do not. This fallacy not only ignores the different immigration experiences of Asians but blatantly denies the distinction between and legacies of voluntary immigrants (Chinese, Japanese), refugees (Vietnamese, Thai), slaves (Africans), and conquered peoples (American Indians, Mexicans). In order to begin to unravel some of this and explore the various myths and omissions about Asian Americans, we will examine some of the stories of Chinese Americans, Vietnamese Americans, and Japanese Americans. As we explore these immigration experiences, it is important to remember that this is not Asian history but U.S. history.

Chinese Americans

In the 1860s a Chinese laborer could earn $3–$5 a month in China and $30 a month in California working on the railroad or in the gold mines. Chinese men came to the United States of their own accord, borrowing money from brokers to cover their transportation. Race discrimination began to be widespread toward the Chinese, often forcing them out of the employment they came for and into self-employment. Many Chinese laborers found a niche in the development of laundries. This was not a trade that was learned in China but one learned for survival mechanism in a needed service with a low overhead (Takaki 1993, 193–202).

In 1854, a Chinese man was murdered, and the suspect was white. In the initial trial, the suspect was convicted on the basis of testimony by two Chinese witnesses. The conviction was later overturned when the higher court determined that no one who was nonwhite would be allowed to testify against a white person (Takaki 1993, 229). By 1882, Congress had passed a law that prohibited further Chinese immigration and prohibited any current Chinese citizens from becoming American citizens. Asian Americans are often stereotyped as passive, but during this period of history many Chinese immigrants fought for their civil rights in court (Takaki 1993, 206).

In previous sections regarding African Americans, American Indians, and Latinos we analyzed the impact of U.S. laws and informal treatment on the development and disruption of families. For Chinese immigrants, both Chinese culture and American policy made it almost impossible for Chinese women or families to come to America. The Page Law of 1875 restricted the number of female Chinese immigrants and in 1882 the Chinese Exclusion Law created a total ban. It was not until the late 1960s that miscegenation laws prohibiting the marriage of Chinese Americans and European Americans were lifted. For most Chinese men, it was their full intent to earn enough money to return to China to reunite with and support their families in their home villages. But in the meantime, this created a culture of Chinese bachelors, which in turn created a culture of prostitutes and a double life for these laborers. It was a full century after Chinese immigration began that children began to be born to these immigrants (Dill 1995, 247–48). And it was not until 1952 that the McCarran-Walter Act finally made it legal for Asians to become citizens (Segrest 1994, 222–23).

European Americans used the concept of Manifest Destiny as justification for U.S. aggression and violence. It was widely believed that these white Americans were preordained to be the trailblazers and the beneficiaries of westward expansion. This idea not only devastated the lives of American Indians and Mexicans, but it also obscured the role played by Asian immigrants in the building of United States (Hamamoto 1994, 32). For example, railroad work in the mid-nineteenth century was accomplished largely through Chinese labor, and although 90 percent of all workers on the Central Pacific Railroad were Chinese, famous historic photographs of the completion of the transcontinental railroad show no sign of Asian participation (Hamamoto 1994, 48).

The eighth grade text book *Discovering Our Democracy* speaks of the diversity of Asian groups and states that it was the early economic success of these groups that instigated laws excluding further immigration (Davis and Fernlund 1996, 12). There is no mention of the disruption of the Chinese family, of Japanese internment in the United States during World War II, nor of the orphans created by the Vietnam War. There is no mention of racial discrimination. If you read this textbook or others much like it, the passages about Asians would allow you to think that there were no problems for Asians, other than a brief period of limited immigration. If your experience with Asian Americans was limited, it would allow you to believe the myth of the model minority. Most of us have had little exposure in our formal education to any knowledge of the way that opportunities and barriers have been constructed for different immigrant and racial groups.

"By focusing on the achievements of one minority in relation to another, our attention is diverted from larger institutional and historical factors which influence a group's success" (Woo 1995, 224). While achievements of Asian Americans are part myth and part reality, it is the myth that often serves as the rationale for not supporting programs for African Americans or Latinos or American Indians or even Asian Americans. The argument goes something like this—if Asian Americans can be successful, then other groups just have to work harder and not depend on government handouts. This logic ignores how racism has operated in the United States and the way it has dictated who will have more opportunities and who will have limited life chances. The myth of the model minority is based on the assumptions of the level playing field and the American Dream, which tell us that only individual effort and merit count when it comes to success. This fiction discounts the widely varied experiences of voluntary and forced immigration, as well as the legacies of slavery and conquest.

Japanese Americans

As was the case with the Chinese, Japanese immigrants came to the United States in search of economic opportunity. Japanese began arriving during the 1890s when severe economic hardship in Japan resulted in massive immigration both to Hawaii and the continental United States. Unlike their Chinese counterparts, 35 percent of Japanese immigrants were women, which resulted in more Japanese Americans than Chinese Americans (Takaki 1993, 246).

Japanese immigrants were able to find work as farmers, shopkeepers, railroad laborers, and cannery workers. Their initial labor and economic success triggered a backlash in the United States. By 1908 many states began to prohibit Japanese immigrants from owning or leasing land. In 1922, the Supreme Court ruled that Japanese immigrants could not become naturalized citizens (Takaki 1993, 267).

As the country of Japan emerged as an enemy during World War II, Japanese Americans, most of whom were American citizens, became suspect of treason by the government and many other European Americans. In 1942, Japanese Americans, many of whom had been in the United States for several generations, were declared enemy aliens. Ultimately, over 10,000 people were evacuated from their homes to internment camps. In a tragic irony, 33,000 Japanese Americans served in the United States armed forces during World War II and at least 600 men were killed (Takaki 1993, 382–383).

Even J. Edgar Hoover, director of the FBI, insisted that mass evacuation of Japanese Americans was not necessary for national security and referred to such measures as hysterical. But despite Hoover's recommendations and other government reports that described the U.S. loyalty of Japanese American citizens, General John L. DeWitt of the Western Defense command pursued his plan of mass action. This was fueled by West Coast news media, which described Japanese Americans as spies and vipers, pushed by so-called patriotic organizations that were thoroughly anti-Japanese.

The move for mass evacuation operated in a context of "racism and war hysteria. The Japanese Americans on the West Coast were extremely vulnerable. They were not needed as laborers in the mainstream economy and many white farmers viewed Japanese farmers as competitors." Despite Hoover's belief that it was unnecessary, and Secretary of War Henry L. Stimson's belief that it was unconstitutional, President Franklin Roosevelt issued an Executive Order to place all Japanese Americans into internment camps (Takaki 1993, 381–382).

The evacuees were taken to assembly centers, which were crowded and dirty racetracks, stockyards, and fairgrounds in which hundreds and sometimes thousands of people were crowded into single buildings. After a brief stay in these centers, they were herded into trains and sent to ten different internment camps. Whole families lived in one room inside a larger barracks that most closely resembled a military base or prison. Each family was issued one electric light, army cots, and one blanket per person (Takaki 1993, 383).

It is important to note that despite the fact that the United States was also at war with Germany and Italy, neither German Americans nor Italian Americans were rounded up, taken from their homes, and thrown into internment camps. Why were Japanese Americans treated differently than Italian or German Americans? Why was it determined that the risk for traitorship was so high among Japanese Americans that it was necessary to violate their human and civil rights? Some of these answers revolve around what it takes to become white and what it means to be white in the United States. The descendants of German and Italian immigrants of the early twentieth century had assimilated. They were European and their appearance was white. They had become part of what was understood to be mainstream American and as such were not considered a threat to national security.

Japanese immigrants had great hopes of being considered both Japanese and American, but continued to be viewed as strangers. While other immigrants from European countries could assimilate through changing language, clothing, and customs, this was not an available option for Japanese immigrants no matter how many generations they had been in the United States. For Japanese Americans, changing their names or adopting American culture still would not change the fact that in the United States it was their race that marked them as the "other."

Southeast Asians

The newer Asian immigrants—Vietnamese, Laotians, and Cambodians—differ substantially from earlier Asian immigrant groups. They have been refugees from Southeastern Asian who have come to the United States as a group that are largely poor, young, and uneducated. These groups have had some economic success, yet by and large have not lived up to the myth of the so-called model minority (Hamamoto 1994, 168). Half of the Vietnamese American population in California receives some form of public assistance (Hamamoto 1994, 28) and more than 25 percent live below the federal poverty guidelines (Tatum 1997, 161).

The Vietnam War had a devastating impact on Vietnam, Laos, and Cambodia. One million soldiers of the army of the Republic of Vietnam and an equal number of Viet Cong and North Vietnam regular soldiers were killed. Civilian deaths are estimated at 3.5 million. In fact, more bombs were dropped on Vietnam than on all of Europe during World War II. By 1975, when South Vietnam fell, the war had created 200,000 prostitutes, 879,000 orphans, 181,000 disabled persons, and 1 million widows. The war transformed the country from a prosperous and self-sufficient agricultural region into an impoverished nation no longer able to independently support its people (Hamamoto 1994,26).

By 1980, immigration from Southeast Asia to the United States had swelled. There were 245,025 Vietnamese, 52,887 Laotians, and 16,044 Cambodians. These newer immigrants brought with them the very real trauma and economic and emotional fallout from a devastating war (Hamamoto 1994, 26).

Those of us who were around during the Vietnam War know about it in many ways. It was the first real television war in which daily body counts were a regular part of newscasts and articles. It was a war of great controversy in which those who were prowar were known as "hawks" and those who were antiwar were known as "doves." It was a war of massive protests involving several generations of Americans who walked picket lines and participated in local and national marches in efforts to stop the war. And a president, Lyndon B. Johnson, decided not to run for reelection, in large part because of the massive opposition to his Vietnam policies. The role of the United States in this war that happened so far away from U.S. soil remains controversial. But it is clear that the war ravaged Vietnam and its people.

Yet despite the fact that it has been almost thirty years since the end of the Vietnam War, few history books give it much attention. While visual images of some of the horrors of this war abound, few are found in U.S. textbooks. Rather, the visual images include those of soldiers on patrol or the damage done by violence of the "other side" (Loewen 1995, 247). Quotes are generally exclusively from the two presidents in office during the war, Lyndon Johnson and Richard Nixon.

This small and narrow depiction of the Vietnam War has many implications for future U.S. policy with regard to Third World countries. But for our purposes of examining the impact this lack of information has on race, it means that there was no context for American students who became the classmates of Vietnamese refugees. There was no sense of what their lives may have been like in Vietnam and what they may have lost in both human and material terms. For generations born after the end of the Vietnam War, there was little connection to be made between the U.S. policies that continued the war and the Vietnamese who became the newest Americans.

Multiracial Americans

In a 1908 article, "The Tragedy of the Mulatto," Ray Stannard Baker writes of a meeting he attended in which 1,200 "colored" people were present:

> A prominent white man gave a brief address in which he urged the Negroes present to accept with humility the limitations imposed upon them by their heredity, that they were Negroes and that therefore they should accept with grace the place of inferiority. Now as I looked out over that audience, which included the best class of colored people in Atlanta, I could not help asking myself: "What is this blood he is appealing to, anyway?" For I saw comparatively few men and women who could really be called Negroes at all. Some were so light as to be indistinguishable from Caucasians." (Stannard Baker 1908, 586)

Stannard Baker challenges the standard racist claim of white superiority by challenging the fluid, moving, and often times indistinguishable color line. He discusses the historical relationships primarily between white slaveholders and black women who were slaves. Even in 1908, with the limits of Stannard Baker's understanding of the tragedy and human costs of slavery and racism, he is able to see some of the impact of rape and sexual abuse of female slaves by their white masters: "If there was ever a human tragedy in this world it is the tragedy of the Negro girl" (Stannard Baker 1908, 589).

He also details the post–Civil War practice by some white men of having two families, one white and one black, and notes the range in these relationships. Some wealthy white men took care of their second families sending their biracial children to the finest colleges that would admit them. Some of these interracial families were characterized by deep human emotion and connection. But Stannard Baker is quick to point out, "No legal marriage existed between the races in slavery times and yet there was a widespread mixture of blood. Having concubines was a common practice: A mulatto was worth more in cash than a black man. The great body of Mulattoes now in the country traces their origin to such relationships. And such practices of slavery days no more ceased instantly with a paper Emancipation Proclamation than many other customs and habits that had grown up out of centuries of slave relationships. It is a slow process, working out of slavery, both for white men and black." Despite the dominance of racism of the early twentieth century and the assumption of white supremacy, the author of this article ponders why there is such a fuss about race given that so many people designated as "Negro" are, in fact, racially mixed. "Nothing, indeed," he writes, "is more difficult to define than this curious physical color line in the individual human being."

But the line did exist and, until 1960, the "one drop rule" applied to defining race. A person with any African heritage was defined as Negro or black in the U.S. Census from 1920 until 1960. "Though it is estimated that 75–90 percent of Black Americans have White ancestors, and about 25 percent have Native American ancestry, the widespread use of the one-drop rule meant that children with one Black parent, regardless of appearance, were classified as Black. The choice of biracial identity was not a viable option" (Tatum 1997, 170). This meant, of course, that multiracial children were subjected to the same segregation, inferior schools, and other forms of racism as African American children.

This changed in 1960, when the heads of U.S. households were permitted to indicate the race of the family. Still, there was no box to check for biracial or multiracial identity. In 1908 miscegenation laws that made interracial marriage illegal still existed in all of the southern states as well as Arizona, California, Colorado, Delaware, Idaho, Indiana, Missouri, Nebraska, Oklahoma, Oregon, and Utah. It was not until 1967 that the Supreme Court overturned the last laws prohibiting interracial marriage (Tatum 1997, 168). Since that time, interracial births to families with one parent that is white and one parent that is African American, Asian American, or American Indian have more than tripled. But despite legal progress and the development of healthy multiracial families and children, the multiracial legacy from slavery has not completely disappeared.

Parents generally teach their children during their preschool years how to identify themselves racially. When a biracial child is assumed to be white, there is often shock and curiosity when the darker-skinned parent comes to school. Sometimes, the relationship of the adult to the child is questioned as well. Some children in this situation experience prejudice from their peers when they see the darker-skinned parent. The same shock and prejudice does not occur as frequently when a black-appearing biracial child's white parent arrives on the scene (Tatum 1997, 180–181). While young children may not be able to articulate their feelings at this point, they notice the reactions of children and adults in their world and may feel confusion, discomfort, anger, or sadness. These reactions and their parents' ability to help make sense of them influence the way the child experiences his multiracial identity.

Most of the research, interest, and controversy over interracial marriage and biracial and multiracial children has been directed to relationships between whites and blacks, followed by whites and individuals from other communities of color. There has been little research conducted about the interracial children of two different races of color, primarily because these relationships and children do not threaten or blur the lines of whiteness (Tatum 1997, 168).

In fact, there has been little research in general regarding the experiences of multiracial children and adults. One of the few studies is a doctoral dissertation by Charmaine Wijeyesinghe, who studied the racial self-identification of black and white biracial adults and the factors affecting their choice of how to name or identify themselves by race. Wijeyesinghe concluded that the factors that impact the process and outcome of self-identification include: biological heritage, sociohistorical context of the society, early socialization, culture, ethnic identity and heritage, spirituality, physical appearance, and individual awareness of "self" in relation to race and racism (Wijeyesinghe 1998, 91).

When biracial people experience consistency between their identities and how others respond to them, there is little conflict or serious problem around racial identity. Tension and conflict occur, however, when discrepancies exist. For example, if a black-white biracial child is assigned "blackness" by the parents and the child appears to be African American, other people in their daily lives will not challenge the child when she says that she is black. However, if a biracial child appears white and is assigned "blackness" by the parents, he is likely to experience discrepancies in the form of questions, curiosity, gossip, and challenges often accompanied by rudeness when he announces that he is black. "While it is clear that biracial children can grow up happy and healthy, it is also clear that particular challenges associated with a biracial identity must be negotiated. One such challenge is embodied in the frequently asked question: 'What are you?' —Biracial individuals challenge the rigid boundaries between black and white" (Tatum 1997, 175).

The most recent controversy around multiracial identity once again revolves around the census, this time for the year 2000. This census will allow people to declare more than one race. While many multiracial individuals and organizations have lobbied for this right of self-definition, there remains ambivalence about its potential impact. "Lisa Parks, a 28–year-old program coordinator for a San Francisco non-profit whose father is white and mother Asian, says that while she identifies strongly as multiracial, she's not going to let the Census Bureau know that. 'Because of the power of the census and its ability to shape American political life, just for the census and the census only, I will mark only one race down, that being Asian, because of the fact that this society is so racialized and resource allocation is so determined on numbers of people based on their race,' she said" (Chao 1999, 1). Some government programs that rely on accurate racial data are voting rights laws and health care and education resources that depend on analyses of racial disparity. Employer discrimination charges are also reliant on the availability of racial demographics.

Once again the evolving racial categories and the controversy regarding multiracial identification in the census point out the artificial construction of race. The categories of male and female have not changed over the years, nor have the categories of age. But racial categories are changing again. Based on the new multiracial categories of the census, the Equal Opportunity Commission plans to reassign people who check multiple races to one of the minority race categories they have checked. The Commission's belief is that as they investigate employer discrimination, the effects of discrimination will more likely be equivalent to that of discrimination against the individual's parent of color (Chao 1999, 3).

This controversy around the census points out another fact of life of multiracial people that is embedded in the operation of racism as usual. Regardless of whether multiracial individuals "choose" their identity to be biracial, multiracial, white, black, Asian, or "none of your business," most likely they will be treated as the race that their physical appearance most closely resembles.

European Americans or Whites

While I have studied and worked against racism for most of my life, my experiences as a white person and as a Jewish person are always present and flavor how I analyze and interpret what I read, experience, and observe. As you read some of the standard and often missing history above, I asked that you remember your own personal story and standpoint as you found yourself accepting, resisting, or rejecting various elements of it. If you are white, I ask you now to double those efforts as you read this section. The irony of the socialization of white or European Americans is that it is so thorough and comprehensive that it is also often invisible and requires great efforts to make it visible. "[W]hites are taught to think of their lives as morally neutral, normative, and average, and also ideal, so that when we work to benefit others, this is seen as work that will allow 'them' to be more like 'us'" (McIntosh 1988, 82–83).

Understanding the history of European Americans and their participation in racism is not the same as white guilt. In fact, guilt is fairly useless in this process of understanding race and often acts as a barrier to reconstructing knowledge and arriving at independent conclusions and making decisions about individual and social change. Understanding the history of racism, the role of white people, and structural white privilege are not critical simply to eliminating racism for people of color but to the humanizing of white people as well. It is important for those of us who are white to understand and embrace two concepts simultaneously; that of the impact of white privilege and that of the possibilities of white liberation. As we learned about liberation theory in the first chapter, it became clear that according to these concepts, "We are born without racist attitudes, values or beliefs. Though we are born into social identity groups, we have no information about ourselves or about others. It is through the socialization process that we acquire the sets of attitudes, values, and beliefs that support racism" (Wijeyesinghe, Griffin, and Love 1997, 91).

Racism is dehumanizing for people of color who have been the targets of hundreds of years of violence and discrimination. And racism is also dehumanizing for those whites who have participated in overtly racist acts, for those whites who have actively taken a stand against racism, and for all whites who despite their best actions and intentions, continue to benefit from racism.

As we examine the role of European immigrants and white Americans in the

U.S. history of racism, we will trace how people become "white" in the United States, white-skin privilege, and the benefits that accrue to whites. This history will be different than the stories you have just read. Most of the history and social studies texts and curriculum that most of us have been exposed to in the United States have predominantly featured the stories of white Americans. In fact, in most cases, the word "American" in many contexts has an implicit assumption of whiteness. These stories that have become the sum of standard U.S. history do not need repeating. Rather, as with the rest of the stories of race in this section, it is the inaccessible, the invisible, the out of reach that we will explore.

Becoming White in America

When my students begin the process of exploring their identity in written autobiographies, I ask them to write about their race and their racial and ethnic history and background. Often white students will describe their national origin (if they know it) and for race will describe themselves as "boring" or "normal" and think of racial identity as something for other people. For many white people, and particularly those of us who have lived in communities that are predominantly white, whiteness is an unexamined norm. "Because they represent the societal norm, Whites can easily reach adulthood without thinking much about their racial group" (Tatum 1997, 93).

But according to psychologists Janet Helm and Beverly Daniel Tatum, in a race-conscious society there are psychological implications for whites and their racial identity as well as for people of color. The costs of the kind of individual racism that is characterized by hateful and even violent thoughts, words, and actions are the reduction of one's own humanity, what one of my student's referred to as a "hole in the soul."

For those whites who have never participated in a hateful racial act and have never considered their whiteness, there are also costs. These costs sometimes involve fear of people of color, circumscribed or nonexistent relationships with people of color, and sometimes feelings of guilt and shame. "While the task of people of color is to resist negative societal messages and develop an empowered sense of self in the face of a racist society, . . . the task for Whites is to develop a positive White identity based in reality, not on assumed superiority. In order to do that each person must become aware of his or her Whiteness, accept it as personally and socially significant and learn to feel good about it, not in the sense of a Klan member's 'White pride,' but in the context of a commitment to a just society" (Tatum 1997, 94).

Without this consciousness of one's own whiteness, there is a tendency for many well-meaning European Americans to generalize from their own experience to other racial groups. Most students are taught in school that we live in a just society that has corrected racism with the Civil War and the civil rights movement. For whites who have not experienced racial discrimination directed at them and have neither learned nor observed the way in which people of color continue to be targeted by racism, this teaching of a just society and a level playing field makes sense. Add to that a basically good person who would never consciously participate in a hateful act toward a person of color and thus sees him or herself as free of prejudice. This can result in a more subtle form of racism called "aversive racism," in which there is simultaneously and somewhat ironically a belief in an egalitarian society and an internalization of racial biases and stereotypes. Decent European Americans who have unwittingly been socialized into both of these beliefs may make friendship or dating or housing or hiring decisions with aversive racism at the root of these choices (Tatum 1997, 118).

How do European immigrants become "white" in the United States? An examination of the experiences of Russian and German Jewish immigrants and Irish immigrants serves to illustrate this process of assimilation and the so-called "melting pot."

The experience of Jewish immigrants was both the same as and different from that of other European groups. First, remember that there is power in naming. While Christian immigrants from Germany or Russia were named "German" or "Russian," Jews from these same countries were either named simply "Jews" or "German Jews" or "Russian Jews." In this naming there are two things implicit. The first is that being Christian is the norm and that Jews deviated from that norm. Second, while Jews would eventually be considered white in the United States, they were and are simultaneously considered foreign or "other."

Unlike Chinese and Japanese immigrants of the nineteenth and early twentieth century, Jews did not arrive in the United States with plans to return to their homelands. Anti-Semitism was already virulent in Europe and Jews were often prohibited from owning land or participating in certain jobs or professions. Pogroms in Russia, in which officials massacred Jews and burned their towns, were commonplace. "At the end of the nineteenth century, Jews were being allowed into the white working class in the United States, at the same time they were being cast as the most reviled racial Other in Europe. . . ." (Segrest 1994, 216).

Part of the immigration experience of Jews in America was coming to Ellis Island in New York and standing by as immigration officials changed their names because they could not pronounce or write them. Later, some Jews changed and anglicized their names themselves so as not to be so easily identified as Jewish and easily targeted for discrimination. So while anti-Semitism continued in the United States, there were contradictions in official and unofficial treatment of Jews because they were white. The availability of educational opportunity for Jews and the Jewish cultural emphasis on education meant that by the 1920s, many Jews in New York were entering college. The Jewish population at Harvard reached 20 percent (Takaki 1993, 288–301). "But the increasing presence of Jewish students at Harvard provoked a backlash. In 1923, a writer for *The Nation* complained that the upwardly mobile Jew sent 'his children to college a generation or two sooner than other stocks,' and that consequently there were 'in fact more dirty Jews and tactless Jews in college than dirty and tactless Italians, Armenians, or Slovaks" (Takaki 1993, 302).

Jews have clearly and strongly benefited from white privilege in the United States and have simultaneously been targeted by anti-Semitism. In the last half of the twentieth century Jews have had high access to good housing, health care, employment, and education. But white supremacists often refer to the Jewish conspiracy in banking and media and target Jews for violence along with African Americans.

The nineteenth-century potato famine in Ireland triggered the immigration of millions of unskilled laborers to the United States. These immigrants worked primarily in the construction of railroads and roads and lived in substandard housing. In fact, the Irish laborers were initially compared unfavorably to the Chinese who were engaged in similar work. "The Irish were imaged as apelike and 'a race of savages,' at the same level of intelligence of blacks. Pursuing the 'lower' rather than the 'higher' pleasures, seeking 'vicious excitement' and 'gratification merely animal' " (Takaki 1993, 150). The Irish immigrants were criticized as lazy and as drinkers and gamblers. Signs in New York City barred Irish and blacks from employment and housing.

Yet by the late twentieth century, Irish Americans were considered white and many had dropped the Irish part from their identity. How did this happen for this group of immigrants when it failed to happen for other voluntary and involuntary immigrant groups? Like many other European immigrants, the Irish quickly figured out that in order to be white in America, it was necessary to separate oneself from all that is black. As Irish Americans began to compete with blacks for jobs, they often manipulated the racism they found for their own self-interest. They emphasized their whiteness. A powerful way to transform their own identity from Irish to American was to attack blacks. Thus, blacks, as the "other," served to facilitate the assimilation of Irish immigrants. By the early 1900s, Irish women had gone from being maids to becoming schoolteachers and many Irish men had become prominent in the building trades and the labor movement. It is important to note that even those Irish immigrants who were never slave owners or those who arrived after the Civil War still benefited from anti-black racism.

Other European immigrant groups learned these same lessons. If your skin was white, you could choose to give up your foreign accent, culture, food, customs, and beliefs and then in a generation or two you could receive all the benefits of being white in America. These benefits were and continue to be very real in terms of income and access to education and health care and housing and personal safety. But the trade-offs were also real. Thorough assimilation meant being cut off from one's heritage and often feeling rootless, detached, homogenized. Becoming white was dehumanizing for many European immigrants because it often meant that proof of one's whiteness was demonstrated by competition with, hatred, and even violence toward African Americans, Asian Americans, Indians and Latinos.

"The 'melting pot' was a popular way of describing the assimilation process of

European immigrants to the United States in the late 1800s and early 1900s. Proponents of the model held that immigrants who came to the United States would, within a relatively short period of time, cast aside their European identities, cultures, and language as they forged or were forced to adopt the loyalties, customs, and language of their new home" (Wilson and Gutierrez 1995, 6). In fact, in some factories dramatic ceremonies were held in which immigrants walked onto a stage in their native dress and disappeared behind a huge melting pot, reemerging in the clothing of the American working class. What is clear is that the concept of assimilation and the possibility of the "melting pot" was available only for white European immigrants. It was the immigration and citizenship policies of the United States that made whites the numerical majority. Yet it was the extermination of Native Americans, the enslavement of Africans, the conquering of Mexican land, and the importation of Asian and Latino labor that helped settle this new country in the seventeenth and eighteenth centuries (Wilson and Gutierrez 1995, 7–19).

White Privilege and the Benefits of Being Considered White in the United States

"My schooling gave me no training in seeing myself as an oppressor, as an unfairly advantaged person, or as a participant in a damaged culture. I was taught to see myself as an individual whose moral state depended on individual moral will. At school, we were not taught about slavery in any depth; we were not taught to see slaveholders as damaged people. Slaves were seen as the only group at risk of being dehumanized . . ." (McIntosh 1988, 78). This statement links white privilege with the dehumanization of people of color and the dehumanization of white people who have benefited from racism. Inherent in this logic is the progression that for white people to move beyond their own dehumanization, they must understand white privilege and how they have benefited from racism and be willing to interrupt and change the patterns and power relations that have diminished all races. Many of us are taught that it is rude and racist to even notice racial differences and that it is a badge of our lack of prejudice to say that we do not notice color. In fact, since color or race has had such an enormous impact on U.S. history, being aware of how race sits on our collective shoulders is integral to dismantling the dehumanization of racism.

The first task, then, is to understand how white privilege operates. Peggy McIntosh refers to this process as unpacking the invisible knapsack of white privilege. What are some of the items in this invisible knapsack? We have already learned that when we are taught U.S. history we are taught, by and large, European and white history and that the contributions and experiences of people of color are often left out or marginalized. So, one element of white privilege is that most Americans are taught that people who are considered white made most of the important contributions to the United States. White parents can be fairly sure that their children will learn white history in school (McIntosh 1988).

Another element of white privilege is position and power. White people can be pretty well guaranteed that if they need to speak to the person in charge (of a store, office, corporation, etc.), in most instances this person will have the same color skin as they. White people can count on their skin color working for them when establishing credit, writing a check, seeking a mortgage, or looking for a job. White people normally do not have to worry about themselves or their children being stopped or harassed by police officers because of the color of their skin. While white parents can choose to teach their children about the effects of racism, they do not have to teach their children how to react and survive in environments in which people may ignore or mistreat them because of the color of their skin. White people are not often asked to speak as representatives of their entire race. One final, small but daily fact of white privilege is that white people can go into almost any drugstore and find bandages, stockings, makeup, and blemish cover-up called "flesh-colored" that closely resembles the color of their skin (McIntosh 1988).

The components of white privilege are particularly difficult to tease into visibility when communities or schools are all or predominantly white. The experience of privilege applies to everyone in this circumstance and seems standard and normal to those in the midst of it. In the absence of the voices of people of color, it becomes the challenge of formal and informal educators to notice and discuss the "presence of absence" (Rosenberg 1997, 82), to point out and include the missing voices of people of color and to describe and analyze how white privilege operates.

Over the years, I have heard many white students struggle with this concept of privilege and benefit. If they are working class or poor, female, disabled, and/or gay or lesbian they are often most aware of the discrimination they have faced or the hard work they have had to do to get to and stay in college. Often they feel their experiences of discrimination go unnoticed. Sometimes they feel that they are cheated out of jobs by people of color, who they believe receive unfair advantages. There are two important issues to address in this scenario.

First, it is true that there are many forms of discrimination and oppression. Ranking oppression (e.g., mine is worse than yours) is not useful. Individuals can belong to many dominant and targeted identity groups simultaneously. For example, I am a white, Jewish, heterosexual woman who just turned fifty. I have a mix of benefits from my identities as white and heterosexual, but as a Jew, a woman, and a fifty-year-old, I have some uphill battles. As a second generation American, my family's assimilation and identification as white gives me access to most of the privileges that are listed above. But at fifty, there are already many jobs for which I will not be considered suitable. It is important to acknowledge the ways that class, gender, age, ability, and sexual orientation create privilege and disadvantage and work with and against each other. But they do not erase the benefits of white privilege.

Second, belief in favored treatment for people of color is most often a reflection of a prevailing racial myth. There are no more scholarships designated for African American college students than for white students. Reverse discrimination claims are rare. Between 1990 and 1994, the U.S. District Courts and the Courts of Appeals received 3,000 race discrimination cases. Of these, only 100 were charges of reverse discrimination and only 6 were found to have merit (Kivel 1996, 47–48).

Just recently I observed this myth being played out among middle school students and one of their parents. Four eighth grade girls, three white and one black, applied to a selective private high school for admission. All four girls were bright, but the African American girl stood out. She had achieved scores of 99th percentile on all standardized tests she had taken throughout her school career. She had won spelling bees and essay contests and had been invited to speak at public meetings. She was one of the top students in all of her classes, including the advanced and gifted classes she was admitted into because of her test scores and achievement. The private school accepted her and rejected all three white girls. The next day, one of the white girls confronted the black girl and said, "I know the only reason you got in is because you're black." This same girl's mother proceeded to talk in the community about how terrible it was that the school accepted the other girl just because she was black.

This is based on the same racial myth that is perpetuated in history and social studies textbooks that describe *Brown v. Board of Education* (the Supreme Court decision that struck down the prevailing law and practice of separate but equal schools) and the civil rights movement as having ended all forms of discrimination against blacks. The logical conclusion from this distorted interpretation of history is that unnecessary compensatory programs for African Americans are still in place and that blacks receive all sorts of unfair advantages. The myth, as all racial myths, is based on misinformation and this misinformation feeds white privilege, racism, and internalized racism.

White Allies

My white students often ask, "If even well-intended white people are socialized to believe some of these myths of superiority and inferiority and we benefit from racism regardless of our beliefs, how is it possible to change things?" This is an important question. The pervasiveness of racism and its dehumanizing effects is staggering and often leads people to feel overwhelmed and sometimes hopeless. But in addition to white people's legacy in the history of perpetuating racism, there is also a legacy of individuals and organizations that are role models of antiracism and offer humanizing possibilities and hope for change. Liberation theory is critical to this understanding in its assertion that we are born without racism and with infinite human possibilities. It is misinformation, in this case about race, that damages both people of color and white people. The hopefulness in liberation theory is that because racism is not innate but learned, it can also be unlearned.

There have been many European Americans throughout U.S. history who have taken it upon themselves to unlearn racism individually and act upon their commitment to end racism. In Chapter Two, we learned about the abolitionist activities of Angelina and Sarah Grimké and the creation of a school for African Americans by Prudence Crandall. These women faced ostracism from their families and communities because they took unpopular, dangerous stands and actions to work against racism. We learned in this chapter that Henry David Thoreau refused to pay taxes and that Horace Greeley used the *New York Tribune* to protest the 1846 declaration of war against Mexico. During the American Indian Movement action at Wounded Knee, there were many white people who stood with the Indians as allies at the Wounded Knee Trading Post and who acted as attorneys in subsequent trials. Michael Schwerner and Andrew Goodman lost their lives along with their African Amerian ally James Cheney as a result of their efforts to register blacks to vote in Mississippi in the 1960s.

The late twentieth century antiracism movement is populated by white people who continue to examine their own privilege and racism, as well as institutionalized racism, and have taken strong personal and political stands against racism—David Billings of New Orleans, Mab Segrest of North Carolina, Paul Kivel of California, Joan Olsen of Pennsylvania, and many, many more. These are individuals who have stood as allies with people of color in protests, marches, and courtrooms and have challenged laws, policies, hiring practices, and other forms of discrimination. They are not simply "do-gooders" who want to help other people. These are individuals who are convinced that racism has dehumanized all people and that dismantling racism means a more fully experienced humanity for whites and people of color. These people often see their contributions to ending racism and other forms of oppression as their life work.

There are other ways to be an ally. Not every well-intended white person will decide to dedicate her life to ending racism. But there are daily reminders of how racism operates that anyone can interrupt. White parents can question and object when there is a disproportionate number of white children in advanced classes. They can insist that U.S. history curriculum include the stories of people of color. White allies can also interrupt racist jokes and stories and name calling. Sometimes the people and institutions challenged or interrupted will change, sometimes they will get angry, and sometimes they will do nothing. But the consciousness of white people about the insidiousness of racism, the awareness of white privilege, and the willingness to correct misinformation is all a part of the process of liberation, of unlearning racism.

Chapter Summary

Students in elementary school and high school in the United States receive limited and often distorted information about our country's racial history. Most of us learned primarily about the immigrant experiences of Europeans to the New World and only bits and pieces about the enslavement of Africans and the conquest of American Indians and Mexicans. We have rarely learned about immigration experiences of Puerto Ricans, Cubans, Vietnamese, Chinese, or Japanese. Often the information that we get is limited or glossed over to eliminate elements of racial cruelty, violence, or suppression. Sometimes the information that we get is taught to us as *African American* history or *Asian American* history—as if it is something completely separate from American history. At best, perhaps we have been taught that while there are unfortunate aspects of racism (slavery) and conquest (American Indians) in our history, there have been many efforts to right these wrongs and that racially the United States now has a level playing field in which people from all races have equal life chances. Rarely is there any information that analyzes the connection between individual acts of racial hatred and the institutional or structural racism that occurs in laws or private businesses that discriminate in housing, health care, education, and employment. And seldom is there any mention of the individuals, groups, and movements that have worked to undo the policies and effects of racism.

There are hard facts in U.S. history. There have been times in which dehumanizing a whole group of people has merged with individual acts of hatred and laws and policies that promote violence and oppression in which many, many people have died because of racism. While the omission or revision of this part of our history may be intended to keep children from learning such painful parts of our past, the consequences of the distortion of U.S. racial history are far reaching. "Education as socialization influences students simply to accept the rightness of our society. American history textbooks overtly tell us to be proud of America. The more schooling, the more socialization, and the more likely the individual will conclude that America is good" (Loewen 1995, 307). Education that does not lie is not equivalent to socializing students to believe that America is "bad" rather than "good." Rather it calls for teaching students about the complexities of our stories and how to make inquiries and draw conclusions that allow for critical thinking and autonomous decision making.

The combination of our personal experiences, our formal education, and our exposure to entertainment media add up to our socialization around race. If this socialization tells us that all is well racially and that everyone has equal life chances regardless of race or ethnicity, we are likely to see any racial problem or failure as strictly the fault of an individual. If we believe that there are no racial barriers to employment, then we will see unemployment among people of color as lazy or slovenly. If we believe that education is even for everyone, we will not be open to discuss or vote for remedies to address education deficits for students of color. The lump sum of these distortions can be dehumanizing for everyone.

While our history around race may be painful, we must learn it in much the same way that Germans must learn about the Holocaust: to understand our part in it, to understand how it impacts the present, to learn how to act on its contemporary implications, and to ensure that it will never happen again.

Bibliography

Adams, Maurianne; Bell, LeeAnne; and Griffin, Pat, eds. 1997. *Teaching for Diversity and Social Justice: A Sourcebook.* New York: Routledge.

Bednarz, Sarah; Clinton, Catherine; Hartoonian, Michael; Hernandez, Arthur; Marshal, Patricia L.; and Nickell, Pat. 1997. *We the People Discover Our Heritage.* Boston: Houghton Mifflin.

Brown, Dee. 1970. *Bury My Heart at Wounded Knee: An Indian History of the American West.* New York: Henry Holt.

Chao, Julie. 1999. "Census's Complex Multiracial Nightmare." *San Francisco Examiner,* November 28. http://www.multiracial.com/new/1999news.html.

Compton's Encyclopedia Online. 1999a. http://comptonsv3.web.aol.com/African American History:html, February 1.

———— 1999b. http://www.nara.gov/exhall/originals/sioux.html, February 1.

Croteau, David, and Hoynes, William. 1997. *Media/Society: Industries, Images, and Audiences.* Thousand Oaks, CA: Pine Forge Press.

Davis, Angela Y. 1981. *Women, Race, and Class.* New York: Random House.

Davis, James E., and Fernlund, Phyllis Maxey. 1996. *Civics: Participating in Our Democracy.* Menlo Park, CA: Addison-Wesley.

Dill, Bonnie Thornton. 1995. "'Our Mothers' Grief: Racial Ethnic Women and the Maintenance of Families." In *Race, Class, and Gender: An Anthology,* ed. Margaret L. Andersen and Patricia Hill Collins, 237–49. Belmont, CA: Wadsworth.

Feagin, Joe R., and Sikes, Melvin P. 1994. *Living with Racism: The Black Middle-Class Experience.* Boston: Beacon.

Hacker, Andrew. 1992. *Two Nations: Black and White, Separate, Hostile, Unequal.* New York: Charles Scribner and Sons.

Hamamoto, Darrell Y. 1994. *Monitored Peril: Asian Americans and the Politics of TV Representation.* Minneapolis: University of Minnesota Press.

Kivel, Paul. 1996. *Uprooting Racism: How White People Can Work for Racial Justice.* Gabriola Island, BC: New Society.

Loewen, James W. 1995. *Lies My Teachers Told Me: Everything Your American History Textbook Got Wrong.* New York: Touchstone.

McIntosh, Peggy. 1988. "White Privilege and Male Privilege: A Personal Account of Coming to See Correspondences Through Work in Women's Studies." In *Race, Class, and Gender: An Anthology,* ed. Margaret L. Andersen and Patricia Hill Collins, 82–83. Belmont, CA: Wadsworth.

Madrid, Arturo. 1995. "Missing People and Others: Joining Together to Expand the Circle." In *Race, Class, and Gender: An Anthology,* ed. Margaret L. Andersen and Patricia Hill Collins, 291. Belmont, CA: Wadsworth.

Matthiessen, Peter. 1983. *In the Spirit of Crazy Horse.* New York: Viking.

Mickelson, Roslyn Arlin, and Smith, Stephen Samuel. 1995. "Education and the Struggle against Race, Class, and Gender Inequality." In *Race, Class, and Gender: An Anthology,* ed. Margaret L. Andersen and Patricia Hill Collins, 291. Belmont, CA: Wadsworth.

Moore, Joan, and Pinderhughes, Racquel. 1995. "The Latino Population: The Importance of Economic Restructuring." In *Race, Class, and Gender: An Anthology,* ed. Margaret L. Andersen and Patricia Hill Collins, 227–30. Belmont, CA: Wadsworth.

Moraga, Cherie. 1995. "La Guerra." In *Race, Class, and Gender: An Anthology.* ed. Margaret L. Andersen and Patricia Hill Collins, 60–61. Belmont, CA: Wadsworth.

Reid, Frances [producer/director]. 1995. *Skin Deep: College Students Confront Racism.* Video. San Francisco: Resolution/California Newsreel.

Ritchie, Donald A., and Broussard, Alberts. 1997. *American History, The Early Years to 1877.* New York: McGraw-Hill.

Rosenberg, Pearl M. 1997. "Underground Discourses: Exploring Whiteness in Teacher Education." In *Off White: Readings on Race, Power, and Society,* ed. Michelle Fine, Lois Weis, and Mun L. Wong, 82. New York: Routledge.

Segrest, Mab. 1994. *Memoir of a Race Traitor.* Boston: South End Press.

Stannard Baker, Ray. April 1908. "The Tragedy of the Mulatto." *The American Magazine* 65, 582–98.

Takaki, Ronald. 1993. *A Different Mirror: A History of Multicultural America.* Boston: Little, Brown.

Tatum, Beverly Daniel. 1997. *"Why Are All the Black Kids Sitting Together in the Cafeteria?" and Other Conversations About Race.* New York: Basic Books.

U.S. Bureau of Census. 1990. "Characteristics of American Indians by Tribe and Language." CP-3–7.

West, Cornel. 1995. "Race Matters." In *Race, Class, and Gender: An Anthology,* ed. Margaret L. Andersen and Patricia Hill Collins, 557. Belmont, CA: Wadsworth.

Wilson, Clint C., and Gutierrez, Felix. 1995. *Race, Multiculturalism, and the Media: From Mass to Class Communication.* Rev. ed. Thousand Oaks, CA: Sage.

Wijeyesinghe, Charmaine L. 1998. "Diversity and Learning: Identity, Community, and Intellectual Development." Unpublished presentation at American Association of Colleges and Universities Conference, November 13.

Wijeyesinghe, Charmaine L.; Griffin, Pat; and Love, Barbara. 1997. "Racism Curriculum Design." In *Teaching for Diversity and Social Justice: A Sourcebook,* ed. Maurianne Adams, Lee Anne Bell, and Pat Griffin, 91. New York: Routledge.

Woo, Deborah. 1995. "The Gap Between Striving and Achieving: The Case of Asian American Women." In *Race, Class, and Gender: An Anthology,* ed. Margaret L. Andersen and Patricia Hill Collins, 224. Belmont, CA: Wadsworth.

Zinn, Howard. 1995. A People's History of the United States: 1492–Present. New York: Harper Perennial.

Chapter 5

Stories of Race in Popular Culture

> [E]ven the most seemingly benign TV programs articulate the relationship between race and power, either explicitly or through implication.
>
> —*Hamamoto*

> [H]istorically, the U.S. media have taken "whites" to be the norm against which all other racial groups are measured. The taken-for-granted nature of "whiteness" means that it need not be explicitly identified. For example, we generally do not talk about "white culture," or "the white community" or the "white vote," and so forth. We do, however, often hear reference to "black culture" or "the Latino community," and so on. The absence of a racial signifier in this country usually signifies whiteness. The pervasiveness of white perspectives in media is perhaps its most powerful characteristic.
>
> —*Croteau and Hoynes*

Entertainment Media and Race

The study of entertainment media and race is complex. Many people have studied the images of various racial groups in film and television and music. There are competing theories about how to evaluate and understand the impact and meaning of these images and themes. As we discovered in Chapter Four, the historical experiences of various immigrant and racial groups in the United States are profoundly different from each other. With these varied histories inaccessible in our schools and personal lives, their representation in media takes on added significance. Still further, there is complexity within each racial group. For example, images of Asians and Asian Americans are often collapsed and homogenized as one in media when, in fact, the experiences and cultures of various immigrant groups (Chinese, Japanese, Vietnamese, Filipino, etc.) vary widely. And to add one more complicating factor, the research and work that has been done regarding the representation of various racial groups in popular culture is wildly uneven. There is far more information available about images and themes of African Americans and American Indians in entertainment media than there is of Asian Americans or Latinos. There has been very little research conducted on popular music in relation to Asian Americans, Latinos, or American Indians.

So, how do we sort through what is available, make sense of what is not available, and begin to have some understanding of the construct of race in popular media without oversimplifying or making it so complex that it becomes unreachable and daunting?

In order to take a close look that is historical, analytical, and experiential, I have framed this section on entertainment media and race around eight questions:

1. What role does entertainment media play in socializing us about race?
2. What are the messages and themes about various races in entertainment media?
3. How do these messages and themes differ by race?
4. How have these messages and themes changed over time?
5. How are these messages and themes conveyed in different forms of popular culture—film, television and music?
6. What are the messages of the dominant culture with regard to race and how do themes and characters in entertainment media reinforce these messages?
7. What are some examples of entertainment media that challenge dominant culture messages about race?
8. What is the impact of entertainment media and race on audiences?

We will use content analysis, media history, economics, and cultural studies as the primary methods to analyze entertainment media and race. Readers are invited and challenged to consciously and deliberately bring their understanding of their personal experiences and their current intellectual understanding of race to this study.

That is the context and overview. Now we will bring this study of entertainment media into your living room. Follow the instructions in Media Activity 5.1 to begin your exploration of racial messages in prime time television.

Depending on when you grew up, you will find different results. Most people age twenty and older discover that there were few, if any, major characters of color and very few themes that involved race. If you are under twenty years old, you may find a few major African American characters and an isolated theme or two about race; but in general you will find that few major characters were Asian American, American Indian, or Latino.

What can we begin to conclude from this rough data? Until very recently, depictions of families and workers and neighborhoods on prime time television have

Media Activity 5.1
Childhood Television Favorites and Race

Instructions

List your five favorite television programs from ages 6 to 12. Limit these programs to those with a narrative story line (either comedy or drama). This eliminates such programs as *Sesame Street, Saturday Night Live,* and variety and news programs.
1.
2.
3.
4.
5.

For each of these five programs answer the following questions:

1. What was the total number of major characters combined in these five programs? (Remember that major characters are those without whom the plot would make no sense.) ___

2. Of these major characters write in the numbers of each race:
   a. African American (black) ___
   b. Asian American ___
   c. American Indian ___
   d. Latino ___
   e. European American (white) ___
   f. multiracial ___

TOTAL NUMBERS OF CHARACTERS OF COLOR
(add a, b, c, and d) ___

3. In general did the character development and plots commonly revolve around any of the following major themes?
   a. exploration of various cultures according to race (e.g., music, dress, attitudes, beliefs) ___
   b. exploration of the family relationships of people of color ___
   c. exploration of interracial friendships ___
   d. exploration of interracial romance ___
   e. depiction of racial conflict ___
   f. depiction of barriers to racial equality or racial discrimination ___
   g. depiction of racial pride ___

TOTAL NUMBER OF THEMES RELATED TO RACE ___

been predominantly white and middle class. Most comedies and dramas have been a reflection of the standards, values, customs, lifestyles, family patterns, and physical manifestations of this group. For a variety of reasons that we will explore in this chapter, prime time television has historically reflected the standards of the dominant culture and portrayed it as "normal." This is not always apparent or visible to the viewing audience. While we may at times be aware of the absence of characters of color, we are often unaware of the invisible repetition of certain sets of experiences and values that sit squarely in the white middle class.

What is challenging about identifying the signs and reflection of dominant culture in popular media is that most of us have been so thoroughly immersed in popular culture that its messages and values seem "normal" to us as well. We are looking to be entertained primarily, not to analyze the way we are being socialized. Yet the constant repetition in popular culture of the things that stand for "normal" impact all of us regardless of our race and ethnicity. In order to continue our quest for independence in defining our beliefs, it is important to tease out these invisible messages of dominance in entertainment media, for "images in the mass media are infused with color-coded positive and negative moralistic features. Once these symbols become familiar and accepted, they fuel misperceptions and perpetuate misunderstandings among the races" (Dates and Barlow 1990, 4).

We will begin to explore the portrayal, images, messages, and themes about race in popular music, film, and television. As we do this we will examine how the standards of the dominant culture are reflected, reinforced, or challenged. Part of your work will be the understanding that we all have been influenced by the invisible messages of race in entertainment media and that our task is to make the illusive messages tangible and accessible to us. Once we identify these messages, we then have conscious choices of how and whether we are influenced, persuaded, or socialized by popular culture.

American Indians in Entertainment Media

In Chapter Four we explored some of the history of American Indians that was not available to many of us in our social studies or history classes. We learned that there was vast and violent extermination of much of the Indian population, land, and culture and that these measures were justified by the U.S. government as necessary to the pursuit of Manifest Destiny and to expand the United States to its "natural" borders. Characterizing American Indians as savages and uncivilized helped fuel these policies and actions. To what extent has entertainment media reinforced or challenged these messages?

Prime Time Television and American Indians

In early television the most common representation of American Indians was of characters such as Tonto in the "Lone Ranger," who rode a pinto pony, dressed in fringed buckskin, spoke broken English, and served the Lone Ranger as a faithful sidekick. "During the era when television was dominated by 'westerns' (1960s), Indians were relegated to their movie image, serving as either foils or backdrops to the stories of how the West was won" (Wilson and Gutierrez 1995, 95–96). Even the common phrase "how the West was won" is synonymous with the selling of Manifest Destiny.

There were essentially three features of Indian representation in prime time television throughout the 1960s, 1970s, and 1980s. First, there were very few Indian characters or themes. Second, those few characters and themes available were almost always simple and stereotyped. Third, the scarcity of American Indian images combined with the repetition of the same images reinforced two messages: that Indians were not important and that they served only as secondary companions (and clearly not as intelligent) to white men.

An alternative image of American Indians was presented in the ground breaking television program *Northern Exposure* (1990–95). *Northern Exposure* was set in Alaska and its major story line involved a young white Jewish doctor who was paying back his medical school loans by doing service in a very small Alaskan town. What distinguished this program was that its central theme was the education of Joel Fleischman rather than his noble service to the Alaskan people. There were many recurring and occasional characters of color who were full and complex. One such character was native Alaskan (Eskimo) Marilyn Whirlwind, who served as Fleischman's assistant. She was depicted as wise and spiritual but also with an offbeat sense of humor and a strong and clear set of values. It was largely through Marilyn that Fleishman's lack of understanding and appreciation for native Alaskans was revealed. Ed Chigliak was another multiracial (white and Indian) character in this ensemble cast and offered a contrast to Marilyn. Ed single-mindedly pursued a career in filmmaking. While Marilyn was portrayed as intelligent and wise, Ed was portrayed as simple and somewhat limited in his abilities. There were also many Indian and Eskimo characters frequently appearing on the program, as well as themes that involved discrimination and stereotypes. *Northern Exposure* was on the air for five years and was quite successful, a good example of how quality programming can entertain and offer alternative images of race.

American Indians and Film

Images of American Indians in film were predated by images in nineteenth-century literature in which Indians were described as noble savages, with emphasis on the word *savage*. The theme of Manifest Destiny was constantly underscored in the literature of the time, depicting Indians as the less-than-human "other," who by their very "otherness" served as the rationale for bloody wars and land grabs. Images of Indians typically showed burning, looting, and scalping the good white guys who were simply pursuing their right to Manifest Destiny.

In early film, Indians as well as other people of color were often portrayed in ways that emphasized the myth of white superiority. Indians were frequently depicted as less intelligent than whites and less moral. Many images of Indians in Westerns involved the vicious attack of the wagon train and hostile Indian warriors. But surprisingly, silent films offered some alternative and complex views of American Indians and the history of western expansion.

Silent films produced by Thomas Ince were mixed in their portrayal of American Indians and the conquest of the West. In the 1912 film *Custer's Last Fight,* Ince presented a traditionally patriotic view of Custer as a brave Indian fighter of the stereotypically vicious Sioux Indians, who opposed the advance of the white man and civilization. But in the 1912 film, *The Indian Massacre,* Ince showed how whites shot and killed Indians for sport and slaughtered buffalo. In this film Ince portrayed Indians as fully human, grieving over the loss of children (Aleiss 1995, 3).

But as sound appeared in film, any sympathetic and complex representation of American Indians disappeared from the screen. The 1930s and 1940s depictions of American Indians solidified a series of clichés. The first of these was the reinforcement of the myth of Indian's place in the fulfillment of Manifest Destiny. To serve this purpose Indian characters were the requisite savages in films such as *Drums Along the Mohawk* (1939) and *Northwest Passage* (1940). Second, Indians were lumped together in film as one, with no distinction among various tribes. Third, until the 1960s, much of film depicted Indians through the concept of "Old Custerism."

"What is this Custerism? The celluloid residuals of Manifest Destiny, played out as emotional climax" (Seals 1991, 2). In fact, Ronald Reagan himself played General Custer in the 1940 film *Santa Fe Trail.* The 1940s film, *Cheyenne Autumn,* directed by John Ford, focused on a love story between two white characters rather than the deathly trip of the Cheyennes from Oklahoma to Montana in the 1870s (Seals 1991, 3). In these images, the old "cowboy and Indian" films replayed over and over the "good guys" (whites, cavalry, U.S. army) triumphing over the "bad guys" (the Indians) (Wilson and Gutierrez 1995, 75).

The civil rights movement, which focused on the discrimination toward and the rights of African Americans, also served as momentum to shift images of Indians in film. "White America (in the midst of the Black-inspired civil rights movement) experienced a guilt complex over the historical and persistent mistreatment of Native American Indians" (Wilson and Gutierrez 1995, 87). The late 1960s and 1970s were a decade of pro-Indian films, or "New Custerism," which began with the 1970 film *Little Big Man. Little Big Man* still featured a white man as the central character, but significantly revised the image of Custer as hero to Custer as a violent perpetrator of atrocities toward Indians. Custer's own violent death is portrayed in this film as well deserved (Seals 1991, 3).

Idealized images of Indians became trendy in 1990s films such as *Dances with Wolves,* in which Indians were romanticized as spiritual and good. This continued the era of "New Custerism" by creating a new stereotype that despite its more positive characterization was still oversimplified. Even with these new sentimen-talized images of American Indians, the plot of *Wolves* still revolved around major characters who were white. Shifting from images of the oversimplified bad Indian to the oversimplified good Indian may provide temporary relief from negative stereotypes, yet ultimately it continues to dodge the stories of racism, the slaugh-tering of Indians, and the human complexity of individuals.

As we learned in Chapter Four, one of the consequences of being a conquered people has been devastating poverty on American Indian reservations and in ur-ban communities. It seems that the "Old Custerism" created an image of the vio-lent and hostile Indian and revised history in a way that glorified the cavalry and Manifest Destiny. While "New Custerism" may have had better intentions, in its attempt to paint the noble and romantic Indian and even to demonstrate the massa-cre of the Indians, it has done little to depict the consequences to contemporary American Indians of hundreds of years of conquest, land evictions, and bloody wars. This can leave the audience feeling angry or guilty about white violence toward Indians, but relieved with the sense that it is all in the past.

There are a few films in the last decade that have had some measure of com-mercial success and have depicted an alternative view of American Indians as characters as well as the impact of history on contemporary Indians. One of these is *Thunderheart,* which you can rent at most popular video stores. After you have viewed it answer the questions in Media Activity 5.2.

As you analyze this film, you will begin to see that it has departed from both the "Old Custerism" and the "New Custerism." It has offered a predominantly Indian cast of characters with themes that depict relationships and struggles. The film has a wide range of Indian characters. These characters include the somewhat roman-ticized character of Sam Reaches, the spiritual wise man; Jack and Richard, who wish to profit from the suffering of their people; and Maggie, Walter, and ulti-mately Ray, who take great risks to reveal how the government has exploited the reservation and its people.

The use of visions to explore history and the visual devastation of the reserva-tion offers still another alternative to classic Indian stereotypes. The film demon-strates contemporary devastation and poverty and does not fix responsibility for it squarely on the shoulders of individuals but rather on a multilayered history and set of politics and policies. While the film is not entirely true to the factual infor-mation of the American Indian Movement's occupation of Wounded Knee, never-theless it attempts to show the complexity of the politics and the economics of the situation. The secret strip mining of the reservation is representative of centuries of exploiting Indian land.

While the film's ending, with its requisite chase and modern-day cavalry and Indian confrontation, may be entertaining, it ultimately detracts from the serious and intricate messages in the film. Still, it is a reversal of most traditional Westerns in which the cavalry surrounds the Indians and mounts an impressive, dramatic, and righteous victory.

Media Activity 5.2
Analysis of Racial Images and Themes in *Thunderheart*

Instructions

Answer all of the questions based on your observations of the film, *Thunderheart*, directed by Michael Apted.

Question Set One: The first set of questions are identical to the questions you applied to your five favorite TV programs as a child.

1. How many major characters were there? (Remember that major characters are those without whom the plot would make no sense.)   ——

2. Of these major characters write in the numbers of each race:
   a. African American (black)   ——
   b. Asian American   ——
   c. American Indian   ——
   d. Latino   ——
   e. European American (white)   ——
   f. multiracial   ——

TOTAL NUMBER OF MAJOR CHARACTERS OF COLOR: ——

3. Did the film have any of the following major themes (e.g., did character development and plots centrally revolve around any of these topics)?
   a. exploration of various cultures according to race (e.g. music, dress, attitudes, beliefs)   ——
   b. exploration of the family relationships of people of color   ——

(cont'd)

A discussion of images and themes of American Indians would not be complete without the analysis of two very different films: the Disney production of *Pocahontas* and the independently produced *Smoke Signals*.

Pocahontas, released in 1995, emerged out of a history of racial criticism of Disney animated films of the 1980s and 1990s. The 1992 *Aladdin* was criticized for its stereotypical depiction of Arabs and the 1994 *Lion King* was criticized for depicting the hyenas as stereotypical black and Latino ghetto characters. As a result, Disney executives began the creation of *Pocahontas* with an eye to sensitivity and avoidance of criticism about depiction of American Indians (Edgerton and Jackson 1996, 2).

The results were mixed. Disney hired a number of American Indian consultants and performers to serve as the voices of the Indian characters. One particular coup

c. exploration of interracial friendships   ___
d. exploration of interracial romance   ___
e. depiction of racial conflict   ___
 f. depiction of barriers to racial equality or racial discrimination   ___

Question Set Two: Character Exploration
For each of these characters—Ray Levoi, Richard Yellow Hawk, Grandpa Sam Reaches, Walter Crowhorse, Jimmy Looks Twice, Maggie Eagle Bear—answer the questions below.

4. Was the character simple or complex?

5. Did the character challenge or reinforce Indian stereotypes (e.g., fringed buckskin and broken English, vicious savage, or romanticized hero)?

6. Did the range of American Indian characters depict diversity among characters or reinforce similarity?

Question Set Three: Themes and History

7. How was the FBI depicted? Were they good guys, bad guys, or mixed?

8. How was the income level on the reservation depicted?

9. How was the political struggle between the Indian reservation government and AIM depicted?

10. How was the historical image of the battle at Wounded Knee depicted through Ray Levoi's visions?

was the casting of American Indian Movement (AIM) activist Russell Means as Chief Powhatan, Pocahontas's father. Means's involvement and support of the film was an attempt to demonstrate a commitment to authenticity (Edgerton and Jackson 1996, 3).

Pocahontas was a tremendous commercial success, earning $91 million in its first four weeks and promoting and selling a number of tie-ins including musical tapes, Burger King toys, and moccasins, and a doll that looked suspiciously like Barbie. "Pocahontas, the 400–year-old legend, was expertly redesigned to Disney's usual specifications—meaning a full-length animated feature with a host of commodity tie-ins-thus becoming the version of the Pocahontas story that most people recognize today" (Edgerton and Jackson 1996, 4).

What was this version and how does it reflect on American Indians and history?

The film was never intended to be historically accurate. While Disney's goal was to offer more positive and sympathetic Indian characters, it was never their intent to convey the history of the time. Disney becomes part of a long-time tradition in mythologizing the story of Pocahontas as a symbol of assimilation and how the natives could be civilized and made Christian. This myth was certainly not challenged in the Disney version.

In fact, the real Pocahontas was twelve and the real John Smith, twenty-seven when they met in 1607; they were never lovers. "In relying so completely on their romantic coupling, however, Disney's animators minimize the many challenging issues that they raise—racism, colonialism, environmentalism, and spiritual alienation" (Edgerton and Jackson 1996, 6). Once again, history is revised in film to show the triumph of the individual and of love, rather than the more complex racial relations and conquest themes.

Finally, the process of designing the drawing of the character Pocahontas is revealing of the whitewashing of the film. The original order from Disney executives to the artist was to offer a fine creature who is not a cookie-cutter replication of white females in past Disney features. The artist's original drawings were based on four real women: paintings of the real Pocahontas, an American Indian woman, a Filipino model, and a white supermodel. The artists and decision makers of the final image of Pocahontas were all white males, and the ultimate drawing, while exotic, remained most true to the image of the white supermodel. Ultimately, Disney's version of Pocahontas offered some sensitivity to Indian characters but succumbed to a dominant view of American Indians that "pushes native perspectives to the margins of society, if not entirely out of view. Disney's Pocahontas is thus another example of the 'white man's Indian.' . . ." (Edgerton and Jackson 1996, 8–9).

The 1998 release of *Smoke Signals* was a breakthrough in that it was written, directed, and cast with American Indians. *Smoke Signals* was not an epic or revision of history such as *Dances with Wolves* or *Thunderheart,* nor was it an idolization of Indians such as in *Pocahontas.* Rather, it was a character study of Victor and Thomas, two young American Indian men on a journey to rediscover one of their fathers and in the process to reclaim their own selves. The use of humor in the film was striking as it highlighted Indian stereotypes and satirized them at the same time. In one classic scene in which Victor and Thomas are on a bus, they begin their musical satire of John Wayne's teeth, poking fun at Wayne's classic depiction in Westerns as the great white man who conquers the savage Indians. This was the first feature film in the United States to be directed and co-produced by American Indians.

Stereotypes of Indians as savages and noble savages, princesses and sidekicks still abound. In the absence of personal experience with American Indians and the lack of education regarding the complex American history vis-à-vis American Indians, it is these images, themes, revisionist histories, and stereotypes that fill a void and constitute what we come to believe as real. But the success of films such as *Thunderheart* and *Smoke Signals* seem to signal possibilities for offering alternative and complex images that can be both commercially successful and true to authentic Indian stories and history.

Asian Americans in Entertainment Media

As we begin to take a close look at images of Asians and Asian Americans in popular media, there are several important concepts to bring forward from Chapter Four and reconstructing knowledge. First, there is a tendency for European Americans and those in power to homogenize Asians and Asian Americans into one group rather than recognizing and understanding various countries of origin, cultures, and the differences in immigrant experiences. The second tendency is the belief in the myth of Asian Americans as the model minority. Does entertainment media reinforce these two misconceptions? Are there examples of more complex and alternative images of Asian Americans? These are the questions we will explore in this section.

Asian Americans and Popular Music

Here is an easy exercise in content analysis. Listen to the top forty and rock radio stations in your community for two hours this week or look at the hit charts for the genres of top forty and rock. Observe if there are any artists with Asian first names or surnames and if there are any songs with Asian or Asian American themes. I can almost guarantee that your numbers will be zero. In a scan of top forty singles in the last thirty years I found one specifically Asian song from 1963—"Sukiyaki"— written by Japanese composers Rokusuke Ei/Hachidai Nakamura. The lyrics are Japanese and the translation reveals the loneliness of love lost (Lyrics World 1999).

While there are some aspects of popular music such as karaoke that originated in Asia and are popular in some Asian American communities, there are no Asian-influenced musical genres that have become mainstream. Rather, music that is popular in Asian American communities has become an interesting amalgam of immigrant cultures and roots and mainstream American popular music. The popularity of this uniquely hybrid music has remained exclusively in Asian American communities. "Popular music has frequently been portrayed as a homogenizing influence on minorities, but Asian-Americans frequently appropriate the styles and sounds of popular music to their own culture. The Filipino-American rapper La Quian asserts his multicultural identity within the context of rap music. Many Vietnamese-Americans enjoy Karaoke because it allows them to explore both their Vietnamese heritage and their current concerns. Rather than stifle creativity, these popular music forms are transformed by the Asian communities" (Wong 1994, 1). These developments in music that is popular in various Asian American communities have had little impact on the images of Asian Americans in the wider society.

Asian Americans and Film

Early silent films typically perpetuated the "yellow peril" stereotypes of Asians. In the 1916 film *The Yellow Menace,* Asians (of no particular ethnicity) were portrayed as diabolical as they joined with Mexicans to launch a subversive plot against the United States. With the notable exception of Japanese actor Sessue Hayakawa, who played lead Asian roles in early silent films, many Asian film characters were played by white actors (Wilson and Gutierrez 1995, 73–74).

The passage of the 1924 Immigration Act effectively halted the portrayal of Japanese or Japanese Americans in film until they were resurrected once again as the "yellow peril" directly before, during, and after World War II. During the early twentieth century attention in film focused on China with the development of the thoroughly evil villain Fu Manchu. In the series of Fu Manchu films that were popular from 1933 to 1936, "The American audience was given the impression that Chinese people are prone to violence, anarchy, corruption, vice and prostitution. . ." (Wilson and Gutierrez 1995, 82). Another interesting Asian character in film in the 1930s was Charlie Chan, the mysterious crime solver whose lines read like the one-liners in a fortune cookie. Once again, none of the actors who played Chan were Asian. Even in the 1930s film *The Good Earth,* in which Chinese workers were portrayed sympathetically, the lead Chinese roles went to European American actors Paul Muni and Luise Rainer ("The Long March from Wong to Woo" 1995, 2).

The attack on Pearl Harbor reinstated the Japanese as the "yellow peril" in film. While Chinese images of Fu Manchu and Charlie Chan were clearly stereotypical, Japanese images were more directly evil. In films such as *Wake Island* (1942), *Guadalcanal Diary* (1943), and *Objective Burma* (1945), the Japanese were shown attacking Red Cross ships and children and reveling in torture (Wilson and Gutierrez 1995, 84). These negative Japanese images continued for almost ten years after World War II. In most of these films Chinese and Korean actors played the roles of Japanese. The ruling Hollywood wisdom determined that Asians of one nationality were replaceable by any other Asians ("The Long March from Wong to Woo" 1995, 3).

There is no direct evidence of how these media depictions could prompt or justify internment of Japanese American citizens during World War II. Yet these films repeatedly portrayed a dehumanized, monolithic, and thoroughly evil series of fictional Japanese characters. This may well have contributed to the political hysteria that characterized Japanese American citizens as the "other" and the enemy. This racist construct served as the justification for imprisoning thousands of innocent American citizens of Japanese origin. During this period surrounding World War II, there were no complex, sympathetic Japanese or Japanese American characters in film. Regardless of the intent of the filmmakers, the combination of this film and newspaper coverage of the evil "Japs" constituted U.S. propaganda that influenced the American public's opinion and fear of anything or anyone with Japanese heritage.

The post–World War II United States was characterized by the Cold War and an almost obsessive fear of communism. The wars in Korea and later in Vietnam were ostensibly fought to save the free world from the so-called domino effect of communism. This phenomenon was also reflected in postwar film as the focus of the "yellow peril" shifted from Japan, defeated and no longer the enemy, to China as the newest symbol of Asian evil, this time in the guise of communism.

As sympathetic portrayals of Japanese Americans began to appear in films such as *The Bridge on the River Kwai* (1959) and *Sayonara* (1957), the Chinese were portrayed as an evil and devious threat to the United States and its way of life. Two films, *The Manchurian Candidate* and *The Sand Pebbles*, both released in 1962, typify this menacing image. In *The Manchurian Candidate*, GIs were captured and brainwashed by the "evil" North Koreans and Chinese, who were joined by the Soviets in this frightening experiment in political control through mind control (Internet Movie Database 1999). The evil portrayed here was explicitly Communism, and two-thirds of the communists represented were Asian.

Throughout film history there has also been the image of the beautiful and exotic Asian woman, most frequently involved in a tragic love with a white man. This theme and character stereotype was present in the 1960 film *The World of Suzie Wong*, starring William Holden and Nancy Kwan (Internet Movie Database 1999). Holden plays an artist who unknowingly moves into a hotel in Hong Kong populated by prostitutes. When one of the more beautiful prostitutes (you guessed it, Suzie Wong) models for him, he falls in love with her.

The end of the Vietnam War sparked the production of a large number of films that analyzed, probed, criticized, and exonerated the controversial war. One similarity of both the pro-war and anti-war films of this era was the depiction of Vietnam soldiers as crafty and devious. Critically acclaimed films such as *The Deerhunter* (1978), *Coming Home* (1978), and *Apocalypse Now* (1979) focused on the devastating impact of the war on white U.S. soldiers, using minor Asian characters and Vietnam itself as backdrop to the central antiwar message. The devastating impact of the war on the country of Vietnam, its people, and Vietnamese immigrants was not forefronted.

Of this genre of films it was only *The Killing Fields* (1984) that featured a major character who was both Cambodian and complex and depicted the impact of the war on him and his country. The film followed the horrors of war through the characters of an American journalist and a Cambodian journalist, their relationship, and the difference in how the war impacted each of them and their families. Significantly, the role of the Cambodian journalist, Dith Pran, was played by Cambodian actor Haing S. Ngor (Internet Movie Database 1999). *The Killing Fields* is a strong example of the possibilities of alternative themes and complex characters regarding even highly controversial and politicized subjects such as the Vietnam War. It was nominated for several Academy Awards and grossed $34.6 million. That *The Killing Fields* was both an artistic and economic success is significant. It provided an opportunity for many Americans to see a well-made film that didn't glamorize, villainize, or oversimplify the Vietnam War. And it serves as a model of the potential for feature film to portray difficult topics and themes with depth and texture.

The 1980s replaced the evil Asians with two new contrasting stereotypes: the benign Zenlike master and the martial arts hero. A glut of popular martial arts movies were produced that ranged from Bruce Lee films to *The Karate Kid* (1984). Another new minor Asian character emerged in the 1980s and 1990s—that of the forensics expert, the systems analyst, or the above-average-intelligence Asian, subtly reinforcing the model minority image.

The Joy Luck Club (1993), written by Amy Tan, produced by Oliver Stone, and directed by Wayne Wang, is another example of the possibilities of a successful feature film that depicts complex Asian characters, themes and history. The film, based on Tan's novel, explores the lives of Chinese women who immigrated to the United States and their American daughters and the relationships between these two generations of women. In a series of flashbacks to the immigrant women's lives in China, the audience learns something of the role of Chinese history and the treatment of women in these particular characters' lives. Their stories intertwine with the difficulty, love, and complexity of the lives of their assimilated daughters to tell a poignant story of immigration, tragedy, and triumph. Yet, despite the depth of both the themes and characters, only one of the actresses cast in the six major roles was clearly Chinese or Chinese American. Of the other five actresses, one's ethnicity was not available, one was born in Vietnam, one in France; one in Macao, and one in Japan. Even in this film, anyone who looked Asian could be recruited to play the part of a Chinese or Chinese American woman.

Asian Americans and Prime Time Television

Early prime time television repeated the stereotype of the stock domesticated and emasculated Chinese bachelor. In programs such as *Bachelor Father* (1957–62) and *Bonanza* (1959–72), the Chinese cook or "houseboy" was a regular character (Wilson and Gutierrez 1995, 103). In *The Courtship of Eddie's Father* (1969–72), it was a Japanese woman who took care of Eddie and his father. In other television classics such as *Hawaii Five-O* (1968–80), Hawaiians were often depicted as childlike speakers of broken English who served as part of the exotic background. By the time another popular program set in Hawaii, *Magnum, P.I.* (1980–88), came to the small screen, there were no recurring Hawaiian characters in the series at all (Hamamoto 1994, 11–18).

Originally released as a film, the television program *M*A*S*H* (1972–83) received critical acclaim, more than its share of television awards, and had an enormous loyal following. Set as a medical unit in the Korean War, it was understood that both the film and TV program were implicitly critical of the Vietnam War. And although set in Korea, the program had no recurring Korean characters and few Asians or Asian Americans appeared even infrequently in the series (Internet Movie Database 1999).

Asian and Asian American characters appeared from time to time in TV Westerns. One example of this was in the *Annie Oakley* episode titled "Annie and the Chinese Curse." In this program an evil white man tries to buy or steal the property from a good Chinese man who had immigrated to the United States. In the course of the episode, the Chinese man became the target of broken windows and racist notes. Annie's kid brother Tagg is very upset by this unjust treatment and Annie explains to him that some people just don't take the time to get to know those who are different from them (Hamamoto 1994, 57).

On one level this program provides a message of justice and equality, squarely against hate and discrimination. Annie and Tagg are clearly the "good guys" and they are deeply disturbed and take action to interrupt the racism of the "bad guys." Yet on another level, the episode revises history and misinforms. During the time of the episode, California law forbade Asians from owning property. The premise of the land theft begins with the misinformation that it was even possible for Asians to own land. The actions of the good guys and the bad guys focused on racism and prejudice as acts that individuals perpetuate and that individuals can counteract. While there is always the possibility of hateful acts and the hope of individuals interrupting them, there are some institutional, legal, and policy issues that are the underpinnings of racist acts. As we learned in Chapter Four, there were laws barring Chinese immigration and citizenship, there was blatant institutional and individual discrimination. "One of the tendencies of popular art is for its creators to apply liberally a revisionist gloss on events drawn from the historical past. Nowhere is this more evident than in the art of the television Western. . . . The normative social order is restored through main force by either military (Calvary) or police power (sheriff/marshal). On occasion, lone heroic individuals substitute for state power" (Hamamoto 1994, 49).

By contrast, in 1871 fifteen Chinese immigrants were lynched in Los Angeles. In 1877 a Chinese community was burned in Chico, California, and four Chinese immigrants were burned to death. There was an 1886 massacre of twenty-eight Chinese miners in Wyoming, and in 1850 a high foreign-miners tax was placed on all mining performed by immigrants. (Hamamoto 1994, 52).

The message that American audiences have received about this time in U.S. history is that while there were some instances of anti-Asian racism, it was not the norm. Television characters portraying the lawmakers, sheriffs, marshals, and good men and women were not racist and stood up for racial justice. With little information about this chapter in American history, TV viewers are left with the belief that anti-Asian racism was rare and when it existed, the local people usually corrected it.

The series *All American Girl* (1994) featured comedian Margaret Cho as a first-generation Korean American girl whose parents and grandmother were Korean born. Cho's character was a feisty, assimilated American girl and the show centered humorously around the conflicts between the values and culture of her old world family and her own defiant identification with contemporary American culture. The program was simultaneously entertaining and silly, and it featured interesting issues of culture and assimilation. But it lasted for only one season.

Close examination of Asian and Asian American characters and themes in entertainment media reveals several important trends. The first is that characters have largely been invisible, minor, and extraordinarily simple. The stereotypes of characters as well as themes that have emerged have included the evil "yellow peril," the benign houseboy, the martial arts expert, the male housekeeper, the exotic female beauty, and model minority. Characters and programs set in historical contexts focus on the good and evil of individuals and the restoring of justice and order with virtually no revelation regarding the anti-Asian institutionalized racism that prevailed in much of the nineteenth and twentieth centuries. The combination of low exposure of Asian Americans in popular culture and the repetition of certain themes and stereotypes produces a socialization of audiences that unconsciously take in this misinformation as the "truth." This is particularly true of viewers who have little or no contact with Asian Americans in their real life, little education about this part of U.S. history, and therefore no tools to recognize and challenge the messages in film and television and music.

The production of films such as *The Killing Fields, Joy Luck Club,* and even TV programs such as *All American Girl* demonstrate the possibilities of providing complex themes and characters that reveal more solid information while they entertain.

Latinos in Entertainment Media

A 1988 *Time Magazine* article said, "In 1974, several years before she turned her attention to the decadent doings of wealthy Wasps, 'Dynasty' co-creator Esther Shapiro brought NBC a script for a much different sort of TV show. Called *Maid in America,* it was a bittersweet movie about a Hispanic girl who goes to work for an upper-middle-class Anglo family. NBC executives praised the script but ultimately turned thumbs down. The reason, Shapiro recalls, was expressed in one blunt comment: 'Tacos don't get numbers'" (Zoglin 1988, 134). Apparently this has not changed much. A 1977 study of prime time television on ABC, CBS, NBC, and Fox networks revealed that only 2.9 percent of characters in entertainment television were Latino. This compares to the actual 10.7 percent of Latinos in the U.S. population (Gerbner 1998, 1).

There are several key factors that characterize images of Latinos in film, television, and popular music:

- Latinos are underrepresented in mainstream film, television, and music.
- Those images of Latinos that do exist in film and television are often simple, stereotyped, and/or negative.
- Portrayals of Chicanos, Puerto Ricans and other Latino groups emphasize sameness and blur differences between immigrant groups.
- Spanish-speaking television and radio have drawn enormous Latino audiences.

As early as the 1830s, popular literature began demonizing Mexicans. "In fact, there is much to suggest that American literature of the period was primarily designed to stir up local sentiment for the overthrow of the Mexican government in Texas and New Mexico. . . . Americans were generally persuaded to visualize the Mexican as an inhuman enemy a decade before war with Mexico was officially declared" (Wilson and Gutierrez 1995, 66). Mexican stereotypes in this literature were lazy, stupid, and cruel. In the nineteenth-century literature, generals of Mexico were portrayed as cruel and evil while literature rhapsodized about folk heroes such as James Bowie and David Crockett. Even a century later Crockett was mythologized in song as Davy Crockett, king of the wild frontier.

These stereotypes and their application are similar to the misinformation about American Indians that allowed the government to justify conquering their land and livelihood. They also run parallel to the characterization of Japanese American citizens as the disloyal and "evil Japs," thus providing the ammunition to move a whole group of people to internment camps. These Latino stereotypes in literature remained constant in film and television to be joined subsequently by the simple images of Latin lover and exotic seductress.

As we explore the twentieth-century world of popular media and images of Latinos, recall your personal and educational experiences. For most of us, formal education supplied little information about the histories of Mexican Americans, Puerto Ricans, and other Latinos. If you are Latino or lived in a community with many Latinos, you may have some personal experience to contradict your mediated world. If you are not Latino and lived in a community where there were few Latinos, the world of entertainment media may have been your primary source of information. According to the American Psychological Association, the less real world information viewers have about a group the more likely they are to accept the media reality. Let us examine that media reality.

Latinos and Film

The earliest silent filmmakers were often European immigrants who did not initially have the same socialized racism as second and third generation Americans. Latinos participated as actors and directors in these early films. The first Charlie Chaplin film had a Latino cameraman. "However, when the denigration of people of color became profitable, these same producers developed the same attitudes and participated in either excluding or exploiting the images of people of color. . . . At this point Latinos were excluded from the industry except in front of the camera where they generally played stereotypical roles" (Rodriguez 1997, 2).

Images of Latinos in subsequent silent films were primarily of Mexicans and Mexican Americans as bandits attacking white people. The pejorative word "greaser" was even used in some silent film titles such as the 1911 *Tony the Greaser* and the 1914 *The Greaser's Revenge*. By 1922, the Mexican government banned the distribution of such films (Wilson and Gutierrez 1995, 75).

Other Central and South American countries eventually joined the Mexican banning, and its economic consequences had an impact on later Latino film images. Hollywood began to create stories of hot Latin romance, featuring the new stereotype of the Latin lover. While this provided some opportunities for some Latino actors, many Latino parts were still cast with white actors such as Paul Muni and Noah Beery in the 1928 film *The Dove* and the 1935 film *Bordertown*. *Bordertown* featured the Latin lover as attracting two white women, one who went to jail and another who eventually died. While the Latin lover may have been hot, he was not allowed to succeed in interracial love (Internet Movie Database 1999).

As with American Indians and Asian Americans, Latino characters were an integral part of the classic American Western genre. Typically male, the stock Mexican Western character was the greasy bandit (who spoke broken English), the sidekick (who spoke broken English), or the exotic hero such as *Zorro*. Film was the first of the popular media to develop a separate Spanish-speaking industry, particularly in Latin America. By the 1960s, Latin themes in Hollywood had further diminished and the "greaser" stereotypes reemerged in the form of Puerto Ricans and Puerto Rican gangs in films like *West Side Story* (1961). This trend continued through the 1970s. Much of the 1980s and 1990s continued to feature few Latino characters and themes in film with minor characters the rule and drug lords and gangs abounding.

There are, however, some examples of Latino themes and characters that offered complexity and alternative images and themes. Two of these are *Stand and Deliver* (1988) and *El Norte* (1983). *Stand and Deliver* cast Edward James Olmos as a Bolivian-born math teacher in a poverty-stricken Latino barrio in East Los Angeles. He eventually was able to motivate kids whose response to poverty and racism had been to become tough, hardened, or apathetic. He cajoled and inspired them to succeed in calculus and the Advanced Placement test. The film portrays several striking instances of institutionalized racism. The academic testing company challenged the high test scores of these young people from the barrio, accused them of cheating, and insisted that they retake the test. It is the inspiration and toughness of their teacher that spurs the students to higher self-esteem and success. The film's message involves the power of one person to overcome the power of racism. It is an extraordinary film in its depiction of the barrio and the hopelessness of some low-income Latinos and the hopefulness that one man can bring. The film exposed the low expectations that the school system had for Latino students and the racism of the testing organization. Ultimately, it begs the question of structural racism and focuses, instead, on the individual. Its characters were vivid and complex and dispelled stereotypes about Latinos. So on one level, *Stand and Deliver* is inspirational and leaves the audience with hope; on another level it reinforces the concept that one individual can undo structural racism. Nevertheless, *Stand and Deliver,* at a $14 million box office gross, had little chance for its messages about racism to be seen by a wide audience (Internet Movie Database 1999).

The Mexican-made *El Norte* involves the escape from Guatemala of a teenage brother and sister after their father had been killed for political reasons. The film follows the young people through a tortuous journey through Mexico to California where they have great hopes of wealth and success, the American Dream. They eventually find jobs as a busboy and a housemaid. The young man is turned in to the immigration authorities and his sister becomes very ill from rat bites she received on their journey. While the film is grim and tragic, it reveals the underbelly of immigration and the American Dream. Clearly, some immigrants succeed materially and professionally and others, like the two teenagers who are political refugees in *El Norte,* become part of a permanent underclass. One of the questions raised by this film involves immigration policies. As viewers watch the horrors the characters experience, they may want to ask what U.S. policies and programs are available to help people in these circumstances. They may want to investigate the phenomenon of the real lives before and after immigration of undocumented workers. But like *Stand and Deliver, El Norte* grossed little—less than $14 million (Internet Movie Database 1999)—and the audience available to ask these questions was negligible.

While films such as *Stand and Deliver* and *El Norte* do not offer filmmakers much hope that they will become rich, both films received strong and wide critical acclaim. The late 1990s phenomenon of the success of relatively small and or/independently produced films such as *Smoke Signals, Sling Blade, Shine,* and others raises hopes of the possibilities for complex themes and characters. With the growth rate of the Latino population projected at 53 percent over the next decade, this will be a movie audience whose economic potential filmmakers will need to consider.

Latinos and Television

The phenomenon of television has two separate implications with regard to the Latino community. The first involves the television viewing habits of Latinos and the boom of Spanish-speaking television. The second issue is the representation of Latinos in prime time television.

Spanish-speaking cable television has skyrocketed in its viewing audience, audience spending, and advertising. As a group, Latinos watch more television than the general population. Significantly, three-fourths of Latino viewers spend their time watching Spanish-language programming (Braus 1993, 48). A 1993 study revealed that those Latino audiences watching prime time television viewed only one show in common with the rest of the U.S. population. At that time, the Latino population of 25 million spent $190 million dollars annually and their growth rate was five times that of the rest of the United States ("Hispanics: Last Frontier for Marketing," 1993, 54).

This population and its buying power have become a force for television and advertisers to reckon with. As a result of this viewing pattern, advertisers and demographers have chased this audience—first to analyze it and second to sell to it. Interestingly, the analysis of the Latino population has led advertisers to look more closely at the demographics of Latinos and to determine that they are a multifaceted demographic group in terms of income, generations since immigration, and national origin. "Some firms are helping businesses approach the Hispanic market by dividing it extensively with a sharp knife. Donnelly Marketing Information Services (DMIS) of Stamford, Connecticut, recently introduced a marketing tool that splits U.S. Hispanics in no fewer than 18 ways. Its Hispanic Portraits system ranges from 'Puerto Rican, high income, younger, established with single/ multifamily homes' (3 percent of U.S. Hispanic households) to 'Mexican, lowest income, younger, low mobility, Hispanic neighborhoods' (16 percent of Hispanic households)" ("Hispanics: Last Frontier for Marketing," 1993, 56).

Even the study of Latino immigration and assimilation patterns has become grist for marketing plans. According to *American Demographics Journal,* Latino immigrants originally buy the products, such as Colgate toothpaste, that they used in their country of origin. But, according to demographers, in their desire to become more American lies the opportunity for advertisers to entice Latinos to switch product brands. One marketing consultant found that Latinos thought that within fifty years they would lose their culture and language and become like everyone else in the United States. The job of advertising, apparently, is to help this assimilation by identifying and selling the most American products. However, marketers are equally concerned with U.S.-born Latinos and conclude, "Perhaps the safest way of attracting U.S.-born Hispanics is by placing references to Latino culture in English-speaking advertisements. Such advertisements appeal to Hispanics who primarily speak English but still have pride in their culture. . . ." ("Hispanics: Last Frontier for Marketing," 1993, 58).

For the present, these marketing strategies appear to be focused primarily on Spanish-speaking television, since only one-fourth of the Latino audience regularly watches prime time television. The catch-22 of this situation is that it was the lack of Latino characters and themes that drove the Latino audience to cable, and as we will see, prime time television producers have continued that void.

One study of prime time television of the 1988 season revealed that there were more extraterrestrial characters on television than Asians and Latinos combined. In 1997, only 2.9 percent of network prime time television characters were Latino (Gerbner 2, 1997). Another study of prime time television from 1955 to 1986 indicated that 75 percent of Latino characters were villains as compared to 39 percent of white characters (Rodriguez 1997, 27).

Early Latino characters on television ranged from *The Cisco Kid* (1950–56) with a blend of oversimplified heroes and the stereotype of the faithful, broken-English-speaking sidekick Pancho, to Ricky Ricardo, the hot-tempered but tolerant Latin lover husband in *I Love Lucy.* From 1955 to 1964 only one character in 100 on television was Latino (Rodriguez 1997, 59).

In the course of prime time television there have been few leading characters who were clearly Latino and even fewer themes that revolved around issues facing Latinos and various Latino communities. From 1954 to 1963, *Father Knows Best* episodes occasionally included Frank (pronounced "Fraunk") as the Mexican gardener. From 1957 to 1963, *The Real McCoys* featured Pepino García as a farmhand.

From 1960 to 1961 *The Steve Allen Show* introduced and featured a new character, José Jiménez, played by Bill Dana. Dana, decidedly not Latino, played this character as a simple-minded fellow who spoke broken English. His stock phrase, which viewers repeated and roared about throughout the United States was "My name José Jiménez" (Internet Movie Database 1999). *The Bill Dana Show* (1963) capitalized on the popularity of this character and was a one-season situation comedy in which Jose Jimenez went through life in a daze of simple-minded errors.

Chico and the Man (1974–79) was one of the few prime time network television series to feature characters, themes, and a context that were Latino. Chico Rodríguez, played by Freddie Prinze, teamed up in business with Ed Brown, played by Jack Albertson. The series was set in a Mexican barrio in East Los Angeles. The later 1970s and early 1980s included two Latinos in major television roles. The first was Ricardo Montalbán (as the aging, no longer active, Latin lover) in *Fantasy Island* (1978–83) and Erik Estrada as a California highway patrolman Francis "Ponch" Poncherello in *ChiPS* (1977–83). Montalban's accent made his Latin heritage clear, while it was only Estrada's character's name that was Spanish with little Latino context or background in the program. From 1984 to 1989 Edward James Olmos played the Latino police lieutenant in *Miami Vice* against regularly appearing Latino drug lords (Wilson and Gutierrez 1995, 100–101). This began an interesting pattern in television cop shows that has continued through the 1990s. The major characters in *Miami Vice, NYPD Blue,* and *Law and Order* have almost all been white and many of the criminals have been people of color. But in each of these programs, the police lieutenant, with some amount of authority, is a person of color. These regularly appearing characters, however, are not the characters around whom the action revolves nor whose personal lives are regularly uncovered and revealed.

The actors Jimmy Smits and Benjamin Bratt, both Latino, have brought a new kind of Latin lover to the small screen, both with great cross-over appeal. Smits first appeared in *L.A. Law* (1986–94) as Víctor Sifuentes, a Mexican American lawyer and one of the major characters in an ensemble cast. While the character's racial identity was always clear, his women were usually white and there was almost no mention of any racial context or barriers or problems he faced. Later, Smits became one of the two main characters on *NYPD Blue* (1993–). As Bobby Simone, he continued to be the hot love and sex interest on the program, but neither his surname nor his character development was specific about his racial identity, heritage, or any racial issues. Again, his love interest and wife was a white woman.

Benjamin Bratt played the role of Detective Reynaldo "Rey" Curtis on *Law and Order.* The audience does not know that "Rey" is short for Reynaldo. The spelling of his name (which of course the audience rarely sees) is one of the tip-offs to his Latino heritage. Occasionally, we see Curtis speaking in Spanish to witnesses or suspects or being called derogatory names (such as "beaner") by criminals.

The contemporary characters played by Bratt and Smits are attractive, interesting, and complex. They are not simple or stereotyped in the older molds of Latin lover, faithful sidekick, or evil bandit. In that regard, there is some progress in the characters they play. However, the characters of Sifuentes, Simone, and Curtis were rarely immersed in their own cultures, and did not face racial barriers to their personal or professional success. Their characters were the model of assimilation and conveyed the message that if you are a good person (which all are) and you work hard (which all do), you will experience few barriers to success. Once again, the American Dream appears on the little screen.

As you will see in the next section, "African Americans in Entertainment Media," there are some, if infrequent, themes that explore racism and discrimination. However, "When television has explored discrimination, prejudice or the appropriateness of inter-racial relationships, it has almost always staged them as a black versus white issue. Whatever racial tensions exist between Latinos and other groups in American society, they have rarely made it to the small screen" (Rodriguez 1997, 68).

Is it beginning to sound like a broken record? American Indians, Asian Americans, Latinos. Recall the section in Chapter Four on reconstructing knowledge. Remember the histories of conquest and destruction, and the laws and policies that reduced opportunities for citizenship and full American rights, and recall the violence. Juxtapose this information with the entertainment images and themes that are scarce and, when available, most often stereotyped and simple. The few examples of complex characters from these three racial groups on television have somehow managed to assimilate in such a way that allows them to be treated as white and refrains from examining any themes of racial tension or discrimination. Once again, this allows viewing audiences with little personal experience or educational exposure to these groups to conclude that there are few problems. One of the dangers in this conclusion is that it almost always implies a subtle political message that is drenched in racism. That message is, if these Latino characters can succeed, compete with, and get along with white people on television, then it must be the fault of the real Latino people out there if they are stuck in poverty and dead-end jobs or unemployment. The trend of blaming poverty and racism on its targets has been a phenomenon since the late 1970s. While entertainment media cannot bear the full brunt of these disturbing messages and misinformation, it perpetuates and reinforces a set of beliefs that denies any structural racism in the United States. If a society cannot see the consequences of racism, it is exceedingly difficult to address it and seek solutions.

African Americans in Entertainment Media

African Americans and Film

The 1988 film *Mississippi Burning,* directed by the British Alan Parker, was loosely based on the disappearance and murder of three civil rights workers in 1964. The film received one Academy Award for cinematography and was nominated for six others including best actor, best supporting actress, best director, and best picture; it grossed over $34 million (Internet Movie Database 1999). This film was controversial when it was released because while it was based on the actual disappearance of local black activist James Chaney and white activists Andrew Goodman and Michael Schwerner, it deliberately deviated from important historical elements of the story. *Mississippi Burning* provides an excellent opportunity to analyze the ways in which popular media can reflect upon or revise the history of race in the United States.

The exercise in Media Activity 5.3 below involves two parts. First, it asks you to draw some conclusions after viewing the film, and second, to reach subsequent conclusions after conducting a bit of research. The film can be rented at most video stores. As you grapple with these questions you will find conflicting information and reviews. The film powerfully depicts the racial climate in the deep South during the Freedom Summer of 1964. The visceral, vicious, and violent racism dominates the screen and is relentless and stunning. The *feel* of racism in this small town is palpable and frightening. For most viewers with little experience or education about this chapter in U.S. history, the film initially creates a sense of outrage at the depth of racism in the 1960s and a sense of relief that things are better.

But on closer examination there are several aspects of the film that are clear mismatches to historical truth. First, an examination of the characters reveals that all of the major characters are white. All of the heroes are white and, in fact, all of the villains are white. There is diversity among the white characters; they are not all the same or similar. The white characters are the only ones who have any complexity (e.g., Ward, Anderson, Mrs. Pell). Mrs. Pell and Agents Ward and Anderson exhibit a disdain for discrimination and bravery amid violence. With the exception of one young black man, the black citizens of this small town are portrayed as frightened into passivity.

What is wrong with this picture? Director Alan Parker claimed that the film could not have been made even in the 1980s if the heroes were not white. He believed that audiences could accept the premise of racism in the film if those who solved the disappearance of the civil rights workers and worked for justice were white (Kempley 1988, 1). It is debatable whether the film would have reached such a wide audience or grossed as much at the box office with African American characters in the lead roles. But the central question is how did *Mississippi Burning* revise history and what impact does that have?

While there may have been individual FBI agents who were driven to overcome racial injustices in the 1960s, your research probably uncovered the fact that the Director of the FBI J. Edgar Hoover had a different agenda. Hoover developed a counterintelligence program called COINTELPRO in which he targeted activists in the civil rights movement (as well as other movements for change), including Martin Luther King, to undermine their efforts to transform racism. His strategies

---

Media Activity 5.3
The Truth in *Mississippi Burning*

Instructions

View the 1988 film *Mississippi Burning* and answer the first set of questions. After answering this set of questions, conduct some research about the particular incident. You can find film reviews of *Mississippi Burning* on the Internet Movie Database (http://us.imdb.com) and academic articles and reviews on the Internet by using keywords *Mississippi Burning* and/or Chaney, Schwerner, and Goodman.

Question Set One:

1. Describe the basic plot of the film.
2. Describe the major characters. Discuss their personalities, their behavior, their goals and apparent motivation. Indicate whether each character is simple or complex and whether they perpetuate or dismantle any stereotypes.
3. How are white people characterized in the film? Are they all portrayed in a similar fashion or is there diversity and range among the white characters?
4. How are black people characterized in the film? Are they all portrayed in a similar fashion or is there diversity and range among the white characters?
5. How are various organizations portrayed in the film? Include discussion of the FBI, the Ku Klux Klan, civil rights organizations, churches, and so forth?

(cont'd)

---

included planting agents within activist organizations and spreading rumors of interracial sex, sexual promiscuity, and connections to communism among the leaders of civil rights organizations. This is the same FBI that is portrayed with universal and overwhelming zeal for justice in the film. "[T]he film strays when it comes to FBI methodology. But if it didn't, there would be no catharsis for an audience beset with brutality—there's no heroism in witness payoffs and bureaucratic paperwork" (Kempley 1988, 1).

In addition, black churches and civil rights organizations played an enormous role in the civil rights movement in small southern towns. Black and white students regularly committed acts of great courage as they organized voter registration drives and conducted sit-ins and other activities to end segregation and Jim Crow laws. Black residents knew they were risking their lives through the simple but courageous act of registering to vote and actually voting. Yet, in the film, most of the black characters were part of the background and scenery, simple, fearful, and passively allowing the white FBI to seek justice on their behalf.

6. Who are the heroes and who are the villains in the film? Who exhibits courage or bravery and who exhibits cowardice or fear? How does this line up in terms of race?
7. Summarize how the audience is left to understand what happened in this small town in Mississippi.
8. What do you come to know and feel about racism after viewing *Mississippi Burning?*

Question Set Two:

9. Locate at least one article on Schwerner, Chaney, and Goodman and the circumstances of their civil rights work and subsequent deaths. Summarize what you learned about the events and the key players.
10. Research information in the article above or others that indicates the role of the FBI, the Ku Klux Klan, civil rights organizations, churches, and so forth. If you cannot find specifics about the roles of these groups in this case, find information about their roles in the larger civil rights movement.
11. As you summarize the information above, do you find courage and bravery? Do you find cowardice or fear? Discuss your findings on these issues.
12. Following your research, what are you left to understand about what happened in this small town in Mississippi?
13. What do you come to know and feel about racism after conducting research?
14. How is your research similar or different to the information and messages in the film?
15. If you had seen only the film without the research, what would you have concluded about this situation?
16. What are the truths and what is the misinformation in *Mississippi Burning?*

The characters of Ward, Anderson, and Mrs. Pell are complex and interesting, and the film itself creates a palpable sense of the horrors of racism. But it also creates illusion and misinformation. The uninformed viewer leaves this film with the same kind of sense the old Westerns evoked. We are invited to believe that even the worst injustices can be made right through the "good guys" in authority and that the public authority (this time the FBI instead of the sheriff's office) is dedicated to lawfulness and equality. The film suggests that black people were in need of saving and had been frightened away from the possibility of standing up for themselves and being heroes in their own liberation. "[I]t views the black struggle from an all-white perspective. And there's something of the demon itself in that. It's the right story, but with the wrong heroes. There's this nagging feeling that it begins where it ought to have ended—with the deaths of the three young activists" (Kempley 1988, 3).

The issue of poetic or dramatic license in this film is worth mentioning. Dramatic license is the right of the artist; in this case, the filmmaker, to take liberties with facts in order to create his or her art. Certainly, director Alan Parker had the right to make the decisions to develop the film he wanted. He never claimed that it was a documentary; it was fiction based on a real story. The problem, as you can see from your own experience with this film, is that most of us have not been taught and do not know the "real story" of Cheney, Schwerner, and Goodman or some other important aspects of the civil rights movement, hence the version of the "truth" in *Mississippi Burning* becomes what we believe to be real.

A closer look at the history of the portrayal of African American characters and themes demonstrates how the kind of misinformation and distortion in *Mississippi Burning* could have evolved. Edward Guerrero identifies five chronological phases of African American images in film. These include the stereotypes of the plantation genre from 1915 to 1965 (*Birth of a Nation, Gone with the Wind, The Littlest Rebel*); contemporary revisionist images of slavery *(The Color Purple, The Toy)*; the civil rights movement, black power, and blaxploitation films from 1969 to 1974 (*Shaft, Superfly, Sweet Sweetback's Baadasss Songs*); Hollywood conservative backlash films from 1975 to 1989 (e.g., *Caddyshack, Stir Crazy*); and the resurgent boom of black films in the 1990s *Boyz N the Hood, Do the Right Thing*) (Guerrero 1996).

As we examine some of these films, it will be important to put their analysis in a broader economic and social context. It is clear that the film industry responded at various points such as the 1960s and the 1990s to calls for social justice and demands for inclusion of African Americans in both the industry and the content of the films themselves. It is equally clear that the film industry is a business that has evolved through its history and has been driven primarily by economics and profit. For example, from 1964 to 1974 there was a boom in the production of cheaply made films with both blacks casts and content. On the surface it may seem that the civil rights and black power movements' call for African American inclusion in film triggered this growth. In 1963 the NAACP and the ACLU were joined by film stars such as Marlon Brando, Burt Lancaster, and Paul Newman in attacking racism in the film industry. In 1969 the Justice Department announced plans to sue six film studios and two television networks for discrimination in hiring (Guerrero 1996, 82). This is only part of the picture.

Concurrent to developments in the civil rights movement and calls for more participation and fewer stereotypes of African Americans in film were other developments in the industry. Hollywood's once united audience was becoming increasingly fragmented. The huge epics that Hollywood had once relied on as a primary source of profit were no longer predictably successful formulas. The average weekly box office draw sunk to $15.8 million in 1971 as compared to $90 million in the years immediately after World War II. African Americans comprised 10–15 percent of the 1971 population and 30 percent of the film-going audience. White flight to the suburbs left movie theaters in the cities whose audiences were largely African American. As the industry was trying to figure out how to recoup audiences and profit, a strategy dropped itself in their collective laps.

In 1971 Melvin Van Peebles scraped together $500,000 in funds and cast himself and friends in *Sweet Sweetback's Baadassss Song* and took only three weeks to shoot the film. By the end of one year, *Sweet Sweetback's Baadassss Song* had grossed $10 million and Hollywood had stumbled on a winning formula that it repeated many times during this period. The lead character was a violent rapist, but he also challenged white oppression and won. (Guerrero 1996, 86).

The images and stereotypes in *Sweet Sweetback's Baadassss Song* (and other films of this genre, such as *Superfly*) of violent, supercharged sexuality, drugs, and crime were highly controversial in the African American community and were challenged by many civil rights groups during the years in which these films were popular. But the so-called blaxploitation era of film only ended when these films were no longer economically viable for the film industry.

"[T]he black image on the commercial screen, principally Hollywood's ideology of racial domination and difference [,] . . . constructs black people as *other* and subordinate, while it naturalizes white privilege as the invisible but sovereign 'norm' " (Guerrero 1996, 5). But African Americans have not simply been victims of Hollywood. Because of the fluctuating market for film and dynamics of economics and audience, there continue to be times in which both mainstream and independent filmmakers have created complex African American characters and themes that challenge this dominant ideology.

In D.W. Griffith's *Birth of a Nation* (1915), a pattern of portraying blacks as inferior was established that would last for decades (Wilson and Gutierrez 1995, 74). While this film used techniques that made it a film classic, it also glorified the Ku Klux Klan. The film grossed $18 million and was denounced by the NAACP for its racist portrayal of blacks. "In its presentation of the KKK as heroes and Southern blacks as villains, it appealed to white Americans due to its mythic view of the Old South, and its thematic exploration of two great American issues: interracial sex and the empowerment of blacks. Ironically, the film's major black roles (stereotypically played) were filled with white actors—in blackface" (Dirks 1999, 2).

While *Birth of a Nation* was a silent film, it was loud in its establishment of two basic slave stereotypes. One was of the "good old days of slavery" in which slaves were portrayed as docile and content as compared to the second stereotype depicted of the dangerous and insolent freed slaves. These images on the screen were particularly dangerous in the context of its 1915 release in the middle of a period in which segregation was being solidified and lynching was at its height. While direct cause and effect of the film's relation to violent racism cannot be conclusively established, it is clear that the public's tolerance of the Klan drove its membership to 5 million, the highest ever, by 1924 (Guerrero 1996, 13).

Other early silent films such as *Wooing and Wedding of a Coon* (1905) and *The Nigger* (1915) continued these hate-filled stereotypes of African Americans (Wilson and Gutierrez 1995, 75). By contemporary standards, even their titles seem preposterous—unabashedly and outrageously racist. But the acceptability of such titles and the images of blacks that were portrayed is reflective of the widespread acceptance of antiblack racism during the early twentieth century.

African Americans protested these images and stereotypes with few results. It was not until the United States was on the brink of World War II that Hollywood began to rethink the images and stereotypes of slavery and race.

The 1930 self-regulation of the film industry through the Hays Code (the same code that governed the depiction of sex and sexual orientation) was explicitly racist. "It prohibited scenes and subjects which, however distantly, suggested miscegenation as desirable, thereby building a color barrier in Hollywood's dream world as rigid as the color line in America's real world. By casting the issue of racial mixing in black and white terms, the Code proclaimed an assimilationist ideal for European ethnic groups and a segregationist ideal for the 'colored folks'" (Guerrero 1996, 17).

During the Hollywood heyday of 1930–45, the stereotypes of blacks in film began to change from the early images spawned by hate to happy slaves and servants. African American actors and musicians such as Lena Horne and Louis Armstrong were cast as musicians in films in which there was little interaction with other characters. Prior to World War II, black characters were cast as people who knew their place and whose "inferiority" was used to make audiences laugh. The character known as Stepin Fetchit was the classic example of this use of black actors and black characters, as were the young black characters and actors in *Our Gang.* Comedian Ed Lee created an act he called "Step and Fetch It." The roles he played in film used stereotypes of laziness, sloth, and slow-wittedness to create comic effect (Bogle 1998,4). This character clearly knew his place in society, and the films with Stepin Fetchit underscored the subordination of blacks. In *The Little Rascals* films of the 1920s the African American characters of Buckwheat, Farina, and Stymie were immersed in humor that often depended on large-eyes, eye rolling, and the exaggerated use of black dialect. These portrayals often crossed the border into stereotypes. Despite these obvious stereotypes, there was also the depiction of interracial friendships in these children's relationships that was highly unusual for the times.

The 1935 Shirley Temple films *The Little Colonel* and *The Littlest Rebel* were depression-era escapist films but contained important racial images as well. In both films, Shirley Temple's character interacted and danced with an African American man who was portrayed as a childlike servant, preserving the early slave stereotype of docility and dependency (Guerrero 1996, 26).

The 1939 classic *Gone with the Wind* spanned the historical period of pre–Civil War, Civil War, and Reconstruction and once again portrayed the happy and loyal slave and servant. The black characters—particularly Mammy, Prissy, and Pork— had no doubt where they belonged during and after the Civil War. While each of their personalities reflected different stereotypes, it was their extreme loyalty to their "masters" that these characters shared. Notably, Hattie McDaniel, in her role as Mammy, received an Academy Award for best supporting actress. This was the first academy award ever received by a black actor. Nevertheless, there was an African American protest led by the NAACP that challenged the "plantation genre" of *Gone with the Wind.* The concern was that *Gone with the Wind* was a tamer and subtler version of *Birth of the Nation* in its revisionist image of slavery with happy and devoted slaves bemoaning a Civil War that disrupted their lives. Many contemporary film critics contend that in order to transcend the ongoing impact of slavery and its racist legacy, the story of slavery must be told by filmmakers in its full horror so that African Americans and European Americans can squarely face its reality in the past and its legacy today. The United States needed the support of the African American civilian population and the military participation of 1 million African Americans who were drafted. The government needed a way to reconcile the contradictions of fighting the European "master race ideology abroad while allowing racism and racist films at home" (Guerrero 1996, 27).

After World War II there was a transition in the portrayal of blacks. Stereotypes once again shifted and themes of discrimination began to emerge in films such as *Pinky* (1949) and *Blackboard Jungle* (1955). Sidney Poitier emerged as the actor who epitomized Hollywood's portrayal of black men during this time. He was intelligent, handsome, spoke standard and elegant English, was respectful and proud, and mostly depicted as asexual. In *Lilies of the Field* (1963), *Guess Who's Coming to Dinner* (1967), and *In the Heat of the Night* (1967) Poitier played characters who were good men who handled prejudice with dignity. His characters could be admired by any race and they posed no threat (Wilson and Gutierrez 1995, 87). The characters played by Poitier were often criticized for being so thoroughly assimilated that there was no trace of connection to the African American community or culture.

Still another shift of black characters occurred in the mid-1960s and early 1970s with the so-called "blaxploitation" films. These were action films featuring defiant black male heroes victorious over white people and sexually conquering black women. The year 1971 was a big year for these films. As mentioned previously, *Shaft* and *Sweet Sweetback's Baadassss Song* appealed primarily to black audiences and were also financially successful. Sweetback, played by Melvin Van Peebles, who also directed and produced the film, beats two white policeman after they brutalize a black suspect. While Sweetback is a violent rapist, he is also a hero in that he disrupts racist business as usual and wins.

Richard Roundtree's character, Shaft, is a suave black detective who according to the soundtrack is "a bad mother—shut yo' mouth." *Shaft* was produced by MGM for $1.2 million and grossed $10.8 million within a year (Guerrero 1996, 86).

This genre of film had ambiguity in both message and production. While they were widely touted as black films, many of them were produced, written, and directed by whites. Some African Americans welcomed any film that portrayed defiant black characters who triumphed over white oppressors; other groups, such as the NAACP, denounced any repeated portrayal of blacks as drug pushers, pimps, and gangsters (Bogle 1994, 242). Despite all these drawbacks and stereotypes, these films were significant for the number of black actors they employed. This was to change once again in the 1980s.

By the early 1980s, roles for black actors and films with black themes once again became scarce. In 1974, at the height of the blaxploitation era, Hollywood produced a total of 295 films, 45 of which were primarily black themes or casts. By 1981, there were a total of 240 Hollywood films and only 6 of them were primarily African American (Guerrero 1996, 107).

The 1980s included complex images of African Americans as well as the remaking of old stereotypes. The theme of slavery was reconstituted in films such as *The Toy* in which Jackie Gleason buys Richard Pryor as a toy for his son (Guerrero 1996, 82). Films with African American characters shifted from African American themes and casts to the use of isolated superstars. The popularity of Richard Pryor, Eddie Murphy, and Whoopi Goldberg was on the rise. Films that appealed to both black and white audiences, so-called crossover films, became the norm.

These shifts took place in the context of Reaganism and the political backlash aimed at feminism, the civil rights movement, and affirmative action. Under Reagan's presidency, there was a political and social movement afoot to restore the United States from what the public perceived as a decline due to Watergate, Vietnam, and social change movements. Deregulation also characterized this time period, and Hollywood was not immune to this trend. During the 1980s, the film industry steadily became part of larger conglomerates in which movies came to be viewed increasingly as "product." The combination of the political climate and the changes in the corporate structure of the industry swept Hollywood into the conservative political backlash. By using the combination of new film technology and conservative ideology, the industry began to produce films that emphasized the triumph of the white working class, individualism, and the American Dream. Sylvester Stallone's *Rocky* series exemplifies this trend. From 1977 to 1990 there were five *Rocky* films made (Guerrero 1996, 115).

The Color Purple (1985), directed by Steven Spielberg and based on the novel by Alice Walker, demonstrated an interesting mix of the trends in the 1980s. The film was one of the few during this time period with a predominantly African American cast and was based on a novel by an African American woman. But *The Color Purple* also converted the antiracist themes of the novel into a mainstream film that reflected the dominant ideology.

In the novel, Walker explored abuse and internalized racism as experienced by Celie, Sophia, Mister, and Harpo. The male characters, Mister and Harpo, were abusive to black women, but were depicted as complex characters who "learned" to hate themselves and abuse women as a result of racism. In the book, Mister begins to change at the end. Celie also forms a tender sexual relationship with Mister's lover, Shug, and the fullness of the two women's love for each other is expressed on many levels. In the novel, Shug rejects her father, a minister, and his church because they mimic white oppression.

In the film, little of this political consciousness remains. The black male characters are overly simple, and their abuse and cruelty to women, void of the political context, appears to be solely the result of individual evil. The relationship between Shug and Celie is tender but superficial, and their sexual relationship is reduced to a chaste kiss. At the film's climax, Shug symbolically leaves singing at a juke joint to go to her father's church in a way that symbolizes her return from immorality to the purity of the church. The only remaining image of racism is the confrontation between Sophia and the white mayor and his wife (Guerrero 1996, 51). Aside from this scene, the film erases racism from its center, and the blame for African American problems seems to be placed primarily on the African American men in the film.

The film grossed $94 million at the box office and almost $50 million in video rental (Internet Movie Database 1999). In addition to Goldberg, it starred Danny Glover and was a film debut for Oprah Winfrey. Criticism of the film was wide-ranging. Some critics touted it as an extraordinary film that stayed true to the spirit of the book in reflecting the pain of racism and the triumph of the human spirit. Other critics said that it portrayed a brutal, misogynistic image of black men to the glorification of black women. Still others had political objections to the film because its message was about individualized racism and triumph rather than about systemic racism and organizational change (Bobo 1995, 54).

The careers of Richard Pryor and Whoopi Goldberg exemplify what was available to black stars in the 1980s. Both of their standup comedy routines were based on reflections of African American characters and culture and the hard-edged comic criticism of racism. But in film, Pryor's economically successful biracial buddy comedies with Gene Wilder (*Silver Streak* and *Stir Crazy*) featured Pryor teaching Wilder how to act black and scary. Dramatic and more complex roles for Pryor, such as *Blue Collar* (1978), were box-office flops and the lesson was not lost on Hollywood. Crossover, attracting the broadest possible audience, became the central force of mainstream films with black characters. These biracial buddy films became a genre of their own with films also featuring Eddie Murphy and Danny Glover in tandem with white actors such as Dan Akroyd and Mel Gibson. These buddy films conveyed a sense of fictional racial equality through partnership while ignoring the more factual state of race relations. Once again, this sent a false message that all is well.

Eddie Murphy and Whoopi Goldberg continue to have wide crossover appeal to both black and white audiences. While Murphy has played largely comedic roles, Goldberg's roles have ranged from the comic *Sister Act* and *Sister Act II* in the early 1990s to the dramatic *The Color Purple* (1985) and *Sarafina* (1992), and *Boys on the Side* (1995). Often both Murphy and Goldberg have played the classic black "buddy," the only person of color in the film.

By the 1990s several films emerged that examined life in black communities in central cities. In 1990 and 1991 alone, there were more films focused on African Americans than during the entire blaxploitation film period (Guerrero 1996, 159). This boom in African American films was kicked off by director Spike Lee's production of *She's Gotta Have It* (1986). Using what came to be known as "guerrilla cinema," Lee built on the successful formula of the blaxploitation era by making the film with his family and friends in twelve days for $175,000. The film grossed over $7 million (Guerrero 1996, 145). But this film and several that followed were produced independently. This independence allowed Lee to create African American characters that were complex as individuals and represented a range of different types of individuals.

During the 1990s, other African American directors emerged including John Singleton, Robert Townsend, Charles Burnett, and Julie Dash. Some of the films they produced used Lee's guerrilla cinema tactics and were made and distributed as independents, while others were financed and produced through major studios. Ironically, the ability to use the best technology and financing through a major studio to produce a film that would be seen by a wider audience meant that these directors were under the constraints of the industry to produce a profitable product. The mainstream pressure to sell the product often meant diluting insurgent ideology that challenged stereotypes, replacing it with what the studios thought would sell.

Do the Right Thing (1989) and *Boyz 'N the Hood* (1991) were directed by Spike Lee and John Singleton respectively. *Do the Right Thing* was financed by Universal Studios for $6.5 million and grossed $27.5 million. *Boyz 'N the Hood,* financed by Columbia, grossed $57.5 million. These films demonstrated the artistic and economic possibilities for the collaboration between African American directors and screenwriters with major studios. Both films introduced complex themes and frankly explored racism, using contemporary rap music as background and as political commentary.

Do the Right Thing took place on one hot summer day in a New York neighborhood in which relationships, racial dynamics, bigotry, and confusion were portrayed among white Italians, Asians, and African Americans in the community. The poverty, heat, and racism created a pressure cooker that ultimately exploded. This is a warning from Lee that if poverty and antiblack racism are not seriously addressed it can become explosive and life-threatening. Lee addressed racism in the exchanges between the Italian pizza shop owners and their black customers. He also employed a sort of modern-day chorus, with older African American men hanging out in the neighborhood commenting on the action and relationships. The danger of losing its political edge rested in the risk that the audience would reduce complex social issues to disputes between individuals. But Lee reduced this risk with his closing image of a handshake between Martin Luther King and Malcolm X, suggesting that it is the combination of their political approaches that offers the promise of racial justice.

Boyz 'N the Hood was set in South Central Los Angeles where gang and police violence are depicted as regular occurrences. The film follows a young Tre Styles (Cuba Gooding. Jr.) and his relationship with his father Furious (Laurence Fishburne), and their effort to fight the violence and damage of racism while living in the midst of it. *Boyz* was also the film debut of rapper Ice Cube as Doughboy, a young man whose violence was portrayed as a complex but inevitable result of personal and societal factors. In one scene, the complexity and systemic nature of racism is explained by Furious to Tre and some of his friends. Furious wants these young men to know the source of the guns and drugs that have invaded their lives and he discusses redevelopment and gentrification and who benefits and who suffers from it. Tre, Furious, Doughboy, and his brother Ricky are all complex characters who demonstrate varying degrees of internalized racism and varying methods of fighting the internal and external results of racism.

Despite the complexity of male characters and sophisticated portrayal of racism in these films, both paint portraits of one-dimensional black women. In *Do the Right Thing* the women are the main character's sister and girlfriend; the first is an archetypical virgin and the second is stereotypically highly sexed and sexy. In *Boyz 'N the Hood,* the women are in the background as mothers and girlfriends. But Ricky and Doughboy's mother is shown to favor Ricky and verbally and physically abuse Doughboy—one explanation of Doughboy's violence. Still another mother in the "hood" is shown as a crackhead, abusing and neglecting her children. Tre's mother and girlfriend are shown as "good women," but one-dimensional. The range and depth of the women in the film are thin and shallow as compared to the depth and complexity of the male characters.

The 1990s was an interesting decade for black characters and racial themes in film. Actors Denzel Washington, Morgan Freeman, Wesley Snipes, Samuel L. Jackson, Laurence Fishburne, Eddie Murphy, Whoopi Goldberg, Angela Bassett, and Whitney Houston played a range of characters from Malcolm X to the Nutty Professor and from Tina Turner to a revolutionary teacher in South Africa. Some of these actors and their films have received critical acclaim, such as Denzel Washington in *Glory* or Angela Bassett in *What's Love Got to Do With It.* Some of these films have had complex characters and themes that wove in race and racism and others have been simpler stories of love and sex or comic relief. In addition to these mainstream films, independent filmmaker Julie Dash produced the 1992 *Daughters of the Dust,* a rich and textured story of black families and black women, critically acclaimed but not economically successful.

For all its flaws, the 1995 film *White Man's Burden* took some interesting risks and twists on the theme of racism and power in black and white relations. Written and directed by Japanese American Desmond Nakano and starring Harry Belafonte and John Travolta, the film asked the audience to suppose what would happen if African Americans were in power. Some of the image reversals in the film cause viewers' heads to spin as we begin to ponder what we have come to consider as "normal." In one scene, wealthy African Americans sponsor a benefit for inner city white children who appear in their rag tag clothes as their black benefactors talk about how cute they are. In another scene, a young white boy channel surfs his television to find that most of the characters are black, and when he goes with his father to select his birthday present the only "cool" action figures are black.

While stereotypes of African Americans in film have not disappeared, an important phenomenon emerged in the 1990s. There were many films with black characters and themes that had a wide range of images and messages. This means that the same messages (blacks as subservient, blacks as ridiculous, blacks as violent) are not hammered regularly into audiences. This is a new trend, which if continued could mean an expansion of characters and themes that could provide a wider array of African American images and explore the impact of racism. "[T]he black filmmaker must struggle to depict the truth about black life in America while being inextricably tied to the commercialized sensibilities of a mass audience that is for the most part struggling to deny or avoid the full meaning of that truth" (Guerrero 1996, 168). It remains to be seen whether the boom of African American films in the 1990s is an irreversible trend or like the blaxploitation phenomenon, just another isolated moment in time in which content and economics come together temporarily.

African Americans and Popular Music

The relationship between blacks and whites in the United States and the history of race and racism are intricately woven into popular music written, produced, and recorded by African Americans. From the phenomenon of cover music to the Motown sound to rap and hip-hop, the music is often simple but the context is complex.

A quick scan of four decades of music from 1955 to 1995 reveals a different phenomenon than any other minority representation in popular culture. The songs that made the top forty charts for the years 1955, 1965, 1975, 1985, and 1995 were scanned for the presence of African American recording artists. During that time period, the African American percentage of the U.S. population never exceeded 12 percent. However, in 1955 the percentage of black recording artists to hit the top forty charts was 9 percent, 1965 was 20 percent, 1975 was 9 percent, 1985 was 13 percent, and 1995 was a whopping 34 percent (Lyrics World 1999). To begin to make some sense of this unusual occurrence in popular culture, we will examine cover music, the Motown sound, and rap and hip-hop music. This analysis will primarily focus on the widespread popularity across racial boundaries of music that has a "black sound." The crossover phenomenon we have seen in film with black actors has emerged in a different way in popular music.

Cover music is the term originally used to describe a 1950s strategy to promote white singers who recorded music that imitated or "covered" music created by black recording artists. This racist practice was based on the premise that white singers would sell more records, and the result was that many black singers and songwriters were relegated to the background at the expense of their careers and their bankbooks. White singers such as Pat Boone and Georgia Gibbs were cover artists for many black singers. Gibbs covered the sexually suggestive song "Roll with Me, Henry," which became "Dance with Me, Henry" in her version. At the same time that even the Beatles and the Rolling Stones covered black songs in the 1950s, white teenagers were exploring black music. "For the popularity of white covers or imitations of black rhythm and blues in the 1950s had conferred a mystique on the original black versions, which led many curious white teenagers to seek out the real thing. . . . The cultural and economic consequences were large. These teens, with more expendable money than their parents had when they were teenagers, became a real presence in the mass marketplace by the 1950s" (Early 1991, 13).

Part of the declaration of independence of adolescents from their parents in the United States has been their choice of music. Swing in the thirties and forties; rock and roll in the 1950s and 1960s; heavy metal, rhythm and blues, rap, and hip-hop have all at one time or another been part of popular youth culture. But it was in the 1950s that large numbers of white teenagers first became taken with black music. Whether it was the rhythm and blues of the 1950s or rap and hip-hop of the 1980s and 1990s, these white adolescents were not necessarily making a political statement that identified with antiracism and black liberation. Rather, by and large, they liked the sound, the music, and its sense of hipness or coolness.

In 1959 Berry Gordy founded Motown, a black owned and operated recording studio and record production company that promoted and recorded black artists. Gordy understood the historical context of the movement toward civil rights, the growth of black identity, and the phenomenon of the white youth fascination with black music. Ultimately, Motown became the most successful independent record company and the most successful black business in the United States. The tremendous success of Motown was in part because of the strength and appeal of the music and in part due to Gordy's understanding of business, politics, and culture.

Gordy employed a two-tiered marketing strategy. He marketed some rhythm and blues songs to be covered by white artists, and he marketed the original black recording artists as well (Early 1991, 13). Artists, songwriters, and superstars associated with Motown in the early years included Smokey Robinson and the Miracles, Diana Ross and the Supremes, Stevie Wonder, the Temptations, Mary Wells, and Marvin Gaye.

Motown was a predominantly black business, but from the beginning Gordy also hired white producers, promoters, and sales representatives. Gordy managed to establish an organization that appealed to blacks and whites in its strong black identity, successful economics, and its interest in racial integration. These organizational characteristics fit well with the 1950s historical context. "These were the years, then, in which America recognized, and cringed before, the social reality that would not hide itself anymore. . . . And the 'new' popular music helped to expose the false separation of America from itself, by revealing the culture's essential fusion all the more inescapably" (Early 1991, 14). The 1950s and 1960s Motown organization and sound and its wide appeal across racial lines gave a sense of hope and promise to blacks and whites who wanted integration. Here was a place where black and white people worked side by side to make and appreciate something together—music. In its organization, its recording artists, and in its audiences, the business and sound of Motown was the first major crossover phenomenon.

Hip-hop originated in New York in the 1970s. It began as a youth movement of sorts, a musical declaration of pride and identity amid urban poverty and alienation. Hip-hop was music, and it was clothing, language, and neighborhood identity and culture. The early days of hip-hop predated its discovery by mass media and a wider audience. Its musical form followed the African tradition of story telling and oral history of the "griots" or African storytellers. "Rappers have become urban griots, using their lyrics to disperse social commentary about what it means to be young and black in the late twentieth century" (Croteau and Hoynes 1997, 220).

Hip-hop and its most popular form, rap, changed from the 1970s to the 1990s. In its earliest form and in some of its contemporary incarnations, hip-hop and rap were political protest. Cultural studies scholars analyze political forms of rap as a popular and original form of music that has challenged and resisted the dominant culture. "In the face of under- and/or misrepresentation in traditional media, black youths have turned to hip-hop as a means to define themselves. In terms of resistance, hip-hop provided a forum from which black youth can portray what it means to be young and black in America and protest against it" (Croteau and Hoynes 1997, 222).

A strong example of political resistance in rap is Public Enemy's "Fight the Power," which was used as an anthem in Spike Lee's film *Do the Right Thing*. Public Enemy's lead rapper, Chuck D, was very explicit about the group's name and the political purpose of their music: "The sociopolitical meaning of Public Enemy came after we decided the group would be called that, because the meaning and the connection of what we were about fit right in. The Black man and woman was considered three-fifths of a human being in the Constitution of the United States. Since the government and the general public follow the Constitution, then we must be the enemy" (Croteau and Hoynes 1997, 84). While the political messages, establishment of an alternative culture, and resistance to dominant culture still exist to some degree in contemporary hip-hop, another trend emerged in the 1980s that changed it. This was the enormous surge in the white audience for rap. "[A]lthough rap is still proportionally more popular among blacks, its primary audience is white and lives in the suburbs" (Early 1991, 24). Rap crossed over to white audiences in 1984 with Run-DMC and King of Rock. The 1970s rappers were immersed in urban street culture while the rappers in these 1980s crossover groups were middle-class young men dressed according to the urban hip-hop mode (Samuels 1991, 26).

Public Enemy's message was clearly that of political resistance and black nationalism accompanied by a number of contradictory elements. But Public Enemy was formed not on the streets of New York, but in suburban Long Island, where the group's members grew up. Their protest was not from the urban streets but from suburban college students who were standing up to inequality. This type of protest was valid, yet removed from the urban street authenticity of early hip-hop. Their song "Fight the Power" (1989) became the biggest college hit to cross racial lines (Samuels 1991, 27). In fact, hip-hop culture, language, and dress have become a subculture among young white men and teens.

In some ways the popularity of rap and hip-hop culture in suburban white communities is the continuation of the popularity of the Motown sound and rhythm and blues in general among white audiences. The separation of youth from their parents and from the dominant culture is a familiar strain in the United States and is often reflected in musical tastes that are substantially different from those of the previous generation. In this regard, white youth's attraction to rap is not unlike similar attractions to rock or heavy metal or punk music.

What differentiates the attraction of vast white audiences to rap from those audiences drawn to Motown in earlier years is the message in the music. Motown was doo-wop and love songs with simple messages of love lost or love gained. With the exception of some of Marvin Gaye's more political songs (e.g., "What's Going On?"), the most political thing about Motown was that it was an African American business. The political messages in rap run from protest of racism and police brutality to the brazen social messages of violence and abuse to women in gangsta rap. Why would these messages have such deep and wide appeal to young white men?

Some critics speculate that in addition to a declaration of generation independence and an attraction to the beat of the music, young white men are opposing racial discrimination in their musical tastes, and this is their form of musical protest. Other critics see it as a door for young white people to try to see and understand black culture. Still others see it as a way for white youth to appropriate black culture without ever being required to have personal contact: "The ways in which rap has been consumed and popularized speak not of cross-cultural understanding, musical or otherwise, but of a voyeurism and tolerance of racism in which black and white are both complicit" (Samuels 1991, 29).

Whichever explanations seem reasonable to you, the fact is that since 1991 most popular music charts identify black music as occupying at least seven of the top ten positions on the chart. This phenomenon is unlike any other in popular forms of media, where African Americans are in the minority or are stereotyped or segregated.

African Americans and Prime Time Television

It is your turn again. Complete the exercise in Media Activity 5.4 below to begin to look at African Americans in television. How many of the programs had casts that were predominantly African American? How many of the programs had casts that were predominantly white? How many of the casts were racially mixed with significant numbers of African Americans and whites? In 1999 you may have found some dramas such as *The Practice* and *Homicide* with racially mixed casts and other dramas such as *E.R.*, *Chicago Hope*, and *Law and Order* with some recurring and/or major African American characters, but by and large you probably

Media Activity 5.4
Black and White Television

Instructions

Use a listing of local television programming from your local newspaper or *TV Guide*. Choose two weeknights and make a list of the narrative programming offered from 7 to 10 p.m. central time or 8 to 11 p.m. eastern time that is offered on ABC, CBS, FOX, and NBC. Do not list any movies, news, infotainment or variety programs, or special broadcasts. List only narrative programs that are either dramatic series or situation comedies. Next to each program place an X in the appropriate column to indicate whether the regular cast is predominantly African American, predominantly white, or racially mixed of African Americans and whites or other races. Indicate racially mixed only when there is more than 25 percent of any racial group. Indicate "other" when the cast is predominantly a race other than African American or white. Feel free to ask other people about the cast of any of the programs with which you are not familiar. Determine the percentage of each column in relation to the total number of programs

	Predominantly African-American cast	Predominantly white cast	Racially mixed cast	Other races	Total number of programs
List of programs					
Total numbers: _____	_____	_____	_____	_____	
Percentage of total programs: _____	_____	_____	_____	_____	

discovered that situation comedies are as segregated as most churches are on Sunday morning.

Racially mixed casts are a very new trend in entertainment television programming. We will examine this emerging pattern and others throughout television's history and take a close look at the industry, the racial content and messages of programming, and the impact on audiences.

Understanding the relationship of advertising to entertainment television is key to understanding the evolution of African American images. Because television in the United States is part of private industry, the success of individual programs has always been based on a particular program's ability to reach a wide audience. This popularity or projected popularity is what generates advertising, profit, and the length of the run of a program. Advertisers' pursuit of larger audiences has played a critical role in shaping prime time content. Until recently, a widely held belief was that since the majority of the audience was white, this was the group that constituted the mass to whom programming should be directed. "It was the task of the mass media to find commonalities among members of the audience; common themes, ideas, interest areas that would attract and not offend the mass audience. With few exceptions, this meant that the content of the mass media reinforced, rather than challenged, the established norms and attitudes of society. To do otherwise would be to risk offending significant numbers of the mass audience, and in the process, lose the large audience demanded by the advertisers" (Wilson and Gutierrez 1995, 41–42).

There have been few prime time programs with serious African American themes and messages. Among these are *Frank's Place* (1987–88) and *Under One Roof* (1995). Both received extraordinary critical acclaim. *Under One Roof* was a mid-season replacement for *Rescue 911* and was poorly publicized. It was one of the only television dramas with a predominantly African American cast. The recurring characters demonstrated a range in class, use of language, dress, and values with identities that ranged from Afrocentric to assimilated. The short-lived series offered universal themes of family life, love, and conflict, but also focused on plots revolving around interracial friendship, racist business practices, and the intersection of poverty and race. *Under One Roof* was the victim of a changing of the guards in CBS's entertainment division with an accompanying change in vision. Leslie Moonves, the new President of Entertainment, wanted to change the image of CBS as the network for older Americans to include younger, hipper programming. When *Under One Roof,* with a star the caliber of James Earl Jones, could not pull a wide audience in its six weeks on the air, it became a casualty to economics and network politics and CBS pulled it off the air after six episodes.

Images of African Americans on television changed throughout the decades in part according to the racial climate and culture of the times, but the bulk of these changes can be attributed to shifts in viewing patterns and profitability. Since the 1950s, much of prime time television has reflected and reinforced the stereotypes, race relations and prejudices of the dominant culture. "[R]acial images in the mass media are infused with color-coded positive and negative moralistic features. Once these symbols become familiar and accepted, they fuel misperceptions and perpetuate misunderstandings among the races" (Dates and Barlow 1990, 4).

In the 1950s African American characters as servants were the norm on prime time. *Beulah* (1950–53), played by Louise Beavers, was a wide-eyed, grinning, heavy-set woman who served as a maid to a white family. This was the first television show to star an African American actor. But while Beulah was the title character of the show, her whole life revolved around the white family she served and her own family and independent life were invisible.

In *The Jack Benny Show* (1950–1964), *The Stu Erwin Show: The Trouble with Father* (1950–55), *My Little Margie* (1952–55), *Make Room for Daddy* (1953–64), *The Great Gildersleeve* (1955–56), and *Father of the Bride* (1961–62), the only black characters were butlers, maids, or handymen in minor or one-shot roles. "The domestic was a symbol that a White family was successful. Therefore, it was this decoding of the servant role that antagonized the NAACP and Black middle class. While it is true the Black middle class were antagonistic toward the portrayals of Black men and women as maids and butlers in film, radio, and television, their quest for a piece of the American dream was the critical element to understanding their strategy for censorship in these popular forms" (Nelson 1998, 81).

Like *Beulah, Amos and Andy* (1951–53) was based on an old radio show. While African American actress Hattie McDaniel originated the role of Beulah on radio, it was two white men who played Amos and Andy before it made the jump to TV. The male characters (Andy, Amos, Kingfish, Lighting) on *Amos and Andy* were alternately sly, cunning, and conniving, while the women (Sapphire and Mama) were domineering, loud, big, and shrewish. The stereotypes on *Amos and Andy* were so strong that the NAACP made the protest of this program central to its 1951 convention and platform.

The messages about African Americans in the 1950s were abundantly clear. Their overall absence on TV marked their perceived insignificance in the dominant culture. The fact that the few roles available to African Americans were as servants and/or buffoons reinforced stereotypes and reflected the misinformation and belief in their inferiority to whites.

The 1968–71 series *Julia* signified a new kind of African American character. Played by Diahann Carroll, Julia was a nurse and single parent and the program was the first to feature a black star since *Amos and Andy*. In 1968 Martin Luther King was assassinated and the Poor People's Campaign occurred in Washington, D.C., but in the world of *Julia* the message was assimilation and the invisibility of race. Race was rarely mentioned. Racism and racial struggle did not exist in this television land (Dines and Humez 1995, 416).

The primary 1970s programs with African American characters were *Room 222* (1969–74), *Sanford and Son* (1972–77), *The Jeffersons* (1975–85), *Good Times* (1974–79), and *What's Happening* (1976–78). All of these programs were situation comedies. Three of them *(Good Times, Sanford and Son,* and *What's Happen-*

ing) were set in low-income black urban areas and foregrounded fun and laughter amidst the mostly unaddressed background of poverty and struggle. *The Jeffersons* represented the flip side of these programs—the "hilarious" antics of upward mobility and attempted assimilation of an African American family. Unlike the others, *Room 222* was set in a school and involved African American teachers as the main characters. But overall, the decade of the 1970s conveyed the message of the happy but poor black family and failed to demonstrate much about the structural barriers of racism faced by urban black families. Using entertainment media assessment tools to examine complexity in individual characters and diversity among black characters as a test to determine the extent of stereotypes reveals that most of these characters and programs failed. The same message was repeated over and over to once again reinforce the fallacy of the inferiority of African Americans.

The miniseries *Roots* (1981) was significant on many levels. It was one of the most watched television programs of all times. Families of all races remained glued to their television sets during that week. This created a second element of significance. After each daily installment of this epic, which followed a black family from Africa to slavery to freedom, were the discussions at work and at school. These discussions, often across racial lines, were for some people the first time they had ever discussed race and racism in U.S. history with someone of another race. *Roots* was significant in visually portraying the horrors of slavery and contradicting stereotypes and myths of white superiority. In the end, this phenomenal miniseries reinforced the myth of the American Dream "[W]ith *Roots* the popular media discourse about slavery moved from one of almost complete invisibility (never mind structured racial subordination, human degradation, and economic exploitation) to one of ethnicity, immigration, and human triumph. This powerful television epic effectively constructed the story of American slavery from the stage of emotional identifications and attachments to individual characters, family struggles, and the realization of the American dream" (Gray 1995, 78).

Throughout television's history, "Televised comedies helped Americans adjust to the social order as transmitted myths and ideology reinforced society's implicit rules and codes of behavior. In their portrayal of African American images, these comedies picked up threads of the established pattern of white superiority and black servitude and continued to weave them back into the popular culture" (Dates and Barlow 1990, 261). This was the trend in prime time television until the mid-1980s, when *The Cosby Show* marked a shift in the way African Americans were portrayed in television and presented a more complex set of images . . . and problems.

The Cosby Show (1984–92) was a phenomenal success among both black and white audiences. It was ranked number one during most of the years it was broadcast. The program was a situation comedy that featured an upper middle class African American family, the Huxtables, in which Cliff was a doctor, and Clair was a lawyer. The story was set primarily in their home and revolved around the interactions between the parents and their five children. Bill Cosby and African American psychiatrist and program consultant Alvin Poussaint, were aiming to accomplish two objectives with *The Cosby Show*. The first was to entertain. The second was to create a situation comedy that depicted exceptional African Americans who were financially and socially successful in order to depart from previous black stereotypes of poverty, servitude, and buffoonery. Ironically, the extraordinarily successful Cosby characters let the white audience off the hook with respect to any complex understanding of continued racism in the United States.

In fact, Bill and Camille Cosby funded a study to determine the impact of *The Cosby Show* on black and white audiences. This study, conducted by cultural studies scholars Sut Jhally and Justin Lewis, involved identifying messages through content analysis and conducting small racially separate focus groups to discuss responses to various aspects of the program. Jhally and Lewis concluded the following:

- *The Cosby Show* was successful in generating racial tolerance among white viewers and racial pride among black viewers.
- Racially, the United States remains a deeply divided society in desperate need of major structural changes to rectify its profound racism. *The Cosby Show* joined other programs in promoting the fiction that the civil rights movement had "won." By touting the exceptions rather than the rule of class and race oppression, the program contributed to the myth of the American Dream.
- The debate among viewers regarding whether the Huxtables were "too white" was really a debate about class and resulted in confusing both black and white audiences about both race and class.
- *The Cosby Show* contributed to a strong belief among some whites that there was no need to act on racism in this country, because it is no longer a serious problem.
- The term "enlightened racism" refers to the complex concept indirectly fostered by *The Cosby Show,* which left white viewers to believe that black people who do not succeed like the Huxtables are individually to blame for their problems and are lazy, and/or stupid (Jhally and Lewis 1992, 83).

The Cosby Show was powerful in its signaling of these messages both because of its popularity and because of the extent to which it weekly visited both white and African American homes. But its power also stemmed from the fact that it was among the scarce prime time images of African Americans during that time. Without a wide range of class representations among African Americans, and with few themes regarding the continued structural barriers of race, the themes, characters, and messages of this one program became increasingly important and potent.

Politically, the 1980s were dominated by a shift in politics marked by the presidency of Ronald Reagan and what was known as Reaganomics. Central to the ideology of the Reagan years was the return to the Western theme of individualism and the belief in the power of the one person or one family to create their own destiny. The intersection of class and race and their impact on a person's ability to be well educated and find solid employment, housing, and so forth were not a consideration in these times. Rather, the political message was the same as that of the American Dream—your success or failure is in your hands and your hands alone.

Racially, this meant that a shift was made from the 1960s ideology of low income African Americans as victims of racism to a new belief that it was middle
class white people who suffered from unfair treatment as a result of social welfare,
affirmative action, and other so-called special treatment for blacks. "In short,
Reaganism had to take away from blacks the moral authority and claims on political entitlements won in the civil rights movement of the 1960s" (Gray 1995, 17).

While *The Cosby Show* and other 1980s programs such as *Benson, Different
Strokes,* and *227* unwittingly bought into this political shift, there were also programs such as the short-lived *Frank's Place* and *A Different World* that created
more serious and complex characters and images, raised questions about race and
racism and challenged the dominant ideology that the individual is the only source
of racial problems.

There were several different historical, economic, technological, and cultural
issues in the 1980s that set the stage for new trends for African Americans in 1990s
prime time television. First, the decline in network viewing due to cable and video
forced the networks to rethink and redefine their audiences. This takes us back to
the relationship between programming and advertising. Second, the success of
The Cosby Show signaled that there was a potential for marketing African American programs and casts to both African American and crossover white audiences.
Third, the concept of "narrowcasting" was born amid cable and video. This concept was based on research that demonstrated that black audiences watched prime
time television more than any other group and that low income black audiences
were less likely to have cable. All of these factors contributed to the proliferation
of black programming and casts and a renewed segregation on prime time.

In 1998, the top ten TV programs watched by black households were strikingly
different than those viewed by white households. African Americans watched programs with predominantly black casts and whites watched programs with predominantly white casts. The number one show for African Americans was *Between Brothers*
on Fox. This same program was ranked 117 for white viewers. The remaining nine
popular programs for black viewers in 1998 were: *Living Single, 413 Hope Street,
The Steve Harvey Show, The Wayans Brothers, Good News, Malcolm & Eddie, Sparks,
Moesha,* and *Smart Guy.* White households preferred *ER, Seinfeld, Veronica's Closet,
Friends, Touched by an Angel, NFL Monday Night Football, Home Improvement,
Union Square,* and the *CBS Sunday Night Movie* (Richmond 1998, 1).

The following are two examples of contemporary situation comedies that serve
as models for the possibility of addressing race and racism in ways that while
staying within the context of humor of the particular program raise important questions that transcend stereotypes and the focus on the individual.

Robert Townsend's contemporary television program, *Parent 'Hood* (1995–)
paid an interesting tribute to the young actor, William Thomas Jr., who played the
role of Buckwheat in *The Little Rascals.* The situation comedy revolves around an
African American family, and in this episode the young son Nicholas was required
to choose an African American person that he admired and to portray this person
in a student production. To his parents' dismay, Nicholas chose Buckwheat. The

plot of the episode involved many twists and turns in which his parents tried to dissuade him from selecting a character who exemplified some of the worst of African American stereotypes.

Ultimately Nicholas was determined to stick with his original choice and proceeded to dress as Buckwheat for the production. But his discussion of the actor William Thomas Jr. turned serious as Nicholas explained to the audience how few options were available to black actors during the 1930s and that William Thomas Jr. was a hero because of his acting talent, his ability to maintain some dignity amid the racist times, and because his work was groundbreaking for African American actors who came after him. Implicit in this tribute was that the work of William Thomas Jr. paved the way for Curtis Williams, the young African American actor who played Nicholas, to portray a character who did not have to conform to rigid racial stereotypes.

In the situation comedy *Third Rock from the Sun* (1996–) the central premise is that of a group of aliens inhabiting human forms in order to study the earth and its people. While the Solomons have studied many documented aspects of American people and culture, it is clear that their education has gaps. The comedy of this program often revolves around these gaps in informal societal rules and the kind of information that we have learned is typically absent in history texts.

The episode in question revolves around the observations of Dick Solomon (a university professor played by John Lithgow) of his African American secretary Nina's participation in an African American pride group. Solomon and his cohorts, unaware of the finer points of racism, puzzle over this notion of black pride and begin to inquire about the existence of "white pride" groups. Through their inquiry they discover a white supremacist group meeting, which in their ignorance they believe will be equivalent to Nina's black pride group. When they attend this meeting, to their horror they discover the virulence of racism. When the group burns a cross, the Solomons are once again puzzled and question what this white group has against the "small letter 't.'" The story goes on to simulate and mock white paternalism in a variety of ways, consistently remaining faithful to the program's premise and the source of its humor. However, in selecting the topic of race and revealing it through the untainted eyes of these "aliens," this episode also mocks racism and its absurd ranking of people according to skin color.

As with recent developments of African American characters and themes in film, these two examples of prime time television offer some promise that even within the limited genre of the formulaic thirty-minute sit-com exist possibilities to raise serious questions about race.

Chapter Summary

With racially segregated neighborhoods and schools still prevalent in the United States, there are only a few ways that we can learn about races that are different from our own, the way racism has operated throughout our history, and the contemporary face of racism. We can learn in school; we can learn through our own independent reading or participation in multiracial cultural, social, and political events; and we can learn from the media. As we discovered in Chapter Four, U.S. schools have been notoriously superficial and misleading in the way curriculum and texts explain race and racism. The majority of people do not have the information, inclination, or time to seek independent multiracial ideas or activities. One of the few sources of information about race that is universally available to Americans is popular media in the form of music, film, and prime time television.

Stretched across these three popular forms of media and the decades of the twentieth century is a widely varying picture of how Asian Americans, American Indians, African Americans, Latinos, and European Americans, their relationships to one another, and the story of race in America are portrayed. There are, however, some common features.

The evolution of popular media in the United States has been located exclusively in the private sector and has been largely dictated by economics. When it has been profitable (such as films of the blaxploitation era, Motown, or *The Cosby Show*), themes and characters of color have proliferated. But even in times of relative abundance, these characters, themes, and interracial relationships have tended to reinforce a dominant ideology that promotes the dual myths of white superiority and the American Dream. There have been isolated examples in which complex characters, relationships, and themes about race have presented oppositional ideologies that question the racial status quo. Toward the end of the twentieth century we saw an increase in the number of people of color who were musicians and filmmakers and TV producers offering thoughtful alternatives to standard racial representations.

Nevertheless a 1998 study revealed that only two out of ten Latino and Asian children, and four out of ten African American children say they see people of their race "very often" on TV, compared to seven out of ten white children. The impact of this lack of images of people of color is significant for everyone in that it signals who is important in U.S. society.

While the relatively recent trend of more participation and representation of people of color and racial themes is significant to production of more diverse images and stories, the role of the audience or media consumer is equally significant in changing the media racial terrain. The extent to which consumers are able to detect invisible racial and racist messages in media and to question and challenge them is the extent to which we are able to untangle the web of racial fallacies and misinformation.

Bibliography

Aleiss, Angela. 1995. "Native Americans: The Surprising Silents." *Cineaste* 21 no. 3 (Summer): 34.

Bobo, Jacqueline. 1995. "The Color Purple—Black Women as Cultural Readers." In *Gender, Race and Class in Media*, ed. Gail Dines and Jean M. Humez, 54. Thousand Oaks, CA: Sage.

Bogle, Donald. 1994. *Toms, Coons, Mulattoes, Mammies, and Bucks: An Interpretive History of Blacks in American Films.* New York: Continuum.

Braus, Patricia. 1993. "What Does 'Hispanic' Mean (How Marketers Perceive the Hispanic American Consumer Group)." *American Demographics* 15, no. 6 (June): 46.

Croteau, David, and Hoynes, William. 1997. *Media/Society: Industries, Images, and Audiences*. Thousand Oaks, CA.: Pine Forge Press.

Dates, Jannette L., and Barlow, William, eds. 1990. *Split Image: African Americans in the Mass Media*. Washington DC: Howard University Press.

Dines, Gail, and Humez, Jean M., eds. 1995. *Gender, Race and Class in Media*. Thousand Oaks, CA: Sage.

Dirks, Tim. 1999. http://www.filmsite.org/cato.html.

Early, Gerald. 1991. "One Nation Under a Groove: The Brief, Shining Moment of Motown—and America." *New Republic* 205, no. 3: 30.

Edgerton, Gary, and Kathy Merlock Jackson. 1996. "Redesigning Pocahontas: Disney, the 'White Man's Indian,' and Marketing of Dreams." *Journal of Popular Film and Television* 24, no. 90 (Summer): 2–9.

Gerbner, George. 1998, November. "Casting and Fate in '98: Fairness and Diversity in Television: An Update and Trends Since the 1993 SAG Report." In *A Cultural Indicators Project Report to the Screen Actors Guild*, pp. 1–4.

Gray, Herman. 1995. *Watching Race*. Minneapolis: University of Minnesota Press.

Guerrero, Edward. 1996. *Framing Blackness: The African American Image in Film*. Philadelphia: Temple University Press.

Hamamoto, Darrell Y. 1994. *Monitored Peril: Asian Americans and the Politics of TV Representation*. Minneapolis: University of Minnesota Press.

"Hispanics: Last Frontier for Marketing. (Television Show Viewer Ratings of Hispanic Americans)." 1993. *Broadcasting and Cable* 123, no. 36: 54–58.

Internet Movie Database. 1999. http://us.imdb.com.

Jhally, Sut, and Lewis, Justin. 1992. *Enlightened Racism: The Cosby Show, Audiences, and the Myth of the American Dream*. Boulder, CO: Westview Press.

Kempley, Rita. 1988. "Mississippi Burning." washingtonpost.com. http://www.washington.com, December 9.

"The Long March from Wong to Woo: Asians in Hollywood." 1995. *Thi Thanh Nga* 21 (4 Fall): 38.

Lyrics World. 1998–2000. http://lyrics.natanet.com.br.

Media Awareness. 1998. http://www.media-awareness.ca/eng/issues/STATS/issmin.html.

Nelson, Angela M.S. 1998. "Black Situation Comedies and the Politics of Television Art." In *Cultural Diversity and the U.S. Media,* ed. Yahya R. Kamalipour and Theresa Crilli, 81. New York: State University of New York Press.

Richmond, Ray. 1998. "TV Sitcoms: The Great Divide-Few Shows Bridge Black, White Audiences." *Variety* 370, no. 9: 1.

Rodriguez, Clara E., ed. 1997. *Latin Looks: Images of Latinas and Latinos in U.S. Media*. Boulder, CO: Westview Press.

Samuels, David. 1991. "The Rap on Rap: The 'Black Music' That Isn't Either." *New Republic* 205, no. 20: 24–29.

Seals, David. 1991. "The New Custerism." *The Nation* 252, no. 18: 634.

Thomas, Rebecca. 1996. "There's a Whole Lot o' Color in the 'White Man's' Blues: Country Music's Selective Memory and the Challenge of Identity." *The Midwest Quarterly* 38, no. 1: 73.

Wilson, Clint C. II, and Gutierrez, Felix. 1995. *Race, Multiculturalism, and the Media: From Mass to Class Communication*. Thousand Oaks, CA: Sage.

Wong, Deborah. 1994. "I Want the Microphone: Mass Mediation and Agency in Asian-American Popular Music." *TDR* 38, no. 3 (Fall): 152.

Zoglin, Richard. 1988. "Awaiting a Gringo Crumb: Hispanics Have Gained on TV—But Oddly, Not Much." *Time Magazine* 132, no. 3: 76.

Chapter 6

Sexual Orientation and the Fabrication of "Normal"

We are your gay and lesbian children: "You must not seek
vengeance, nor bear a grudge against the children of your
people" (Lev. 19:18); [W]e are the stranger: "You must not
oppress the stranger. You shall love the stranger as yourself for
you were strangers in the land of Egypt" (Lev. 9:34); [W]e are
your gay and lesbian neighbors: "You must not oppress your
neighbor" (Lev.19:13). "You must judge your neighbor justly"
(Lev. 19:14). "You shall love your neighbor as yourself"
(Lev.19:18)

—Olyan and Nussbaum

Best advice I ever got was from an old friend of mine, a black
friend, who said you have to go the way your blood beats. If you
don't live the only life you have, you won't live some other life,
you won't live any life at all.

—James Baldwin

Personal Experience

Most of us have an ironic blend of huge gaps in information about gays, lesbians,
and bisexuals mixed with strong negative messages. In this chapter we will examine the sources of our information and misinformation and reconstruct what we
consider to be true about sexual orientation. As you begin to think about, or continue, your journey in understanding sexual orientation and identity, consider the
following questions. Your answers will help you locate your current beliefs and
values and questions about sexual identity. Your responses to the four questions in
Personal Inventory 6.1 constitute elements of your current beliefs, attitudes, openness, knowledge, and experience about sexual orientation and identity. Your clarity about your starting perspective will help you observe and analyze your response
to what you read in this chapter. As always, you are never required to change your

Personal Inventory 6.1
Locating My Beliefs

Instructions

Choose the statement that comes closest to matching your current beliefs.

1. The following statement comes closest to matching what I think
   about what it means to be gay, lesbian, or bisexual:
   a. I think it is wrong to be gay, lesbian, or bisexual.   ____
   b. I believe it is important to judge the "sin" and not the "sinner."   ____
   c. I am confused and not sure what to think.   ____
   d. I respect other people's choices, but I don't agree with the
      gay, lesbian or bisexual "lifestyle."   ____
   e. I think that gays, lesbians, and bisexuals are as natural as
      heterosexuals and should have all the same rights.   ____
   f. I think that being gay, lesbian or bisexual is liberating and
      frees people from the constraints of heterosexuality.   ____
   g. Other (please indicate) _____

2. The following phrase comes closest to describing my academic
   or intellectual knowledge and understanding of sexual orientation
   and sexual identity.
   a. Very little or none.   ____
   b. A moderate amount.   ____
   c. Some reading and studying.   ____
   d. Extensive reading and studying.   ____
   e. Other (please indicate) _____

(cont'd)

beliefs, but only to remember that they are your beliefs, which is not always the same as the "truth." It is important to understand how what you believe influences your openness to new information and experience.

More than any other topic of cultural diversity, sexual orientation and sexual identity in the United States is more controversial and confusing to many people. We receive less information about this issue than gender or race or even socioeconomic class. Many religions teach that to be gay or lesbian or bisexual is a sin or a sickness. Many people go through much of their lives without ever knowingly interacting with someone who is gay, lesbian, or bisexual. While jokes about race in the twenty-first century are considered out of line in most social circles, gay jokes still abound. While it is rare to hear anyone publicly express disdain about people of different races, it is not so unusual to hear someone speak publicly and

3. The following statement comes closest to describing my personal knowledge and understanding of sexual orientation and sexual identity.
   a. I have never known anyone who was openly gay, lesbian, or bisexual. ___
   b. I have met a few people who are openly gay, lesbian, or bisexual but have not been friends with them. ___
   c. I have one or more friends or family members who are openly gay, lesbian, or bisexual. ___
   d. I am part of a community that has many members who are openly gay, lesbian, or bisexual. ___
   e. I am part of a community that is exclusively gay, lesbian, or bisexual. ___
   Other (please indicate) _____

4. Choose the sentence that comes closest to your thoughts as you begin studying sexual orientation and sexual identity.
   a. I hate the idea of even reading this chapter. The topic disturbs me. ___
   b. I am uncomfortable about the topic of sexual orientation and identity and am hesitant to study it. ___
   c. I am confused and unclear about approaching the study of sexual orientation and identity. ___
   d. I am neutral and have no strong thoughts or feelings about sexual orientation and identity. ___
   e. I am somewhat curious and open to learn more about sexual orientation and identity. ___
   f. I am very curious and very open to study sexual orientation and identity. ___
   g. I am excited that sexual orientation and identity are part of this work and eager to learn more. ___
   h. Other (please indicate) _____

negatively about homosexuality or people who are gay or lesbian. While it is clear that racism and sexism are still alive in the United States, the culture has changed in many ways to make their most blatant expression unacceptable to many people. Not so with homosexuality. This lack of experience, information, and cultural acceptance of intolerance makes this an especially challenging topic. The fact that many people's beliefs about homosexuality are in some way tied to their religion creates another layer of challenge.

Some of you who are reading this are gay, lesbian, or bisexual and are interested in learning more about history, oppression, and liberation of your community and may be impatient with the careful attention to those who judge or discriminate against you. Some of you reading this are friends and allies of people who are gay, lesbian, or bisexual and want to learn more about what you can do to support the liberation of this community. Some of you reading this may have given little or no thought to this issue. Some of you reading this may feel confused about the issue or negative toward people who are gay, lesbian, or bisexual. Whoever you are, this chapter is for you. This chapter is for those people who identify with targeted or marginalized groups, those who are in the majority, and those who may not have thought about how cultural dominance and marginalization around sexual orientation and identity occurs and affects us all.

Now that you have begun to identify your current beliefs and attitudes about sexual orientation, we will examine what contributed to this perspective. As we explore the experience of socialization, it is important to remember that people who are gay, lesbian, and bisexual are subject to the same information, misinformation, and distortions as people who are heterosexual. Answer the questions and total your score in Personal Inventory 6.2.

If you scored a total of 20–25 points, you have been socialized to understand homosexuality as a natural phenomenon and have been told that people who are gay, lesbian, or bisexual can be good family members and friends that deserve all of the privileges and rights of heterosexuals. If you scored 15–19 points, you have been taught that homosexuality is acceptable but with some limitations. For example, your parents may have taught you to respect people who are gay, lesbian, or bisexual, but you overheard them telling gay jokes. Or your religion may have taught you that you should feel sorry for people who are homosexual but your parents had good friends who were gay, lesbian, or bisexual who you thought were terrific. If you scored 10–14 points you were socialized to believe that homosexuality was mostly wrong. You learned from at least one group (parents, religion, peers) that to be gay, lesbian, or bisexual was unnatural or wrong. You may have had at least one or two groups tell you something positive about gays, lesbians, or bisexuals but it contradicted other things that you learned. This may have created some confusion for you. If you scored 5–9 points, chances are you were told nothing or very little and what little you were told was very negative about homosexuality. If you scored under 5, you were socialized to believe that to be gay, lesbian, or bisexual was either a forbidden topic to discuss or it was sinful, evil, and wrong. Each group reinforced this message and what you learned was consistent.

As I was growing up, I received no formal information about sexual orientation. I assumed, without any conscious awareness of the assumption, that I was "normal" and expected that I would grow up and marry a man. The first time I can remember being directly told anything about gays or lesbians was the summer before seventh grade when my best friend's older sister had a talk with us. She told us that we had to stop holding hands when we got to junior high school because everyone would call us "fairies." Now at that point, I was not sure what a fairy was, but I could tell from the way that she said it that it was not something good. From that point until much later in my adulthood I ceased holding hands or having much physical contact with girls or women. My other early memories consist of adults joking about and mocking hairdressers and interior decorators who they assumed were gay men. The mocking always involved a limp wrist and an exaggerated feminine accent. Other than these two experiences, I had absolutely no other formal or informal information about gays, lesbians, or bisexuals. I am not sure I even knew the words. The words I heard were queer, fairy, fruit, and sissy. I knew that while it was acceptable for a girl to be a "tomboy" and do "boy type things" such as sports and getting dirty, it was not acceptable for a boy to do "girl type things" such as play dolls, cry, or hang out too much with girls.

I was born in 1949, and it was not until the late 1960s and early 1970s that I became aware of any other information or experience about what it meant to be gay, lesbian, or bisexual. During the 1960s I became involved in what was then called the women's liberation movement and voraciously read everything about women and feminism that I could get my hands on. Some of the books I read discussed coming out as a lesbian as a natural and evolving phenomenon and other books addressed being a lesbian as the ultimate feminist political statement. In the 1970s I knew women who had publicly identified as heterosexual who either experimented with relationships with women or "came out" as lesbian. I was not close enough to any of these women to share the intimate details of this coming out process. It was not until the mid-1970s that I became close friends with men and women who were gay and lesbian. One friend disclosed to me that she was lesbian with much trepidation. She feared that I would reject her. She feared telling her parents.

I had one male friend whose religion had taught him that to be gay was a sin. For the first four years of our friendship I thought he was heterosexual. It was not until we had been good friends for that long that he told me of his struggle to address his sexuality. In the early stages of this struggle, he was convinced that he needed to do everything possible to transform, be "normal," and be accepted by his church. He told no one of his sexual identity. He tried dating women. He had a brief encounter with the priesthood. He had a longer encounter with alcohol. It was a more than ten-year process for him to come to grips with and accept his sexuality and the full range of who he is. He is now in a long-term committed relationship with a man. Being a witness to this painful process moved me. Here was an extremely bright, funny, professionally successful, interesting, and compassionate person whose sexual identity and its rejection from society served to torture him for many, many years. It was during that time that I made a conscious decision to be an ally to people who are gay, lesbian, and bisexual.

Since that time I have had many friends who are gay, lesbian, and bisexual. They are part of a larger group which I consider my community. I never "taught" my children about sexual orientation when they were very young; it was a fact of their life and experience. My students frequently ask me how I could teach such young children about homosexuality and sex. My answer has been that when my children were preschoolers, I never taught them about how heterosexuals have sex and would not teach them about homosexual sex either. Rather, I have told them that sometimes boys and girls love each other and become life partners or get

Personal Inventory 6.2
How Do I Know What I Know?

Instructions

Choose the answer that comes closest to your experience and circle this response. When you complete all of the questions add your total score.

1. As a child, my parents told me that people who were gay, lesbian, or bisexual were:
    a. sinful   ___ (0 points)
    b. sick   ___ (1 point)
    c. unfortunate people who deserved our sympathy   ___ (2 points)
    d. they never said anything   ___ (0 points)
    e. simply homosexual without attractive value judgment   ___ (0 points)
    f. a minority that was subject to unfair discrimination   ___ (3 points)
    g. a group of people that deserved the same rights as
       people who are heterosexual   ___ (4 points)
    h. a group of people to be respected for their courage
       to be who they are   ___ (5 points)

2. Mark the answer that comes closest to what you heard or overheard your parents say or do:
    a. As a child, I heard my parents say hateful or violent
       things about people who are gay, lesbian, or bisexual.   ___ (0 points)
    b. As a child, I heard my parents use derogatory words
       or terms to describe people who are gay, lesbian, or
       bisexual.   ___ (0 points)
    c. As a child, I heard my parents make gay jokes or
       mock people whom they thought were gay, lesbian,
       or bisexual   ___ (0 points)
    d. As a child, I heard my parents say a mixture of
       positive and negative things about gays, lesbians,
       or bisexuals   ___ (3 points)

(cont'd)

married, and that sometimes boys and boys or girls and girls do the same. This was confusing for them sometimes because the rest of their environment gave them such strong messages about heterosexuality and marriage.

One time we were having a barbecue and invited many of our close friends, one of whom was a single gay man. My son, who was then three years old, asked me if Andy's [not his real name] wife was coming. I said, "No, Andy doesn't have a wife. Remember—he's gay." To which my son responded, "Who's he gay with?" That's been a joke between Andy, my son, and me for almost ten years now. When

---

    e. As a child, I heard my parents talk with or about their
       gay, lesbian, or bisexual friends and about the joys
       and challenges in their lives.   ___ (5 points)
    f. I never heard them say anything.   ___ (0 points)

3. As a child my parents' friends, my friends' parents and
   my neighbors were:
    a. all heterosexual   ___ (0 points)
    b. 1 or 2 people were gay, lesbian, or bisexual   ___ (1 points)
    c. a few people were gay, lesbian, or bisexual   ___ (2 points)
    d. many people were gay, lesbian, or bisexual   ___ (5 points)

4. As a child my peers said the following things about
   people who were gay, lesbian, or bisexual:
    a. It's evil.   ___ (0 points)
    b. It's nasty.   ___ (0 points)
    c. It's stupid.   ___ (0 points)
    d. I don't get it.   ___ (2 points)
    e. It's okay for them, but not for me.   ___ (2 points)
    f. It's fine.   ___ (5 points)
    g. It's cool.   ___ (5 points)
    h. Nothing.   ___ (0 points)

5. As a child my religion taught the following about
   homosexuality:
    a It's a sin and an abomination against God.   ___ (0 points)
    b. It said nothing.   ___ (0 points)
    c. It's a sin, but we should hate the sin and not the
       sinner.   ___ (1 point)
    d. It's a sickness that we should try to heal.   ___ (1 point)
    e. It is a natural part of some people's lives that they
       can't help.   ___ (3 points)
    f. It constitutes an oppressed minority that we should
       work to help.   ___ (4 points)
    g. It is a natural lifestyle that is part of God's plan that
       we should embrace.   ___ (5 points)

TOTAL SCORE ___

I told Andy about my son's question, Andy said, "Be sure and tell him that as soon as I find someone to be gay with, he'll be the first to know."

Another time when my son and daughter were eight and nine years old, they each had a friend spend the night. The next morning the four of them were sitting at the kitchen table having breakfast. These were the days for them when playing house and assigning people familiar family roles was common. One of their friends said, "Let's pretend we're two married couples having breakfast together." My son responded, "I know, we can pretend to be two gay couples having breakfast together."

My own socialization kicked in during this conversation. My first reaction was, "Oh no! What if these kids tell their parents that they came to our house and played gay?" That was the reaction of my own homophobia and fear of what other people would think of me based on my children's comfort level and openness about sexual orientation. During my second reaction, my intellect kicked in, and I found myself quite proud of my open-minded children.

As an ally to people who are gay, lesbian, or bisexual, I have made some choices in my adult life—some about which I feel very good and some of which I am not particularly proud. I am committed to interrupting jokes or comments that discriminate against or mock gays, lesbians, or bisexuals. I have spent much time reading and writing and teaching about the history of both discrimination against and liberation for homosexuals. I support domestic partnership benefits in the workplace as well as other issues that make work a safe environment for gay people. I support hate crime legislation that makes it a criminal and enforceable offense to participate in violent or nonviolent acts of hate against gays, lesbians, and bisexuals. I have attended commitment ceremonies and anniversary parties of my gay friends as well as cultural events in the community.

I have worked to understand the advantages that I have by being identified as heterosexual, but I have not always been consistent in addressing these privileges. Several years ago I asked some of my gay and lesbian friends about the issue of the illegality of civil marriage for homosexuals, which meant that if they were a couple, they could not make a choice to get married and have it sanctioned by the government. At that point I had the advantage of being married publicly with the approval of the state for over fifteen years. I asked my friends if they would consider it an act of solidarity for me to begin to refer to my husband as my "partner" rather than my spouse or husband. I felt this was parallel to non-Jews wearing yellow armbands in solidarity against anti-Semitism. My friends liked this idea. But the truth is I never did it with any consistency or regularity. True, it was a bit awkward to change a reference to someone from husband to partner. But deeper than that, I realized that I did not want certain people to think I was a lesbian. I wanted my children's teachers to know I had a husband to make sure they knew they were dealing with a two-parent heterosexual family. I wanted my kids to have every edge possible. When I had a customer service complaint, I wanted the store to know that I had a husband who was mythically in the background to back me up if they did not respond to my complaint. I have realized that in many instances, while I am committed to serving as an ally to people who are gay, lesbian, and bisexual, I have not been willing to relinquish the privileges and advantages of being seen as heterosexual. Yet, in order to work toward a more level playing field, some of us may need to relinquish some of our privilege and work to create the same privilege and opportunities for gays, lesbians, and bisexuals.

One more story that was an eye opener for me: I have a close lesbian friend who has children and is in a long-term committed relationship. We have talked about how heterosexuals often say, "Look, I don't care who you sleep with. Your personal life is your own business, but I don't want to hear about it. Keep it in your own mind and in your own bedroom." My friend's response is that people in heterosexual relationships "out" themselves all the time without talking about sex itself. She described a time when she went to pick up her daughter from swim team practice, and the coach was running over thirty minutes late. She said that within the first five minutes, the other parents all "came out" as heterosexual. One woman said, "Boy I wish he'd hurry up. I told my husband I'd meet him in ten minutes." Another man said, "I'd better call my wife and let her know we'll be late for dinner." This kind of common and casual conversation went on for a few minutes, and my friend wondered what would happen if she would say, "I'd better call my partner Jane and tell her we'll be late." She imagined, as did I, that while there may not have been any direct nastiness or discrimination, that the conversation would not have continued so fluidly or naturally. There may have been awkwardness or tension because her "outing" would have been perceived as outside the norm.

Now it's your turn. Write or tape record the answers to the questions in Personal Inventory 6.3 that continue your autobiography and discuss them with others to determine what patterns or distinctions emerge. As you think about your answers to these autobiographical questions, try to articulate your beliefs about sexual orientation and what about your convictions is clear and what is perhaps confusing.

Then try one more exercise. Imagine that the world is primarily homosexual and that it is the norm to be gay, lesbian, or bisexual. It is legal to have same sex marriages and illegal to marry someone who is another sex. It is dangerous to be an openly heterosexual couple. If you are heterosexual, you may be subject to discrimination or even violence in housing, education, in your job, and in your community. You will need to make constant decisions about where and with whom to be out as a heterosexual. People who are gay, lesbian, and bisexual—or perceived to be so—are typically the ones who are in charge of major businesses, educational institutions, and government. Employee benefits, parties at work and in school, health insurance and other benefits revolve around gays, lesbians, and bisexuals. Most books, movies, and television shows that portray families are those with gay, lesbian, or bisexual parents and children. Popular music and music videos are all about romantic love and pain between gays, lesbians, and bisexuals.

Now whether you identify as gay, lesbian, bisexual, or heterosexual—imagine going through your day with the rules and norms changed as described above. What would be the same about your day? What would be different? What kinds of decisions would you need to make? What kinds of things would be easier and what kinds of things would be more difficult?

The combinations of the exercises and autobiographical information above are elements of your story about sexual orientation. They will help you find your place in the larger story of oppression and liberation of gay, lesbian, and bisexual people. If, like me, your childhood and early adulthood were void of any formal information about sexual identity and the only informal information you had was

Personal Inventory 6.3
Autobiography on Sexual Orientation

Instructions

Write or tape record your answers to these questions in order to develop a deeper understanding of what you were taught and what you learned about sexual identity.

1. What are your first memories of being told or overhearing anything about gays, lesbians, or bisexuals? Were these things positive, negative, or neutral?

2. As a child and teenager, what words did you hear your parents use about homosexuals or homosexuality? Were these words positive, negative, or neutral?

3. As a child and teenager, what words did you hear your friends and other peers use about homosexuals or homosexuality? Were these words positive, negative, or neutral?

4. As a child and teenager, what words did you use about homosexuals or homosexuality? Were these words positive, negative, or neutral?

5. Did you or your friends or family ever engage in any conflict around sexual orientation?

(cont'd)

by instructions on how not to be mistaken for someone who is homosexual, and by jokes and mocking—you were socialized to assume that heterosexuality was good, right, and normal and that any other sexual orientation was by extension bad, wrong, and abnormal. If you identified as heterosexual this information and misinformation probably underlies assumptions that you made about dating, relationships, and marriage and in this area of your life you were most likely to feel acceptance from people around you. If you identified as gay, lesbian, or bisexual and were socialized like I was, this information and misinformation challenged, criticized, and rejected an important part of your identity. You may have chosen to defy these messages, you may have chosen to keep your identity hidden, or you may have even tried to transform your sexual orientation. In any case, it was fairly likely that some people in your life rejected, mocked, or were disappointed in this important part of your identity.

When you reflect on the information, misinformation, and missing information you received as a young person from your religion, family, and peers, you can begin to reconstruct the influences on your views, attitudes, and behavior about sexual orientation. It is this knowledge of what forces have shaped you that you

6. Did one or both of your parents identify as gay, lesbian, or bisexual? What kind of experiences did you have as a result?

7. PLEASE ANSWER THESE QUESTIONS REGARDLESS OF YOUR SEXUAL IDENTITY. How old were you when did you become aware of your sexual orientation? Are you gay, lesbian, bisexual, or heterosexual? How is your sexual orientation accepted among your peers, family, larger community? How did your sexual orientation affect you when you were in school? Are you "out"? If so, what was the coming out process like for you? If not, what is it like for you having a part of your identity that is not widely known?

8. As a young or mature adult, have your views about sexual orientation changed? What experiences or relationships have you had that confirmed or challenged your early beliefs and experiences?

9. What are you proud about regarding your sexual orientation? Is there anything about your sexual orientation that makes you frightened or causes you embarrassment or shame?

10. Is there anything about your beliefs and attitudes and behavior toward gays, lesbians, and bisexuals that makes you proud? Is there anything about your beliefs and attitudes and behavior about and toward gays, lesbians, and bisexuals that makes you frightened or causes embarrassment or shame?

can use as a touch point as you begin to consider new information about sexual orientation. The way that you were socialized and the way that you accepted or challenged that socialization will affect the way that you respond to the information, history, and theories below. It is important to notice and pay attention to your personal thoughts and reactions to the information and track it back to your earlier informal learning experiences. In this way you will be able to make conscious and deliberate choices about what to believe, what information to retain, and what information to reject.

Reconstructing Knowledge and Sexual Orientation

Many of us who were raised in western cultures learned that there were at least three subjects that were taboo in polite conversation: a person's income, their religion, and their sex life. A discussion of the history, theories, and beliefs about sexual identity and orientation involve at least two of these taboos: religion and sex. To the extent that you were taught to avoid or severely limit conversations about these two issues you may experience some discomfort or resistance to this material. It will be important to keep several things in your thoughts simultaneously. First, stay aware of your personal experience and socialization about sexual orientation and about sex. Second, be mindful of any aspects of religion or sex that you believe are too private or should not be discussed. Third, attempt to separate your emotions from your best, clear thinking. Fourth, remember that as you consider what may be new material or information that is contradictory to what you learned elsewhere, your task is to sort through old and new, formal and informal learning experiences and make conscious independent decisions about your own values and beliefs.

Historically, western cultures have considered sex to be a dangerous and destructive force whose only possible redemption could be if there was little pleasure involved and if its purpose was for procreation in marriage. The norm in most modern western cultures has been to view sex hierarchically, with married, reproductive sex at the top of the hierarchy and nonreproductive, unmarried, same-sex, promiscuous sex at the bottom. Most of the sexual activity at the lower end of the scale comes complete with cultural stigmas that are often psychological, social, and religious (Abelove, Barale, and Halperin 1993, 11).

Same sex relationships and sexual orientation have been controversial topics in the western world since at least the mid-eighteenth century. Opinions, beliefs, and even theories and history have been hotly contested about what it means to be gay, lesbian, bisexual, transsexual, or transgendered. This section will explore the controversies, the oppression, and the efforts for liberation regarding sexual identity and sexual orientation by examining the following:

- terminology regarding sexual identity and orientation and its evolution;
- the history of sexual minorities in the United States;
- institutionalized religions and sexual orientation; and
- the current cultural and legal status of gays, lesbians, and bisexuals in the United States.

Terminology and Its Evolution

A discussion of labels, language, and terminology regarding sexual identity and sexual orientation can be paralyzing if it is interpreted as a lesson in political correctness. In order to talk about individuals or groups, we need to have words to communicate with each other. Understanding the history and politics of terms used for homosexuality is not intended as a reason to cease discussion, but rather as a reflection of how the limitation of the language and naming of sexual orientation and identity reflects the various ways discrimination and liberation have occurred.

The term *homosexuality* originated in Germany in 1869 in a pamphlet that was distributed in efforts to repeal the German sodomy law (Miller 1995, xv). Before this time, same sex attractions and relationships existed, but were not named. In the naming of "homosexuality," a group was culturally created or constructed.

This is parallel to the naming and the construction of race that was discussed in Chapter Four. Fluid political and cultural definitions of race have been reflected throughout the twentieth and twenty-first centuries in the constantly changing racial categories that are listed as options for the U.S. Census data collection. For individuals with same sex attraction, a group was constructed when it was named homosexual and has subsequently taken on political and social meaning as its definition has evolved over time. Part of the story of homosexuality is the story of the "naming" of it according to political, social, cultural, and often religious thought in various time periods.

The early sexologists in Germany and England were sympathetic to same sex relationships and opposed laws that criminalized it. While some of them used the word homosexual, eventually they adopted the word *invert* to refer to lesbians and gay men. This new name was based on the sexologists' beliefs that people who were attracted to the same sex were part of a third or intermediate sex. Their belief was that men who were inverts took on characteristics that were traditionally feminine and women inverts assumed traditionally masculine characteristics. There were others in the mid-nineteenth century that viewed same sex relationships as sinful. But while the sexologists had limited information about same sex attraction, their contribution to its evolution was the belief that it was natural and unchangeable. Thus if the "inverts" could not change, most of the sexologists concluded that they should not be punished or penalized (Miller 1995, 13).

The work of the German and British sexologists was known by some scientists and doctors in the United States but was not widely known nor accepted by the larger population during the nineteenth century. In fact, the concept or construct of homosexuality was largely underground. During the mid-nineteenth century through the early twentieth century in the United States, there was virtually no public concept of gay, lesbian, bisexual, homosexual, or invert. Some women participated in what were called "romantic friendships," which often had a private sexual dimension. The sensibility in the United States at the time was such that there was virtually no concept of sexual relationships between people of the same sex and thus there was neither suspicion nor condemnation.

In an 1843 essay in the *Evening Post,* William Cullen Bryant rhapsodized about the beautiful female friendship between two maiden ladies and their dedication to each other throughout their forty-year relationship. There was an innocence and an ignorance of even the possibility that such a relationship might be sexual (Faderman 1991, 2).

By the early twentieth century the work of the European sexologists had reached the United States. Rather than the limited but sympathetic view held in Germany and England regarding sexual inverts, in the United States the so-called inverts were considered freaks (Faderman 1991, 45). By the mid-1930s the concept of homosexuality and individuals who were involved in same sex relationships were largely reviled in the United States.

After World War II, another label was applied to gays, lesbians, and bisexuals—

this time by the medical and psychiatric professions. Ground-breaking psychiatrist Sigmund Freud regarded homosexuality as the result of fear of the opposite sex that was created in childhood and could be changed through psychoanalysis. He laid the foundation for blaming detached fathers and seductive mothers for "creating" gay men and reproaching passive fathers and dominant mothers for "creating" lesbians. Subsequent U.S. psychiatrists, such as Sandor Rado and Charles Socarides, claimed that same sex relationships were "sick," a function of mental illness, and as such were doomed to failure. The American Psychiatric Association's first catalog of mental disorders listed homosexuality as a sociopathic personality disturbance (Miller 1995, 248). The emphasis of psychiatry was to attempt to cure this "disease." Parallel to this development were evolving and quite public religious beliefs in many mainstream religious institutions that claimed that the Bible said that same sex behavior was a sin.

Both the phenomena and trends in psychiatry and religion will be explored in greater depth later in this chapter. But for now, the important thing to observe is that by naming homosexuality as "sick" and/or as "sinful," the construct of same sex attraction and behavior became extremely negative and potentially dangerous to people who identified as or were perceived to be gay or lesbian.

The terminology for homosexuality continues to be contested. Some lesbians and gay men have rejected the term homosexual for self-identification for two reasons. The first reason is that this was the term used for many years to describe same sex relationships as pathological and/or sinful. A second reason was that the word "homosexual" suggests a person's identity is exclusively sexual, rather than suggesting that sexual attraction and behavior exist in the context of a broader culture (Jagose 1996, 31).

The terms *heterosexual* and *straight* are those words most commonly used to refer to men and women who are attracted to and/or have sexual relationships with individuals of the opposite sex. While there are currently no other widely used words to describe this kind of sexuality, both terms are problematic. "Heterosexual," like homosexual, has the implication that it is descriptive exclusively of sex rather than part of a larger cultural context that is assumed to be regular and normal. The word "straight" implies that heterosexuals are upright and good as well as the obverse: that homosexuals are bent or crooked and bad.

The word *gay* began to be used in the last half of the twentieth century as an alternative to homosexual. "Gay" originally had a political as well as a sexual connotation. Gay liberation was a political movement in which various groupings of gay men, lesbians, and their allies engaged in activism to claim their rights. But politically, many women who identified as gay experienced an exclusion from the Gay liberation movement in the 1960s and 1970s. They observed that most of the gay organizations, their leadership, and issues were largely for, about, and run by gay men. Many women began to identify separate women's issues and women's organizations were formed to advocate for "gay" women. The term *lesbian* became commonly used to distinguish the identity, issues, and organizations of homosexual women from those of gay men.

Bisexual refers to men and women who are attracted to individuals from both sexes. There have been times in U.S. history, such as in the 1920s in Greenwich Village or in Harlem, in which bisexuality was regarded as hip (Faderman 1991, 67). There have been other times in which some lesbian feminists regarded bisexuality as sexual confusion or the unwillingness to make a commitment. However, people who identify as bisexual are neither inherently hip, confused, nor promiscuous.

The history of oppression and liberation of *transsexual* and *transgender* people is complex and requires more attention than is within the scope of this book. This chapter will only briefly touch upon this subject since neither term is specifically about sexual orientation. The terms transsexual and transgender are often confused with homosexuality. In fact, people who identify as transsexual or transgender can have sexual orientation that is heterosexual, homosexual, bisexual, or asexual.

People who identify as transgender or transsexual cross the boundaries of what most people think of as masculine or feminine. This may be a person whose life choices, behavior, and appearance more closely resemble those that are commonly associated with the opposite sex. Transgender and transsexual people are distinguished by their biological sex being distinct from their sense of themselves as masculine or feminine. They often have the sense that their biological sex does not match their gender identification. For example, someone who was born with the genitals and hormones of a woman may feel, often since childhood, that her sense of herself and orientation to the world is male.

Outside of the transgender/transsexual community the distinction between the two terms is generally thought of as this: transgender people live with the complexities of their mismatched sex and gender identity, perhaps with hormones, but not with surgery. In contrast, transsexual people have undergone sex change surgery. Within the transgender/transsexual community the lines between the two terms and people are not as distinct but rather more part of a continuum. For some people the main distinction between being transgender and transsexual is the money needed for surgery. For others, it is a long and complex process of "coming out" and finding a way to live in a world that is often rejecting or mocking (Adams et al. 1997, 162). It is important to understand that transgender and transsexual people run the gamut in their sexual orientation; they are not exclusively gay, lesbian, or bisexual.

The terms transgender and transsexual are discussed here to clarify their meaning and to distinguish them from sexual orientation. Because transgender and transsexual people's identity and appearance differ from traditional gender boundaries they are often targeted by the same kind of discrimination and oppression that is directed at gays, lesbians, and bisexuals.

Coming out, short for coming out of the closet, refers to the individual process in which gays, lesbians, and bisexuals choose to move from secrecy to openness in their sexual identity and expression. It is a process of self-acceptance and public declaration that moves from the secrets of sexual identity and perhaps the shame and guilt of internalized homophobia to a personal identity that integrates sexual orientation into a broader sense of self.

The word *queer* has historically been a derogatory term used to deride gays and lesbians. More recently it has been reclaimed by some gays, lesbians, bisexuals, transgender, and transsexual people to describe and dramatize that biological sex, gender identity, and sexual desire do not always line up neatly and match (Jagose 1996, 3). Along the same lines some gay men and lesbians have reclaimed other formerly derogatory terms such as *faggot* or *dyke*. While these words have been recently recovered from their previous exclusively disparaging context, they retain a bitter sting when used outside of the gay, lesbian, and bisexual community as well as to some individuals within the community.

> If there is one major point to be made . . . it is that perceptions of emotional or social desires, formations of sexual categories, and attitudes concerning "mental health" are constantly shifting—not through the discovery of objectively conceived truths, as we generally assume, but rather through social forces that have little to do with the essentiality of emotion or sex or mental health. Affectional preferences, ambitions, and even sexual experiences that are within the realm of the socially acceptable during one era may be considered sick or dangerous or antisocial during another—and in a brief space of time attitudes may shift once again, and yet again. (Faderman 1991, 119)

In reviewing the terms that have been used about sexual orientation for the last hundred years, it becomes increasingly clear that the language reflects the culture and reality of the time and that reality is constantly shifting. Because the language is imperfect, the words I will use in this chapter will also be imperfect. Generally I will interchangeably use the words homosexual and gay and lesbian to refer to men and women who have same sex orientation. I will use gay to refer to homosexual men and lesbian to refer to homosexual women. I will use the term bisexual when appropriate to refer to men or women who have sexual affinity for both men and women. The words transsexual and transgender will be used specifically to address people whose biological sex and sense of gender are aligned unconventionally. The term sexual minorities will be used as a broad umbrella to include all of those individuals and groups whose sexual orientation or gender identity differ from the cultural norms and are consequently targeted for discrimination.

Understanding the change in the language in this section and the historical shifts described in the next section is important in observing your own evolving thoughts, perspective, and understanding. The topic of sexual orientation is cluttered with misinformation and distortion. The discovery and analysis of clear factual information and the quest for understanding are critical to making independent decisions about our values and beliefs.

Theories and History of Sexual Minorities in the United States

Theories of Oppression and Liberation and Sexual Orientation

The theories of cultural diversity and oppression introduced in Chapter One are an important foundation to understanding the history of oppression and liberation of sexual minorities in the United States. You may recall that the cultural competence continuum progresses from cultural destructiveness at the bottom of the scale through cultural neutrality in the middle to cultural competence at the top of the scale. As we study this continuum in relation to sexual orientation, it is important to know who is standing on the continuum. The continuum suggests that the individual or institutional standpoint is one that is different from the culture considered on the continuum. So, in the case of sexual orientation, it is heterosexual individuals, and institutions that are characterized by heterosexual norms, who need to determine where they begin on the cultural competence continuum and where they would like to travel on it.

Cultural destructiveness suggests a belief that heterosexuality is superior to homosexuality. An individual or institution that is culturally incompetent sees no need and makes no effort to learn more or understand the experience, culture, or history of gays, lesbians, and bisexuals. Individuals who are culturally destructive with respect to sexual orientation may make hateful comments or jokes or may resort to violence against people they perceive to be outside the sexual "norm." An extreme example of individual cultural destructiveness was in 1998, when two young men tortured and killed Matthew Shepard, a student at the University of Wyoming, simply because he was gay.

A culturally destructive institution would not knowingly hire someone who is gay or lesbian or bisexual. A culturally incompetent government would pass laws making sex between two people of the same sex illegal. An example of this occurred after World War II, when the federal government sought to fire anyone it believed to be a "sexual deviate."

Cultural neutrality is the point on the continuum at which an individual or institution believes that sexual orientation is irrelevant. On the face of it, cultural neutrality has a certain innocence to it that adheres to the belief that everyone is equal and that no one needs to know or notice another person's sexual orientation. However, this point on the continuum is also neutral or oblivious to discrimination and cultural differences. Individuals who are culturally neutral to sexual orientation may disregard the concrete and damaging discrimination that a gay or lesbian person has endured or may not understand the need for a gay or lesbian community of support. They also may find it unnecessary for someone who is gay or lesbian to be open about their sexual orientation and relationships. People who are at the culturally neutral position often make statements such as, "I don't care what you do in your bedroom, just keep it in your bedroom." What they are often unaware of is the way in which heterosexual people are constantly "out" about their sexual orientation. Every time a young girl speaks about her boyfriend or a man refers to his wife, they have been open about their sexual orientation without ever mentioning sex.

Culturally neutral institutions may, with good intent, ignore the kind of discrimination and lack of safety that is often present for sexual minorities in the workplace. Because the institutional assumption is that it is a level playing field with regard to sexual orientation, they may not see the ways that heterosexuals are privileged in the workplace. They may be oblivious and thus, neutral, to the fact that life partners and children of homosexuals do not have the health insurance benefits that their heterosexual peers have. They may refuse to think of ways to protect sexual minorities against harassment or job discrimination because they do not see the problems. Governments may decide that specific legislation to protect gays and lesbians from hate crimes is unnecessary because they believe that gays and lesbians are just like everyone else and do not require special protection or laws.

Cultural competence suggests that an individual or institution has worked hard and continues to work to understand the experience, history, and deep and surface culture of gays, lesbians, and bisexuals. An individual may read extensively, attend cultural or political events in the gay and lesbian community, and serve as an advocate or ally for the rights of sexual minorities. An individual who is culturally competent does not have the equivalent of certification in understanding sexual orientation, but rather understands that the learning process is ongoing. An institution that is culturally competent may offer workshops or courses on sexual orientation and may have policies that offer benefits to domestic partners that are equivalent to those offered to people whose heterosexual relationships are sanctioned by the state in marriage. Governments that are culturally competent may include the protection of sexual minorities in civil rights legislation or anti–hate crime legislation.

Individuals and institutions that are culturally competent will still continue to make mistakes as they work to move past their privilege and socialization to understand and accept diverse sexual orientations and to serve as allies. Despite the academic research and personal work I have done to unlearn homophobia, I can be reasonably sure that somewhere in this chapter I have made an error in judgment or understanding. The mistakes—and more important, their corrections—are part of the learning process.

According to the fabric of oppression, homophobia or heterosexism are the individual and cultural beliefs that assume that heterosexuality is the only natural and acceptable sexual orientation. Homophobia and heterosexism discriminate against people who are *perceived* to be gay, lesbian, bisexual, transgender, or transsexual. The word "perceived" is critical to this definition because homophobia can target homosexuals as well as heterosexuals who are believed to be gay or lesbian. Recently, at an elite private high school, two girls were best friends during their freshman year. They spent a lot of time together, and frequently put their arms around each other's shoulders as they walked down the hall and hugged as part of their greeting. Many other students perceived them to be lesbian and began to tease, harass, and ostracize them from social activities. These girls identified as heterosexual, but because they were perceived to be lesbian, they suffered extreme harassment and discrimination. "[H]omophobia, like other forms of oppression, serves the dominant group by establishing and maintaining power and mastery over those who are marginalized or disenfranchised. Individuals maintain oppressive behaviors to gain certain rewards or to avoid punishment; to protect their self-esteem against psychological doubts or conflicts, to enhance their value systems, or to categorize others in an attempt to comprehend a complex world" (Blumenfeld 1992, 8).

Homophobia operates on a number of different levels. On a personal level it reflects a belief system that pities or despises gays, lesbians, and bisexuals. On an interpersonal level, this bias turns into namecalling, jokes, harassment, rejection, and even violence. On an institutional level homophobia is at the root of why some businesses, schools, religions, and government agencies have laws, codes, and policies that discriminate against or ignore the existence of sexual minorities. Some organizations will not hire or promote people they believe to be homosexual. Until 1973, the American Psychiatric Association considered homosexuality a mental illness. Culturally, homophobia has a list of invisible rules that restrict "normal" behavior to attitudes and actions that are viewed as appropriately masculine for men and traditionally feminine for women. Traveling outside of these norms makes a person suspect as gay or lesbian and thus potentially a target of discrimination (Blumenfeld 1992, 4).

Heterosexual privilege is available to individuals who, once again, are perceived to be sexually attracted to or in primary relationships with someone of the opposite sex. This privilege involves personal safety and protection from discrimination, harassment, and violence directed at gays, lesbians, and bisexuals. Heterosexual privilege also includes government sanction and cultural approval of marriage. Marriage provides a couple with tangible tax and insurance benefits, the legal right to care for each other through sickness, and the legal right to custody or visitation of children should there be separation or divorce. Heterosexual marriage also bestows an invisible set of privileges for couples who can casually refer to their "wife" or "husband" and establish a measure of credibility and sense of "normality" that may be shaken when one refers to the intimate person in one's life as "my partner." Heterosexual marriage means that when a couple applies to be adoptive or foster parents, they will not be rejected on the grounds of their sexual orientation. Assumed heterosexuality means that during divorce proceedings, an individual will not be denied child custody based on sexual orientation. It means that an individual never has to go through a day wondering if she should disclose or hide her sexuality or weigh the relative danger and safety of being "out."

Throughout this section, we will explore the ways that homophobia has discriminated against and endangered the lives of sexual minorities. There are also ways that homophobia impacts people who identify as heterosexual. On a personal level, homophobia restricts the way all people dress, talk, and express themselves. In cultures that are extremely homophobic, any deviation from strict gender roles of masculinity or femininity are regarded as suspicious. A woman who identifies as heterosexual who does not want to be accused of being lesbian may feel the need to wear soft and perhaps frilly dresses and refrain from activities such as car repair or certain sports or occupations.

On an interpersonal level, homophobia limits expression between friends and families. If someone is afraid of being called gay or lesbian, he will be less likely to be physically warm and affectionate with his same sex friends. As parents, people may carefully restrict information about sexual orientation to their children and clearly communicate to them that to be gay or lesbian is unacceptable. If one of their children has questions about sexual orientation or is gay or lesbian themselves, the parents' homophobia would limit their ability to communicate with their own children and limit the children's ability to be open about their own identity and sexuality. Homophobia can pressure young people, as well as adults, to prove themselves to be heterosexual. This phenomenon often is reflected in the ridicule and mistreatment of gays and lesbians. Any time we deliberately mistreat others, we diminish our own humanity. For young people who question their own sexual orientation or are accused of being gay or lesbian, it often pressures them to have, and increases the likelihood of, premature heterosexual sex in order to prove themselves (Blumenfeld 1992, 11). Because of the cultural stigma against homosexuality, as well as the homophobia of many parents, schools, and high school students, the suicide rate of gay and lesbian teens is alarmingly high.

"Males in our society are saddled with the heavy burden of masculinity. . . . We must 'keep it all together'; we cannot show vulnerability, awkwardness, doubts. . . . To keep us in line, faggot, pansy, wimp, sissy, girl, and homo are thrown at us like spears to the heart" (Blumenfeld 1992, 37). Men and boys learn very early that there are certain things that can make them subject to ridicule and harassment. Playing with dolls, cooking, and crying because of hurt feelings all transgress the traditional rules of what it means to be male. Whether a boy is heterosexual or homosexual, he is subject to the same discrimination and often makes decisions about his behavior, based not on what interests him or that he enjoys, but rather on whether other boys will find it acceptably masculine.

Homophobia and the fear of appearing homosexual also reinforce gender stereotyping for women through lesbian baiting. Many women make choices to reject traditionally masculine (and often more comfortable) clothing because people might think they are lesbian. Some women consider jobs such as the military or construction as off-limits because people might think they are lesbian. Some women who challenge male power or sexual advances or demand equal rights as women or identify themselves as feminists are accused of being lesbian and are consequently more cautious as they make these kind of choices. Both men and women may refrain from emotional and physical displays of affection of their same sex friends for fear that people might think they are homosexual. Homophobia is so strong in U.S. culture that the fear of simply *appearing* homosexual often dictates and limits our behavior.

It is commonly thought that ending discrimination against sexual minorities would exclusively benefit people who identify as gay, lesbian, bisexual, transgendered, or transsexual. Yet, there are many ways that ending homophobia is in the interest of and of benefit to those who identify as heterosexual. Ending homophobia would benefit heterosexuals in the following ways:

- It would expand options for men and women to transcend rigid gender boundaries.
- It would permit men and women to have closer and more intimate relationships with friends of the same sex.
- It would increase the sense of safety and decrease the sense of danger if one is perceived to be gay or lesbian.
- It would allow for greater appreciation and range in one's own expression of sexuality since this would not be limited by strict gender roles and expectations.
- It would allow more range in heterosexual relationships by allowing people to safely transcend traditional assumptions of what it means to be masculine or feminine.
- There would be a greater possibility of connection and love between people without the existence of homophobic fear. This could create the possibility of more love and justice in the world (Thompson 1992, 241–242).

In fact, the work that gays and lesbians have done to win the rights for same sex domestic partners to be entitled to workplace benefits such as health and life insurance has also benefited opposite sex domestic partners.

Liberation theory explains that homophobia, heterosexism, and internalized homophobia are the result of misinformation and distortion and omission of information. The same misinformation that heterosexuals receive is also received by homosexuals who, as a result, may struggle with understanding and accepting their own sexual orientation and identities. The optimism in liberation theory suggests that because patterns of discrimination in our beliefs and actions are learned, they also can be unlearned.

The next two sections on history and religion and sexual orientation are designed to provide accurate information and a variety of theories and beliefs to augment and perhaps challenge information you have received in the past. It will be up to you to decide what you believe and if there are any attitudes or behaviors you wish to change.

Sexual Orientation in U.S. History

Before World War II

While it is difficult to document the earliest examples of same sex attraction and relationships, it is clear that before the twentieth century there was no American name nor concept for individuals attracted to and sexually involved with someone of the same sex. This period of time appears to be an inadvertent age of innocence. With no concept of homosexuality in place, there was no social or political construct that evaluated same sex relationships as right or wrong, good or evil, healthy or sick. There was simply no concept of homosexuality, nor was there the contested meaning that exists in contemporary U.S. culture.

One example of this conceptual absence was the American Indian *berdache* or *winkte,* who appeared in 130 tribes from the sixteenth to nineteenth centuries. These individuals defied neat classification into western cultural categories. Most often, the berdache was a biological male whose gender sensibility and behavior was female. "Berdaches represented a special category among many Native American tribes. They were men who wore women's clothing, occupied themselves with 'women's work' such as pottery and basket weaving, and took a sacred role in tribal rituals" (Miller 1995, 31). Berdaches were awarded a holy status and were highly respected in most tribes. Male berdaches were permitted to have sex and be married to men. While there is less known about female berdaches, there is evidence that they also held a special status in at least thirty tribes (Miller 1995, 35).

When the Europeans arrived in North America, they were determined to obliterate the berdache and its accompanying holy tribal status. As early as the sixteenth century, Spanish conquerors described Indians in Mexico as sodomites and ordered them killed. By the early nineteenth century, the Spanish had successfully eliminated the berdache from California tribes (Miller 1995, 38). By the early twentieth century, Americans had begun to be affected by trends in psychiatry and religion that identified homosexuality as a third sex that was either sick or sinful. By the early 1900s the forced assimilation of American Indians in boarding schools, coupled with the pressure of western values, had socialized most tribes into viewing the berdaches as deviant in their sexuality and gender identity. "In any event, the berdache shows how certain premodern societies took people who would probably be considered homosexual today and affirmed them, instead of stigmatizing them, giving them important—even sacred—cultural roles" (Miller 1995, 40).

Through the early twentieth century, romantic friendships and love between girls and women were commonplace. The Industrial Revolution, which had a strong impact on the roles of women and men and on class mobility, once again had a strong influence. This time it was relationships between women that were impacted by industrialization. Before the end of the nineteenth century, most women needed to be married and part of a family in order to survive economically. By the end of the nineteenth century, middle and owning class white women could attend college and pursue careers. For the first time these women were able to live independently from a father or husband. In these circumstances, romantic friendships flourished (Faderman 1991, 14). Romantic friendships were affectionate and often long term. The women lived together and were often devoted to one another, helping each other through illness and hard times. It was not always clear whether these relationships between women were sexual. Romantic friendships were also known as "Boston marriages," in which college graduates set up households together. These relationships were common on the east coast. "The list of female contributors to twentieth century progress and decency who constructed their personal lives around other women is endless" (Faderman 1991, 24). Both Emily Blackwell, the co-founder of Women's Medical College of the New York Infirmary, and Jane Addams, the founder of Hull House and the Settlement movement and recipient of the Nobel Peace Prize, were involved in long-term romantic friendships with women (Faderman 1991, 5).

But despite the fact that at least some of these romantic friendships were sexual, there was still no concept or construct of homosexuality, nor was there a personal identity as lesbian. "Only when individuals began to make their living through wage labor, instead of as parts of an interdependent family unit, was it possible for homosexual desire to coalesce into a personal identity—an identity based on the ability to remain outside the heterosexual family and to construct a personal life based on attraction to one's own sex" (Emilio 1992, 8).

Class played an important part in cultural acceptance or rejection of women's same sex relationships in the early twentieth century. For women of the middle and owning classes, romantic friendships were accepted and often admired largely because the possibility of the sexual dimension of the relationship was unseen, unacknowledged, or dismissed. For the most part the women in these relationships continued to appear traditionally feminine and their behavior was viewed as acceptably "ladylike."

Working class women's relationships with each other were quite different in the late nineteenth and early twentieth centuries. Romantic friendship, which often blossomed and took hold in the relative independence and privacy of college, was not readily available to lower income women. The Industrial Revolution impacted many working class women as well but in a different way. Many lower income women took jobs and moved to the cities, often sharing rooms or apartments with other women. Some working class women dressed as men to get better paying jobs or join the army. This was most often motivated by economics rather than sexual attraction or gender identity. But the phenomenon of cross-dressing working class women was seized upon by the sexologists who described these women as inverts, a third sex, or women acting like men. This was the first time in U.S. history that the concept of homosexuality was applied.

This is an important U.S. example of the construct of homosexuality evolving according to "experts" who evaluated women by their appearance and economic class rather than by their identity or behavior. "The sexologists conflated sex role behavior (in this case, acting in ways that have been termed masculine), gender identity (seeing oneself as male), and sexual object choice (preferring a love relationships with another woman). . . . And conversely, women who were passionately in love with other females but did not appear to be masculine were considered for some years more as romantic friends or devoted companions" (Faderman 1991, 45).

By the early twentieth century, romantic friendships became suspect as well. For the first time the concept of lesbian was constructed. The sexologists began to warn parents and young women that colleges were breeding grounds for lesbians and that physical affection between young women, earlier considered charming, was now considered dangerous (Faderman 1991, 49). Soon the only place where lesbian relations could survive was in the New York City areas of Greenwich Village and parts of Harlem in "artistic or bohemian pockets, where social rules were relaxed and unconventionality was prized" (Miller 1995, 63).

Around the turn of the century, the construct of homosexuality, the naming of same sex attractions and relations became more widespread. Sexologists in the United States began to use the term "invert," which they thought of as an intermediate sex. They condemned inverts as "sick," yet they also believed that men and women who were attracted to the same sex were born that way and could not change. This was the first time in the United States that the concept of essentialism was introduced and a debate about the "causes" of homosexuality began that has continued throughout the twentieth and twenty-first centuries.

Essentialism is the belief that people are born with a given sexuality and that it is unchangeable. There have been a variety of groups that have believed this in the United States. Some groups believed that this essential part of a person was natural and should be accepted. Others viewed it as a "birth defect." "For many, to claim a birth defect was preferable to admitting to willful perversity" (Faderman 1991, 57). Essentialism stresses the difference between homosexuals and heterosexuals—sometimes with acceptance and sometimes with condemnation. In the early twentieth century and other times of extreme homophobia, many gays and lesbians subscribed to this belief as a political strategy to build their own culture, based on the premise that since they were born different they must find ways to rely on themselves (Faderman 1991, 61).

Another belief about the origin of homosexuality is the theory of *social construction*. Individuals and groups that subscribe to social constructionism believe that while same sex attraction and relationships may exist, certain social and political conditions are necessary for the identity of gay or lesbian or bisexual to be an option for men and women. According to this explanation, some of the social and political conditions that must exist include: the naming and concept of homosexuality, the decrease in pressure to procreate, an atmosphere of sexual freedom, and a shift in society in which the traditional nuclear family is not essential for economic survival. Some gay liberation groups and lesbian feminists in the 1960s and 1970s believed that to be gay or lesbian was a political statement that challenged sexism and patriarchal systems. Ironically, there have been some conservative religions that condemn homosexuality that also believe that same sex attraction and relationships are socially constructed. Their belief differs from radical gays and lesbians in that these conservatives believe that homosexuality has been made possible by an inappropriately permissive society.

The father of the psychoanalytic movement, Sigmund Freud (1856–1939), believed that homosexuality was a combination of biological origin and socialization. He saw same sex attraction as a deviation from normal development that people could outgrow with the help of therapy.

In fact, the so-called causes of heterosexuality and homosexuality are speculative and largely unknown. Sexual orientation and gender identification have complex social origins and there is no definitive conclusion that there is any biological origin. Individual personality and family types for gays, lesbians, and bisexuals are as diverse and multifaceted as those in the heterosexual population (Cruikshank 1992, 26).

Before and during World War I, interactions in Greenwich Village in New York City reinforced Freud's theory of homosexuality as one path on the road to human development and maturity. The Village was a hub of artistic, bohemian, and unconventional behavior in which men and women experimented with all sorts of alternative behaviors and lifestyles, including homosexuality and bisexuality. While there were some individuals who pursued same sex relationships exclusively and/ or monogamously, it was more common for homosexual relationships to be temporary. Another of Freud's theories helped fuel this phenomenon. It was widely interpreted in popular culture that Freud believed that it was harmful to repress sexual urges. For many people, their sexuality was not part of their permanent separate identity. But rather, their same sex relationships or bisexuality became part of a bohemian chic. In the 1920s, many people valued things that were daring and that flew in the face of the ordinary. Bisexuality fit these values perfectly (Faderman 1991, Miller 1995).

During World War I, Greenwich Village was famous for balls attended by gay men in flamboyant evening gowns. Working class bars for gay men began to emerge in lower Manhattan. In gay institutions throughout most of New York City, there was an unspoken agreement with the police that they would not be bothered. This changed in the 1930s when the New York State Liquor Authority developed a policy that prohibited bars from serving alcohol to gays and lesbians (Miller 1995, 145).

Harlem in the 1920s was another center of bohemian chic that added interracial relationships as another dimension of embracing the taboos of conventional U.S. society. Some white people who wanted to experiment with same sex relationships went to Harlem for anonymity. Others bought into the racial stereotype that somehow African Americans were more sexual and therefore more sexually free. In fact, while there was great ambivalence in the black community about homosexuality, the 1920s Harlem night spots were tolerant of same sex dancing and affection. Famous women, both black and white, visited Harlem as an experiment in biracial and/or bisexual relationships. Others maintained heterosexual marriages by day and homosexual relations by night. Women such as Joan Crawford, Tallulah Bankhead, Bessie Smith, and Ethel Waters were Harlem regulars. "These women, who did not take great pains to pretend to exclusive heterosexuality, must have believed that in their own sophisticated circles of Harlem, bisexuality was seen as interesting and provocative. Although unalloyed homosexuality may still have connoted in 1920s Harlem the abnormality of a 'man trapped in a woman's body,' bisexuality seems to have suggested that a woman was super-sexy" (Faderman 1991, 75).

Despite the chicness of bisexuality in urban enclaves such as Harlem and Greenwich Village, the medical concept of homosexuality became increasingly pervasive in the United States from 1900 to 1930. While some doctors called for "decriminalization of homosexuality because 'the poor creatures' are sick, not criminals" others began to attempt to develop and implement so-called "treatment" of homosexuals. These treatment practices included castration, cliterodectomy, lobotomy, electric shocks, and commitment to mental institutions (Adams et al. 1997, 166).

The depression of the 1930s interrupted even the isolated liberal trends in attitudes toward homosexuality. Economic independence became less of an option for women as jobs became scarce, and hostility increased toward women who were perceived as "stealing" jobs from men, the breadwinners. Some working class women became "hoboes," traveling around the countryside like their male counterparts to find odd jobs and income. There is documentation that some of these women traveled together as lesbian couples. Most middle class lesbians, with few economic options, married and led lives in which their sexual identity or behavior was secret. Lesbians were demonized during the depression, in part because many people scapegoated economically independent women as the cause of the severe economic downturn. Because of the economic and social conditions of the depression, which signaled more danger for lesbians and a resulting secrecy, the opportunities for community or solidarity were negligible (Faderman 1991).

Surprisingly, the entry of the United States into World War II provided new opportunities to strengthen both the individual identity and the development of group support for gays and lesbians. Informally the military steered gay men into jobs as clerks and medics and lesbians into jobs as mechanics and drivers. This channeling of job placement according to stereotypes ironically provided opportunities for personal connection and solidarity. Gay men began to discover bars and parks in New Orleans, New York, San Francisco, and San Diego (Miller 1995, 231).

Approximately 80 percent of women in the military in World War II were lesbians, but because women's labor was desperately needed, the military closed its eyes to this fact and ignored their sexual identity and behavior (Miller 1995, 231). Orders were given not to penalize lesbians unless their behavior was disruptive to their work. This is a clear example of how different economic times and needs construct different views, policies, and attitudes toward gays and lesbians. This tolerance of homosexuality during the war was viewed as a practical necessity, much like the need for women in the work force at home.

After World War II, this changed. "A society that agreed once again that woman's place was in the home saw feminists as a threat to the public welfare, and lesbians, the most obvious advocates of feminism, once more became the chief villains. The social benefits of curing lesbians, who were all sick anyway and needed curing, were unquestionable" (Faderman 1991, 134).

After World War II

After World War II, attitudes, policies, and responses to homosexuality took another radical turn. In general, there was a strong national urge after the economic hardships of the depression in the thirties and disruption of war in the forties to return to "normalcy." Anything that seemed out of the ordinary was suspect, criticized, or condemned. Women, who had been in the work force at home and in the military, were expected to return to marriage and domestic life. Gays and lesbians were once again regarded as "sick" as the medical profession swung into high gear in assessing homosexuality as an illness that needed to be and perhaps could be "cured." The era of Senator Joseph McCarthy and the House Committee on Un-American Activities was on the rise and homosexuals, along with Communists, were reviled and hunted down.

For eighteen months beginning in 1950, gays and lesbians were fired from government jobs at a rate of roughly sixty per month. President Dwight D. Eisenhower, who had been one of the military leaders to encourage lesbian employment in the military during the war, issued an Executive Order that made "sexual perversion" sufficient grounds for exclusion and dismissal from federal employment (Miller 1995, 261). Until 1966, the U.S. Post Office monitored men who received "physique" magazines or were part of gay pen pal clubs and put these individuals under surveillance. Regional FBI offices supplied lists of gay bars and other gathering places to local vice squads. Gays and lesbians had little social recourse to fight employment discrimination or raids of gathering places. In the 1950s, even the American Civil Liberties Union (ACLU) was unwilling to provide legal assistance to gay and lesbian organizations and individuals (Miller 1995).

However, there were a few trends and organizational issues that had emerged during World War II which continued to provide support for the embryonic gay and lesbian communities. Although the American Psychiatric Association listed homosexuality as a psychiatric illness in 1952, Albert Kinsey's 1948 and 1953 reports on American sexual behavior challenged this. Kinsey's findings established that homosexual behavior was much more widespread than commonly believed. Kinsey hypothesized that there was a continuum of sexuality that ranged from heterosexual to homosexual and seriously challenged the medical community's sickness and pathology paradigm.

Kinsey's study was shocking to the medical establishment as well as to the sensibilities of the contemporary American public. The Rockefeller Foundation withdrew funding from Kinsey's study and the psychiatric community used his data as additional support for their belief in the threat of homosexuality (Miller 1995). But Kinsey and others continued to study homosexual behavior and life and continually demonstrated that psychological adjustment in gays and lesbians had the same range as in heterosexual men and women.

Post–World War II attitudes and policies made it dangerous for gays and lesbians to organize socially or politically. But the connections made during the war and the beginning sense of solidarity had been so important to many gays and lesbians that turning back to isolation and secrecy was not an option. The need and possibility of developing organizations for support and advocacy for homosexuality was almost inevitable. By the 1950s the first American gay and lesbian groups appeared. Daughters of Bilitis was primarily a social club for middle class lesbians that served as an alternative to meeting and associating with women in bars and was intended to protect women's privacy and anonymity. The goal of the organization was to educate both the lesbian and heterosexual publics. However, informants infiltrated the organization and turned names over to the FBI (Faderman 1991, 149).

Most women believed that to reveal their sexual orientation as lesbians would threaten their jobs and their incomes and pose potential physical danger. Despite this risk, bars became the center of social life for working class lesbians. These bars created strict rules of dress for "femmes," who wore traditionally feminine clothing and behaved in ways that were stereotypically feminine, and "butches," who wore clothing and engaged in behavior that resembled that of working class men (Miller 1995, 314). Long-lasting stereotypes of masculine and tough lesbians came out of this part of the newly emerging lesbian culture. Even inside the lesbian community, criticism of the butch–femme culture hinged on the belief that these relationships mimicked heterosexual relations, copying gender oppression as well.

However, the working class butch–femme culture served two important purposes. First, with such strict rules of dress and behavior, it made it more difficult for informants to infiltrate and thus protected women from arrest and physical danger. Second, it took another step toward creating a lesbian social identity and sense of group that distinguished lesbians from heterosexual women (Faderman 1991, 174).

The Mattachine Society was developed primarily by and for gay men. Its leader, Harry Hay, was concerned that McCarthy would target gays in the same way that Communists were hunted in the 1950s. In fact, the first leaders and members of this organization were primarily Communists. They took the position that as gays they were an oppressed minority and like any other minority were entitled to certain rights. Given the climate in the United States at the time, this was a radical and potentially dangerous position to take.

The Mattachine Society engaged in discussion groups and formed an advocacy group whose aim was to outlaw entrapment of gay men; they also published and distributed their own magazine. Eventually, concern and fear on the part of the Mattachine membership that its Communist leadership would make both the organization and gay men more vulnerable to attack prompted the original leadership to resign. The organization switched from advocacy to public education and assumed a low profile. Its goal was to demonstrate that homosexuals were just like heterosexuals except for their sexual preference. It was this switch in positions and strategies that formed what came to be known as the homophile movement (Miller 1995).

By 1959 San Francisco and New York authorities began to crack down on gay and lesbian bars and meetings. In San Francisco, this prompted the organization of the owners of gay bars as well as other organizations to hold fund-raisers for legal defense. By this time, the ACLU began to defend gay and lesbian individuals who were arrested in bars and other social gathering places. By 1965, liberal leaders of faith-based organizations became supporters of the rights of gays and lesbians. By the mid-1960s, homosexuals and their allies in San Francisco had become a serious political force (Miller 1995).

Raids on gay bars in New York City were common. The New York State Liquor Authority could legally close bars that served alcohol to gays. But it was not until June 28, 1969, that a raid that took place at the Stonewall Inn in Greenwich Village signaled the beginning of gay activism and the end of tolerance for police harassment. The term Stonewall has come to have great literal and symbolic meaning for the movement and organization for gay and lesbian liberation.

Stonewall and Its Aftermath

The police raid at the Stonewall Inn in the Greenwich Village section of New York City occurred in the context of a political atmosphere in which college students were organizing for freedom of speech, African Americans and their allies were organizing for civil rights, and women were organizing for equal rights. It was in this political mood that in June 1969, police served the Stonewall manager with a warrant for selling liquor without a license and ordered customers to leave. This same scenario had occurred many times before and was usually followed by the arrest of some customers, while other patrons departed quietly. But this night at the Stonewall Inn was completely different from the past.

A crowd gathered outside the bar as the police steered those arrested into a paddy wagon. They began to throw beer cans and bottles at the police and at windows and set fire to trash cans. In the end, the police turned a fire hose on the crowd, and thirteen people were arrested. The police returned the next night and so did the crowd, this time with protest signs and a determination to fight this discrimination. This refusal to be victims any longer inspired the beginning of the gay liberation movement and marked the transition from the term homosexual to the term gay (Miller 1995, Cruikshank 1992). "[H]omosexuals became gay when they rejected the notion that they were sick or sinful, claimed equality with heterosexuals, banded together to protest second-class citizenship, created a subculture, and came out in large numbers. Pride followed visibility: for lesbians and gay men, shame and invisibility are inseparable" (Cruikshank 1992, 3).

As in the other movements for change in the 1960s and 1970s, there were several different political perspectives and strategies for change that were based on distinct political goals. Liberals or moderates in the gay liberation movement wanted equal rights, the same treatment as and an equal chance along with heterosexuals. This political position was one of minority rights and access, the goal to have a piece of the American pie and dream. Radicals in the movement wanted to transform the American pie itself. They saw homophobia as a reflection of a broader range of deeper oppression that resulted from patriarchal and sexist behavior, policies, and institutions. Their goal was to change or overthrow the sexist and heterosexist culture and institutions that perpetuated this repressive culture. It is important to understand these distinctions and not to assume that the movement for gay and lesbian liberation was monolithic. As in all groups and organizations and individuals, there was diversity on many fronts.

While the old homophile movement had advocated assimilation of gays and lesbians, gay liberation challenged the dominant culture and its assumption that heterosexual relationships, sexual reproduction, and the nuclear family were and ought to be the societal norms. The movement was committed to challenging traditional notions of what it meant to masculine or feminine. Part of the movement for gay liberation was to support the personal, sexual, social, and political identity of gays and lesbians and to encourage the act of being publicly gay by "coming out" (Jagose 1996).

In 1969 the Gay Activist Alliance (GAA) was formed to raise gay issues in mainstream politics through direct action. The "zap" became their modus operandi. It was learned that a credit agency in New York called Fidelifacts sold information about sex lives to its clients. The president of Fidelifacts was quoted as saying, euphemistically referring to gays, that if it looked like a duck and acted like a duck, it probably was a duck. GAA members dressed in duck costumes, held protest signs, and quacked at the front door of Fidelifacts (Miller 1995, 378).

Different political perspectives and divisions emerged as homophobia and internalized homophobia struck the gay liberation movement and the other movements for change in the 1960s. Bayard Rustin, a gay African American man who was a Quaker and a pacifist, conceived of and developed the strategies and campaign for the Montgomery bus boycott and the famous 1963 civil rights march that featured Martin Luther King's "I Have a Dream" speech. Senators, Congressmen, and the FBI threatened to expose Rustin's homosexuality, even suggesting that they would falsely claim that King and Rustin were involved in a homosexual affair. Civil rights leaders feared that the homophobia of the times was still sufficiently rampant that if these threats were carried out there would be damage to the credibility and support of the civil rights movement. King and his advisors chose to put Rustin in the deep background and he was never publicly acknowledged or recognized for the instrumental role he played in the civil rights movement (Miller 1995).

Other liberation movements were equally susceptible to such homophobia. The National Organization of Women (NOW), spearheaded by Betty Friedan, opposed the up-front leadership role of lesbians. The leaders of NOW believed that the larger population of women that they were trying to reach and that the society they were trying to change would see feminism as one and the same as lesbianism. Some even referred to lesbians as the "lavender menace": they, too, believed that the credibility of the women's movement would be seriously impaired and that their strategies for change would fail if lesbians were out and up front in leadership roles. Many women, such as Rita Mae Brown, author of *Rubyfruit Jungle,* resigned from NOW in protest of its anti-lesbian policies (Jagose 1996, 50).

The women who resigned from NOW first attempted to become part of the predominantly male Gay Liberation Front. They concluded, however, that the interests of lesbians and gay men were different. They believed that gay men were still privileged by being male and as a result repeated the patterns of male dominance even in their liberatory organizations and ideology (Miller 1995, 375).

Like other movements whose goal was to transform society into something that was more just, there were some lesbian feminists who sought to both change oppressive institutions and create their own alternative institutions, culture, and structure. Their belief was that these alternatives could model a way of making decisions, living, and forming families that would be nonhierarchical and liberatory. In this effort, lesbians created women's music and festivals, businesses, health care, and child care centers. Some of these institutions failed and some thrived.

But the legacy of the radical lesbian feminists was important in many ways. It was successful in reducing internalized homophobia. "They were able to take messages from both the women's movement and the gay movement and weave them into a coherent theory of lesbian-feminism. They identified the women's movement as homophobic and the gay movement as sexist, and they fought against both. In the process they not only forced those movements to open up to lesbian and feminist ideas, but they also established their own movement that created a unique 'women's culture' in music, spirituality, and literature that made at least a small dent in mainstream culture" (Faderman 1991, 244). The Michigan Women's Festival has historically been a significant hub of lesbian alternative culture.

By the late 1970s there were several concrete results of the movements for gay liberation and lesbian feminism:

- The U.S. Civil Service Commission stopped excluding gays and lesbians from federal employment.
- The American Psychiatric Association and the American Psychological Association removed homosexuality from its list of mental illnesses.
- Thirty-six cities and towns enacted gay rights laws and 25 states repealed sodomy laws.
- The first national march on Washington for gay and lesbian rights occurred (Adams et al. 1997; Miller 1995).

Elaine Noble of Massachusetts was the first openly gay legislator. Air Force Technical Sergeant Leonard Matlovich came out as gay and thus initiated the challenge of the gay ban in the military. When Matlovich died, the epitaph on his tombstone was, "When I was in the military, they gave me a medal for killing two men, and a discharge for loving one" (Miller 1995, 395).

In the mid-1970s George Moscone, a supporter of gay liberation, was elected Mayor of San Francisco. Harvey Milk, an openly gay man, was elected to the San Francisco Board of Supervisors as was Dan White, a conservative who took a strong stand against what he called "social deviates." White's charge against gays and lesbians marked the beginning of both a local and national shift to the political right that included opposition to abortion, support of school prayer, opposition to the Equal Rights Amendment, and activism against the legal and social rights of gays and lesbians.

In San Francisco this conservative shift was exemplified in the proposed Briggs Initiative of 1978. This initiative was designed to bar gays from teaching in public schools. Dan White was a leader in the effort to pass the Briggs Initiative and Harvey Milk was instrumental in its eventual defeat. In the aftermath of an ensuing political squabble, White assassinated both Mayor George Moscone and Harvey Milk. White was convicted of voluntary manslaughter and sentenced to only 7 years and 8 months in prison. This verdict prompted a mass march on City Hall in which protesters burned police cars and police retaliated by raiding the gay community in San Francisco's Castro district. At the end, 61 police officers and 100 gay men were hospitalized (Miller 1995).

Another challenge to the hard-won victories of the movement for gay rights occurred in Florida. Former Miss Oklahoma, pop singer, and the orange juice industry's commercial spokesperson Anita Bryant launched a campaign to repeal a Dade County, Florida, ordinance that protected gay rights. She collected the necessary signatures for a countywide referendum and in 1977 the ordinance was repealed. Similar ordinances were voted down in St. Paul, Minnesota, and Eugene, Oregon. Oklahoma passed a law to fire openly gay and lesbian teachers. The overturn of these legal protections of gay and lesbian rights spawned protests by gays and lesbians and their allies all over the country (Cruikshank 1992, 16).

In the midst of this backlash, lesbian feminists continued to seek a more just culture through challenging traditional identities and institutions and creating their own. While some lesbians lived private or secret lives and separated themselves from the politics of transformation and the personal commitment to coming out of the closet, radical lesbians continued to pursue political change.

But the radical gay liberation movement that had been primarily populated by men gave way to a more reformist and in some ways conformist strategy by middle class gay men. While there were many examples of gay men who were political activists and others who were part of long-term gay male couples, large numbers of gay men entered into the broader movement of sexual liberation. An urban gay culture emerged in several cities that included gay bars and discos, multiple sexual partners, and bathhouses that were exclusively patronized by gay men. Disco became such a strong part of this culture that Warner Brothers' dance music department spent 10 to 15 percent of its advertising budget in gay newspapers and magazines (Miller 1995, 429).

By the 1980s, coming out for many lesbians was still a political statement, a criticism of the dominant culture, while coming out for many gay men was a statement of sexual freedom and liberation. In 1981, the first case of acquired immune deficiency syndrome (AIDS) appeared (Adams et al. 1997, 168), and its health and political consequences seriously affected both the identity of lesbians and gay men and the politics and goals of gay and lesbian organizations.

Part of the New Right's political and fund-raising rhetoric involved demonizing homosexuality as the ultimate consequence of a politically liberal agenda and government. The religious right tied homosexuality to "sin," which they claimed was clearly spelled out in the Bible. By the 1980s, the New Right began to use the spread of AIDS in the gay male community as proof of their belief in God's condemnation of homosexuality. Syndicated columnist Pat Buchanan wrote, "the poor homosexuals: they have declared war on nature and now nature is exacting an awful retribution" (Shilts 1987, 311). The mainstream news media contributed to this discrimination in subtle ways. First they often referred to the spread of AIDS in the "homosexual" community, ignoring the fact that lesbians had the lowest incidence of AIDS. Second, the news media often referred to children as the "innocent victims of AIDS," with the implication that gay men were somehow, therefore, the "guilty" perpetuators of the disease.

A relatively small radical lesbian subculture survived the 1960s and 1970s. Many lesbians moved into the mainstream in the 1980s, much like their counterparts in other liberation movements. Long-term relationships and families were formed in both urban and suburban areas and educated middle class lesbians pursued careers in the dominant culture. Individual women and lesbian organizations were personally and politically moved by the epidemic of AIDS among gay men, both because of human empathy and because of the way the political right was using AIDS to fuel its conservative agenda. Many lesbian leaders concluded that the right was as dangerous to lesbians as it was to gay men and by the mid-1980s personal and political alliances between lesbians and gay men were on the upswing.

In April 1983, there were 1,300 cases of AIDS reported in the United States. By mid-1985 there were 8,897 cases reported, half of whom had already died. More than 70 percent of these recorded cases of AIDS were gay and bisexual men. In the early days of AIDS, there was panic, fear, and confusion about its proportions and how it was spread. By 1983, the virus that caused AIDS (human immunodeficiency virus, or HIV) had been identified and it became clear that it could not be transmitted through casual contact, but rather through the exchange of bodily fluids—most likely through sexual contact or the sharing of intravenous needles by drug users (Miller 1995).

This information and the quick spread of the disease and resulting deaths had a devastating impact on the gay male community. Personally, many gay men were dazed by their own diagnoses and grieving the loss of friends and acquaintances in their communities. Some studies said that 50 to 60 percent of sexually active gay men in New York City and San Francisco and 25 percent in Pittsburgh and Boston had tested positively for HIV by 1985 (Miller 1995, 440). Gay leaders and organizations were also conflicted about strategies to fight this disease. Some were concerned about the political backlash that could be caused by rampant press coverage and advocated for low-profile tactics. Others took strong action to raise funds for AIDS research, to educate gay men about the spread of AIDS and methods of safe sex, and to find ways to care for men who were already sick with the disease.

On a personal level, the earlier gay male culture of the baths, the discos, anonymous sex, and multiple sexual partners was changed dramatically by AIDS. The conservative political backlash in general, coupled with the right's strategy of using homosexuality as a symbol for all that was wrong with the country, also meant that the government with Ronald Reagan at the helm would do little to advocate for AIDS research funding. Many gays and lesbians were outraged at the lack of support to find a cure for such a major threat to public health.

With the leadership of Larry Kramer, the organization ACT UP (AIDS Coalition to Unleash Power) was formed to use direct action to fight for research funds and the use of experimental drugs to treat or cure AIDS. The slogan of ACT UP was "silence equals death" (Miller 1995, 458).The political energy fueled by AIDS, the alliance between gay and lesbian organizations, and the militant activism of groups such as ACT UP spawned major political and cultural changes. The Food and Drug Administration made significant changes in its approach to experimental drugs, making them more accessible to AIDS patients. In 1987, 700,000 people attended the national March on Washington for Lesbian and Gay Rights. At the march, the Names Project Quilt was first displayed, featuring 2,000 enormous quilt panels handmade by friends and loved ones of people who had died of AIDS. In 1990, the Gay (Olympic) Games in Vancouver attracted 7,000 athletes and by 1994 the Gay Games in New York City attracted 11,000 athletes from all over the world.

By the end of the 1980s, the term "queer" began to be reclaimed and used in many political circles of gay and lesbian organizations. Some gays and lesbians that supported the use of queer viewed the term itself as a serious challenge to conventional understanding of gender and sexual identity. Some queer theorists suggested that the concept of gender identity itself is false and misleading and were critical of gay liberation and lesbian feminism. "According to the liberationist model, the established social order is fundamentally corrupt, and therefore the success of any political action is to be measured by the extent to which it smashes that system. The ethnic model, by contrast, was committed to establishing gay identity as a legitimate minority group, whose official recognition would secure citizenship rights for lesbian and gay subjects" (Jagose 1996, 61). Queer theorists and activists believed that most gay and lesbian organizations had bought into the ethnic model and had consequently become assimilated, losing their radical edge in efforts to be acceptable, accepted, and to get their piece of the American pie.

By the end of the 1980s another organization, Queer Nation, had emerged that used street theater and confrontation tactics to aim for gay visibility. They held kiss-ins at malls and used humor by singing songs such as "It's a Gay World After All" to make their point. They also challenged a long-term cultural belief and practice in the gay community which held that every gay and lesbian person was entitled to come out at his or her own pace and in his/her own way. Queer Nation began the practice of "outing" famous gays and lesbians. There was much evidence that pointed to prominent, but closeted, gays and lesbians, taking strong anti-gay public positions in order to deflect any suspicion of their own sexual identity. Queer Nation's controversial practice of outing was an effort to deflate this kind of discrimination and claim pride in a "queer" identity.

By the close of the decade of the 1990s and the twentieth century, many of the same issues that were present for sexual minorities throughout the century still existed. Employment discrimination; the lack of opportunity for same sex marriage; the frequent failure of institutions to recognize domestic partnerships, thus depriving gays and lesbians of insurance and legal benefits and rights that are automatic for heterosexual partners; discrimination in housing; and high suicide rates of gay and lesbian teens were among some of these stubborn issues. By the late 1980s the Department of Justice had released a study of hate crimes that listed crimes against gays and lesbians as the most frequent of any hate crime. In 1988, there were more than 7,000 physical attacks on gays and lesbians, including 70 murders. By 1989, this number had increased by 67 percent. By 1992, coalitions on the right had targeted gays and lesbians as the cause of what they called the breakdown in family values. A Colorado initiative to ban gay rights legislation was successful and spawned similar efforts in other states. Despite President Bill Clinton's campaign pledge to lift the military ban on gays and lesbians, the outcome of a controversial struggle over this issue was a 1993 policy referred to as "Don't Ask, Don't Tell, Don't Pursue."

Homophobia continued to be one of the most active and intractable forms of overt discrimination and oppression. But despite this and the political setbacks listed above, some states, such as Missouri, passed anti–hate crime legislation that specifically defined hate crimes against gays, lesbians, bisexuals, and transgender and transsexual people and allowed for legal remedies.

Some studies, as well as personal experiences, have demonstrated that when people who identify as heterosexual have interaction with gays and lesbians, fear and discrimination are reduced (Cruikshank 1992). These studies point to the need for education both in and out of school. Yet education and schools are often sites of homophobia. "Curriculum that focuses in a positive way upon issues of sexual identity, sexuality, and sexism are still rare, particularly in primary and secondary grades. Yet schools are virtual cauldrons of homophobic sentiment, as witnessed by everything from the graffiti in the bathrooms and the put-downs yelled on the playground, to the heterosexist bias of most texts and the firing of teachers only on the basis that they are not heterosexual" (Smith 1993, 101).

The documentary *It's Elementary* (Chasnoff and Cohen 1996) highlights curricular projects in elementary and middle schools throughout the country that teach about discrimination toward gays and lesbians and demonstrate the positive response and support of this curriculum by parents and the educational value for children. This documentary was aired nationally by the Public Broadcasting System (PBS), yet some local affiliates chose not to screen it for fear of homophobic backlash in their communities. It is hard to imagine that a documentary on school curriculum to combat racism or sexism would have been censored in this way in the late twentieth century.

As we move into the next section, which examines religious perspectives on sexual orientation, this history of oppression and liberation of sexual minorities in the United States provides a backdrop. You may agree or disagree with the political right or left, the gay and lesbian movements for change, or current legislative and policy initiatives. As you consider the chronology, politics, and dynamics of this history, it is also important to think of the human and personal benefits and costs at various points in the twentieth and twenty-first centuries. "The issue is not only whether certain forms of sexual behavior are natural or moral but whether any form of individual behavior not harmful to others should be regulated by the state" (Cruikshank 1992, 53). Another critical issue, on a more personal and individual level, involves respect and acceptance of all human behavior that does not hurt anyone. Still another issue involves the way in which judgment and ostracism of people who are different from the dominant culture has historically led to hate, hate crimes, and even genocide. These are the central questions you will need to ask yourself as we begin to tackle the topic of religion and sexual orientation.

Religion and Sexual Orientation

We often think of religious beliefs as sacrosanct and immune to challenge or criticism. The tradition of religious freedom in the United States mandates that we respect a wide variety of beliefs and practices as long as they do not break the law or hurt anyone. But public laws and customs as well as religious doctrines and practices have changed throughout our history. For example, there were many Protestant and Reform Jewish denominations that once excluded women from the clergy and now welcome women in these positions. The Church of the Latter Day Saints (the Mormon Church) changed its practice of excluding African Americans from leadership and clergy positions. Many houses of worship still continue to be racially segregated, yet more and more have actively sought racial integration of their membership or have formed partnerships with congregations of different races. While not all religions or denominations have changed according to contemporary secular beliefs, laws, and culture, many have seriously assessed their religious doctrines, policies, and practices to weed out discrimination and to find ways to be inclusive that are compatible with their faith.

The role of religion in thought and beliefs regarding homosexuality is central and critical to many Americans. Those individuals who are deeply committed to their faith and observant of religious doctrine take quite seriously and generally comply with any explicit theology or religious tenet. There are other individuals, also committed to their faith, who find that their personal beliefs on homosexuality are divergent from their religious teachings. This can cause conflict and great anguish for some people. This is not unlike the difficult situation for Catholics who believe that women should be ordained as priests or who believe that women have the right to choose abortion. There are agnostics and atheists who base their beliefs about homosexuality on secular values and traditions. There are also many individuals in the United States who are only minimally involved in their religions. Perhaps they go to church twice a year for Easter or Christmas or to temple or synagogue only for the High Holidays. They may not have studied their religion or even be aware of their religion's position on homosexuality. But because religious language is so prevalent in public debates about homosexuality, they too may adopt this language and its accompanying beliefs.

Some of us have thoroughly studied and have developed thoughtful beliefs with regard to homosexuality, while others of us have not looked below the surface of what we have been told or have come to believe as the "truth." Some of us have clearly separated our religious beliefs from public policy while others of us have interwoven the threads of misinformation, religious beliefs and public policy into an intricate and often inseparable fabric.

To look below the surface of our current beliefs—regardless of whether they are strong and clear, ambiguous or confused—requires separating, studying, and understanding misinformation, religious beliefs and public policy about homosexuality. The information provided below offers some tools for this kind of analysis for three of the major religions in the United States: Protestantism, Catholicism, and Judaism. As you read this, please keep in mind that there are many other organized religions and faiths in the United States including Buddhism, Hinduism, Islam, and Bahai, as well as new age spiritualism, agnosticism, and atheism.

One image of organized religions' response to homosexuality is that of a fishbone in the throat that can neither be ejected nor swallowed (Nugent and Gramick 1989, 7). Different faiths have divergent beliefs about how homosexuality is viewed in the Bible, religious theologies, and traditions, as well as the role gays and lesbians are permitted to play as members or leaders of congregations. Even within certain faiths, Protestant and Jewish, for example, there are widely divergent beliefs and practices. For those Americans who are grounded in their faith, this is a particularly complex and difficult analysis.

In the other issues we have studied—gender, class, and race—religion has mostly played a marginal role in their U.S. histories of oppression and liberation, particularly in the twenty-first century. While women are still banned from ordination in some religions and some faiths still teach that women should be subservient to men, these beliefs and practices are neither widespread nor central to contemporary public policy decisions. Black churches were in the forefront of the organization of the civil rights movement. And there are still some congregations that teach racism and segregation of races. Yet there are no mainstream denominations that teach that people of color are sinful by virtue of their skin color or that they should be denied the same legal or human rights afforded to whites. Racism and sexism are alive in the United States, but religion does not play a central role in their perpetuation. The explicit and implicit role of religion with regard to homosexuality, however, is critical to the understanding of homophobia and heterosexism in this country.

If our faith teaches us that God loves all human beings, including homosexuals, and that it is our religious duty to be inclusive of gays, lesbians, and bisexuals in every aspect of life, we may see other religious beliefs as discriminatory or even barbaric. But if our faith teaches us that God accepts only that sexuality which has the possibility of procreation and that any other sexuality is "sinful," we may see other religious beliefs as misinformed at best and sinful at worst.

Much like the discussion about and controversy over abortion, there are no easy answers nor clear-cut guidelines to civil debate and communication. For this section, I will continue to use the same guidelines and principles I have used throughout the book. I will provide historical information that is not readily accessible in mainstream education and introduce a framework for analysis as well as a variety of theories. As you read this information, keep in mind liberation theory, the cycle of oppression, and other theories that describe the process of socialization that leads to discrimination and oppression, including homophobia, as well as the possibilities for breaking the cycle. As you sort through this section, consider your own socialization as well as old and emerging beliefs and thoughts.

A Framework for Discussion

Most organized religions have official positions on:

- same sex attraction and behavior;
- civil rights for gays and lesbians;
- antigay violence;
- the meaning of same sex relationships; and
- criteria for leadership and membership in the faith institution.

Most religions have a faith-based history and foundation upon which their moral stance on homosexuality is rooted and conveyed to their members. Despite the clarity of institutional religions' beliefs and practices for their own members, many churches, synagogues, and other faith organizations struggle with their role in the larger secular community. Should they take strong positions on employment laws and anti–hate crime legislation that is consistent with their religious beliefs? Should they advocate or oppose domestic partnerships? Should they insist that government and corporations have policies and practices that comply with these beliefs? These are some of the questions that will be raised in this section.

There are four basic positions that organized religion can assume about homosexuality. These different categories of belief will serve as a framework both for understanding the perspectives of different religions and for understanding individual beliefs that are rooted in faith.

The first position is both *rejecting and punitive* toward gays, lesbians, and bisexuals. This view holds that homosexuality is a sin explicitly prohibited in the Bible. This position encourages homosexuals to renounce their sexuality and seek conversion to heterosexuality through spiritual healing. Some religions that hold this view banish gays and lesbians as members and are convinced that they will go to hell when they die. An extreme interpretation of this position is that AIDS is God's punishment to homosexuals for their sinful behavior (Nugent and Gramick 1989, 32).

A *rejecting but nonpunitive* perspective is the second position a religion may take. This position separates the act of homosexuality from the person, condemning the "sin" but not the "sinner." The central belief here is that any sexuality that does not have the potential to result in procreation is unnatural. Homosexuals are encouraged to seek reorientation or to remain sexually celibate (Nugent and Gramick 1989, 37).

The third religious position involves *qualified acceptance* of homosexuality. This belief is that of traditional western culture that in the hierarchy of sex, heterosexuality is always superior. But qualified acceptance is grounded in the belief in essentialism that says that gays and lesbians have no choice in their sexual orientation and therefore cannot be condemned for something they were born with or that is involuntary. The central thesis of this position is that homosexuals will never be capable of reaching the ideal of human existence (Nugent and Gramick 1989, 39).

A final position that organized religions may take is *full acceptance* of gays and lesbians. This position is based on the belief that there is a rich diversity of creation that includes homosexuality. The central thesis here is that "wholesome sexuality is not to be evaluated in terms of procreation, but by the nature and quality of the relationship of the persons involved, regardless of gender" (Nugent and Gramick 1989, 45).

This framework for understanding religion and sexual orientation and the range of possible positions and beliefs will serve as the foundation for examining several religious approaches to homosexuality. The positions of three major religious traditions previously mentioned will be considered. This debate among and within religious communities has had and will continue to have an enormous impact on the acceptance of sexual minorities within faith-based organizations and the broader secular society.

Protestant Perspectives on Homosexuality

The majority of Protestant denominations and churches rely on theology as the basis of their understanding of religion and homosexuality. Different denominations, clergy, and members of churches interpret theology in very different ways. Some of these beliefs, policies, and practices are described below.

With the exception of the Southern Baptist Convention, most Protestant denominations support decriminalization of homosexuality and protection of civil rights. The National and World Council of Churches states that sex should occur only within heterosexual marriages. This same body supports human rights for homosexuals and clear religious disapproval of same sex relations and state-approved marriage. Most Protestant churches (with the exception of the United Church of Christ) oppose ordination of gays and lesbians as ministers, yet encourage pastoral care (Stackhouse 1998, 119). In this view there is somewhat of a separation of the beliefs of the church and the role of the government. The Protestant denominations that subscribe to this point of view see homosexuality as less than ideal but simultaneously believe that the government must protect all of its citizens. This position calls for qualified and limited acceptance of gays and lesbians, which gays and lesbians and their allies challenge as a denial of equality and equal rights.

Another less common Protestant position is that of the Southern Baptist Convention, which believes that homosexuality is a sin, spelled out explicitly in the Bible (Green 1998, 118). Southern Baptists see the central biblical covenant with God as heterosexual marriage with the intention to procreate and create family. Any other kind of of sexuality or family is seen by this denomination as an affront to God. Because of these beliefs, the Southern Baptist convention voted to boycott the Disney Corporation when it adopted benefits for domestic partners. A key element of this religious belief involves the role of the government. Southern Baptists and other Protestants that share their views believe that the state should protect its citizens from "false religion" and the "moral wrongness" of homosexuality and that laws should be passed to prohibit this "immorality" (Green 1998, 114). Depending on the particular church and denomination, these beliefs fall somewhere between rejecting/nonpunitive and rejecting/punitive.

On the other side of the spectrum is the United Church of Christ, the only Protestant denomination that has officially supported ordination of gays and lesbians. Their position is based on the belief that "God's creative intentions for humans is to love our gay sisters and brothers who should be valued by us as by God" (Green 1998, 115). This set of beliefs also sees marriage as a covenant with God—one that is not exclusively based on the possibility of procreation but rather on the development of a committed love and friendship and the possibility of the creation of family. These beliefs most closely adhere to full acceptance of homosexuality. This position also strongly believes that political means and the government must be utilized to fulfill this covenant.

Protestant churches that are predominantly African American can fall anywhere on this continuum but are characterized by some unique features that are not usually present in mainstream white Protestant churches. The first of these features is that African American churches have a history that dates back to slavery and was most prominent during the civil rights movement. This history is a fundamental commitment to ending oppression and supporting human rights.

Black churches have also historically strongly advocated monogamous, heterosexual marriage and the creation of family. Some African American church leaders have deep concerns about what they see as the disintegration of family and parenting structures in the black community. And while many see these patterns of family as a direct legacy of slavery and racism, some leaders of black churches are concerned that gay and lesbian relationships are another way to destroy the traditional family in the black community (Sanders 1998, 178).

Because racism has had such a devastating effect on the African American family and has in many ways discredited and disempowered African American men, many black churches have worked to build up the status and authority of male members. At times these well-intended efforts of elevating black male leaders in the church have also had the effect of elevating a culture of traditional masculinity and heterosexuality while denigrating women and gay and lesbian relationships.

Theologically, many African American churches fall somewhere in the rejection of homosexuality category, sometimes with and sometimes without a belief that gays and lesbians should be punished for their sexual orientation. Some black scholars and theologians believe that these religious beliefs are based on a reliance on white theology and that there is a basic contradiction between the tradition of liberation and social justice in black churches and their position on homosexuality. For some church members and leaders this presents a conflict between what they understand to be the teachings of the church and their loyalty to the advancement of human rights (Dyson 1998, 196).

Catholic Perspectives on Homosexuality

While most Protestant denominations base their beliefs on an interpretation of the Bible, Catholic beliefs on homosexuality are centered on their understanding and interpretation of divine natural law. Protestant beliefs vary from denomination to denomination and sometimes even from church to church, but the teachings of the Catholic church are intended to be the norm for all of its members. In reality, Catholic scholars, church members, and theologians may hold beliefs different from the central position. But what distinguishes Catholicism on sexual orientation is that there *is* a central position.

The dominant theology of Catholicism as applied to homosexuality is consistent with the principle that is applied to birth control and abortion—the belief that procreation and the possibility of the transmission of life is the only kind of sex that is sanctioned by God. But like the issues of birth control and abortion, many Catholic scholars, lay people, and priests disagree about the relationship of the church and the government and the right of the government to make decisions about its citizens' sex lives.

One Catholic perspective is that while every act of sex must be open to the transmission of life, gays and lesbians ought not to be punished by the state and should be treated with human dignity and afforded human rights. According to this belief, the government should intervene for only two reasons. The first is to protect human rights. Anti–hate crime laws targeted for the safety of gays and lesbians are consistent with this approach. The second reason the government may intervene is to protect the common good. According to this perspective, there is no common value in same sex marriage and therefore it should not be considered appropriate (Twiss 1998, 71–74).

Part of the debate about homosexuality in the Catholic church centers around the rights and responsibilities of religion to influence law. The United States was founded on the principle of separation of church and state. But there are some in the Catholic church and other religions who believe that certain moral convictions are so strong and that their violation has such dire consequences that it is essential to impose these beliefs on the wider public by making them the law of the land.

For example, one set of beliefs holds that committed gay relationships are morally good and should only be judged by the same standards as heterosexual relationships. This perspective interprets Vatican II as emphasizing freedom as essential to the common good and translates this into an imperative to urge the state to promote that freedom (Curran 1998, 87). If this belief is joined with the conviction that it is acceptable for religion to influence law, then it would be logical to pursue or endorse nondiscrimination laws at a minimum and perhaps even same sex marriage laws. "The sanctioning of divorce by law negatively affects marriage and the family more than does protecting gays and lesbians against discrimination" (Curran 1998, 92) and "the civil law allows divorce and remarriage and does not discriminate against divorced people, but the Catholic Church still maintains its moral teaching on divorce" (Curran 1998, 96).

But if on the other hand, the belief that homosexuality is a sin and an affront to God is combined with the belief that the church has the right and obligation to influence law, a completely separate set of actions would follow. If this belief was so strong as to say that as "sinners" homosexuals should not have their rights protected by law, then this perspective would lead its followers to pursue repeal of anti-discrimination laws targeted to gays and lesbians and to fight any proposed law that sanctioned same sex marriage or other rights.

Generally, Catholic beliefs range from the rejecting and punitive approach to qualified acceptance. The wide majority of Catholic scholars and the Conference of Bishops see homosexuality as a violation of one of their basic understandings of God's natural law and at the same time take a strong stand against violence against gays and for respect for their human dignity and rights.

Jewish Perspectives on Homosexuality

Judaism is organized into four branches: Reform, Reconstructionist, Conservative, and Orthodox. These branches are diverse in their perspective and approach to homosexuality. And as with Protestants and Catholics, their particular stances and policies vary by individual synagogues and temples, leaders and members.

The debate among Jewish scholars, rabbis, and congregations centers around the understanding of ancient Jewish law and its relationship to contemporary western life. The traditional law is interpreted by the Orthodox and some Conservatives as meaning that homosexuality should be condemned because the divine law calls for procreation and that homosexuality undermines the family and is anatomically and biologically unnatural (Kahn 1989).

Liberal Jewish thinking in the Reform and Reconstructionist branches as well as some Conservative congregations holds that this divine law itself is debatable and that contemporary thinking, values, and beliefs in human rights should weigh heavily in the consideration of contemporary issues—including homosexuality. Some compare discrimination against gays and lesbians to anti-Semitism and "call for a response to contemporary oppression of gay people that is informed by the historical Jewish experience of discrimination, and insist[s] that a heightened sensitivity to homosexuals' calls for justice and liberation must take precedence over the traditional Jewish teaching" (Kahn 1989, 59). This perspective conforms to a civil rights approach that sees gays and lesbians as a minority that must be protected and given full rights.

The progressive Jewish position found in some Reform and Reconstructionist congregations calls for two principles to be upheld. The first is the belief that God does not create in vain, and therefore gays and lesbians have a covenantal obligation to be fully themselves. Rabbi Janet Marder was Rabbi of Beth Chayim Chadashim in Los Angeles, founded in 1972 as a haven for gays and lesbians. This congregation was instrumental in changing Reform policies and positions about homosexuality. Marder says, "The Jewish values and principles I regard as eternal, transcendent and divinely ordained do not condemn homosexuality. The Judaism I cherish and affirm teaches love of humanity, respect for the spark of divinity in every person, and the human right to live with dignity. The God I worship endorses loving, responsible, and committed human relationships, regardless of the sex of the persons involved" (Kahn 1989, 66).

A second principle in the progressive Jewish position on homosexuality criticizes the civil rights approach that regards gays and lesbians as a minority and believes that homosexuality needs to be placed in a larger context of sexual identity and sexual ethics. According to this perspective, broader issues must be questioned including how the dominant system promotes rigid gender roles, compulsory heterosexuality, and the patriarchal social order. Supporters of this perspective believe that without this fundamental overhaul, gays, lesbians, and bisexuals will continue to exist in the margins of Judaism and the broader society (Plaskow 1998, 30).

Generally, Reform and Reconstructionist Jews have official policies of nondiscrimination toward gays and lesbians in leadership, teaching, membership, and other aspects of congregational life. These branches allow for same sex marriage ceremonies to be performed at the rabbi's discretion (Olyan and Nussbaum 1998, 5).

In 1990, The Central Conference of Rabbis voted to admit sexually active and open gays, lesbians, and bisexuals into rabbinic training. With membership numbering 1.5 million nationwide, Reform Judaism became the largest religious denomination to welcome openly gay clergy. Many of these congregations have also taken strong public positions on laws that call for nondiscrimination and protect the rights of gays and lesbians with respect to hate crimes. Some have advocated laws that call for state approved same sex marriage (Olyan and Nussbaum 1998, 6).

The Conservative branch of Judaism generally welcomes gay and lesbian members and prohibits same sex marriages. It is typically the rabbi's decision concerning the level of membership and leadership that is permitted (Olyan and Nussbaum 1998, 5).

The traditional position on homosexuality is reflected in Orthodox Jewish beliefs that procreation is the central and divine purpose of human sexuality and that is the basis upon which homosexuality should be condemned. People who identify as gay or lesbian have traditionally been encouraged to remain celibate and to seek therapy according to this set of beliefs (Olyan and Nussbaum 1998, 15).

For the most part, beliefs and practices in the various branches of Judaism range from rejecting and nonpunitive to fully accepting. Beliefs about the relationship between religion and government seem to be determined by two things: the convictions of the particular congregation and the relationship of the congregation to politics in general. Often, liberal and progressive Jewish congregations see the Holocaust and the failure of religious organizations to take an active stand to stop the government of Germany from its extermination of Jews as a strong rationale for religion to influence law—particularly in reference to discrimination and hate.

Summary of Reconstructing Knowledge

Whether we identify as heterosexual, gay, lesbian, or bisexual, most of us were strongly socialized to see heterosexuality as either the only option or as the norm. Many of us received almost no information about the history, debates, or discrimination regarding sexual orientation. People we trusted, including our parents, teachers, and clergy, generally either told us nothing or told us that homosexuality was wrong. Much as the construct of race changed over time in the United States, definitions and beliefs and laws about homosexuality have changed significantly in the United States over time and across various cultures. There has been a kind of heavy curtain over information regarding sexual orientation which misinformation has penetrated, only recently to be joined by more accurate information and open debate. Given this history, it is not surprising that many people find themselves resistant to new information that challenges their thinking and beliefs. With this kind of deep and widespread socialization as background, it becomes increasingly important to consider a wide array of information and beliefs and reach independent conclusions.

Sexual Orientation and Entertainment Media

The next exercise in Media Activity 6.1 will, no doubt, be the quickest and simplest in the book. If you are over twenty years old chances are your answers were the same as mine—none and none. In this section, we will trace the absence of gay, lesbian, and bisexual themes and characters in entertainment media and the audience impact of this omission. We will also explore the history of the intermittent appearance of gay, lesbian, and bisexual characters and themes in popular media. To place this exploration in a broader context, it is important to take another look at the organization of the industry of entertainment media and its relationship to the choices of content about sexual orientation.

Popular Media Industry and Sexual Orientation

The vast majority of the organizations that produce entertainment media in the United States are large corporations that are economically driven. While individuals who work in these corporations may be interested in the quality of the media content, its artistic value, and its ability to provoke thought, the corporate culture revolves around profit. "Ownership by major corporations of vast portfolios of mass media gives us reason to believe that a whole range of ideas and images—those that question fundamental social arrangements, under which the media owners are doing quite well—will rarely be visible. This does not mean that all images and information are uniform. It means that some ideas will be widely available, while others will be largely excluded" (Croteau and Hoynes 1997, 43).

The centrality of the profit motive limits the range of the content in several ways with respect to gay, lesbian, and bisexual characters and themes. First, the drive for economic success pushes programmers and producers to minimize risk. While in some cases, risk can mean economic success (e.g., *Roseanne*), generally risky subjects are thought to be money losers. Second, when a successful formula is discovered, its format is frequently mimicked or spun off as another effort to chase the dollar. Whether it is the hospital programs that were spawned by the successful *E.R.* or the many clones of 'NSync or the Backstreet Boys, copycat tactics in popular media often work.

Until recently, these fundamental industry rules have meant that images of gays, lesbians, and bisexuals have been almost completely missing. As these images and themes began to emerge they most frequently appeared as stereotypes: gay men with flamboyant clothing, style, and exaggerated feminine mannerisms; evil men or women; carefully coded and barely recognizable homosexual characters and victims. In the 1950s and 1960s, stereotypes of gay men were fair game for prime time television. A limp hand, exaggerated lisp, and the occupation of interior decorator, hairdresser, or florist were standard fare and likely to evoke a laugh. It has only been in the late 1990s that any complex characters and themes have evolved

Media Activity 6.1
Popular Culture and Sexual Orientation

Think of the time during which you were ages eight through twelve
and choose the following:
- minimum of three of your favorite television programs
- minimum of three of your favorite movies
- minimum of three of your favorite popular songs

For each of these three categories answer the two questions below:

1. How many major or recurring characters were gay, lesbian, or bisexual?

2. How many themes (e.g., gays and lesbians in loving relationships or
   families, coming out, grappling with sexual identity, discrimination, gay
   bashing, etc.) in your favorite media involved gays, lesbians, and
   bisexuals?

around homosexuality. The development of these characters and themes will be
described in later sections of this chapter.

Hegemony, as you may recall, allows those in power to rule by consent rather
than force. In democratic countries such as the United States, this is a significant
and often invisible way that people agree to certain world views or universal ways
of thinking. People who are elected or hired into leadership positions also serve
informally as cultural leaders and often encourage and reinforce the idea that certain things are just "common sense" and certain kinds of behavior are "natural."
Entertainment media, along with religion and education, is one of the institutions
that reinforces our sense of what is considered normal. This "normalcy" typically
reflects the beliefs or ideology of the dominant culture.

Most of us think that our beliefs about what is natural cannot be controlled
socially. We believe that is just the way things are. For example, many people
believed and some still do that it is "natural" for women to stay home and raise
children and keep house. Some believe that it is just part of human nature for
people to want to feel superior to others. If we are convinced that something is
natural, we are also more likely to believe that it is legitimate, permanent, and
unchangeable.

The dominant hegemonic belief has been that heterosexuality is natural and
that homosexuality is therefore "unnatural." The scarcity of gay and lesbian characters and themes and the recurrence of negative images has been popular media's
contribution to this set of beliefs or ideology. "The media give us pictures of social
interaction and social institutions that, by their sheer repetition on a daily basis,
can play important roles in shaping broad social definitions. In essence, the accu-

mulation of media images suggests what is 'normal' and what is 'deviant' . . . popular media . . . have a tendency to display a remarkably narrow range of behaviors and lifestyles, marginalizing or neglecting people who are 'different' from the mass-mediated norm" (Croteau and Hoynes 1997, 166).

This does not mean that media professionals and industry leaders are plotting conspiratorially to brainwash audiences to a particular point of view about sexual orientation. They are not necessarily even thinking about ideology as they make programming and content decisions. Rather, they are thinking about and predicting what will sell, and it is the stories and messages and characters that get selected that often create or reinforce our "common sense" and "natural" notions of sexual orientation.

Prime Time Television and Sexual Orientation

It is your turn again. Complete the exercise in Media Activity 6.2 to take a closer look at sexual orientation in prime time television. If you are doing this exercise with a class or a group, select different weekday evenings and different networks and compile your data. What percentage of all the major characters you observed was gay, lesbian, or bisexual? What percentage of minor characters was gay, lesbian, or bisexual? What about the total percentage of both major and minor characters? Of this number, what percentage was isolated and what percentage was part of a larger gay or lesbian community? What was the percentage of recurring gay characters in a series? What percentage of the gay or lesbian characters was in a same sex relationship? What percentage was shown displaying physical or sexual affection?

Chances are the numbers and percentages for all of these questions are well below 5 percent. Yet even this small percentage represents an increase over the last forty-plus years of television. By the 1999 prime time television season, the numbers of gay and lesbian characters had increased significantly, as had the complexity of individual characters and the range of characters presented. Before the mid-1990s the number of homosexual characters on prime time television was so low that their absence has also meant a notable lack of books and articles chronicling homosexuality in television. Yet while the few gay characters that slipped through were minor, they often triggered major controversy.

In 1974, *Marcus Welby* (1969–76) was a popular dramatic series that revolved around a doctor (played by Robert Young, the same actor who played the classic 1950s "father" in *Father Knows Best*). One episode featured a gay man who was a child molester and suggested that his tendencies to molest were connected to his homosexuality and that his homosexuality could be cured. This provoked protests by gay activists who subsequently organized media watch activities.

By the 1980s, there were occasional gay characters in prime time television series. While there were some isolated characters who were depicted as complex and "normal," overall gay characters were external to the "natural" order of these

Media Activity 6.2
Gay, Lesbian, and Bisexual Characters in Prime Time Television

Instructions

Choose an evening of prime time television on ABC, NBC, CBS, FOX, or the WB from 8 P.M. to 11 P.M. eastern time. Make sure the programs you observe are narrative fiction and are neither news, infotainment, movies, specials, nor variety programs. Answer the questions below.

1. List the television programs you watched.

2. List the number of major characters in each program. (Recall that major characters are those within the particular episode without whom the plot would make no sense.) Indicate which of these characters are identified as heterosexual, bisexual, or homosexual or if his or her sexual identity is unclear. Add the total number of major characters. What percentage of these characters is gay, lesbian, or bisexual?

3. List the number of minor characters in each program. (Minor characters are those characters with speaking parts but who do not contribute centrally to the plot.) Indicate which of these characters are identified as heterosexual, bisexual, or homosexual or if his or her sexual identity is unclear. Add the total number of minor characters. What percentage of these characters is gay, lesbian, or bisexual?

4. What is the total number of gay, lesbian, or bisexual characters in the programs you watched? What is their percentage of the total number of major and minor characters?

5. Of the gay characters that you observed, answer the following questions:
   a. Are they part of a gay or lesbian community or depicted as separate from others who are gay or lesbian?
   b. Are they recurring characters in a series?
   c. Are they shown involved in a same sex relationship? If so, are they shown displaying affection at the same level as heterosexual couples in the series?

programs and often generated protest. *Thirtysomething* was a dramatic series that aired from 1987 to 1991 and chronicled and explored marriage, parenthood, careers, dating, abortion, and the affairs of a tight-knit clan of middle class whites in their early thirties. In one episode two men, apparently a gay couple, were shown in a scene talking in bed. The outcry was strong and well organized and several advertisers withdrew their commercials. The characters were never seen again and the episode was pulled from the summer rerun line-up (Crouteau and Hoynes 1997,

164). This event reinforced the already prevailing industry wisdom that creating gay characters as part of an ensemble or regular cast was far too risky for economic success.

But despite the risk, regular characters began to emerge slowly and tentatively on prime time in the 1980s and 1990s. In 1989, *Roseanne* took another kind of programmatic risk by depicting Arnie's wife Nancy coming out as a lesbian. Later in the series, Roseanne's boss and subsequent business partner was a gay man. Even Roseanne's mom revealed at a Thanksgiving dinner one year that she was a lesbian. In the same year Steven Carrington on *Dynasty* was the first bisexual on a prime-time drama. His character endured a murdered lover, a wife, and a plane crash (Epstein 1999, 6). In 1994 *My So-Called Life* was the first program with a regular character who was a gay teen, but the series only lasted for one season.

Northern Exposure (1990–95) was one of the first prime time series that featured gay and lesbian characters and themes from the very beginning. In fact, there were intermittent episodes that revealed the story of the founding and development of the small town of Cicely, Alaska, where the program occurs. A lesbian couple founded the fictitious Cicely. Their sexual orientation and relationship were central to the early days of the town and were never questioned, challenged, or made the butt of humor. The relationship between the two women was depicted as loving and caring and complex; quite unusual for prime time television. In addition, there were occasional gay male couples on *Northern Exposure;* one couple considered buying some property and was later shown dancing a slow dance together at an informal gathering of series regulars.

Throughout the 1980s and 1990s these images, however, continued to be rare. One could watch weeks of prime time television and never see a gay or lesbian character. Yet some programs offered the occasional regular gay or lesbian character. In *Mad About You,* Paul's sister Debbie was engaged to a gynecologist named Joan. From the very beginning of the popular *Friends* series it was clear that Ross was getting divorced because his wife, Carol, discovered that she was a lesbian and developed a live-in committed relationship with Susan. Susan and Carol appeared on the show periodically and were featured on the episode in which they got "married" by none other than conservative politician Newt Gingrich's lesbian sister. The characters and humor of the series remained consistent as gay and lesbian characters and themes were explored. While at the wedding, series womanizer Joey talked about the frustration of being a single man looking for love at a lesbian wedding, to which the consistent romantic loser Chandler replied, "Now you know how I feel all of the time."

It was not until 1997, with the first coming out of a main character—Ellen Morgan of the program *Ellen*—that significant changes in television and sexual orientation emerged. Comedian Ellen Degeneres, who played the character Ellen, had once upon a time been dubbed the female Jerry Seinfeld as her series emerged with a group of unmarried generation Xers sitting around their apartments chatting and cracking wise. The show experienced more than moderate popularity in early 1997. Then the rumors began to stir that the character Ellen and the actor Ellen would be coming out at the same time. The media fanfare was enormous and loud. The episode itself was an hour long and featured, among other celebrity guests, Oprah Winfrey as Ellen's therapist and Laura Dern as the woman to whom Ellen declared her sexuality. Leading up to this episode, the Moral Majority urged sponsors to drop the show and a few did. But ultimately, it was the viewers' reaction that sounded the death knell for *Ellen* in the following season. The month before the coming out episode, 63 percent of audiences familiar with *Ellen* had no interest in this episode and 37 percent thought it was a bad idea for a major television character to be gay or lesbian (Pela 1997, 3).

The program stayed consistent with its dry and off beat humor while exploring sexual orientation. In a dream sequence in one episode, Ellen experienced the world as if the dominant group were gay and lesbian and the minority group heterosexual. Her straight friends were afraid to be "out" and posed as gay or risked ridicule and discrimination. Despite its decline and ultimate demise after the coming out episode, *Ellen* played a significant role in paving the way for other gay and lesbian characters and themes in prime time. A spokesperson for the Gay and Lesbian Alliance Against Defamation said, "The power of Ellen Degeneres' coming out on- and offscreen cannot be underestimated in the annals of gay and lesbian history. . . . It was a giant step forward" (Epstein 1999, 3).

By the late 1990s there were an increasing number of regular gay and lesbian characters on prime time television. There was African American doctor Dennis Hancock on *Chicago Hope* and Dr. Maggie Doyle on *E.R.* There was clerical assistant John Irvin (also known on occasion as "Gay John") on *NYPD Blue* and the emerging bisexuality of *Homicide* major character Detective Tim Bayliss. There was *Spin City*'s mayoral staff person, Carter Heywood and the sexually ambiguous Josh of *Veronica's Closets.*

For the first time several programs that featured teens (and had much longer shelf-lives than *My So-Called Life*) began to explore homosexuality. One of *Dawson Creek*'s six regular characters, Jack McPhee, came out in 1999. And in the same year the popular program *Felicity*, set in a New York college, depicted Felicity offering to marry her gay immigrant boss, Javier, so that he would not be deported. Felicity also encouraged her then boyfriend, Noel, to accept the news that his brother was gay. Other programs with teens such as *That 70s Show, Beverly Hills 90210,* and *Buffy the Vampire Slayer* explored issues such as coming out to one's family and lesbian parenting.

Conservative organizations such as the Christian Action Network have expressed concerns about the impact of these images of teen homosexuality and have protested many of these programs, advocating an "HC" rating for homosexual content. Executives of these same programs, however, have stated that the audience response has been overwhelmingly positive. Youth advocates from gay and lesbian organizations have applauded this new trend because it gives positive images to young people who are grappling with their sexuality and may help curb the severe depression that often strikes young gays and lesbians. Cole Rucker, director of the Los Angeles Gay and Lesbian Center said, "I can't emphasize enough how important these portrayals are. I have gotten phone calls, met youth in person—dozens and dozens of youth—who come in and say, 'I was thinking about killing myself until I saw Ellen come out,' or, 'until I saw *Dawson's Creek*.' Obviously they are trying to entertain people but they are truly saving the lives of young people when they present positive images on television" (Epstein 1999, 4).

The groundbreaking program *Will and Grace* is a direct descendant of *Ellen*. The premise of the program, which premiered in 1998, was two friends moving into an apartment together after breaking off their respective long-term relationships. The twist is that Grace was a straight female designer and Will was a gay male attorney. Will was handsome, often mistaken for straight, and openly gay. In another deviation from the norm of sitcoms, Will's best male friend, Jack, is the third of four main characters. Jack is flamboyant, effusive, and also openly gay. The humor in *Will and Grace* often centers around the characters tenderly poking at each other in a way that seems authentic. In the pilot episode Grace says to Jack, "My dog knows you're gay," and Will adds, "Dead people know you're gay" (Natale 1998, 1).

The significance of two major gay characters on *Will and Grace* is multifaceted. First, Will and Jack have as much complexity and depth as a sit-com character can muster. They explore friendship, romantic relationships, work, and personal ethics, among other issues. But even more importantly, Will and Jack demonstrate at least two very different styles and personalities. Both the individual complexity and the range of the characters go far to dispel gay stereotypes. "The Will-and-Jack dynamic also offers audiences a chance to see how gays relate to one another. Jack is the more flamboyant character, but, say the show's creators, he's probably more comfortable with his sexuality. While Jack's extroverted nature is often the butt of Will's jokes . . . it can also be turned back on Will, the more uptight of the two" (Natale 1998, 3).

But while there had been important gay and lesbian breakthrough programs, characters, and themes on prime time television by the end of 1999, the numbers were still quite small. Even with the more than twenty-five gay characters in prime time, there were only seven appearing regularly on situation comedies. These seven characters represent only 1 percent of the 600 characters who appear regularly on the over eighty-five prime time series (Epstein 1999, 2).

Popular Music and Sexual Orientation

Listen to any popular top forty, rock, or rhythm and blues radio station for an hour. As you listen, make a list of the titles of any songs that speak of love, romance, sex, or intimate relationships. How many of these songs are there? Now, count the number of these titles that involve same sex love, romance, sex, or intimate relationships. As late as the year 2000, this number would most likely be zero.

As we have examined class, gender, and race we have concentrated our media exploration on popular and mainstream film, television, and music because these are the most widespread sources of messages in popular culture. But how can we discuss images of gays, lesbians, and bisexuals in popular music if they simply do not exist? We will examine the music industry and its interaction with gay and lesbian themes and audiences as well as the role of gay, lesbian, and bisexual musicians. We will also take a brief excursion into less mainstream music directed primarily to gay and lesbian audiences.

It seems that the popular music and recording industry has not yet figured out how to make the most of gay and lesbian audiences and markets. "According to a Simmons Market Research Bureau, which polled approximately 25,000 homosexual people in 1993, 76 percent purchased CDs in 1993, while 42 percent bought pre-recorded audio tapes. Further, of the people aged 18–34 who were polled, 60 percent have household incomes of more than $50,000, while 48 percent of respondents aged 35–54 made more than $100,000 a year. Roughly 52 percent of those polled were men, 48 percent women" (Flick 1994b, 1). This would seem to be a potentially profitable market.

The recording industry's overall failure to target and market to this audience through promoting openly gay and lesbian artists and gay and lesbian themes has several dimensions. First, there are striking similarities to prime time television's failure to include any major characters of color in its 1999 fall line-up. While this could be interpreted as a major oversight by producers and directors who are largely white, essentially it was an "oversight" based on demographics. There was the widely held belief that since African Americans and Latinos were among the largest TV watching audiences, they would watch whatever was on television and did not require specific targeting strategies. Perhaps this is also operating in the music industry. If gays and lesbians are already purchasing CDs at a high rate without being targeted as a specific audience, the industry may see no need to single them out with a risky tailored marketing strategy. Decision-makers may believe that sexual orientation has no bearing on musical taste and consumption.

Another dimension to the industry's distance from the gay and lesbian market is its reluctance to take the risk to shift gay themes and artists to mainstream audiences and address a radio promotion strategy. "A major-label A & R executive, speaking off the record, agrees. 'Dealing with openly gay acts and promoting to the gay market is like apples and oranges. There is still a degree of tension and prejudice at big labels like this one, especially when it's time to take that gay act you've been promoting to gays and try to break it in the mainstream. A lot of radio promoters still do not know how to handle it' " (Flick 1994a, 1). Despite the buying power of gay and lesbian consumers, the industry is generally unwilling to take the risk of mainstream marketing for fear of losing an even wider consumer market. The industry's position most likely reflects a combination of a reading and interpretation of homophobia in mainstream audiences as well as homophobia among decision-makers themselves.

As it stands in the early twenty-first century, the music industry has chosen a gay and lesbian marketing strategy that involves minimal risk. The Simmons report indicates that gay and lesbian music consumers are well educated and somewhat affluent and tend to purchase music that "looks into the struggles facing the human condition—and that can be a heavy beat, or a soft, classical violin" (Flick 1994a, 2). Nevertheless, larger labels and small independents are still operating from a stereotype of gay men at discos who prefer dance music with a driving beat and lesbians at coffee houses who want plaintive ballads and folk sounds.

The music industry has employed another marketing strategy that allows it to avoid promoting gay and lesbian artists and themes through mainstream music. This strategy utilizes the connection of concerts and clubs that promote gay and lesbian artists with retail record stores. Independent retail stores often feature in-store appearances following a live concert or club engagement and report that gay consumers come in to buy these CDs (Flick 1994a, 2). From the industry's perspective, this is a profitable strategy that avoids the risk of offending larger audiences.

Epic Records began to further explore the gay and lesbian market following the label's success during the 1994 Gay Games and Stonewall 25 Civil Rights March. More than 1 million people attended this event and the musical events that accompanied it. Subsequently, Epic began circulating a short questionnaire to independent retail record stores throughout the country to take a closer look at the musical interests of gay and lesbian consumers (Flick 1994b, 2). As of 1996, Atlantic Records was seriously considering promoting same sex themes through the creation of a gay marketing division (Hultberg 1996, 6).

Yet even these tentative steps toward thinking about the possibilities of marketing music more extensively and specifically to gay and lesbian audiences are limited to the consideration of promoting more openly gay artists who, up to this point, have not necessarily addressed gay themes and relationships in their music. One major label executive who declined to be identified said that the industry is not likely to launch a trend in openly gay music or artists. "It'll never happen. You can be gay and have a hit—if your record is soft and by a platinum seller like Elton John. But we're years and years away from the day when a gay artist can be broken out of the box. I hate to say it, but gay people are just too frightening to too many people in the straight world" (Hultberg 1996, 3).

The history of gay and lesbian musicians in mainstream popular music and on the big labels has been primarily in the closet. Even as these artists began to come out, many of their mainstream songs continued to embrace heterosexual love, romance, and angst.

In the 1960s, rock music was rebellious, a separation from an older generation and along with the various movements for liberation, increasingly political. Rock had a harder edge than top forty–style music and was dominated by men. Gay men were engaged in rock from the start, but pre-Stonewall, were mainly in the closet.

After Stonewall (1969) and the igniting of the gay pride movement, both heterosexual and gay men began exploring same sex subjects in their music in the form of gay characters, themes, or in the name of shock. The Kinks sang of a drag queen in "Lola," Elton John sang a love song to "Daniel," and Lou Reed told of an Andy Warhol gay scene in "Walk on the Wild Side." "Early 70s glam rock employed shock tactics to shake rock from its post-Beatles doldrums, but at a cost: Androgyny, flirtations with bisexuality, and flamboyant gay imagery was, in retrospect, most often a means to an end, not the sincere expression of proud identity, even if those tactics helped young gay men comprehend their own" (Walter 1997, 8). But even this burst of shock posing as gay pride was short-lived.

Music with lesbian themes and by lesbian musicians was consistent with other forms of lesbian culture and was largely independent, alternative, highly politicized, and directed primarily to the lesbian feminist community via independent recording studios (Walter 1997, 7). The first strongly gay-identified recorded music was written and sung by Alix Dobkin in her 1971 album, *Lavender Jane Loves Women.* Dobkin's music was embedded in lesbian-feminist politics and featured songs such as "Talking Lesbian" (Faderman 1991, 223).

The independent Olivia Records was established in 1973. Its musical content, artists, and nonhierarchical structure reflected the burgeoning lesbian feminist culture. In 1975, Olivia released Cris Williamson's album, *The Changer and the Changed,* which became popular with feminist and lesbian audiences. Other lesbian musicians performed at women's music festivals and recorded songs with explicit same sex themes on Olivia and other budding independent labels. Williamson, Margie Adams, Mary Watkins, and others had a steady following of a concert-going and record-buying crowd that was largely female and feminist. This music never quite made it to the mainstream, however.

In fact, as Olivia Records evolved it reflected the kind of tension that developed in many alternative institutions created in the lesbian feminist community. Olivia's owners and many of its consumers wanted authenticity of lesbian themes in the music, collective and nonhierarchical decision-making, and economic survival, the company was often hard-pressed to be successful at all three endeavors.

Singer, environmentalist, and lesbian Holly Near pierced the mainstream a bit in the late 1970s and early 1980s with her folk-oriented music and identification with the environmental movement. Near's establishment of her own independent label paved the way for lesbian singers in the 1990s whose popularity was on the rise.

Meanwhile, by the 1980s, mainstream rock's brief flirtation with gay themes and androgyny went underground. "After disco hit the glass ceiling of homophobic, racist 'disco sucks' backlash and after the English new wave that generated such gay-leaning pop-dance groups as Bronski Beat, Culture Club, Frankie Goes to Hollywood, Erasure and Wham! subsided, pop's gender-bender boom of the '80s appeared to be over" (Walter 1997, 9).

In 1994, Bruce Springsteen recorded "The Streets of Philadelphia," the title track of the film *Philadelphia.* The song became the first popular song by a heterosexual man in the voice of a gay man. In the mid-1990s, the mainstream popularity of out lesbian superstars k.d. lang and Melissa Etheridge paved the way for the phenomenal success of Ani DiFranco. Etheridge came out as a lesbian after she had established mainstream success.

Despite being wooed by major labels, DiFranco insisted on maintaining her independent status and control and continued to sing of same sex relationships on her own label, "righteous babe." DiFranco's success was built on the experience and tradition of Holly Near's economic and musical independence and Melissa Etheridge's continued popularity even after declaring that she was a lesbian and posing for magazine photos with her life partner. Meanwhile, Ani DiFranco "sings love songs directed explicitly at women, proclaims herself queer, and regularly sells out her concerts, largely due to her dedicated and highly vocal lesbian following. The mood of her shows is much like the women's music circuit, where DiFranco got her start—sisterly, celebratory, and highly cruisy. The difference is that it's taking place under the eye of the mainstream, with plenty of sensitive straight guys in attendance, and for a performer who's considered one of the most vital and of-the-moment musicians in rock. The difference is that DiFranco—and her lesbian-inclusive phenomenon—is not the mainstream" (Walter 1997, 24).

Whether DiFranco's mainstream success is a fluke or a trend remains to be seen. Perhaps her music parallels the popularity of the television series *Will and Grace*. For both, the same sex themes are ironically central in their appeal to gay and lesbian audiences and incidental in their appeal to mainstream audiences. DiFranco's music and *Will and Grace* work because they are successful by the rules of their respective genres: rock music and situation comedy. One is visually and musically edgy and interesting, and the other plays the same sex edge while creating familiar characters, themes, and situations and manages to be very funny.

But, despite the recent and tentative emergence of mainstream gay and lesbian artists and music, we are still hard-pressed to find more than brief same sex themes in popular music. The impact of this absence is significant. Top forty, rock, and rhythm and blues radio stations' greatest following are teens and young adults, developmentally at a point of discovering their sexuality and making difficult choices. Popular music offers very little for young people whose sexual identity is gay, lesbian, or bisexual. In hit music's romances, heterosexuality is the norm or "normal," and homosexuality is largely invisible, and by implication "abnormal." This reinforces the same homophobic messages that many young people receive from family, peers, religion, and school, and contributes to the kind of isolation that leads to depression and the high suicide rate among gay and lesbian teens.

These messages also have an impact on people who identify as heterosexual. Popular music is part of the hegemony, that invisible but powerful ideology that tells us that heterosexuality is good and "natural" and that homosexuality is wrong and "unnatural." When these messages are consistent in the popular culture, there is no need to use force or even laws to convince most people of the "superiority" of heterosexuality.

Sexual Orientation and Film

A quick scan of the American Film Institute's lists of the "Top 100 American Films" and the "All Time Box-Office Hits" (adjusted for inflation) reveals surprisingly similar results about images of gays and lesbians. In the first list (ostensibly the greatest American films) there are only seven films, or 7 percent, that have any overt or subtextual reference to homosexuality. In the second list, the films that have been most popular with the American public, there is only one film with homosexual reference. Together, these two listings of film represent those most widely seen by U.S. audiences and the presence and absence of gay and lesbian images are significant ("Top 100 American Films" 1999).

Of the seven that are listed as best films, six are either barely visible or quite subtextual in their references to homosexuality. The character of Plato (Sal Mineo) in *Rebel Without a Cause* (1955) is suggested to be gay through the male photo in his locker and his more feminine appearance and style, but the character's sexual orientation is never explicitly mentioned or developed. In the *Maltese Falcon* (1941), the sexuality of the character is obliquely suggested only by mention of his gardenia perfume, his feminine style, and the music that announces his first entrance. In the 1967 *Bonnie and Clyde,* Clyde Barrow subtly suggests that it is not Bonnie but his own latent homosexuality that prevents his sexual interest in her. In *A Streetcar Named Desire* (1951), Blanche refers to the suicide of her ex-husband. The man's homosexuality, as written by Tennessee Williams in the original script, disappears from the film.

According to *Ben Hur* screenwriter Gore Vidal, he suggested to director William Wyler that actor Stephen Boyd play his role of *Massala* as if he and Ben Hur (Charlton Heston) had long ago had a love affair. This relationship was so subtextual that Vidal, Boyd, and Wyler never even told Heston of it. And finally, the 1931 *Frankenstein* represents an invisibility of homosexuality that has only been discernible to contemporary film critics as they have looked at the life of openly gay director James Whale and interpreted the monster's exclusion from society and status as an outcast as symbolic of homosexuality. The other film on the best films list that features any gay character is *Midnight Cowboy* (1969). In *Midnight Cowboy,* Ratso Rizzo (Dustin Hoffman) pimps for Joe Buck (Jon Voight), finding desperate homosexuals and a grim homosexual scene.

Ben Hur appears, once again, in the list of Top 100 American Box Office Hits. But the chances of the 1959 audience being even remotely aware of the director's and screenwriter's subtextual suggestion to one of the characters is quite slim. *Tootsie* (1982) and *Mrs. Doubtfire* (1993) appear on this list as well. Both main characters are decidedly heterosexual; in *Tootsie* the character cross-dresses for the purposes of getting an acting job, and the man in *Mrs. Doubtfire* does so in order to spend more time with his children. *Mrs. Doubtfire* also includes a brief appearance of Harvey Fierstein as the gay brother of the main character.

This is it. These are the most prevalent images of homosexuality that have been seen by American audiences from the years 1937 to 1998. The characters and themes are largely invisible, subtextual, circumstantial, or evil. And they are all male.

Now it is your turn. Follow the instructions in Media Activity 6.3 to take a close look at images of gays, lesbians and bisexuals in current films. For example, in 1998, the five films nominated for Best Picture were *Shakespeare in Love, Elizabeth, Life Is Beautiful, Saving Private Ryan,* and *The Thin Red Line.* None of these films featured gay, lesbian, or bisexual characters or themes. You could conduct the same kind of simple content analysis with the year's top box office hits as well and find similar results. As we continue discussing images of gays, lesbians, and bisexuals in film, it is important to keep in mind that the films most widely seen by U.S. audiences have few images of gays, lesbians, or bisexuals.

The few images of gays and lesbians in film have all been governed by a combination of legal rulings, external controls by the Motion Picture Production Code, internal controls by a sometimes timid and risk-phobic (not to mention homophobic) film industry, and the profit motive that drives the production of mainstream films. These images and controls on the industry with regard to sexual orientation have been more thoroughly documented in film than in either television or music and provide fertile ground for analysis. Images have ranged from the "sissy" stereotype of gay men to the villainous or predatory gay man or lesbian to the victim to the barely visible. Yet from the earliest days of film, gay and lesbian images have persisted despite the restrictions. In this section we will explore some of the limitations on and in the industry and the evolution of images and themes of gays, lesbians, and bisexuals in film.

A 1915 Supreme Court ruling opened the way for censorship of film along many fronts, including sexuality. The Court ruled that movies were a for-profit business and therefore not protected by the right to freedom of speech spelled out in the First Amendment of the Constitution. Within a few years of this ruling, several states began to pass censorship laws that addressed obscenity and "inappropriate" topics for film (Russo 1991, 30). But it was not until 1931 that the film industry began policing and censoring itself through the Production Code and the Hays Censorship Office. Reference to homosexuality, gay and lesbian characters and themes, and even words like "pansy" were out. Thirty years later, in 1961, the Production Code changed once again and homosexuality was permitted official visibility provided it was portrayed with "care, discretion, and restraint" (Russo 1991, 48). Despite these cautions, words such as "fag, faggot, fruit, dyke, pansy" were freely admitted on the big screen. By 1968, the Production Code was eliminated completely and homosexuality was, for the first time, fair game for filmmakers.

In the early days of film, there were some images that could be interpreted as gay, lesbian, or bisexual. "Briefly, in the early '30s, gays were familiar screen types: 'pansies' for comic relief and, more heroically, bisexual heroines (incarnated by Garbo and Dietrich) who looked thrillingly glamorous in their tuxedos and bachelor togs. That was old Hollywood's highest compliment to a woman—

Media Activity 6.3
Gays, Lesbians and Bisexuals in Current Films

---

1. Select the most recent full calendar year. For example, if it is March 2000, select the year 1999.

2. Locate the Academy Awards component of the Greatest Films Website at http://www.filmsite.org/oscars.html.

3. Find the year you've selected and search for the five films nominated for the Best Picture Academy Award of that year.

4. If you have seen the films or are familiar with them, determine if they contain any themes or characters that are gay, lesbian, or bisexual. For those films that are unfamiliar to you, you may locate plot summaries and reviews on the Internet Movie Data Base located at http://www.imdb.com.

5. What percentage of these films has gay, lesbian, or bisexual characters or themes?

---

that she acted and thought like a man. . . ." (Corliss 1996, 66). In the 1930 film *Morocco,* Marlene Dietrich's character is dressed in a top hat and tails as she performs in a nightclub. She kisses a woman fully on the lips, takes the flower from her hair and throws it to her love interest in the film, Gary Cooper. The ambiguity of the sexuality of the character and the actor is designed to titillate the audience (Weiss 1992, 32).

Greta Garbo, who had a relationship with Salka Viertel, the screenwriter of *Queen Christina,* was in her real life part of an upper class European lesbian community. Hollywood studios went to great lengths to create an image of Garbo's heterosexual romances. Still, the subtext of Garbo's offscreen life and the film *Queen Christina* itself leave room for an oppositional lesbian reading as her character, the Queen, dresses in male attire and kisses Countess Ebba on the lips (Weiss 1992, 36).

One of the first stereotypical images of gay men in film, the "sissy" or the "pansy," predated the Supreme Court decision by one year. In 1914 Stan Laurel's *The Soilers* established a feminized cowboy for laughs and signaled the kick-off of this image that has appeared throughout film history (Russo 1991, 26). After the Production Code adopted by the Hayes Censorship Office was in operation, these references became more oblique because the mention of homosexuality was forbidden. One of these "sissies" in film was the character of Joel Cairo in the *Maltese Falcon* as described above. David Wayne's character, Kip, in the 1949 *Adam's Rib* with Katharine Hepburn and Spencer Tracy, plays Hepburn's gossipy "girlfriend" in men's clothing. But it was Franklin Pangborn that made the "sissy" a stock character as a white man with a pencil-thin mustache and fussy, feminine ways. "In more than a hundred films throughout the 1930s alone, Pangborn played kaleido-scopic variations on the role and became the archetypal sissy" (Russo 1991, 34).

While the Production Code was in full swing, there were other encoded gay characters and themes in film. As previously mentioned, James Whale, the direc-tor of the 1931 *Frankenstein* and the 1935 *Bride of Frankenstein* was openly gay and as a result subsequently blackballed from Hollywood. Whale's life is por-trayed in the 1998 film *Gods and Monsters*.

But from the earliest days of film through the early 1960s, most gay and lesbian images and themes were under the surface, available only to those most willing and able to look for them in the subtext of the story or in the books or original scripts on which the films were based. In the 1945 version of *Lost Weekend*, Ray Milland's alcoholic character (who in the book version was struggling with his sexual orientation) was depicted as struggling with writer's block. Cole Porter's homosexuality was erased in the 1945 film *Night and Day*. The 1958 film *Cat on a Hot Tin Roof*, the 1959 film *Suddenly Last Summer*, and the 1961 film *Children's Hour* were all distorted by the oblique and almost inaccessible references to gay characters and events.

In *Cat on a Hot Tin Roof*, Brick (played by Paul Newman) is apparently unwill-ing or unable to be sexual with Maggie (played by Elizabeth Taylor). Maggie suggests that she cheated on Brick with his dead friend Skipper and Brick subse-quently refused to sleep with her. In an oblique conversation, Maggie makes an almost indiscernible accusation that Brick and Skipper had a sexual relationship and Brick responds by attempting to attack Maggie ("Top 100 American Films" 1999). In another scene, once again, Brick is on the attack. This time his target is Big Daddy, who also questions Brick's relationship with Skipper. Brick subse-quently accuses Big Daddy of trying to turn the only thing he still treasures into something dirty. The "dirt," we are lead to assume, is that of homosexuality but the film never used the word and remained intentionally ambiguous to escape the radar of the Hays Censorship Office.

In the 1959 *Suddenly Last Summer*, once again Elizabeth Taylor appeared, but this time as Catherine, the cousin of Sebastian, who we later learn (or at least think we learn since the reference is so veiled) is gay. Sebastian's mother Violet (Katharine Hepburn) did not want the "evil" of Sebastian's life exposed and insisted on a lobotomy for Catherine. Yet Catherine persists in telling the truth with the help of a therapist (ironically played by the gay but not out actor Montgomery Clift) and reveals that first Violet and then she served as bait for Sebastian. She never speci-fies exactly what they were baiting, even under the therapist's questioning. How-ever, she does eventually reveal that Sebastian was chased by a crowd of street urchins who ultimately murdered and cannibalized him. This was a gruesome fate for a man whose worst sin appeared to be his attraction to other men. Although once again, the words "gay" or "homosexual" were never uttered by any character in the film, it clearly painted a portrait of evil and dire consequences for those who dare make these choices. This sets the stage for another archetypal gay male character, the evil villain and predator ("Top 100 American Films" 1999).

In *The Children's Hour*, Martha and Karen (Shirley McLaine and Audrey Hepburn, respectively) run a private school for girls. One of the schoolgirls whispers words to her grandmother that the audience never hears and can only assume accuses the two women of being lesbians. As the film reaches a crescendo Martha begins to see that she is in fact attracted to Karen and sobs inconsolably about how she has ruined everything and how "dirty" she is. Martha is not portrayed as being quite as evil as Sebastian, but her fate is much the same. She, too, has to die for her "dirtiness" and commits suicide by hanging herself.

Ironically, *The Children's Hour* and *Advise and Consent* were both made in 1961, the same year that the Production Code shifted and opened new possibilities for the depiction of gay and lesbian characters. Yet both of these films have a narrow range of character depiction, from evil or dirty to anguished or pathetic. Neither provides any positive or even particularly complex images of gays and lesbians.

With few exceptions, gay and lesbian characters and themes in the 1960s and much of the 1970s continued to be simple and to conform to the stereotypes of villain, predator, or victim. There were few characters who were complex and compelling and there was almost no range in type of gay and lesbian characters. In *Advise and Consent,* the married senator, Brig Anderson, was blackmailed by a former male lover. Anderson met the lover at a gay bar, the first gay bar depicted in film, and after an apparent internal struggle ran from the bar, followed by the lover. Anderson stepped into a cab as the lover followed, pleading with him to listen, to which Anderson said nothing but shoved him down to the street where the nameless lover fell into the water near the gutter. The symbolism of the depths of homosexuality is unmistakable. Later in the film the audience learns of the senator's death, a suicide in which he slit his own throat for the same reasons that Martha hanged herself and Sebastian was viciously murdered: he was apparently too "dirty" to live.

But another 1961 film, this time made in England, pierced some of these solidifying gay stereotypes and taboos. The film, *Victim*, was an unabashed plea for the reform of England's antisodomy statutes. It features a married but homosexual lawyer, Melville Farr, who is being blackmailed with sexual pictures of himself with a man. An enlightened police detective believes that the only function of the sodomy laws is to aid blackmailers and helps Farr resolve the case and end the blackmail. In this film, Farr, played by popular British actor Dirk Bogarde, is the good guy (Internet Movie Database 1999). He was not destroyed by his sexuality, but rather was a complex character seeking justice. *Victim* was the first film to insist on acceptance and decriminalization of homosexuality and to actually use the word itself. The revised 1961 Production Code called for "care, discretion, and restraint" in reference to homosexuality and interpreted that phrase as justification to refuse its seal of approval to *Victim* unless it cut the use of the word "homosexual." The updated code had been clarified; reference to homosexuality was acceptable but the use of the word itself was not. The film's director and producer refused to make the cuts and *Victim* was released in the United States without a seal of approval (Russo 1991, 128–129).

"The hero–villain question persisted throughout the Sixties and well into the Seventies, with movie homosexuals increasingly falling victim to their own inherently villainous sexuality—the flaw that always destroyed them in one way or another. Self-hatred was the standard accessory with every new model" (Russo 1991, 136). *The Fox* was emblematic of this continuing trend as one of the women in a lesbian relationship is killed when a tree falls on her (ironically between her legs) and the other woman is then free to pursue her attraction to a man, thus being cured of homosexuality. In fact, from 1950 to 1983 there were at least thirty-three documented murders or suicides of gay characters in film (Russo 1991, 347–349).

When the Production Code was completely abolished in 1968, an increasing number of films began to portray gay and lesbian characters and themes. While villains and victims and sissies were still alive and well, there were also new kinds of gay and lesbian characters and themes and a slowly building but wider range of characters as well.

The 1970 *Boys in the Band* was released after the Production Code was abolished and after gay liberation was heralded by the protest at the Stonewall Inn. It was the first film to feature characters who are all gay. Despite the fact that there are eight gay characters and the film was written by Mart Crowley, a gay man, the stereotypes of self-hatred persisted. Crowley later said, "I knew a lot of people like those people. The self-deprecating humor was born out of a low self-esteem, from a sense of what the times told you about yourself" (Epstein and Friedman 1995). While mainstream media praised the film, it was criticized in the gay community. "[W]hen the Stonewall riots of June 1969 triggered the movement toward gay self-esteem, *Boys in the Band* rapidly became dated. With gays redefining themselves as strong and proud, a play about acid-tongued, self-pitying fairies was bound to resemble the gay equivalent to a minstrel show" (Guthman 1999). But at the time, the film was a breakthrough in its direct portrayal of gay characters and themes. Perhaps even in its limitations, the film reflected the internalized homophobia of the time experienced by the writer as well. Internalized oppression is always involuntary and *Boys in the Band* is a strong example of how gays and lesbians can receive and internalize the same misinformation and negative information as heterosexuals.

In the 1972 *Cabaret* set in Nazi Germany, Liza Minnelli plays the heterosexual and sexually liberated Sally, and Michael York plays the openly bisexual Brian, both of whom become sexually involved with the same man. While the interpretation of Brian's goodness as a character may be contested, his complexity and sympathetic nature as a character are not. This is still another kind of breakthrough for gay characters.

The decade of the 1980s was the first time that gay and lesbian films emerged with characters that are both good and bad, victims and perpetrators, simple and complex, men and women. In Table 6.1, thirteen films of the 1980s that feature homosexual themes and/or characters are evaluated according to some of the standard stereotypes that existed in the past. None of these films made it on the lists of greatest films or top box office hits, but most of them were produced by major film studios and, with the exception of *Desert Hearts,* experienced modest to substantial economic success.

Of these thirteen films, nine had major homosexual themes, and nineteen major characters were gay or lesbian. Twelve of the films had at least one gay or lesbian character that was complex. *The World According to Garp* and *Torch Song Trilogy* featured transsexual or cross-dressing characters, Roberta Muldoon and Arnold, respectively, both of whom were complex and likable characters who survived intact in the context of the film. Arnold (Harvey Fierstein) was the major character in *Torch Song,* and while he struggled with love, self-acceptance, and homophobia in his life, in the end he was in a committed relationship with a man, had adopted a son, and had a successful career. Twelve of the major characters were male and seven were female. Gay or lesbian relationships were depicted in eight of the films. Some of the characters and themes were superficial (*Lianna, Personal Best, Making Love*), but many of the characters in these 1980s films demonstrated more range and complexity than ever before in film history.

The themes in these films were predominantly positive or complex. Love and romance, friendship, coming out, and self-acceptance were explored in eight of the films. The homophobia, violence, and gay bashing that occurs in *Cruising* and *Torch Song Trilogy* are of a very different kind. In *Cruising,* a heterosexual police officer (Al Pacino) poses as gay to search for a mass murderer who is targeting gay men in New York's S & M (sadomasochistic) clubs. The film is replete with graphic images of the murders and features no major characters who are gay—only one-dimensional victims and one villainous murderer. There was an enormous outcry from the gay community protesting the stereotypes and the violence of this film. By contrast, *Torch Song Trilogy* follows the inner life of Arnold as he grapples with and succeeds in accepting himself and insists on love and acceptance from everyone in his life, including his mother. His family's homophobia is woven in and out of the story line. But ultimately, it climaxes when Arnold's life partner, Alan (Matthew Broderick) is murdered in a horrifying scene of mass gay-bashing. While the scene and Alan's death are depicted as tragic, the violence is not exploited. Rather, it is depicted as the horrible but logical consequence of hate and homophobia and is used as an admonition to both Arnold's mother and the audience.

Once again, no films with major gay or lesbian characters or themes made it to the top ten box office hits in the 1990s, but Tom Hanks won the best actor Academy Award in 1993 for his portrayal in the film *Philadelphia* of a gay lawyer with AIDS. The trend of burgeoning themes and characters that began in the 1980s continued in the 1990s with the depiction of homosexuality in mainstream films and an increase of images in independent films. Three of the more economically successful films made in major studios were *Philadelphia* (1994), *In & Out* (1997), and *The Object of My Affection* (1998). Some of independently made films were *Go Fish* (1994), *The Incredibly True Adventures of Two Girls in Love* (1995), and *Chasing Amy* (1998).

Philadelphia, starring Tom Hanks and Denzel Washington, is the story of a successful gay lawyer with AIDS and his battle with the disease and with discrimination in his law firm. *In & Out* tells of a high school teacher (Kevin Kline) who is "outed" while engaged to a woman and apparently before he has figured out that he is gay. *The Object of My Affection* puts a single pregnant woman with a gay male roommate, and as their relationship blossoms, she believes he would make a better life partner and father than her baby's biological father. *Go Fish* is a romantic comedy about a group of lesbian friends, their community, and their intimate relationships. *The Incredibly True Adventures of Two Girls in Love* is a comedy about the first love between two high school girls, one white and one black. *Chasing Amy* is the story of a threesome of comic book creating generation Xers in which one of the men falls in love with the woman, who is a lesbian.

On an obvious level, the mainstream films were about gay men and the independents were about lesbians or bisexual women. The independents often allowed for soulful kisses and explicit sex between the women. Of the mainstream films, *Philadelphia* portrayed a body-to-body slow dance between straight actors (cast as gay men) Tom Hanks and Antonio Banderas, and *In & Out* has one whopper of a kiss between two more straight actors, Kevin Kline and Tom Selleck. The mainstream films took a safer course in characters, actors, and themes to appeal to wider resources and a broader audience; the independents, on a lower budget, were aimed at a narrower audience, and took greater risks in character, themes, and actors.

Another way to analyze the depiction of gay and lesbian characters and themes in film is to examine how they are perceived in the wider culture. Some of this can be determined by exploring reviews, box office success, and ratings and to what degree the meaning and significance of the films are contested. The questions of stereotyping, authenticity, and validity of the messages vary from various publications and perspectives and begin to paint a picture of the changing cultural landscape in the United States. A more in-depth examination of ratings, box office success, and reviews of two of these films, *Philadelphia* and *Go Fish,* reveals some of the contested meaning and cultural terrain.

Roger Ebert, a mainstream reviewer, said *Philadelphia* was ground breaking because it "marks the first time Hollywood has risked a big-budget film on the subject" of AIDS. He compared it to *Guess Who's Coming to Dinner* in its relatively superficial but first widely distributed film addressing interracial romance. Like *Guess Who's Coming to Dinner's* use of stars Spencer Tracy, Katharine Hepburn, and Sidney Poitier to make the film and subject more palatable for larger audiences, Ebert believed *Philadelphia* used the same strategy with likable (not to

Table 6.1

Images of Gays, Lesbians, and Bisexuals in 1980s Films

Year/Film	Major themes	Minor themes	Major characters	Minor characters	Complex characters	Standard stereotypes
1980 *Fame*	no	no	no	yes	somewhat	no
1980 *Cruising*	yes	no	yes	yes	no	Villain: Police officer discovers he is gay and becomes a killer
1982 *The World According to Garp*	no	no	no	yes	yes	no
1982 *Personal Best*	yes	no	yes	no	somewhat	A lesbian is transformed to heterosexuality by a "good man"
1982 *Making Love*	yes	no	yes	no	yes	no
1983 *Lianna*	yes	no	yes	yes	somewhat	Oversimplified characters and themes about coming out
1983 *Silkwood*	no	yes	yes	yes	yes	no
1983 *Victor/Victoria*	yes	no	yes	yes	yes	no

1985 *Desert Hearts*	yes	no	yes	no	no
1985 *Kiss of the Spider Woman*	yes	no	yes	no	no
1985 *The Color Purple*	no	no	no	no	The reference to the love and sexual relationship of Celie and Shug is so oblique that it is almost unrecognizable
1988 *Torch Song Trilogy*	yes	yes	yes	yes	Range of gay male characters
1988 *Long Time Companion*	yes	yes	yes	yes	Range of gay male characters

Sources: Information for this table is from the Internet Movie Database; the filmography is from *The Celluloid Closet* by Vito Russo (1991).

Note: The films listed are major 1980s American-made films with significant homosexual themes, characters, or references that are gay, lesbian, or bisexual. Major and minor themes refer to homosexual themes. Major, minor, and complex characters refer to those characters that are gay, lesbian, or bisexual. Standard stereotypes refer to gay, lesbian, and bisexual characters that conform to the classic oversimplified stereotypes of sissy, villain, victim, etc.

mention heterosexual) stars Tom Hanks and Denzel Washington. Ebert seemed to think that *Philadelphia* had taken about as much risk as it could and still reach a wide audience (Ebert 1994a).

Rita Kempley of the *Washington Post* (also a mainstream publication) disagreed with Ebert. She compared the film with Frank Capra classics that center around traditional American values and noble characters but challenge hypocrisy in the American people. Kempley said that *Philadelphia* asks the important question: "Is not this a land where *all* men are created equal—or must they be *straight* men?" (Kempley 1994) [italics show author's emphasis].

Finally, gay reviewer Andrew Sullivan discussed the film in the liberal *New Republic*. Sullivan acknowledged that most gays found *Philadelphia* to be a moving yet superficial treatment of AIDS and homosexuality. Sullivan disagreed. He saw two important functions of *Philadelphia* that made it all worthwhile. First, he believed that the fact that the well-known heterosexual hunk of an actor, Denzel Washington, played Andrew Beckett's (Tom Hanks) lawyer Joe Miller was a significant challenge to homophobia in the African American community. Joe moved from cringing at gay people and references to an attitude of respect and tenderness toward his client. Sullivan therefore believed that the film opened some doors. On a broader level, he saw *Philadelphia* as a positive act of translation to the heterosexual community about the experience of gay men living with AIDS both on a personal level and within their community (Sullivan 1994, 43).

These various interpretations of the film's meaning and impact mark a range of viewpoints among the audiences as well as the reviewers. Significantly, none of the reviewers found the film or the topic offensive as reviewers did when discussing films such as *Suddenly Last Summer*. The main criticism seemed to be that it did not go far enough or take enough risks to convey the complexity and dimensions of AIDS and homophobia. Nevertheless, *Philadelphia* grossed over $200 million worldwide and its message, limited though it may have been, reached the largest audience that any film about homosexuality had ever reached (Internet Movie Database 1999).

By contrast, *Go Fish* grossed just under $2.5 million. The viewing audience for *Philadelphia* was roughly 200 times larger than the viewing audience for *Go Fish*. As the reviews and contested messages of each film are analyzed, much of the significance of the content is in the context. How many people saw each film and what impact could relative audience size have on cultural views of homosexuality?

The reviews for *Go Fish* were largely positive in both gay and lesbian publications as well as in the mainstream press. Roger Ebert said the film was charming and warm and that it was "honest, forthright and affectionate, and it portrays the everyday worlds of these ordinary gay women with what I sense is accuracy" (Ebert 1994b). Ebert said the weakness was that it was so matter of fact in its recording of everyday life that nothing ever happened and it dimmed in interest.

Rita Kempley of the *Washington Post* liked it too and pointed out the universality of the themes: "An explicit, low-budget tale of lesbians in love, this inventive first film may be aimed at gay audiences, but it turns on a premise familiar to all persuasions: when it comes to relationships, opposites attract (Kempley 1994b). But it is only in explicitly gay publications that reviewers commented on the significance of *Go Fish,* its characters, and themes. For example, in *Lesbian Flicks,* the reviewer said she was pleased that for the first time, a film created a community of lesbians who hung out together without angst about their lesbian identities. She also addressed the significance of the range of lesbian characters: "Another plus is that the women in the film are involved in relationships that cover the spectrum, from the monogamous to the promiscuous" ("Go Fish" 1999). The implication is that in the naturalness of the characters and the community and in the range of characters, there was a reduction of stereotypes.

As you consider these films, their images, and their popularity, think about which of them you have seen. Have the images and messages about gays, lesbians, and bisexuals been simple or complex? Have there been a variety of characters and themes in the films you have seen, or are character types and topics fairly narrow and repeated? Take a closer look at how these films have reinforced or challenged the information you have taken in about homosexuality through personal experience, formal education, and other forms of media to determine how you have been socialized on this issue.

Chapter Summary

The last century has been a time of change in the construct of homosexuality; the oppression and liberation of gays, lesbians, and bisexuals; and in entertainment media portrayals. There have been some shifts in laws and policies that effect gays, lesbians, and bisexuals such as the removal of antisodomy statutes and creation of antihate legislation in some states, domestic partner benefits in some businesses, and the removal of homosexuality as a mental illness from the American Psychiatric Association listing. Nevertheless, in 1999 the largest number of hate crimes were still directed at people who were perceived to be gay or lesbian and the highest proportion of teen suicides were those of gay and lesbian teens struggling with their sexual identity. More than any of the issues we have explored, information about sexual orientation is the least available through formal education, personal experience, and media. What little information we do receive is often distorted or biased. The fact that many religious denominations interpret homosexuality negatively and infuse this with religious explanation often closes open discussion before it even begins. As you examine your personal experiences, formal knowledge, and media exposure to homosexuality it will be important to determine if what you were taught from all three sources line up with the same messages and information or if they challenge or contradiction each other. The more extensive and consistent the information you received, the more likely you were to have been thoroughly socialized about sexual orientation. Unobstructed discussion, accurate information, dispelling of myths, and open airing of disagree-

ments are critically important for each of us to reflect on the extent of our socialization and develop our own independent thinking.

Bibliography

Abelove, Henry; Barale, Michele Aina; and Halperin, David M., eds. 1993. *The Lesbian
and Gay Studies Reader.* New York: Routledge.
Adams, Maurianne; Bell, Lee Anne; and Griffin, Pat, eds. 1997. *Teaching for Diversity and
Social Justice: A Sourcebook.* New York: Routledge.
Blumenfeld, Warren J., ed. 1992. *Homophobia: How We All Pay the Price.* Boston: Beacon.
Chasnoff, Debra, and Cohen, Helen, directors. 1996. *It's Elementary.* Documentary film.
Corliss, Richard. 1996. "The Final Frontier: Two New Movies Pose the Question, 'Can't
Hollywood Treat Gays Like Normal People?'" *Time Magazine* 147, no. 11: 660.
Croteau, David, and Hoynes, William. 1997. *Media/Society: Industries, Images, and Audi-
ences.* Thousand Oaks, CA.: Pine Forge Press.
Cruikshank, Margaret. 1992. *The Gay and Lesbian Liberation Movement.* New York:
Routledge.
Curran, Charles E. 1998. "Sexual Orientation and Human Rights in American Religious
Discourse: A Roman Catholic Perspective." In *Sexual Orientation and Human Rights in
American Religious Discourse,* ed. Saul M. Olyan and Martha C. Nussbaum, 87–96.
New York: Oxford University Press.
Dirks, Tim. 1999. *Cat on a Hot Tin Roof.* http://www.filmsite.org/cato.html, December 14.
Dyson, Michael Eric. 1998. "Sexual Orientation and African American Men." In *Sexual
Orientation and Human Rights in American Religious Discourse,* ed. Saul M. Olyan
and Martha C. Nussbaum, 196. New York: Oxford University Press.
Ebert, Roger. 1994a. "Philadelphia." *Chicago Sun-Times,* July 14, p. 17.
———. 1994b. "Go Fish." Internet Movie Database. http://us.imdb.com.html, July 1.
Emilio, John. 1992. *Making Trouble.* New York and London: Routledge.
Epstein, Jeffrey. 1999. "Prime Time for Gay Youth (Gay Characters on Television)." *The
Advocate,* April 27, pp. 4–6.
Epstein, Robert, and Friedman, Jeffrey, directors. 1995. *The Celluloid Closet.* Documen-
tary film.
Faderman, Lillian. 1991. *Odd Girls and Twilight Lovers: A History of Lesbian Life in
Twentieth-Century America.* New York: Columbia University Press.
Flick, Larry. 1994a. "Major Labels Courting Gay, Lesbian Market." *Billboard* 106, no. 31: 1.
———. 1994b. "Labels Broaden Social Perspectives: Stonewall 25 and Gay Games Major
Factors." *Billboard* 106, no. 25: 1.
"Go Fish." 1999. *Lesbian Flicks* online. http://glweb.com/lesbianflicks/gofish.html, De-
cember 15.
Green, Keith. 1998. "Introduction to Essays Representing Mainline Protestant Churches."
In *Sexual Orientation and Human Rights in American Religious Discourse,* ed. Saul M.
Olyan and Martha C. Nussbaum, 114–18. New York: Oxford University Press.
Guthman, Edward. 1999. "'70s Gay Film Has Low Esteem 'Boys' Attitude Seems Dated."
San Francisco Chronicle, January 15, p. 7.
Hultberg, Jesse. 1996. "'Out' Music's Slow Mainstream Inroads." *Billboard* 108, no. 18:
3–6.
Internet Movie Database. 1999. www/http://us.imdb.com.
Jagose, Annamarie Rustom. 1996. *Queer Theory.* New York: New York University Press.
Kahn, Rabbi Yoel H. 1989. "Judaism and Homosexuality: The Traditionalist/Progressive
Debate." In *Homosexuality and Religion,* ed. Richard Hasbany, 59–66. New York:
Harrington Park.

Kempley, Rita. 1994a. "Philadelphia." *Washington Post Online*. http://www.washingtonpost. com/wp-srv/style/longterm/movies/videos/philadelphiarkempley_aoa3ff.html, July 14.
———. 1994b. "Go Fish." *Washington Post Online*. http://www.washington post.com/wp-srv/style/longterm/movies/videos/gofishnrkempley_aoa472.html.
Miller, Neil. 1995. *Out of the Past: Gay and Lesbian History from 1869 to the Present*. New York: Vintage.
Natale, Richard. 1998. "*Will Power* (New NBC-TV Sitcom) and *Will & Grace*." *The Advocate*, September 15, pp. 1–3.
Nugent, Robert, and Gramick, Jeannine. 1989. "Homosexuality: Protestant, Catholic, and Jewish Issues: A Fishbone Tale." In *Homosexuality and Religion*, ed. Richard Hasbany, 7. New York: Harrington Park.
Olyan, Saul M., and Nussbaum, Martha C. 1998. *Sexual Orientation and Human Rights in American Religious Discourse*. New York: Oxford University Press.
Pela, Robert L. 1997. "Disney Steps Out." *The Advocate*, April 29, p. 3.
Plaskow, Judith. 1998. "Sexual Orientation and Human Rights: A Progressive Jewish Perspective." In *Sexual Orientation and Human Rights in American Religious Discourse*, ed. Saul M. Olyan and Martha C. Nussbaum, 30.
Russo, Vito. 1991. *The Celluloid Closet: Homosexuality in the Movies*. Rev. ed. New York: Harper and Row.
Sanders, Cheryl J. 1998. "Sexual Orientation and Human Rights Discourse in the African American Churches." In *Sexual Orientation and Human Rights in American Religious Discourse*, ed. Saul M..Olyan and Martha C. Nussbaum, 178.
Shilts, Randy. 1987. *And the Band Played On*. New York: St. Martin's Press.
Smith, Barbara. 1993. "Homophobia: Why Bring It Up?" In *The Lesbian and Gay Studies Reader*, ed. Henry Abelove, Michelle Aina Baraley, and David M. Halperin. New York: Routledge.
Stackhouse, Max L. 1998. "The Prophetic Stand of the Ecumenical Churches on Homosexuality." In *Sexual Orientation and Human Rights in American Religious Discourse*, ed. Saul M. Olyan and Martha C. Nussbaum, 119.
Sullivan, Andrew. 1994. "Wouldn't Normally Do (Washington Diaries—Gay Reactions to Film *Philadelphia*)." *New Republic* 21, no. 8: 42–43.
Thompson, Cooper. 1992. "Heterosexual in a Homophobic World." In *Homophobia: How We All Pay the Price*, 241–58. Boston: Beacon.
"Top 100 American Films." 1999. *All-Time Box Office Leaders Online*. http://www.filmsite.org/boxoffice.html.
Twiss, Sumner B. 1998. "Introduction to Roman Catholic Perspectives on Sexual Orientation, Human Rights, and Public Policy." In *Sexual Orientation and Human Rights in American Religious Discourse*, ed. Saul M. Olyan and Martha C. Nussbaum.
Walter, Barry. 1997. "Rock's Queer Evolution." *The Advocate*, December 9, p. 24.
———. 1997. "Rocking the Gay Bandwagon (New Mainstream CDs with Gay Themes)." *The Advocate*, November 25 p. 62.
Weiss, Andrea. 1992. *Vampires and Violets: Lesbians in Film*. New York: Penguin.

Index

About the Author

Linda Holtzman is Associate Professor in the School of Communications at Webster University in St. Louis, Missouri. She is a teacher and an activist and a mother of five, which requires both teaching and activism.